400 ART DECO MOTIFS

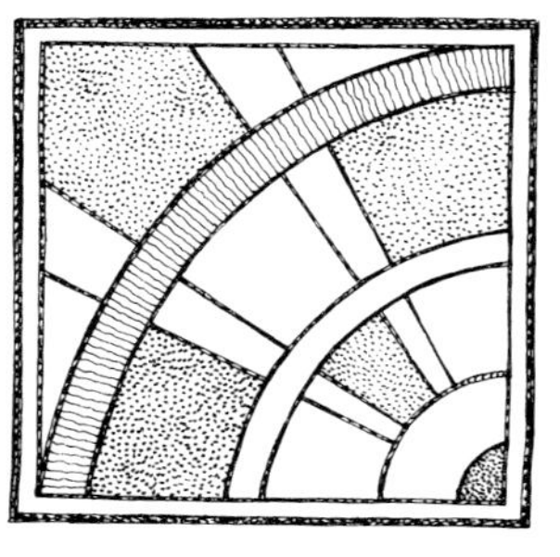
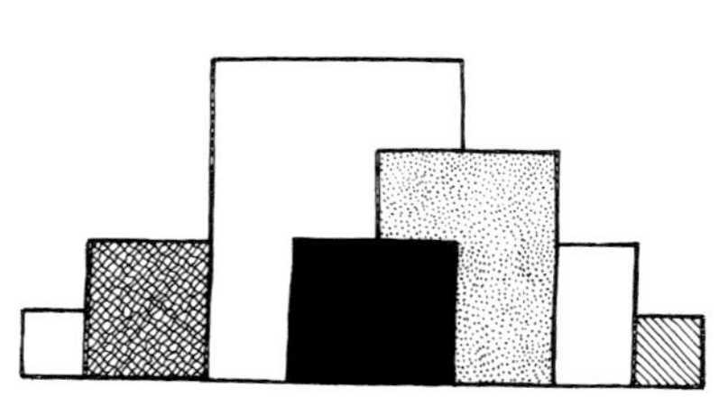
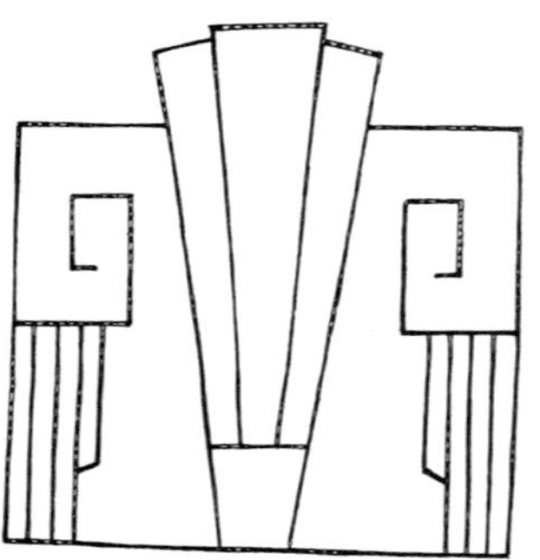

400 ART DECO MOTIFS

Graham Leslie McCallum

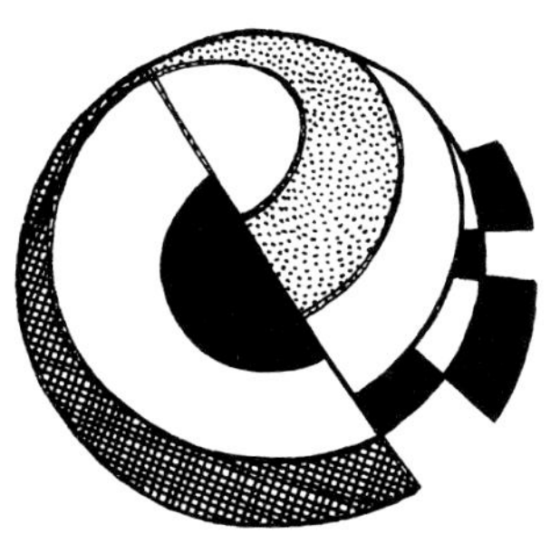
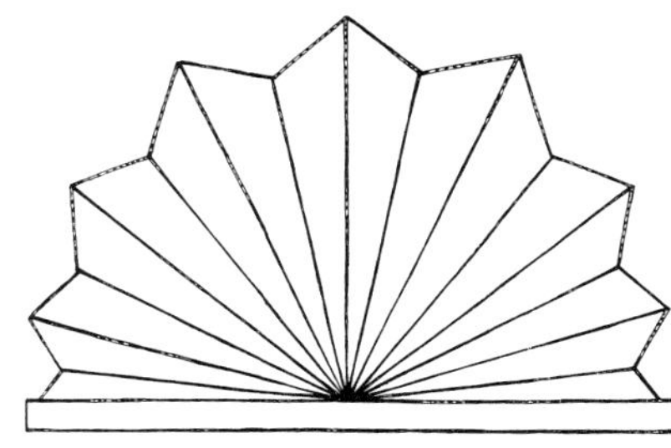
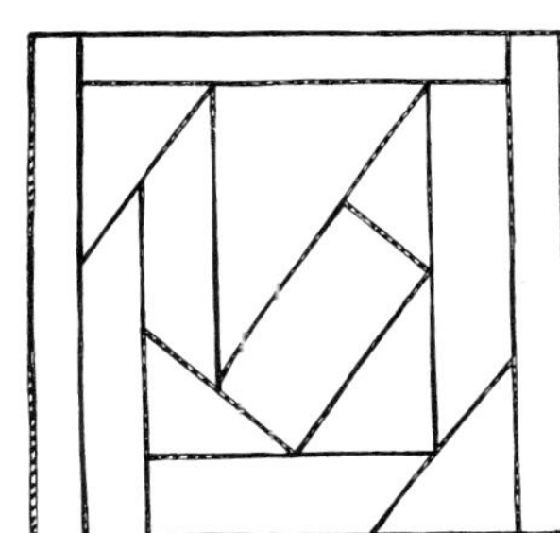

First published in the United Kingdom in 2010 by
Batsford
10 Southcombe Street
London W14 0RA

An imprint of Anova Books Company Ltd

ISBN 9781906388621

A CIP catalogue record for this book is available from the British Library.

18 17 16 15 14 13 12 11 10
10 9 8 7 6 5 4 3 2 1

Reproduction by Dot Gradations Ltd, UK
Printed by 1010 Printing International Ltd, China

This book can be ordered direct from the publisher at the website www.anovabooks.com, or try your local bookshop.

Distributed in the United States and Canada by Sterling Publishing Co., 387 Park Avenue South, New York, NY 10016, USA

CONTENTS

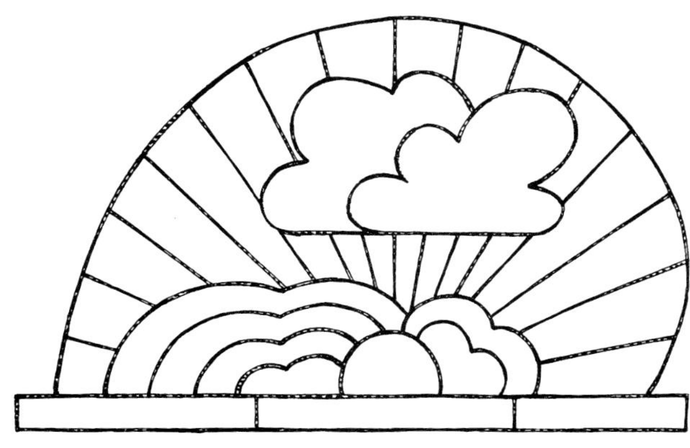

INTRODUCTION

In 1920s Durban, the city where I live, architects suddenly turned their backs on the models of their Edwardian fathers and embraced a new and exciting style. Across the city, commercial and residential buildings were erected with new lines, new forms and new details. Victorian verandahs gave way to modern cantilevered balconies, and mock Gothic and Tudor styling stood down to bold Mayan and Egyptian pyramidal shapes and forms. Gone was the Edwardian fretwork and, in its place, the buildings sported exotic decorations such as sunbursts, scallops, zigzags and spirals. Standing confidently in the bright Natalian light, surrounded by palms and frangipani trees, these new buildings suited the subtropical holiday city of Durban then, as well as now.

The year 1918 had seen the end of World War I and I can imagine the societies that had been brutalized by five years of war wanting to explore something new and fresh. Across the world, from Durban to Djibouti, from Sydney to Auckland, Miami to New York and London to Vienna, this new style, now called Art Deco, was to influence virtually all artistic expression. Motifs such as sunbursts and cloud billows illustrated this new-found optimism and freedom.

These motifs and forms glorified the modern age and especially the new inventions and discoveries of the time. This is especially evident in the structured forms of the buildings. Time-saving electrically driven machines appeared, bringing with them a new enthusiasm for convenience. In the Art Deco style this is manifested by the liberal use of electricity bolts and sparks. Motifs such as wings and gears also conveyed society's keen interest in fast locomotives and motor cars. Record-breaking was the craze and crossings of the Atlantic by ocean liners such as the *Queen Mary* inspired many illustrations. Not only did these subjects engender new motifs, but the subjects themselves came under the sway of stylists. The cabins and ballrooms of the liners were decorated in the current forms and patterns, and vehicles and locomotives were streamlined to the shape of the time.

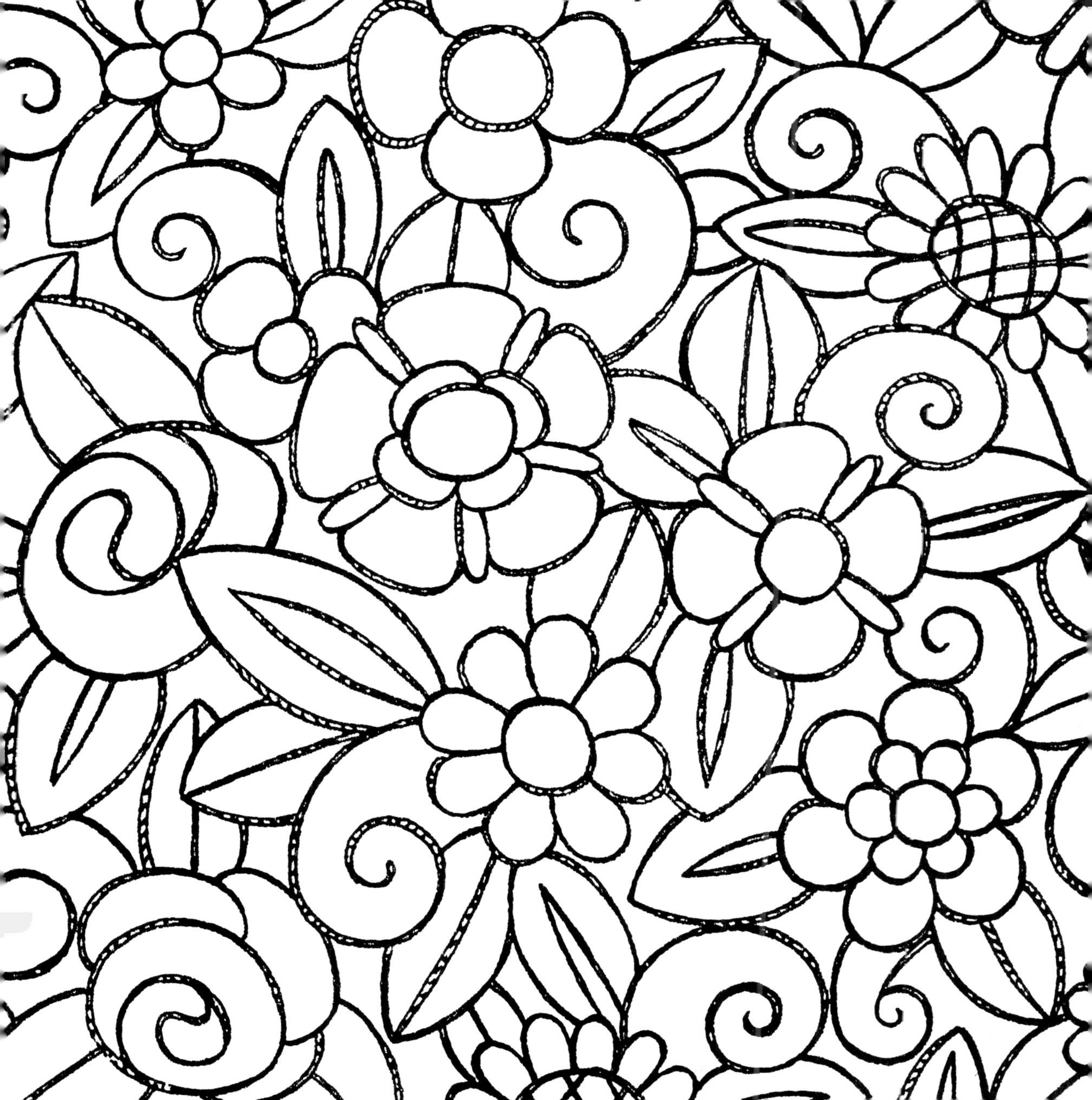

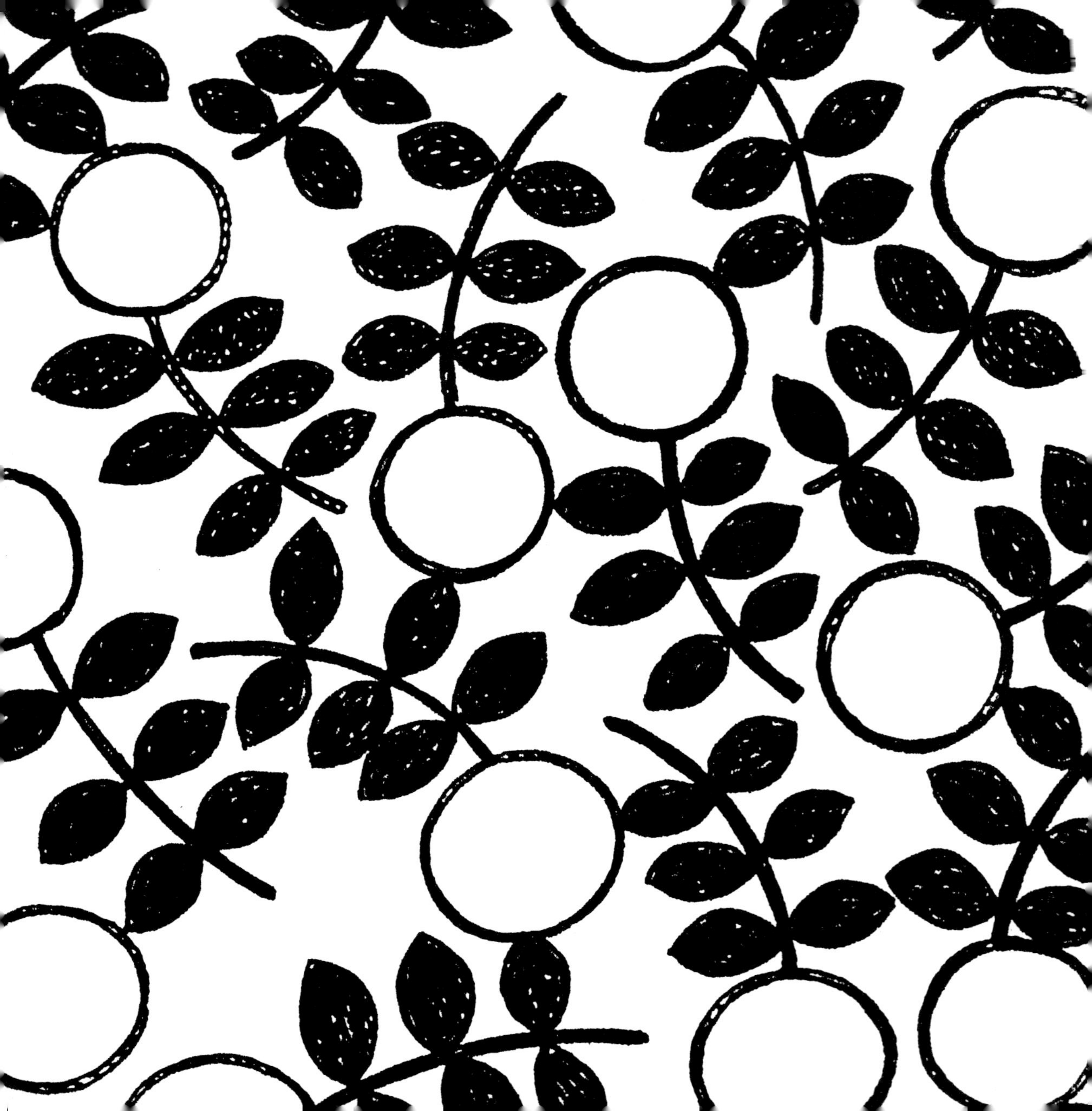

Not only was Art Deco a decorative style as its name implies but, more than this, it was a style encompassing form and mass, evident in the structural forms of the buildings. This book comprehensively explores the form as well as the decorative; presenting these designs in a functional fashion for your use and inspiration.

The enthusiasm and life-joy of the style is one of the reasons for the popularity of Art Deco today. Heritage societies have sprung up all over the world seeking to preserve this art. Today enthusiasts collect and trade Art Deco jewellery, art pottery, statues and artefacts around the world, and architects are again building new structures in this style.

Art Deco's chameleon-like character blends in with modern living and styling. Yet even more than this, the wide subject matter of Art Deco – embracing everything from motor cars to jewellery – presents to artists an amazingly rich legacy, with wide present-day application and adaptability.

I have sourced the motifs in this book from this varied expression. Some of the sources are architecture, machinery, fabric, ornaments, advertizements, sculptures and household appliances. It is this breadth that explains why the style lends itself to all modern day crafts, hobbies and pursuits. If you are an embroiderer, quilter, wood carver, fabric painter or scrap booker (to name a few) this publication will supply you with a wellspring of inspiring images. I know that from within this collection of motifs, borders and patterns from around the world, you will find the precise image you are looking for to complete your project.

So too the creative professions – cabinet makers, architects, illustrators, advertizers and teachers of the arts, who are always looking for inspiration or the right design. You will be able to take full advantage and benefit from Art Deco's generous endowment.

Graham Leslie McCallum

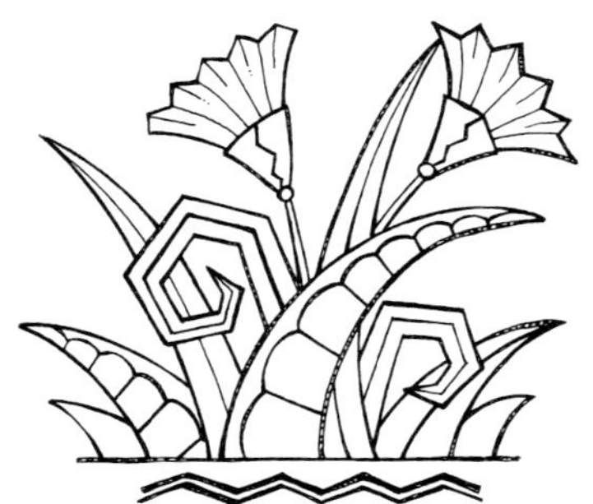
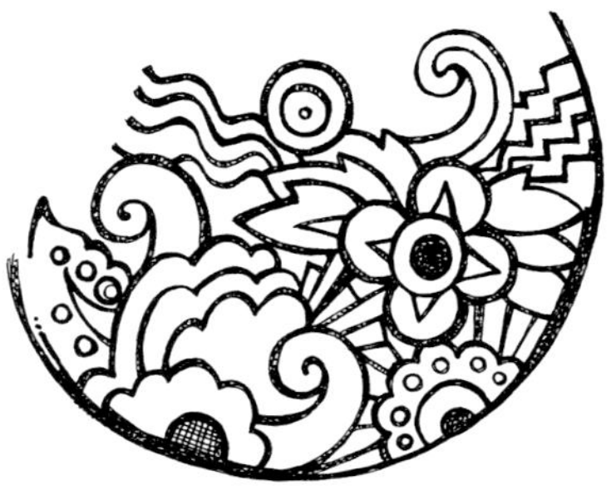
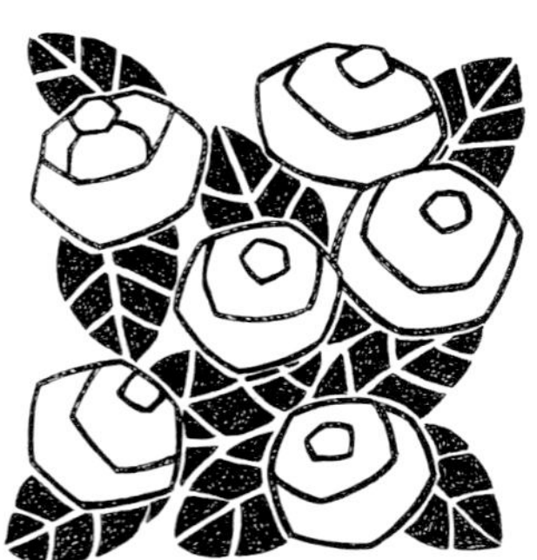

FLOWERS AND PLANTS

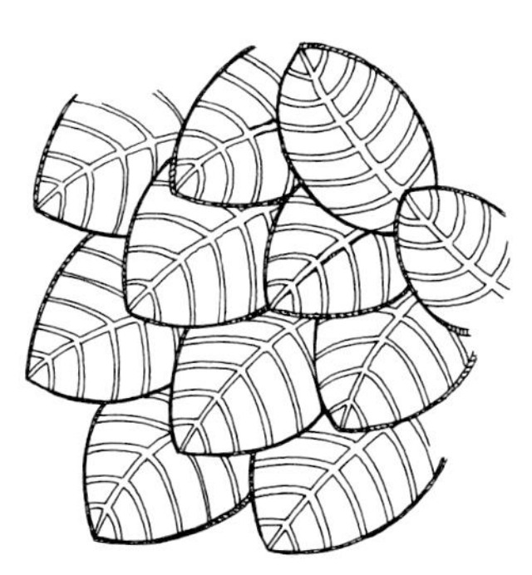

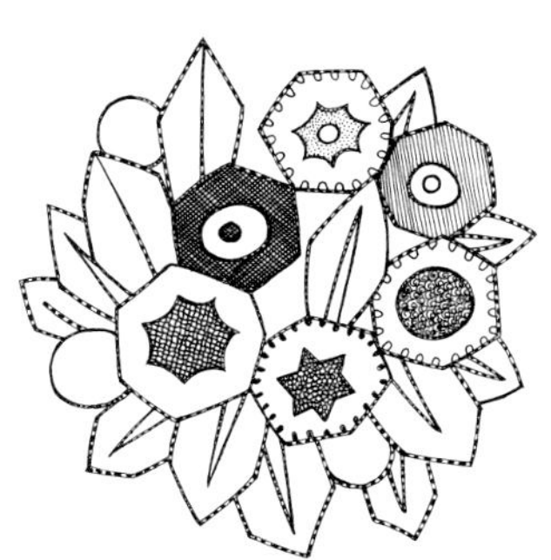

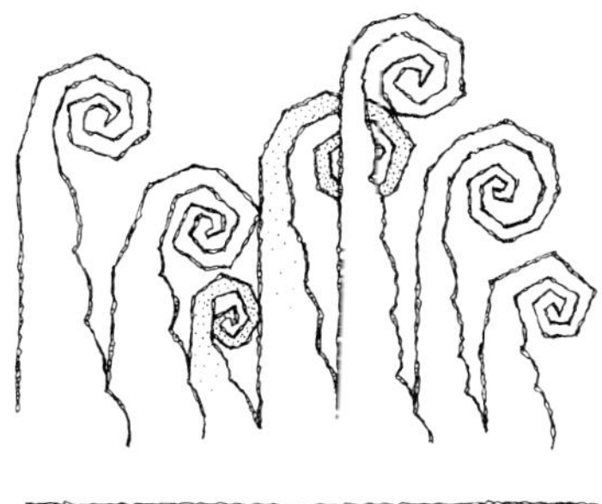

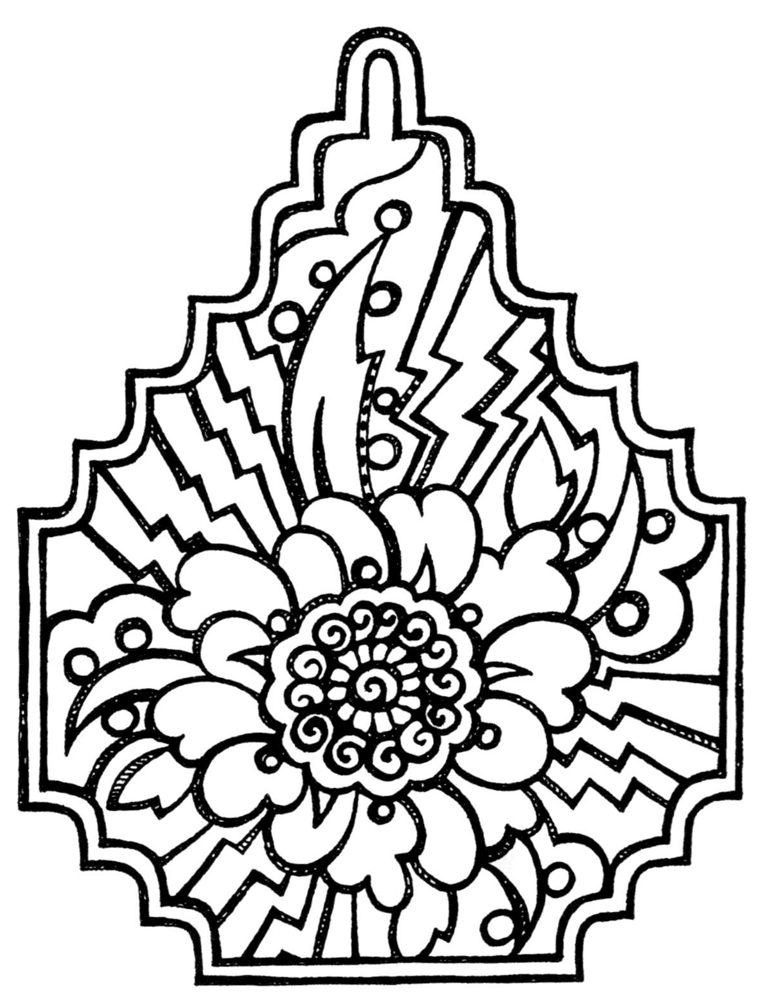

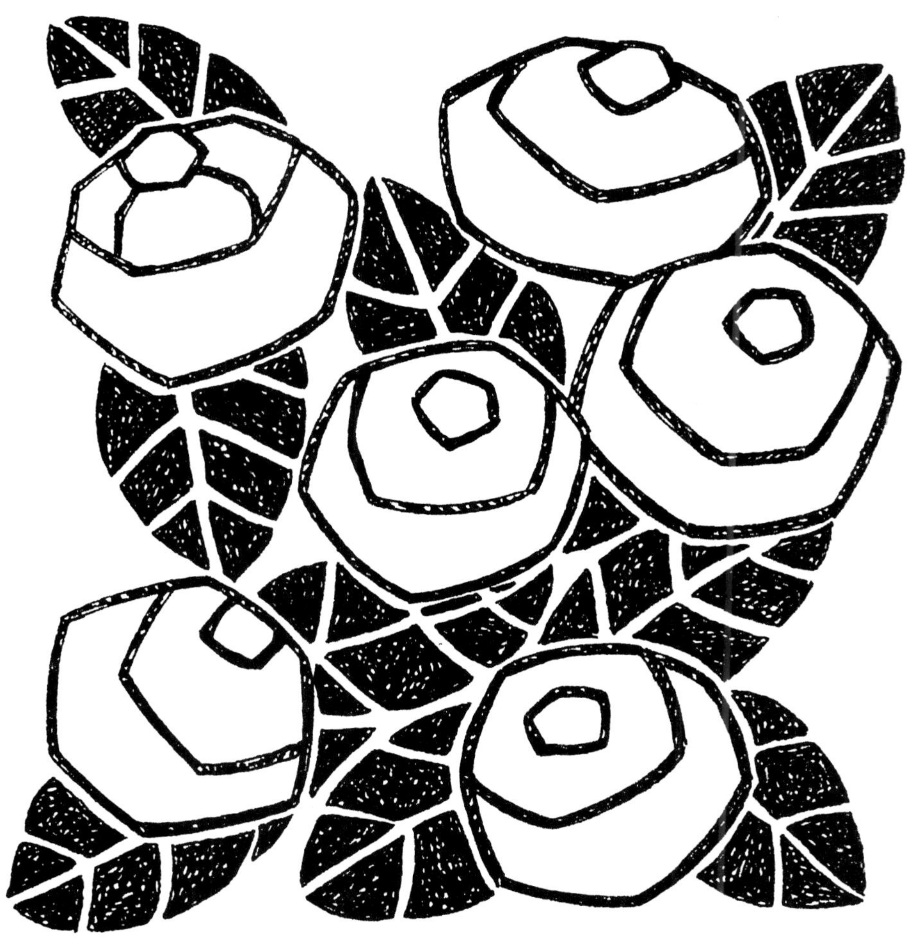

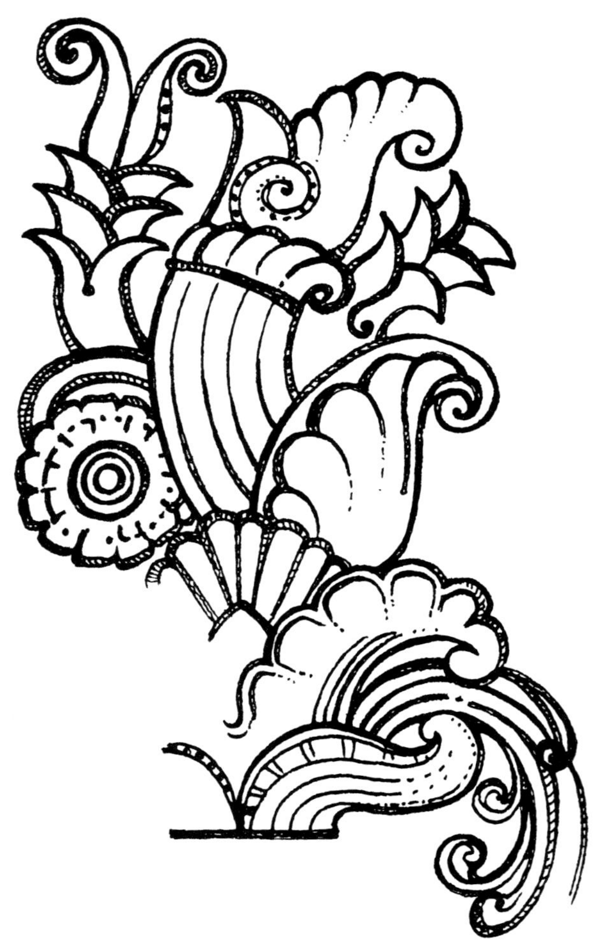

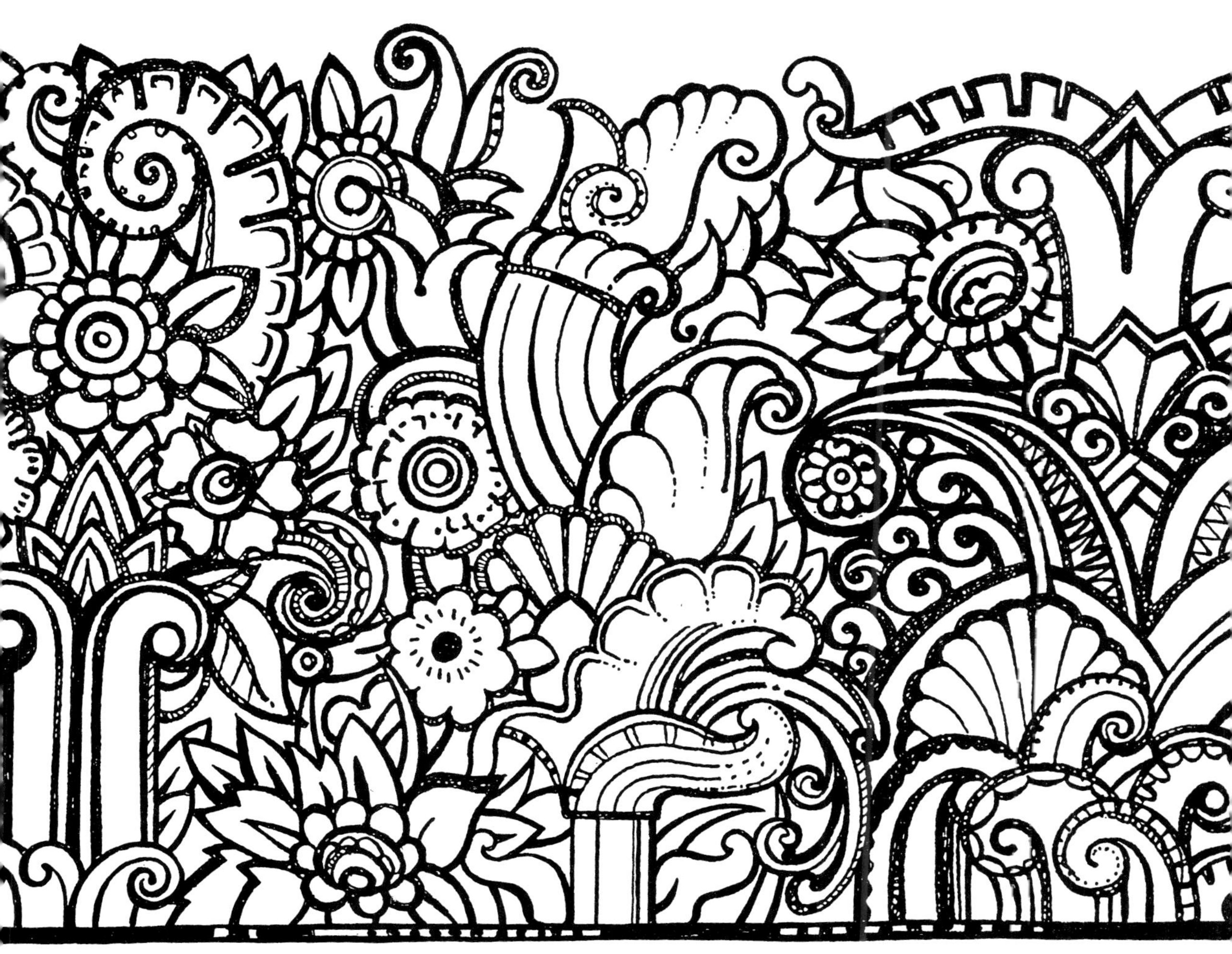

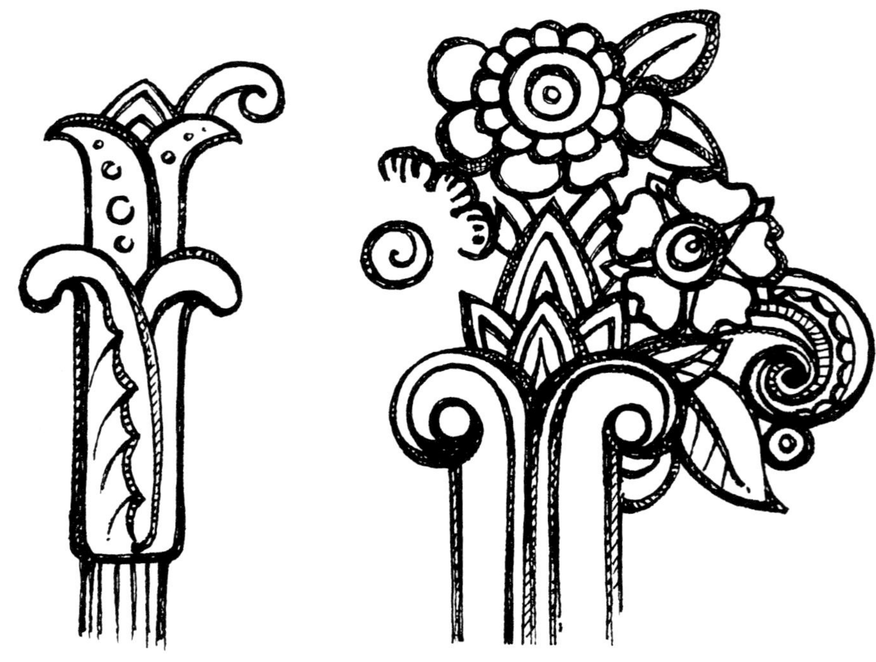

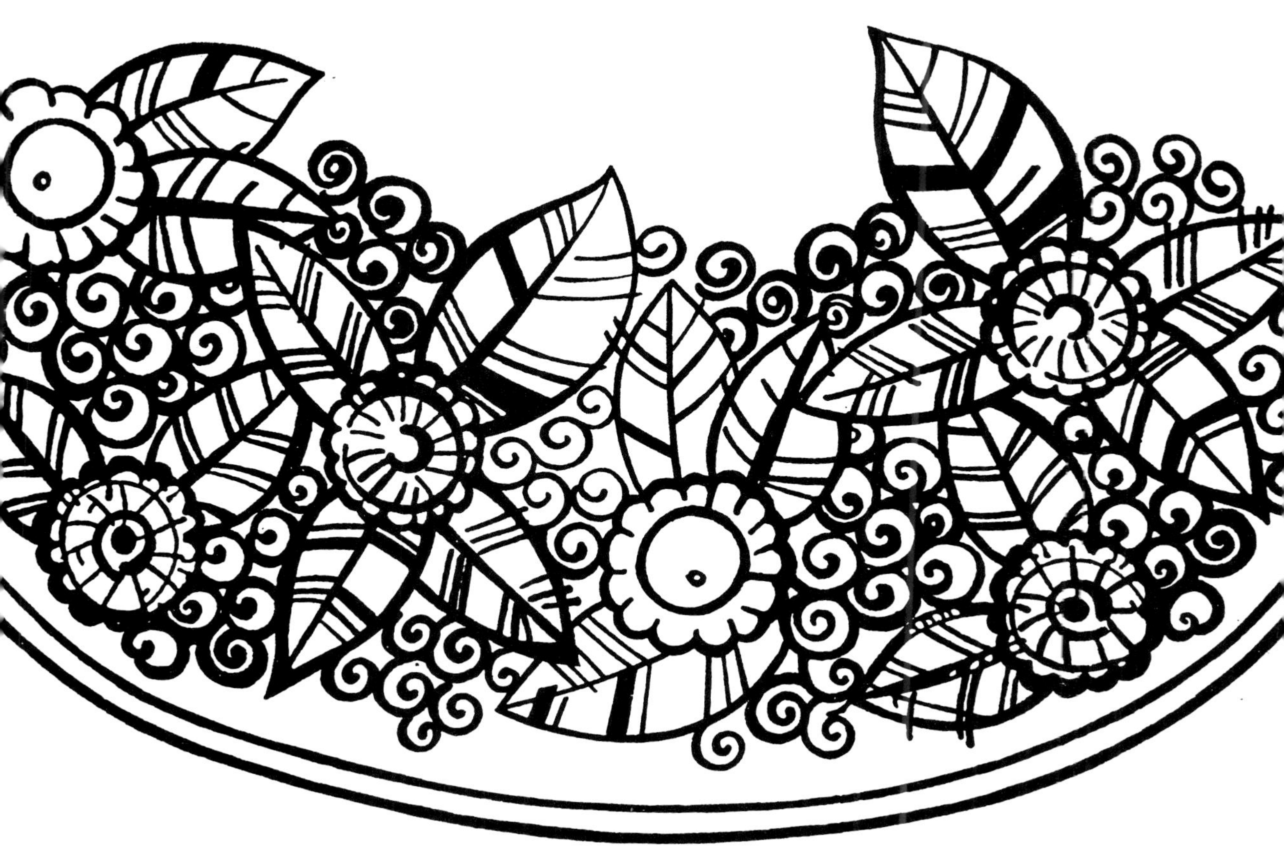

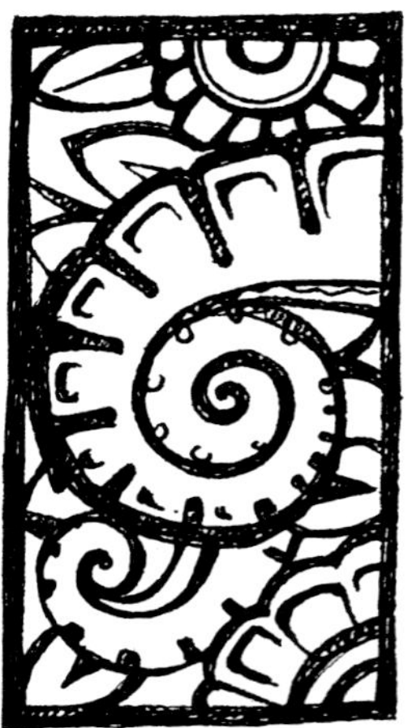

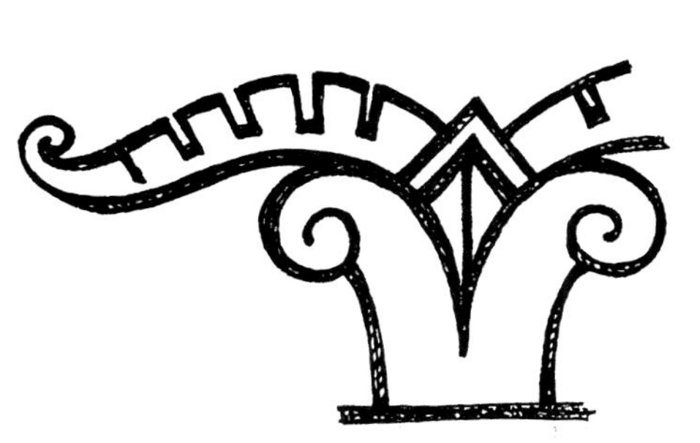

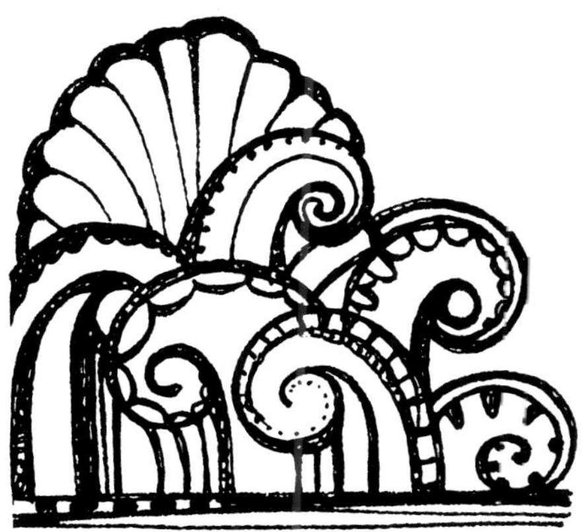

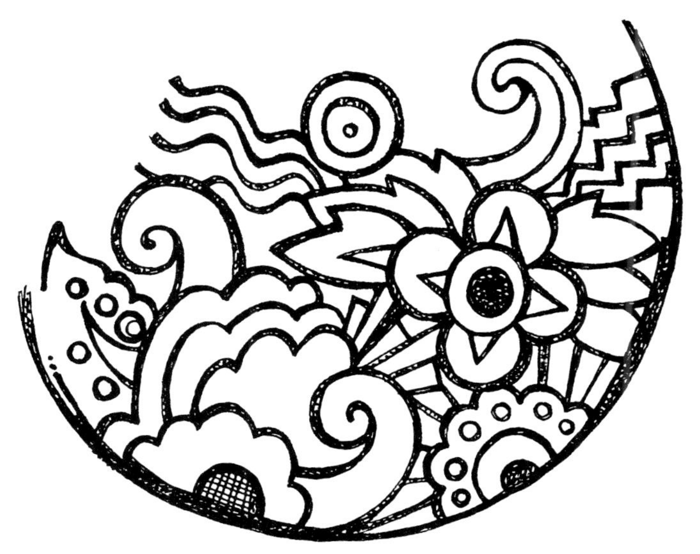

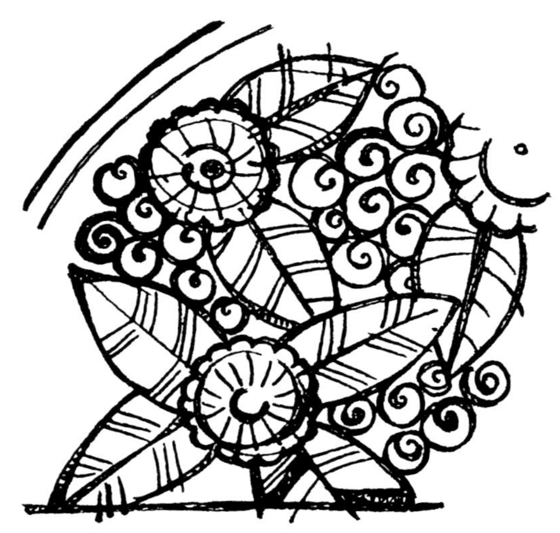

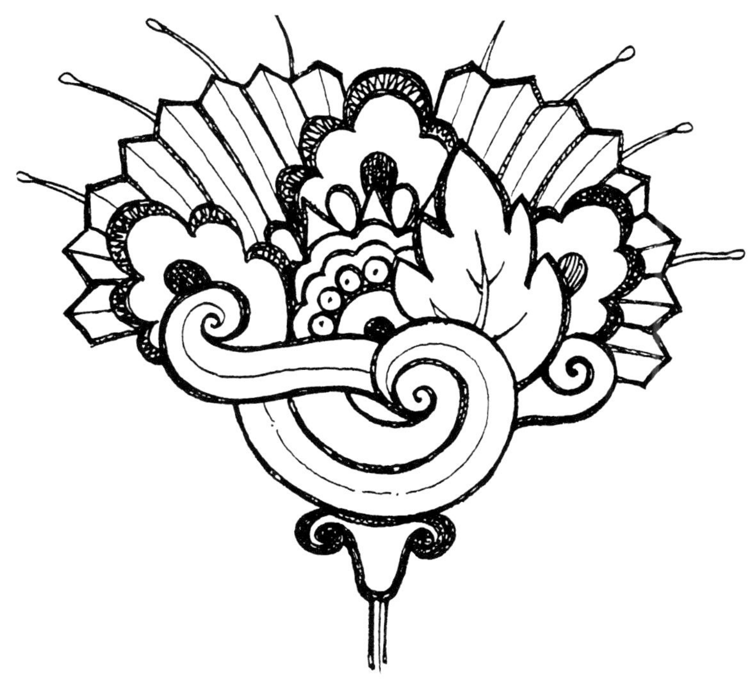

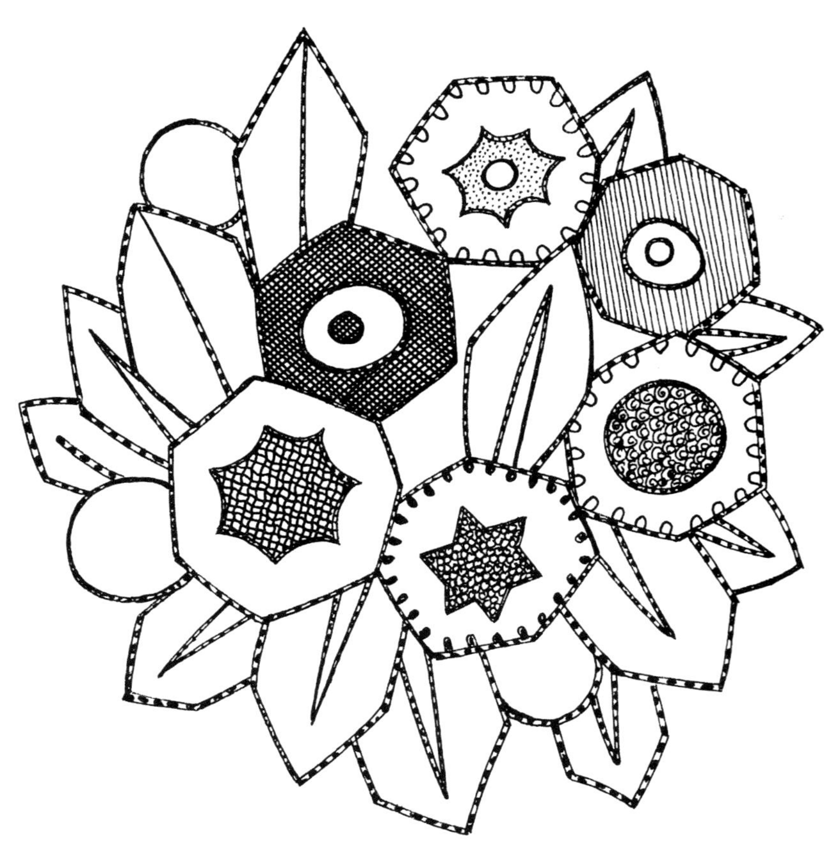

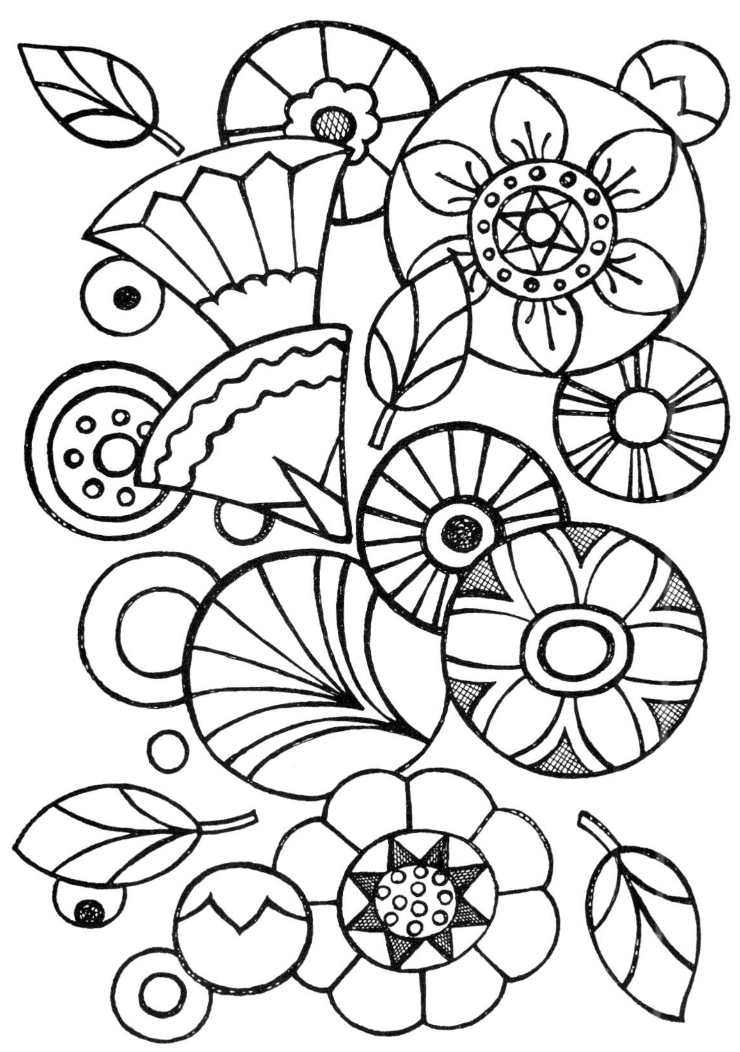

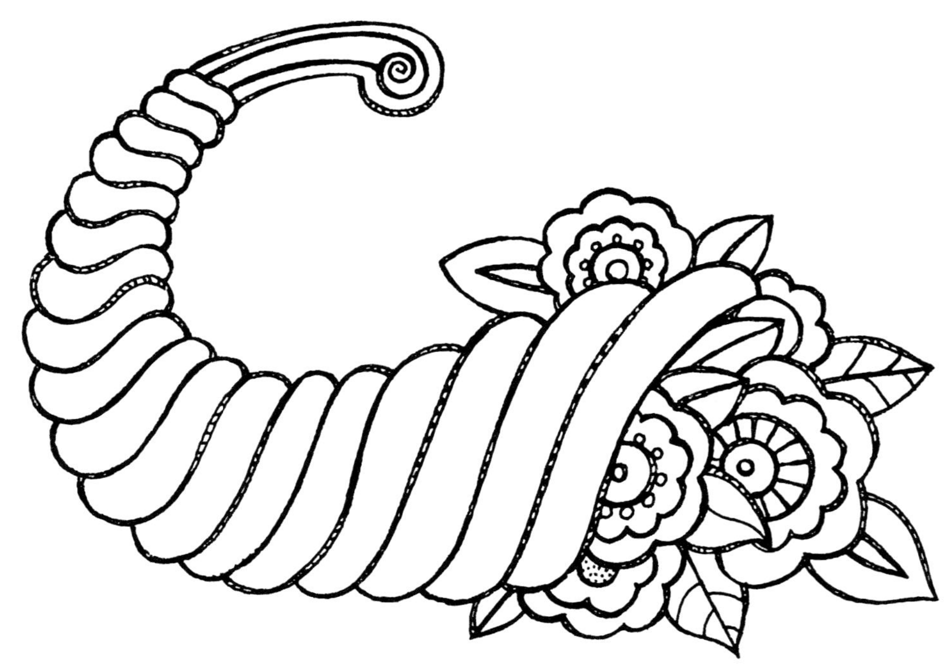

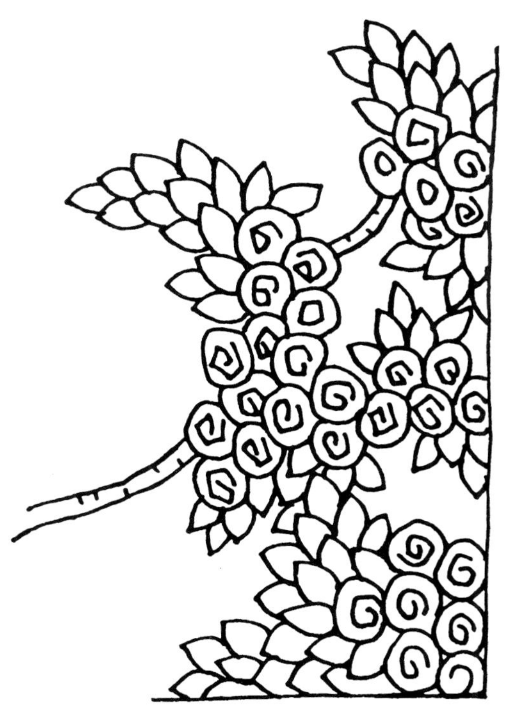

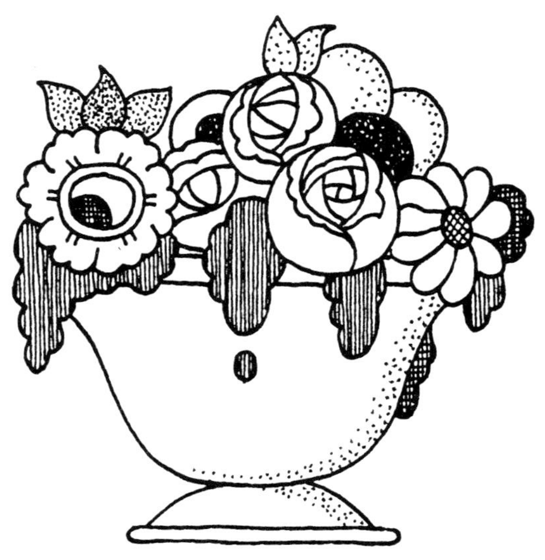

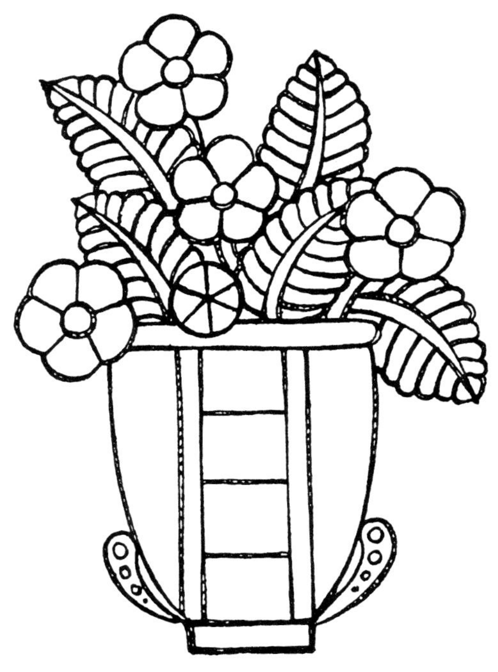

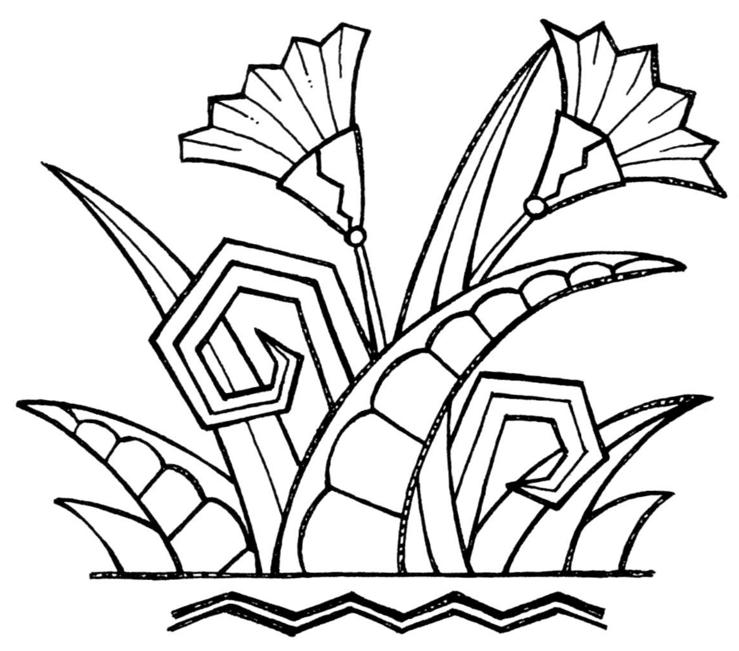

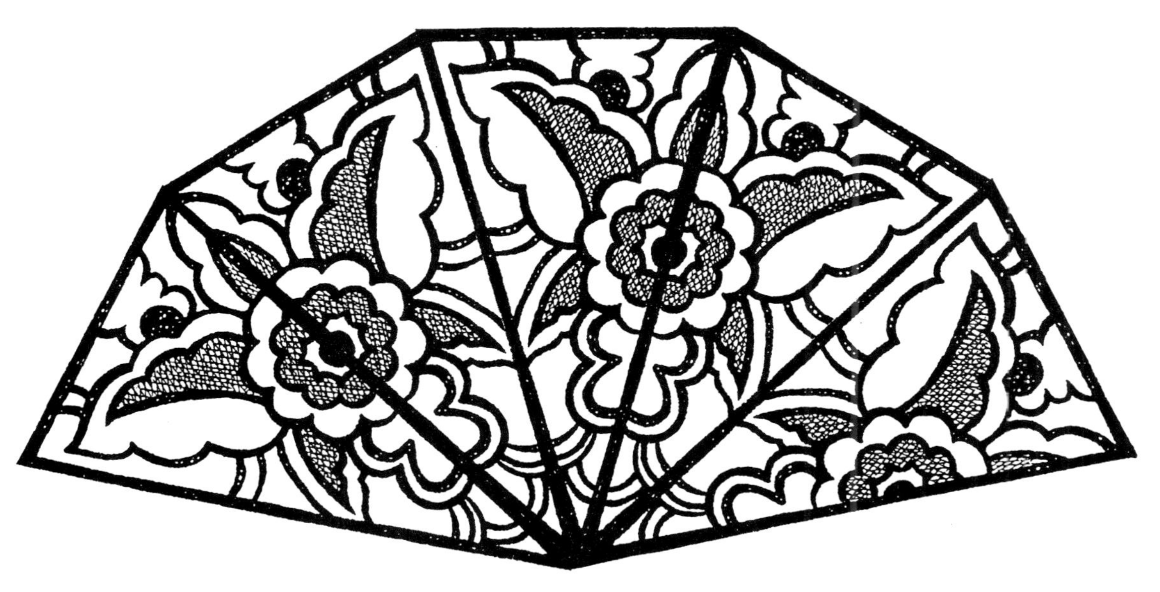

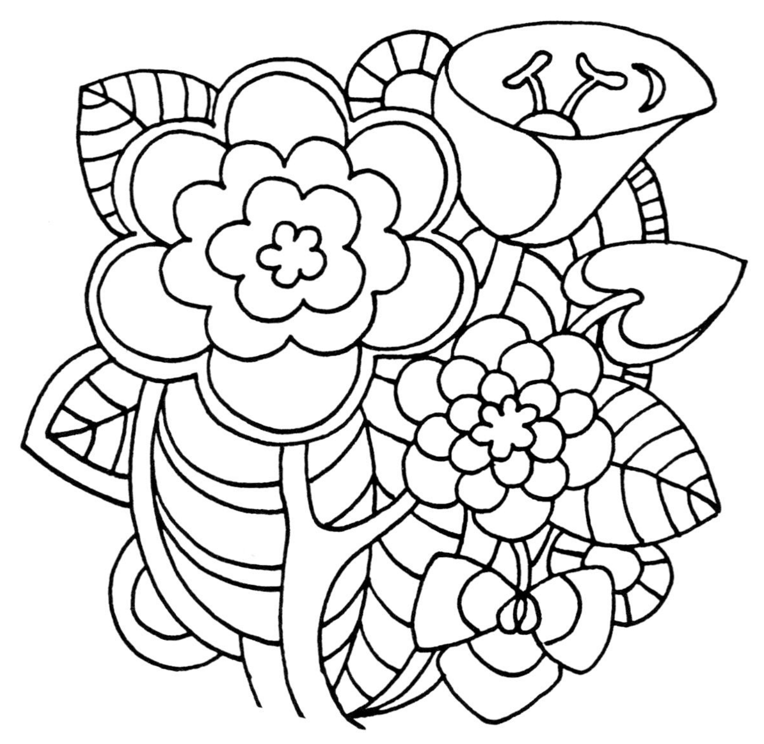

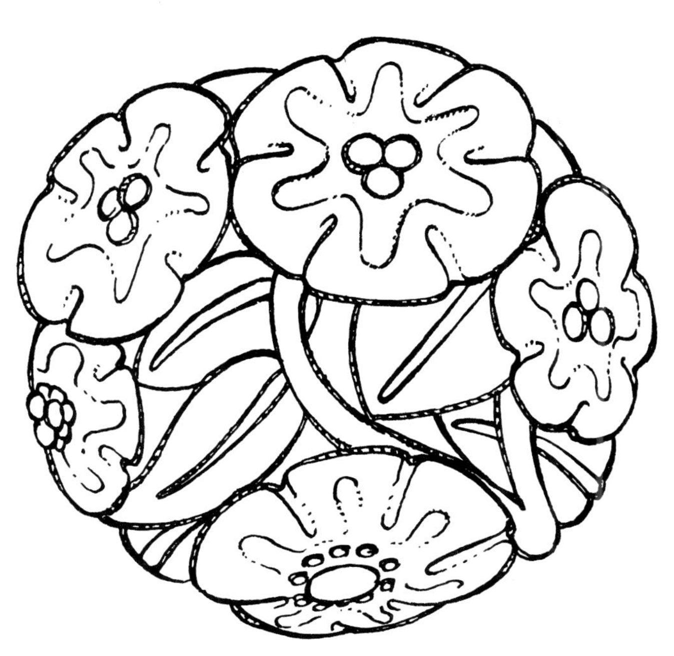

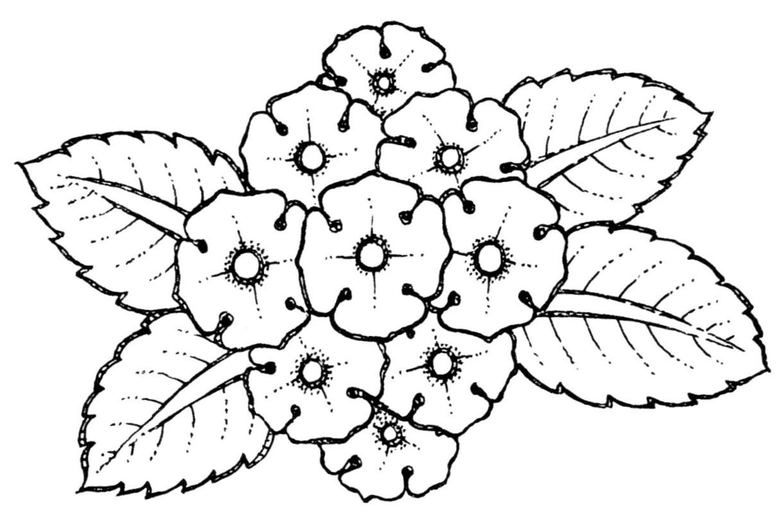

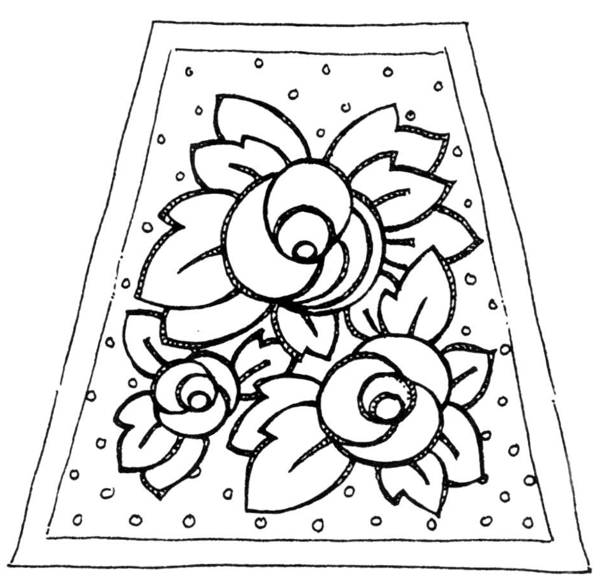

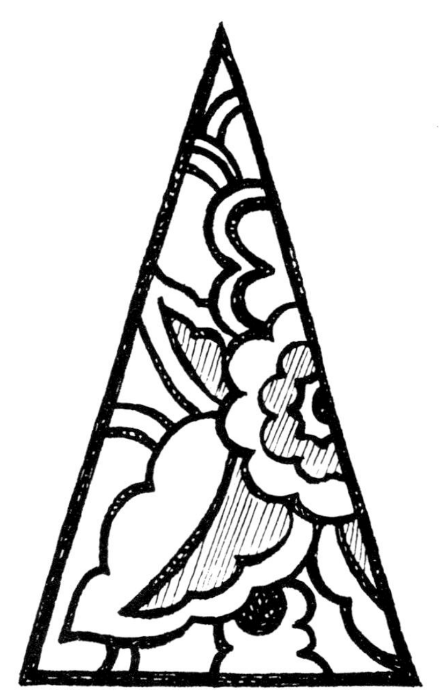

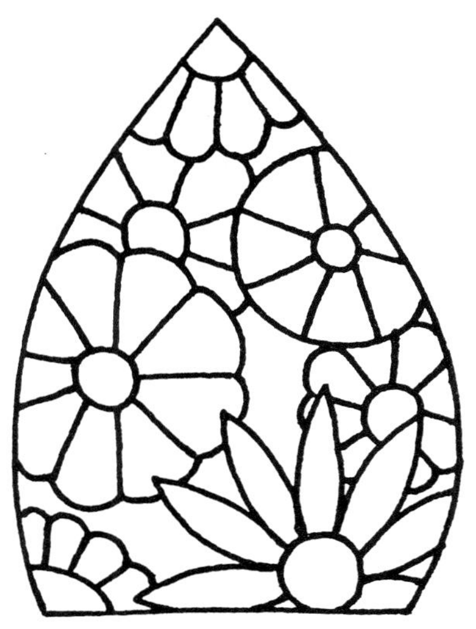

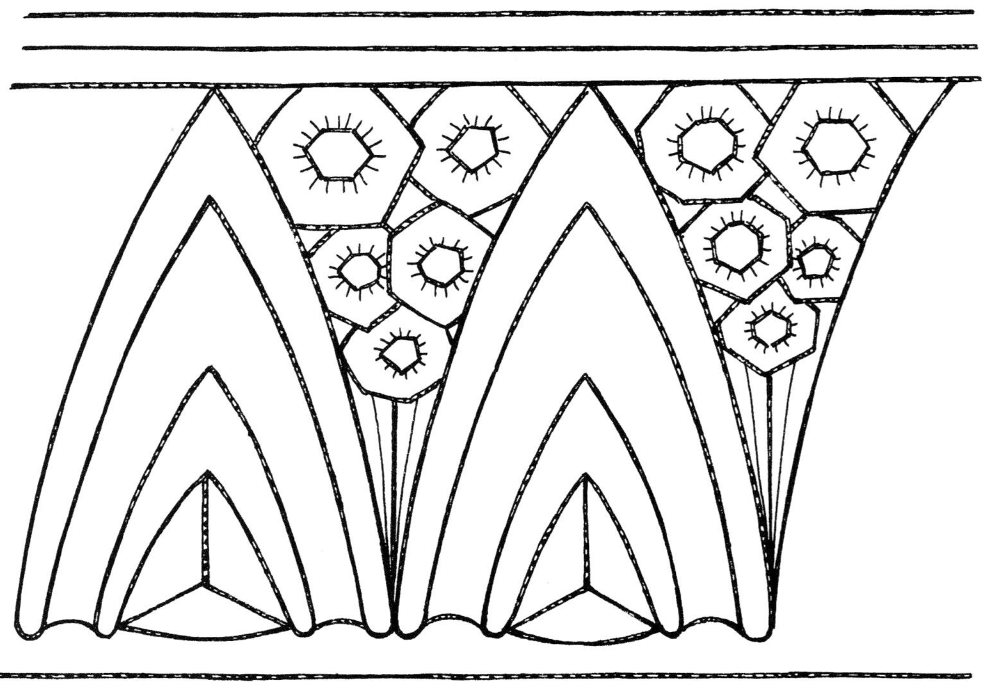

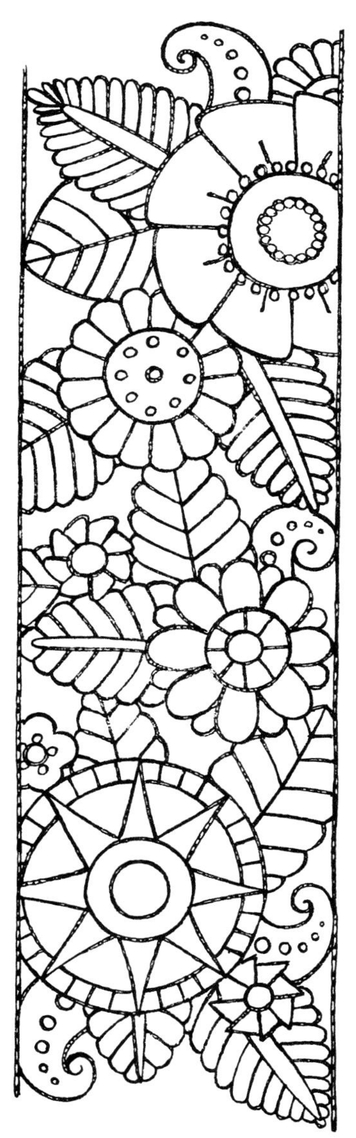

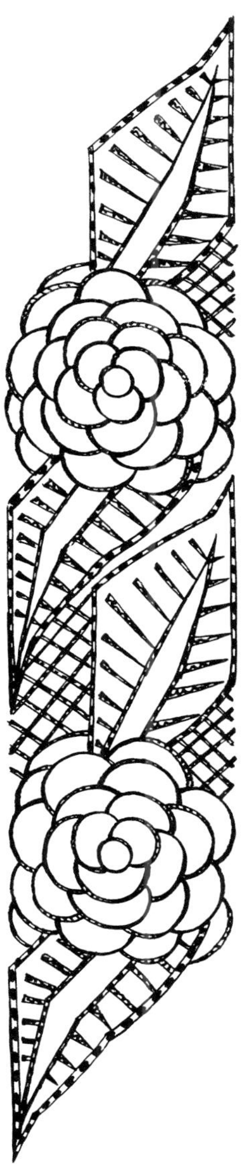

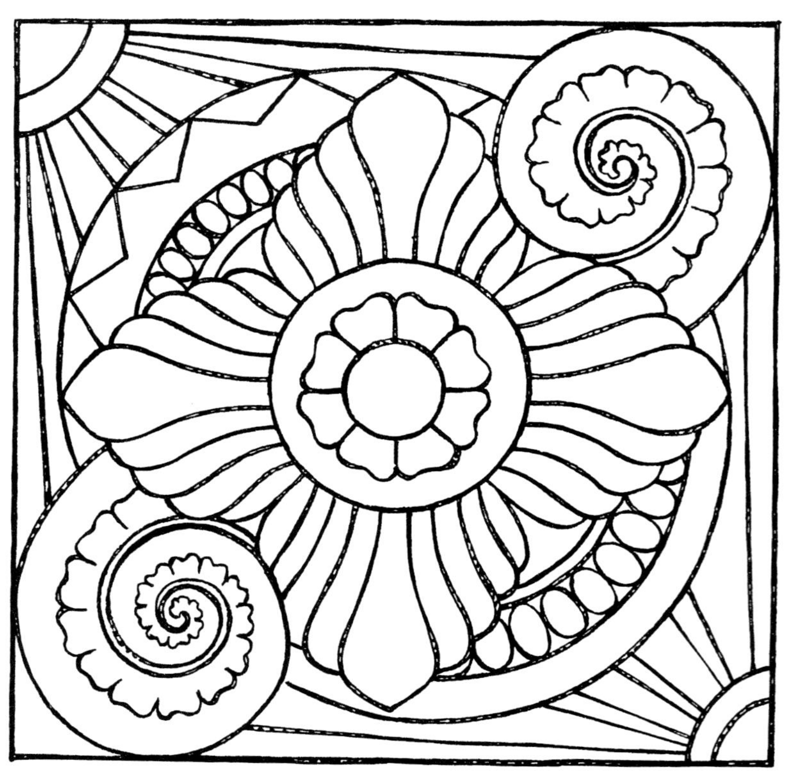

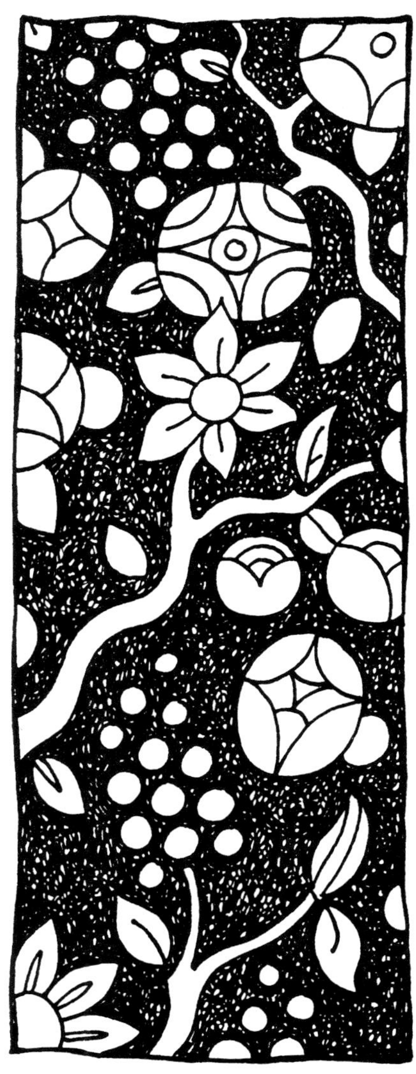

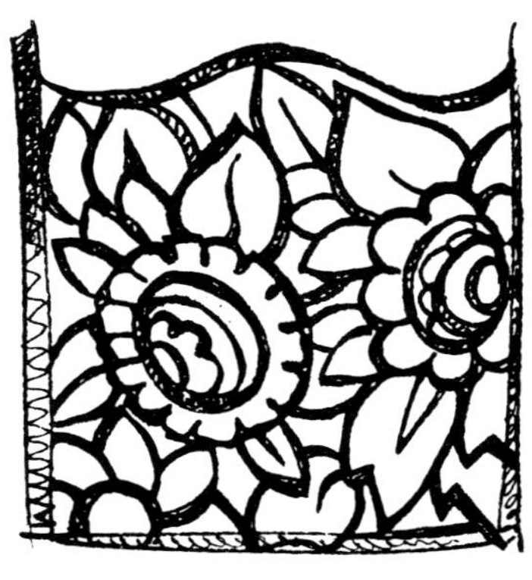

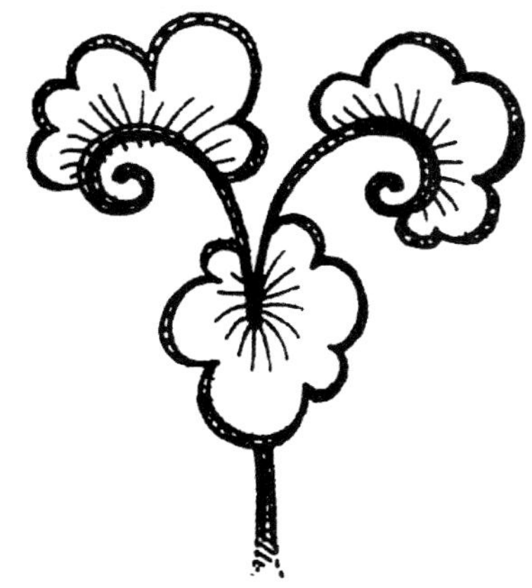

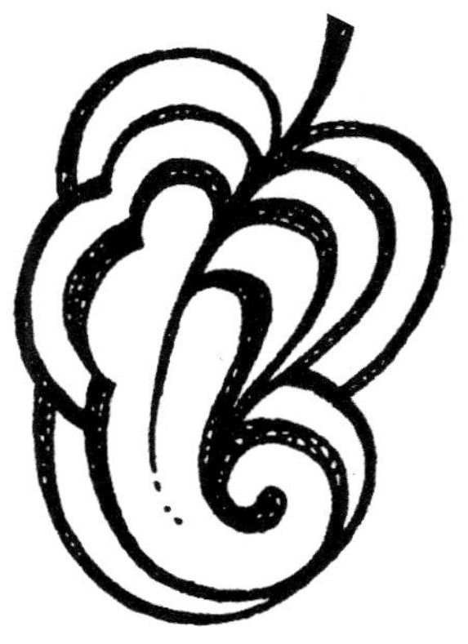

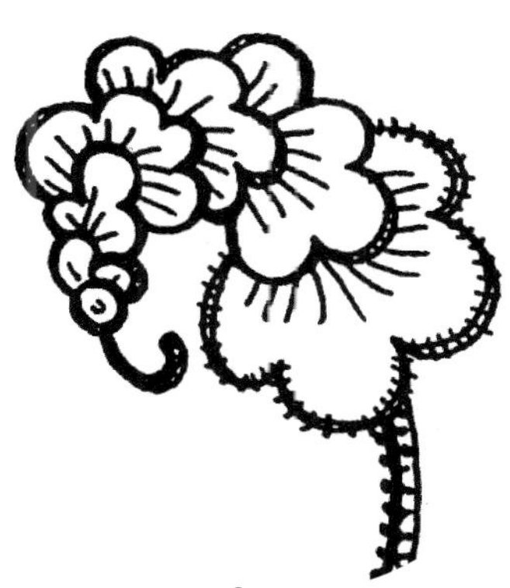

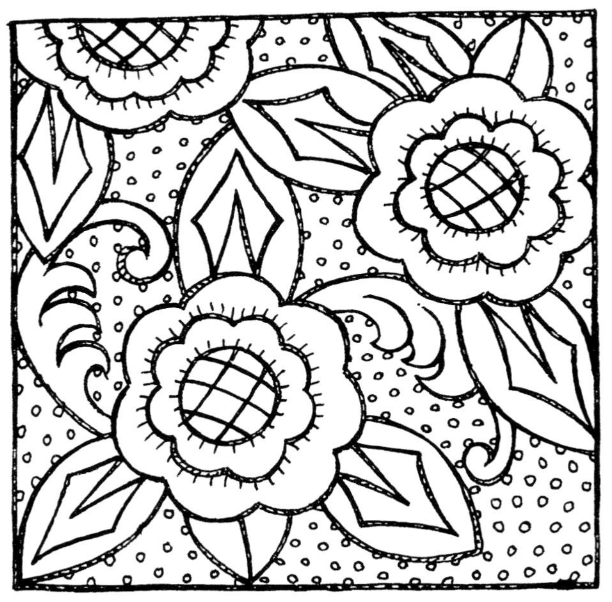

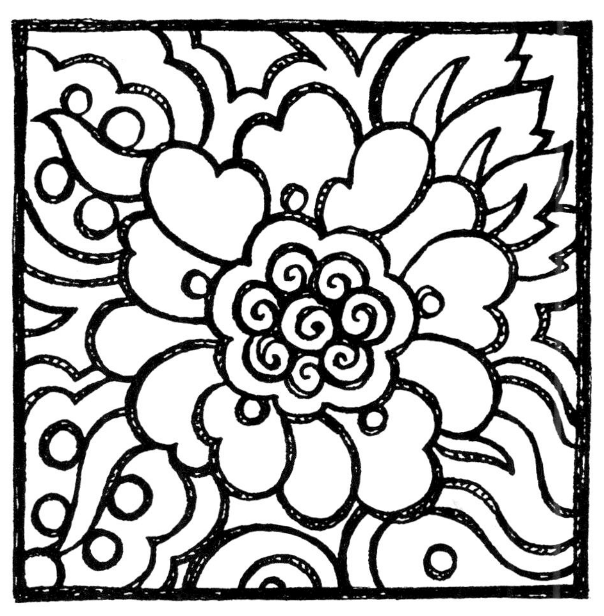

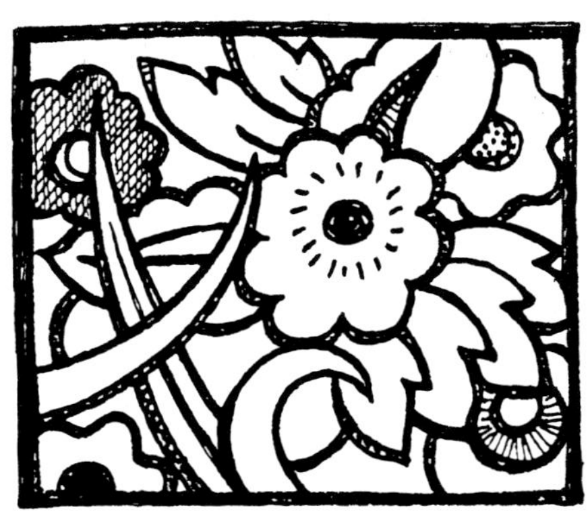

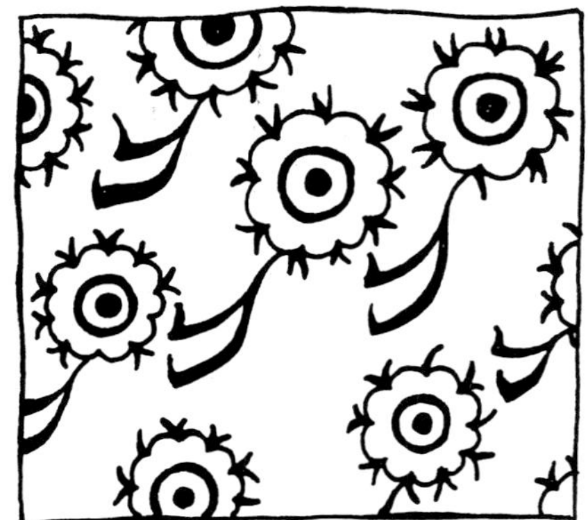

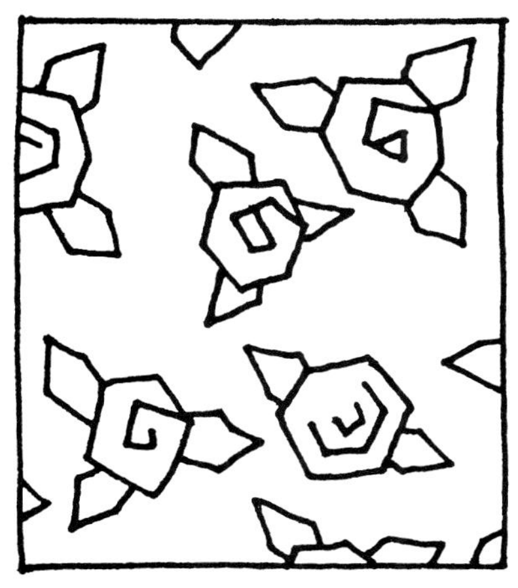

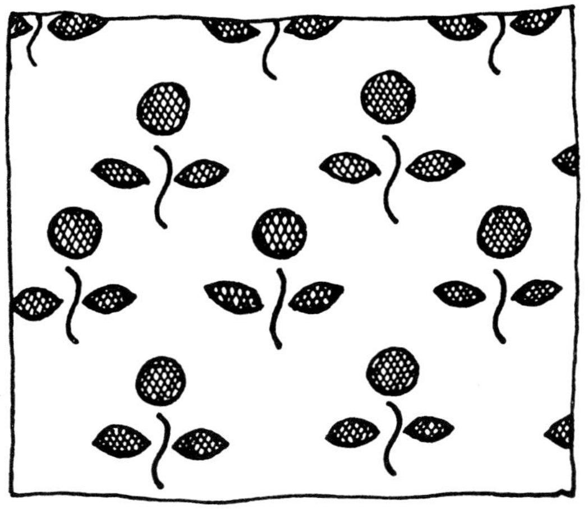

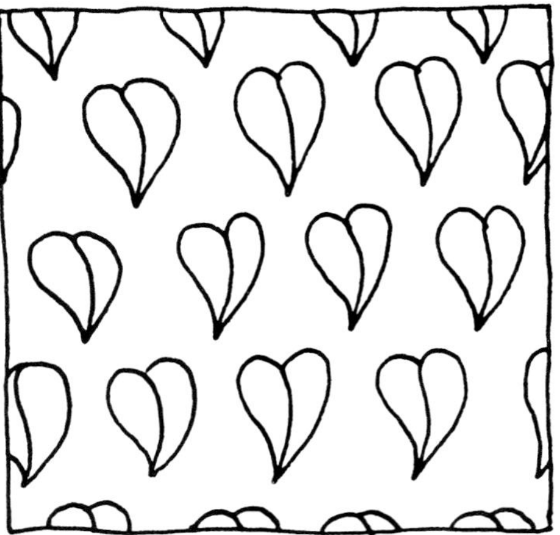

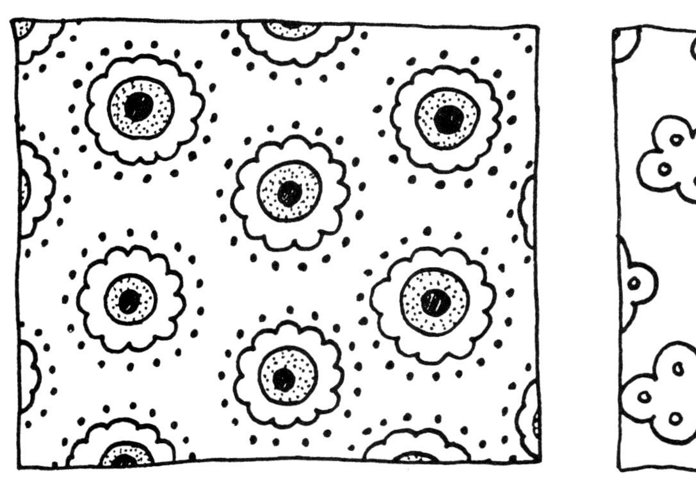

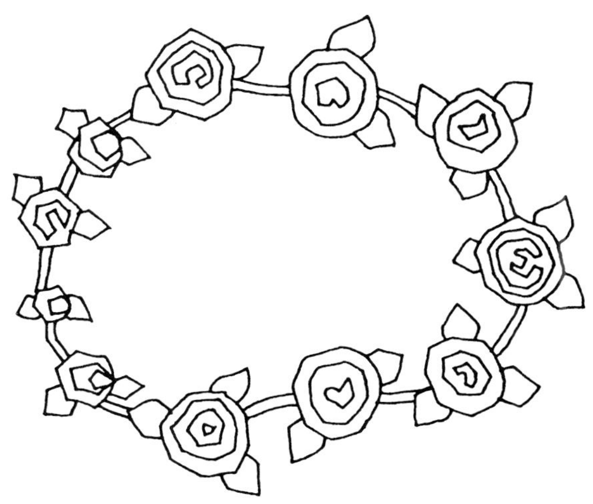

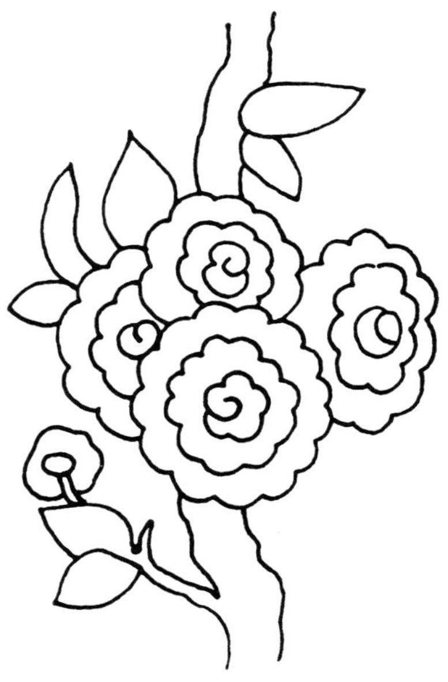

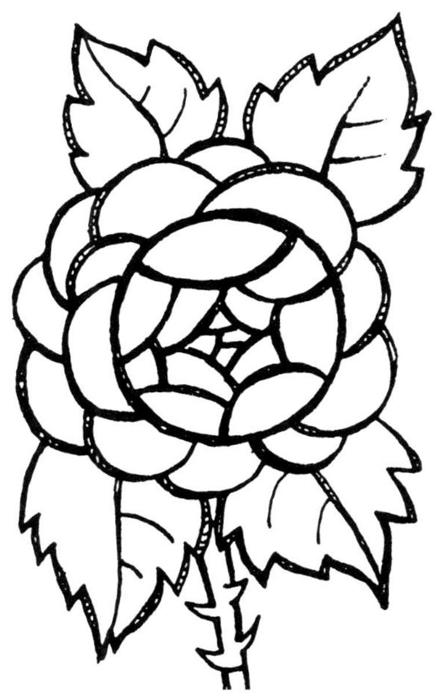

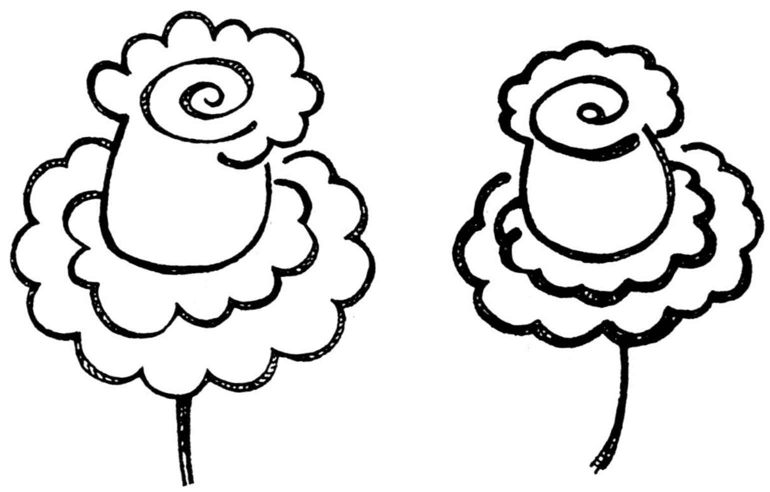

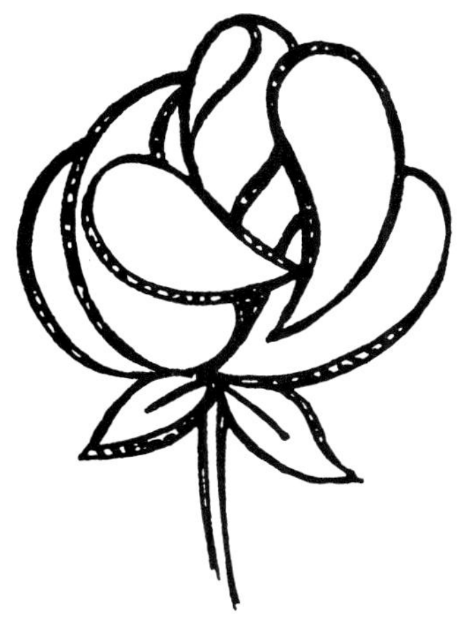

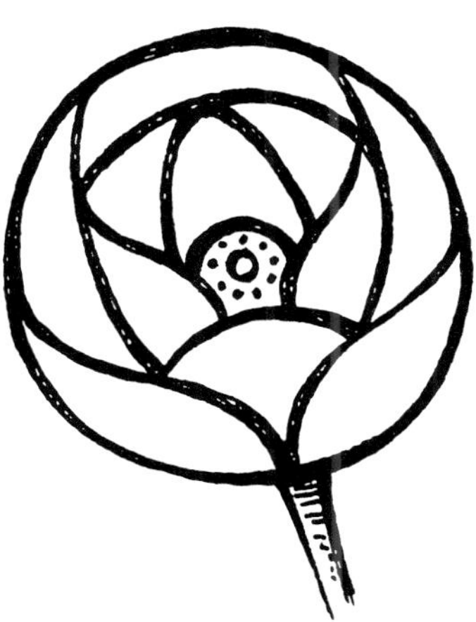

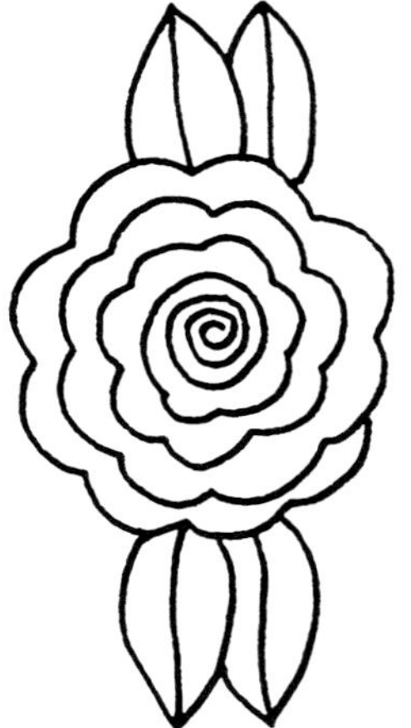

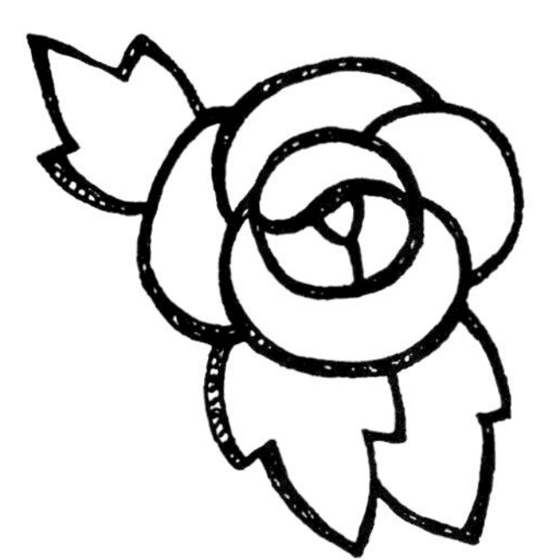

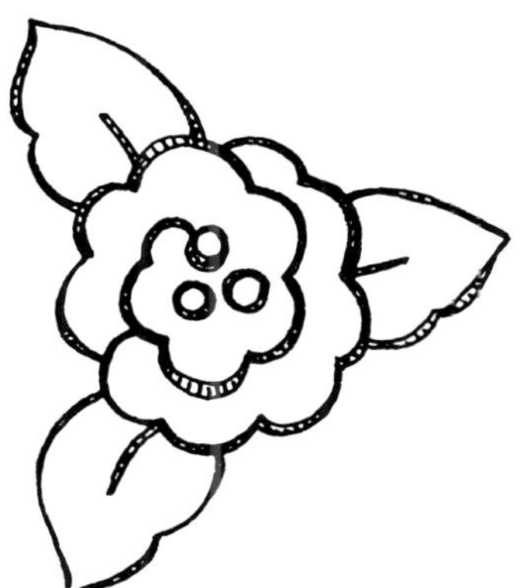

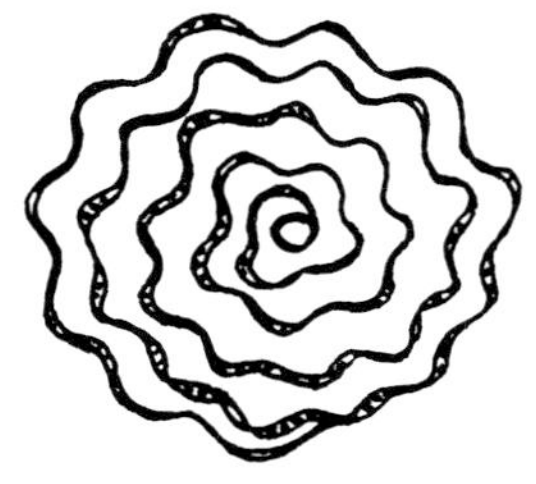

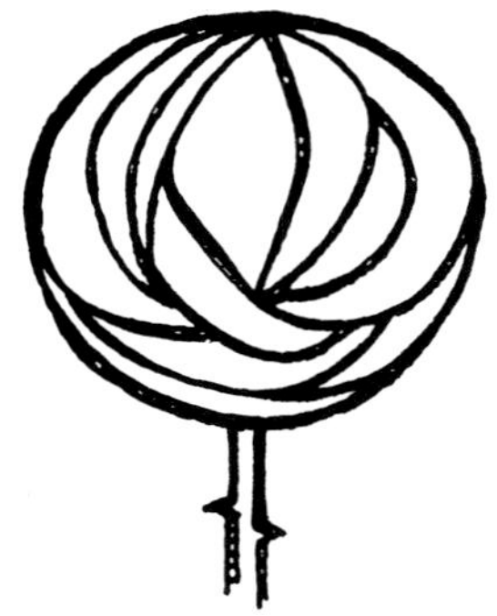

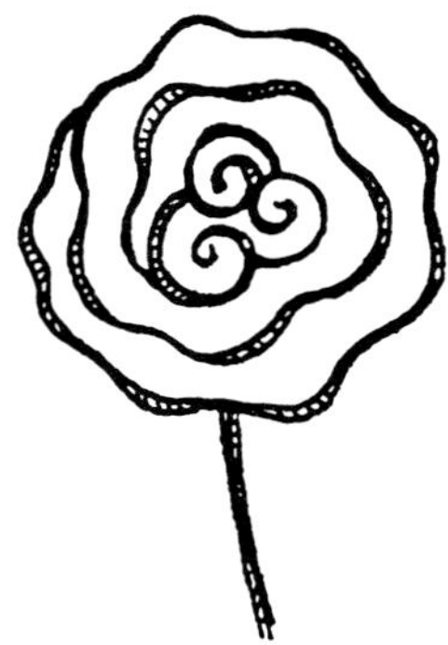

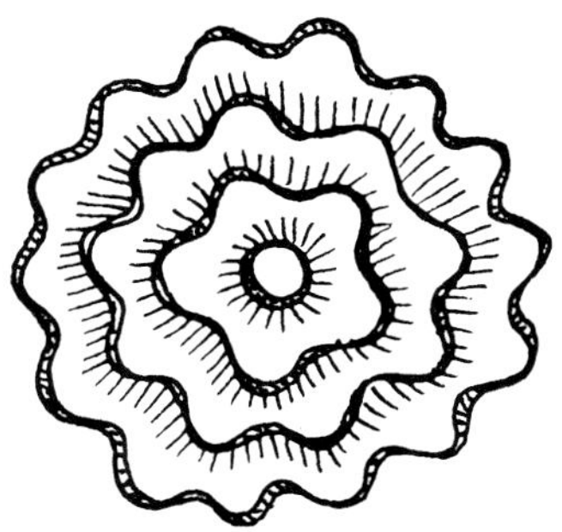

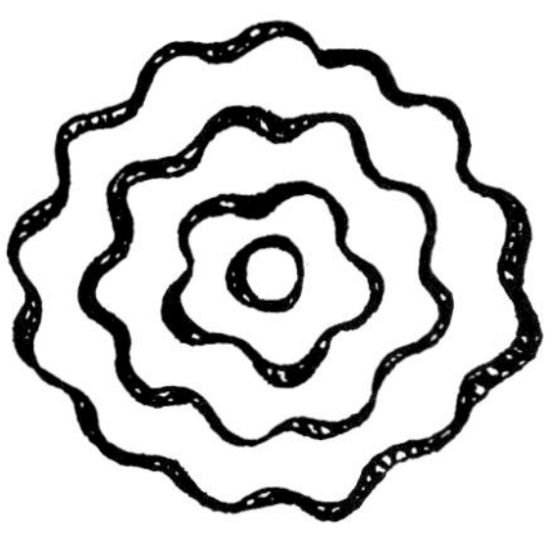

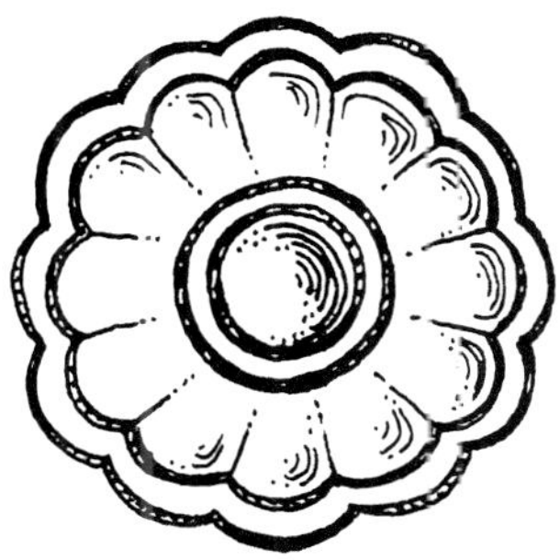

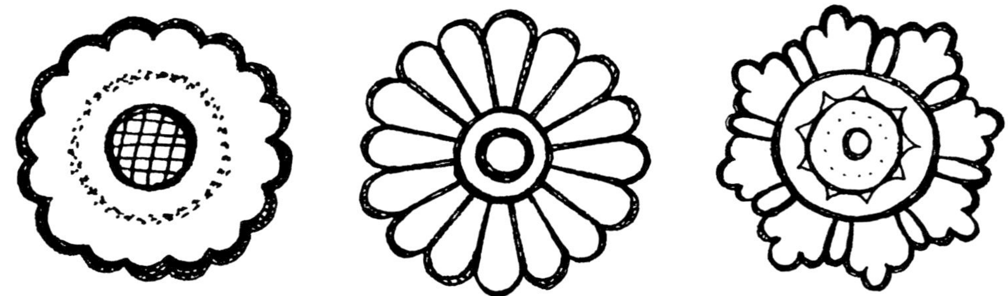

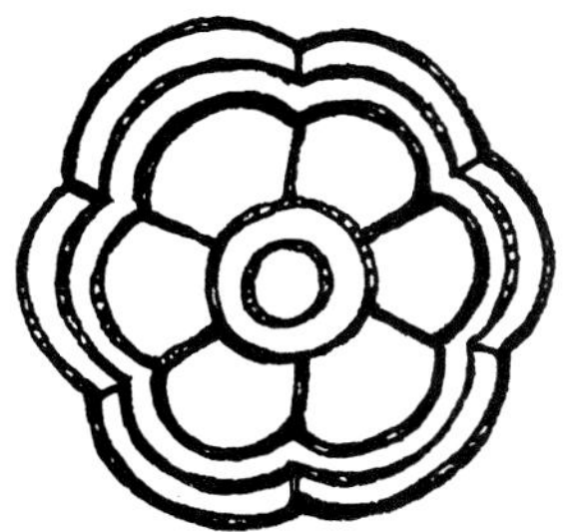
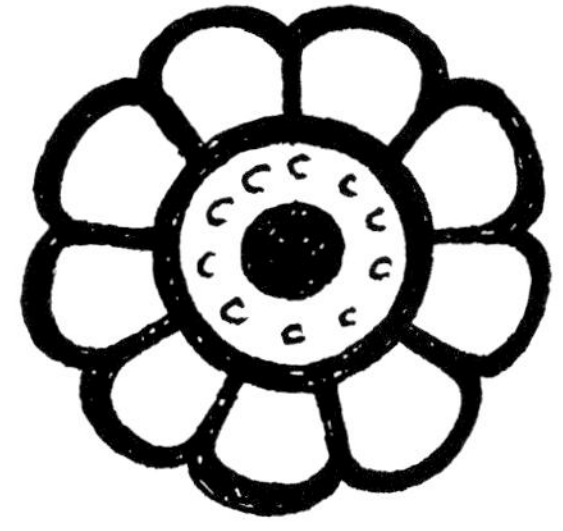
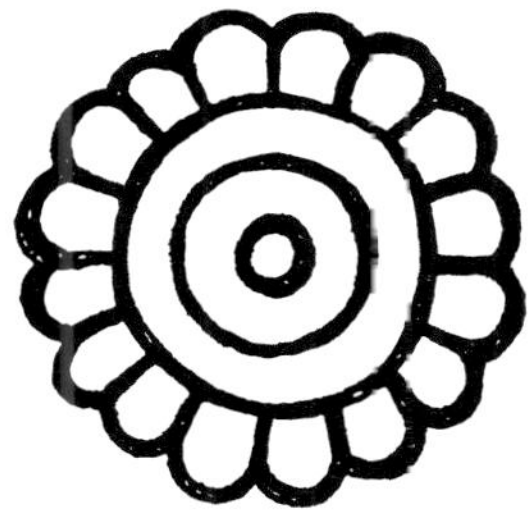

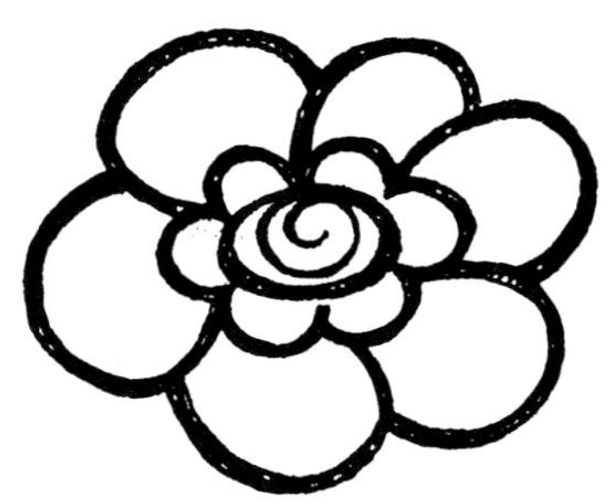

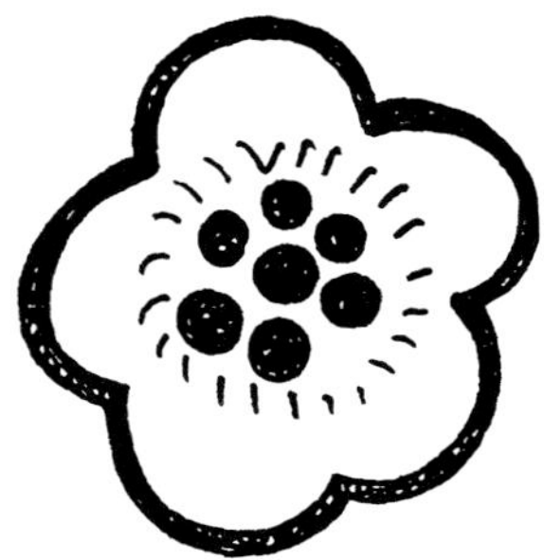

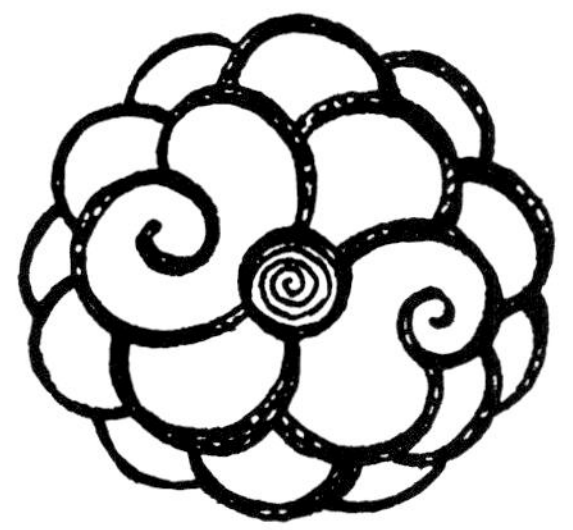
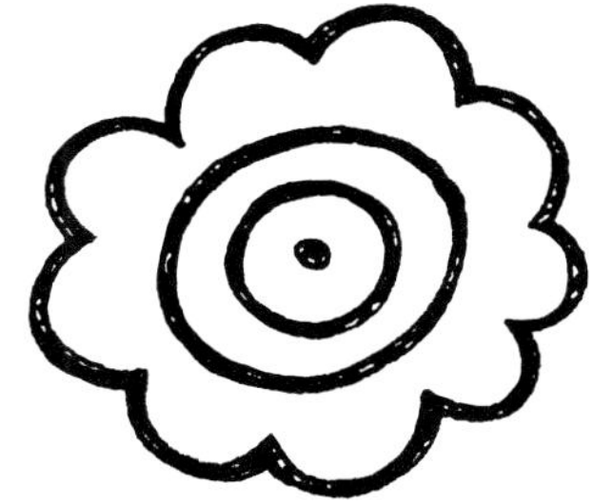
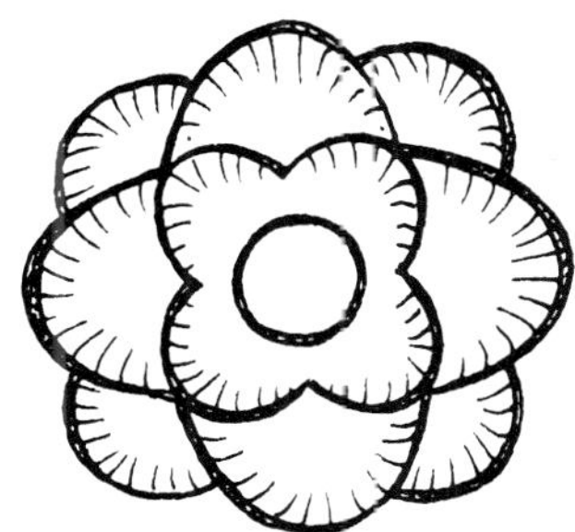

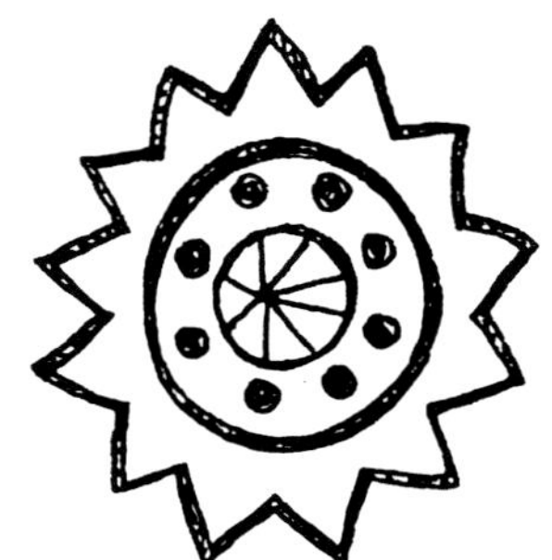

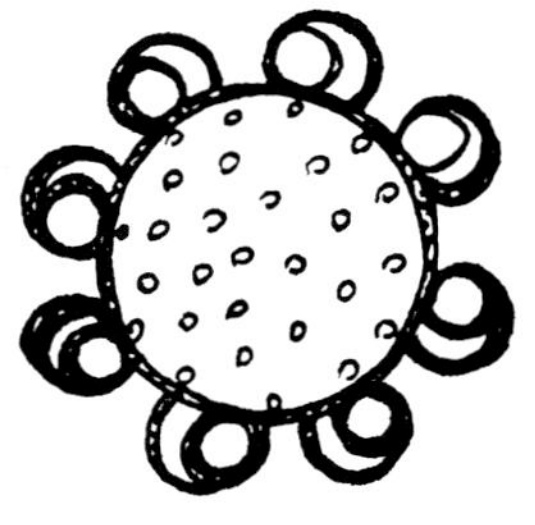

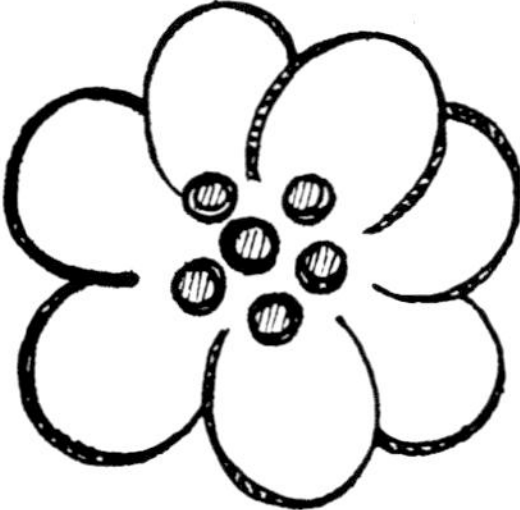

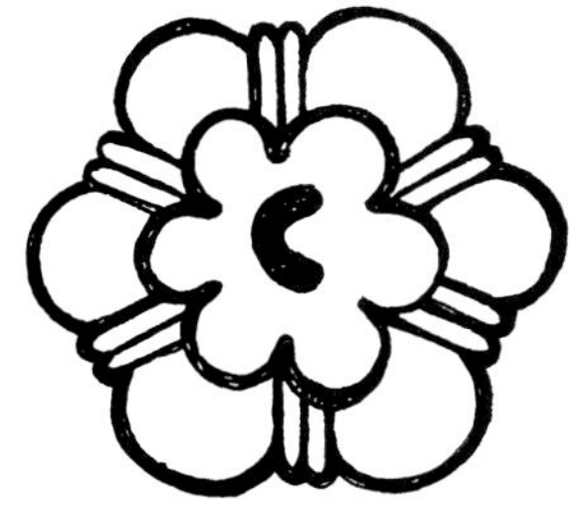
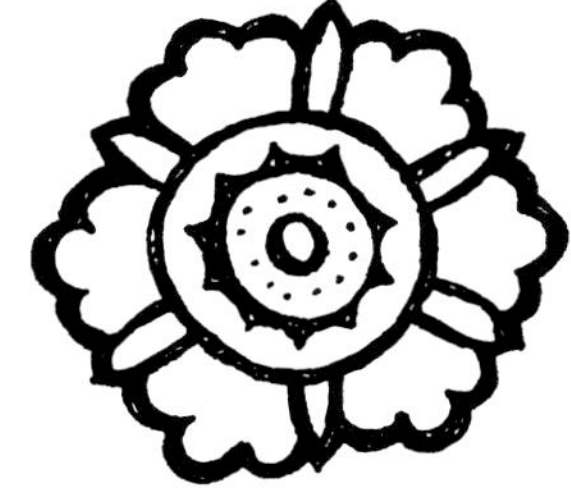
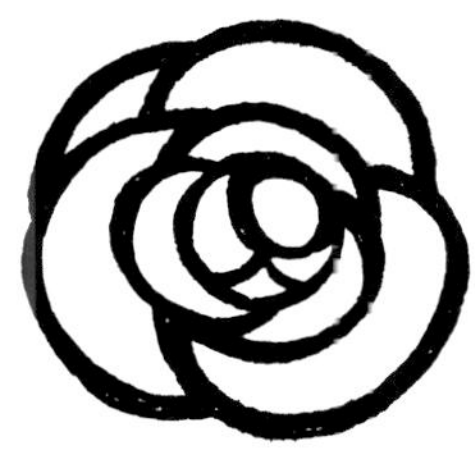

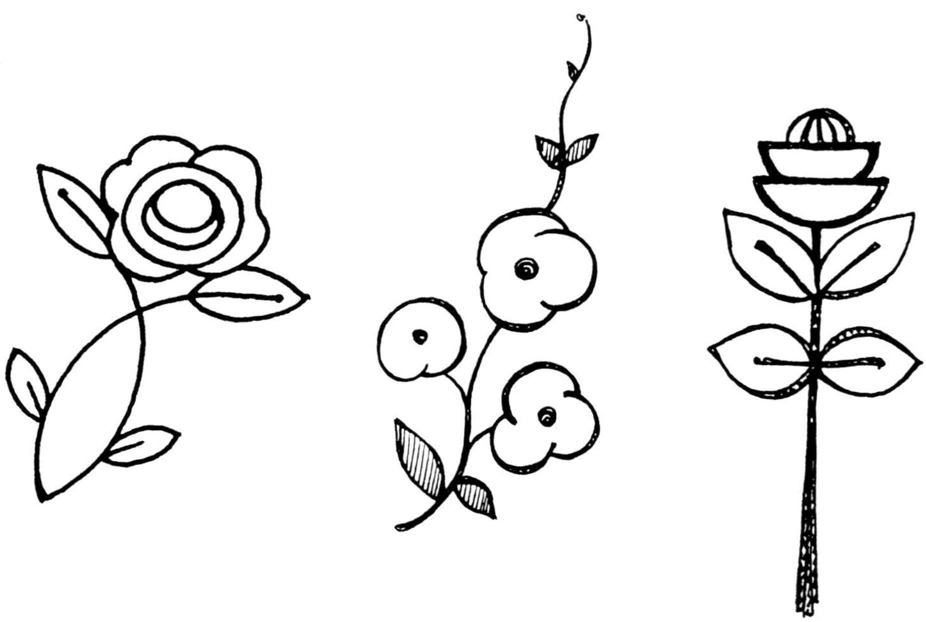

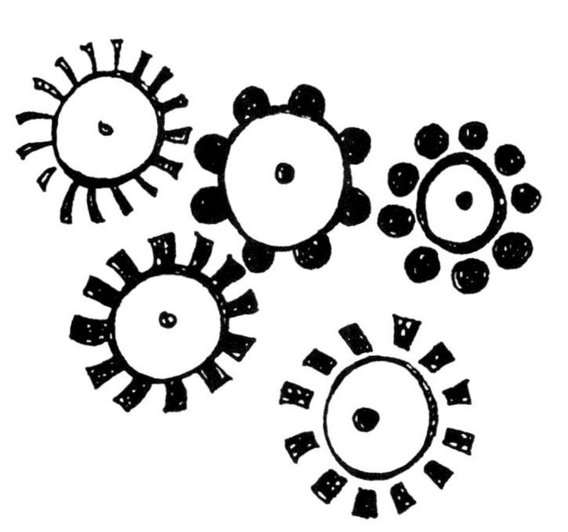

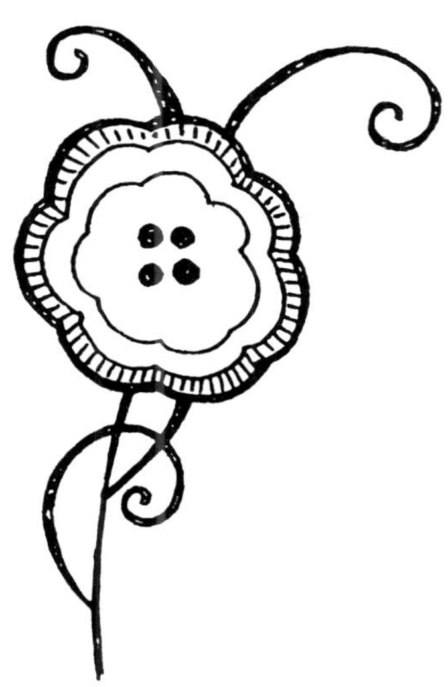

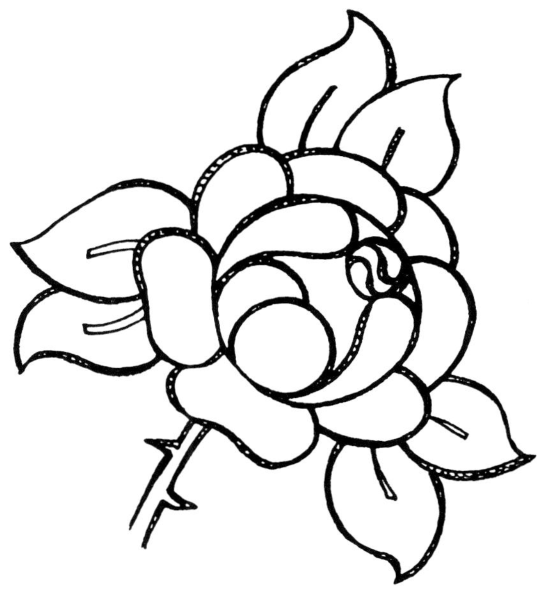

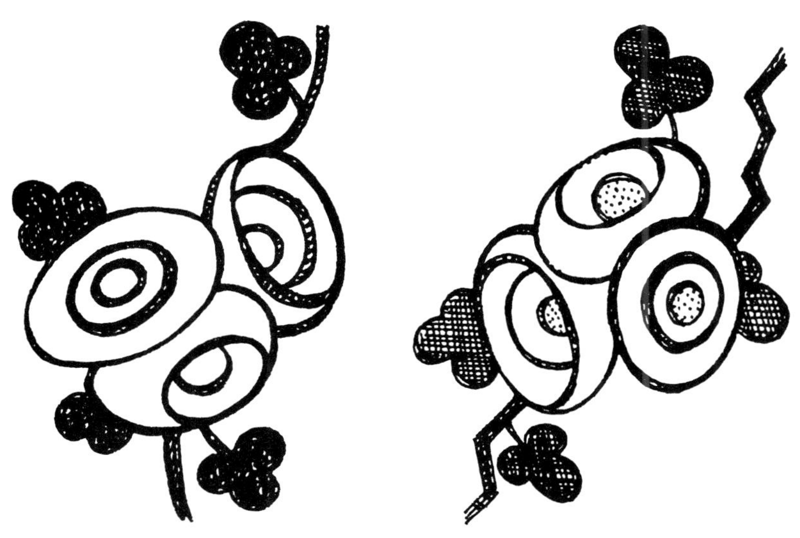

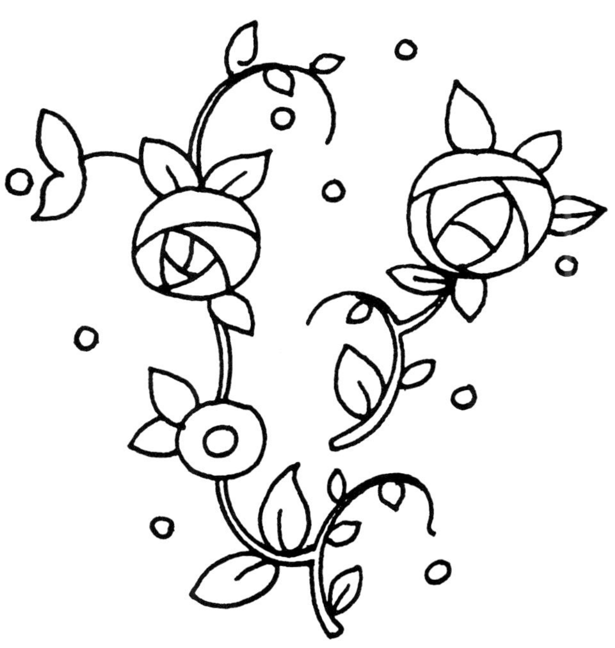

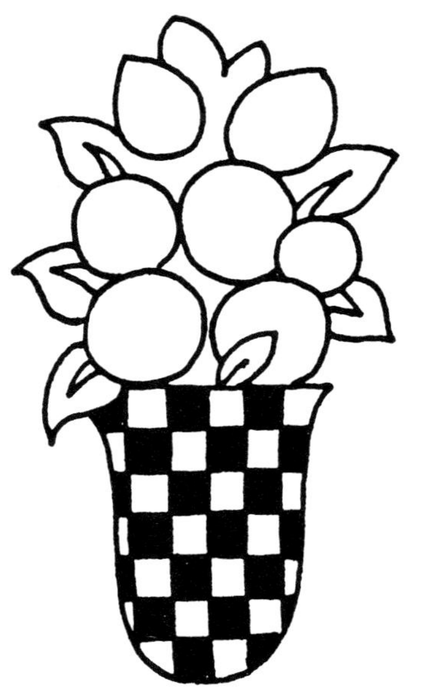

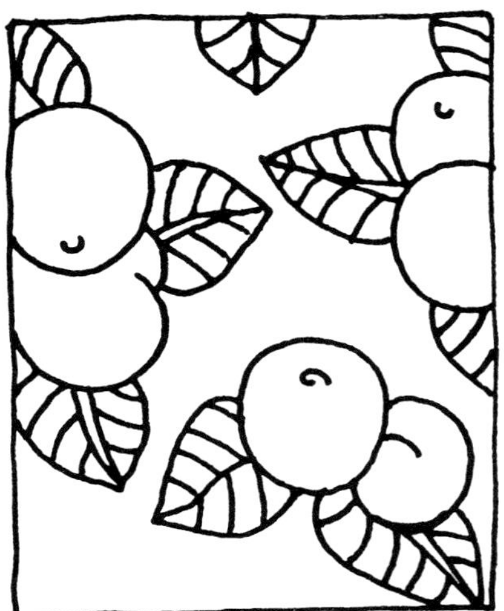

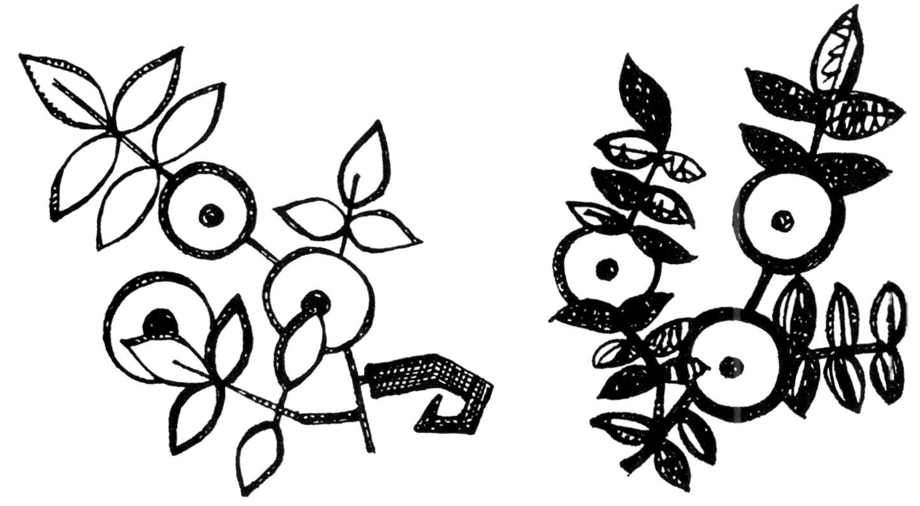

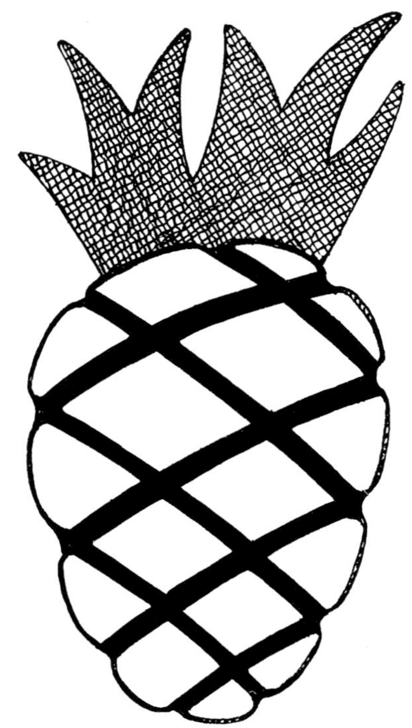

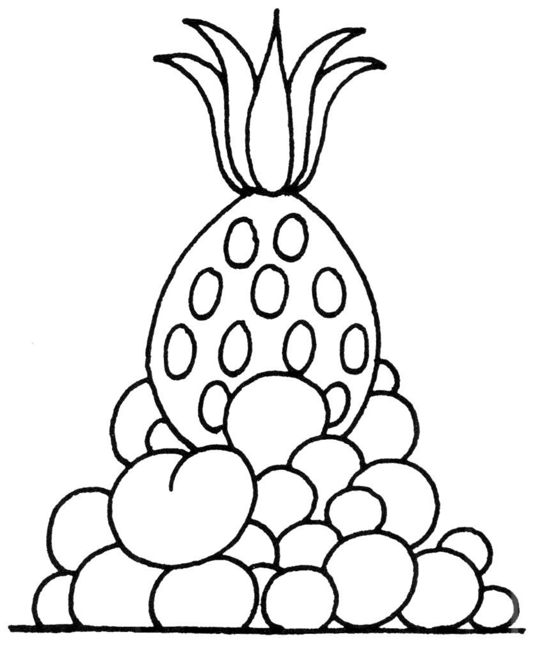

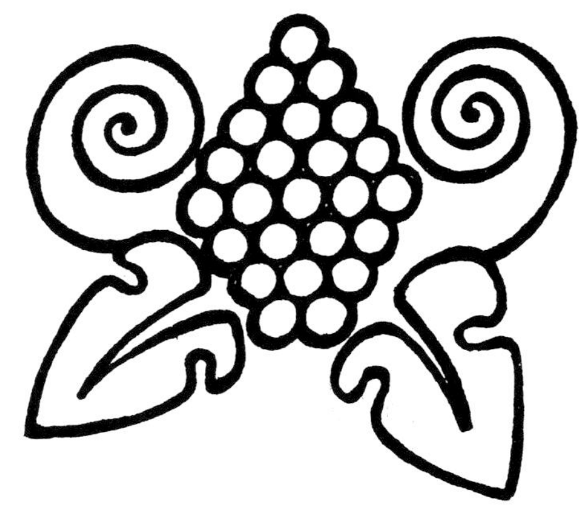

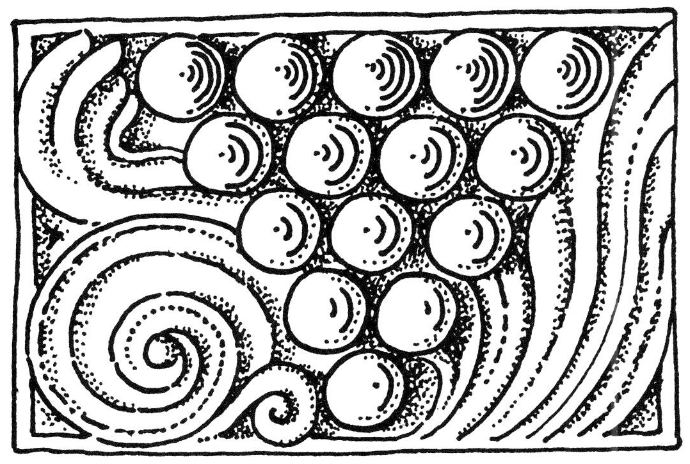

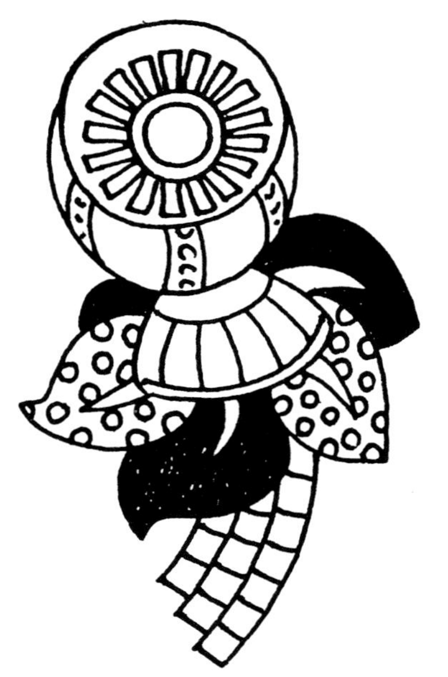

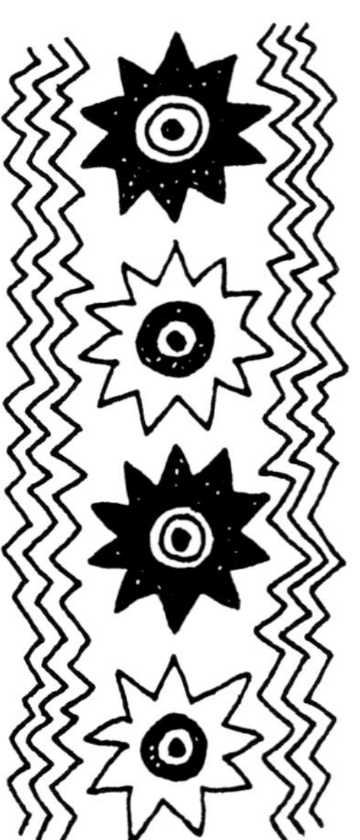

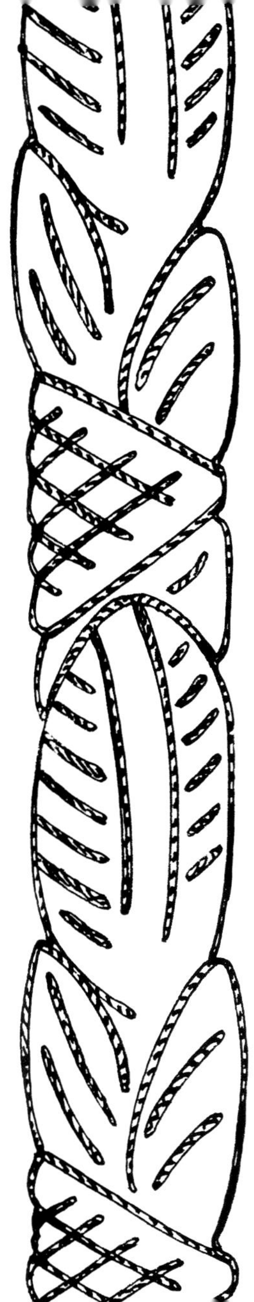

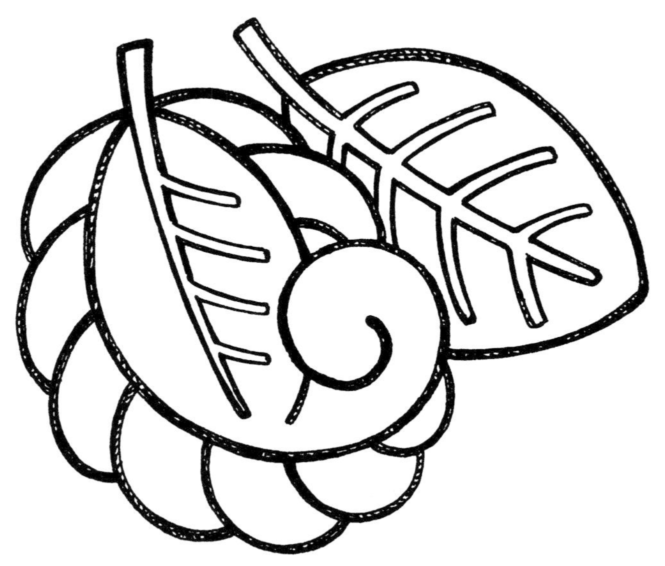

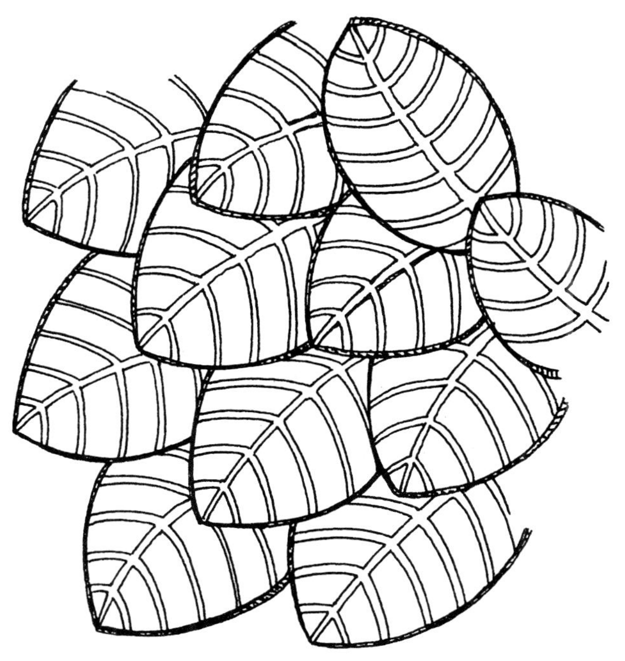

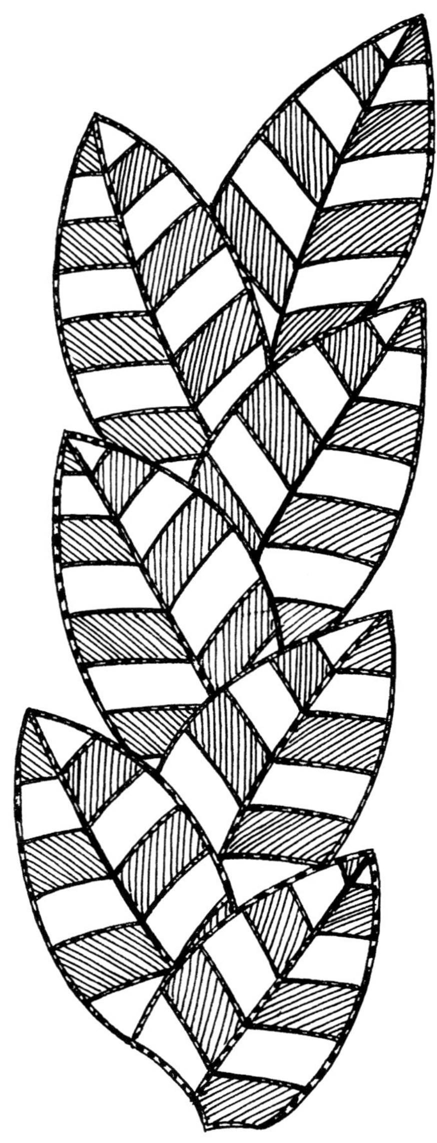

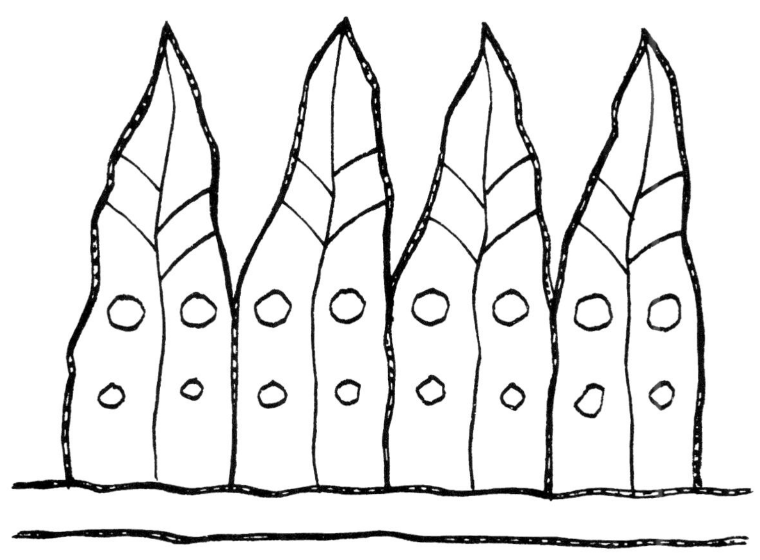

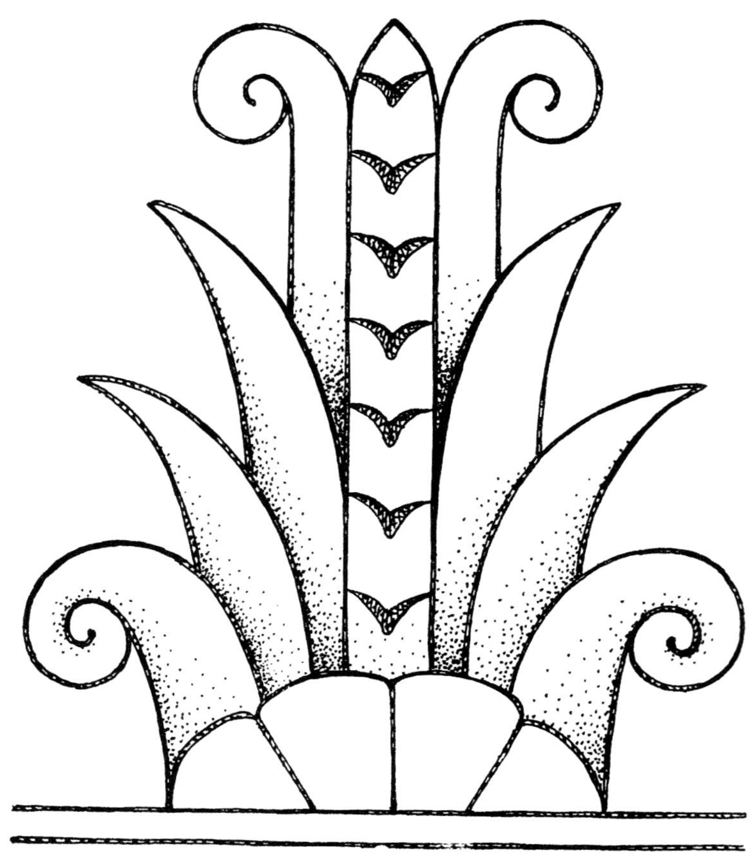

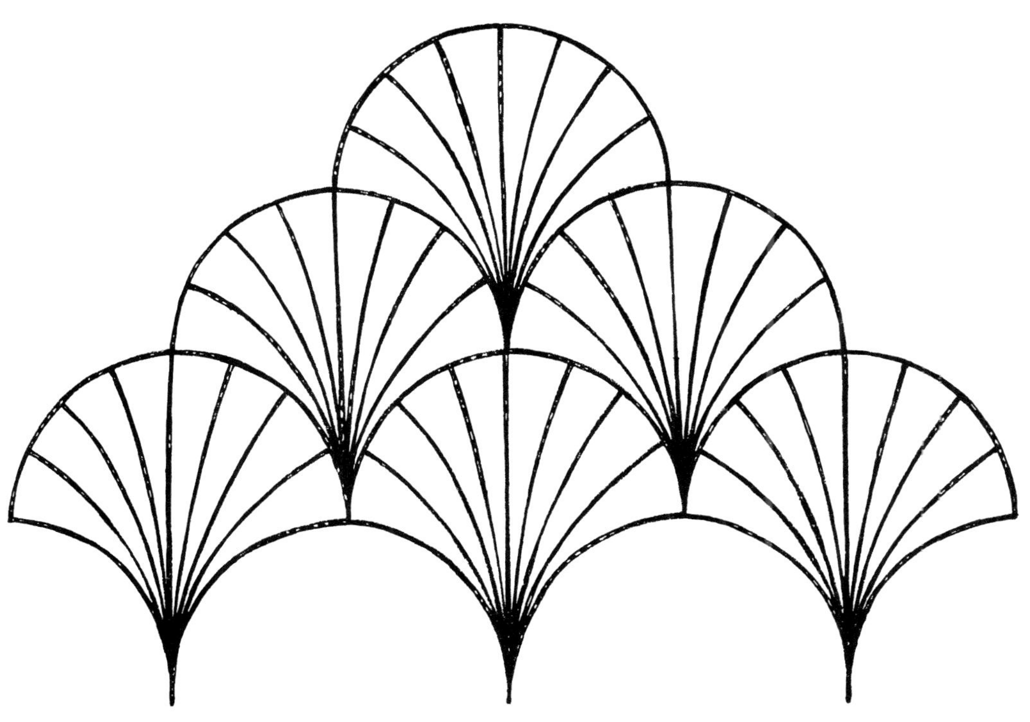

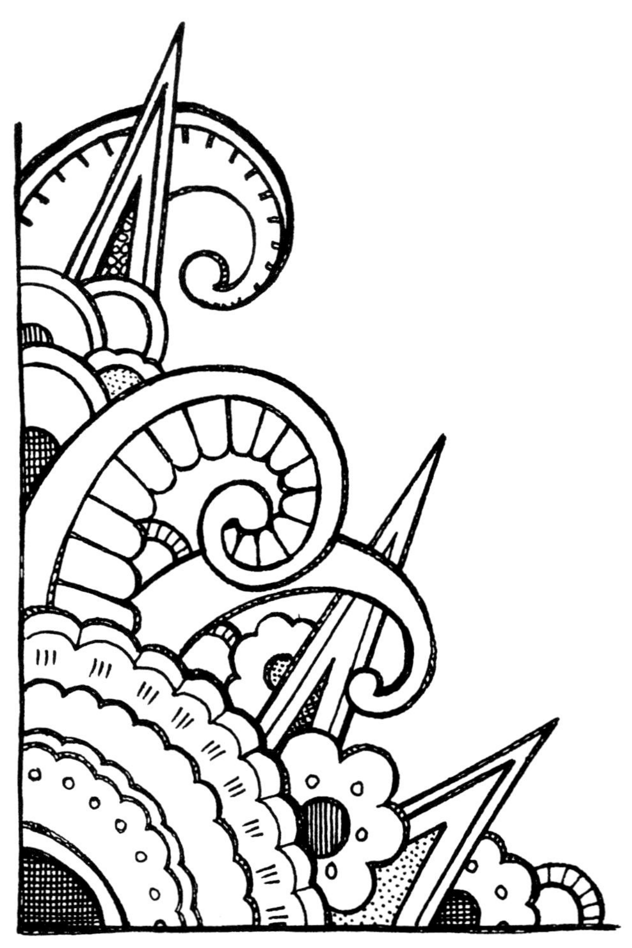

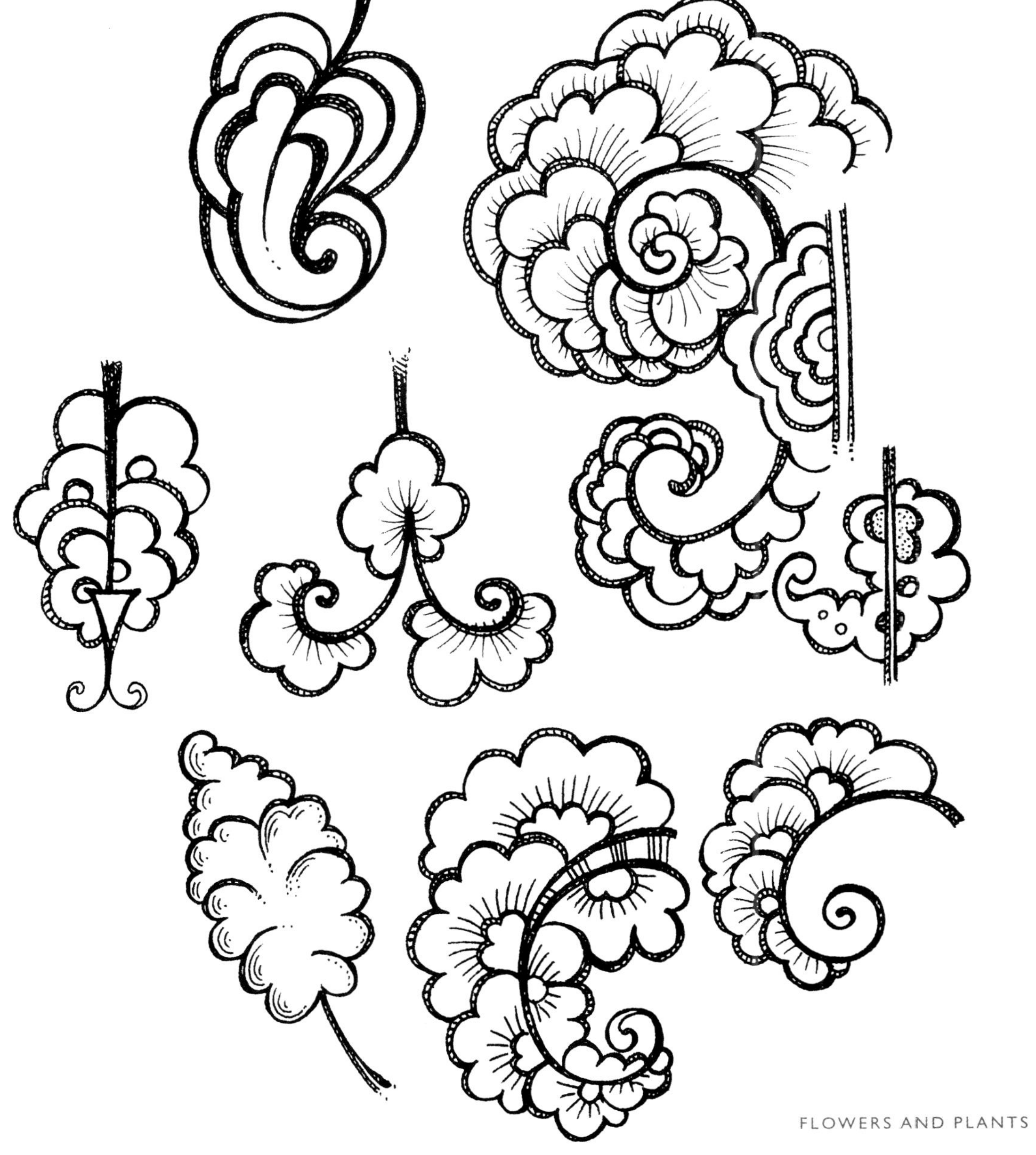

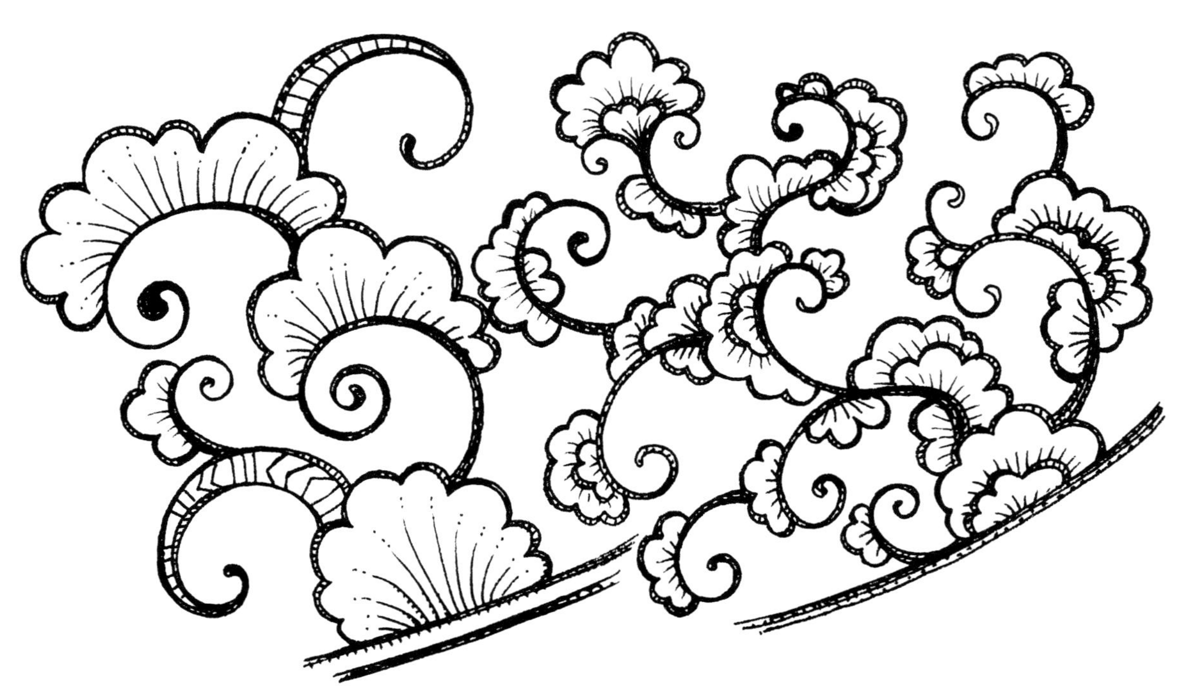

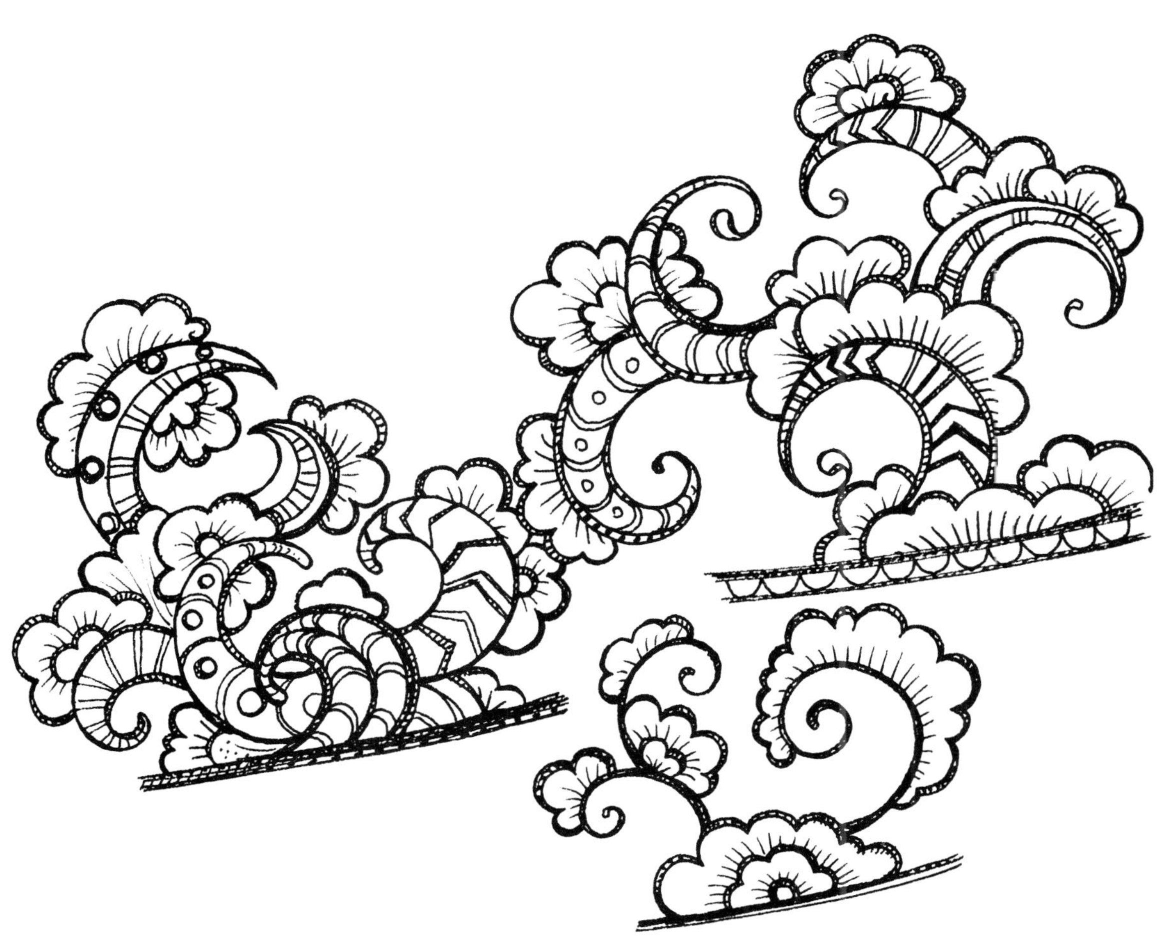

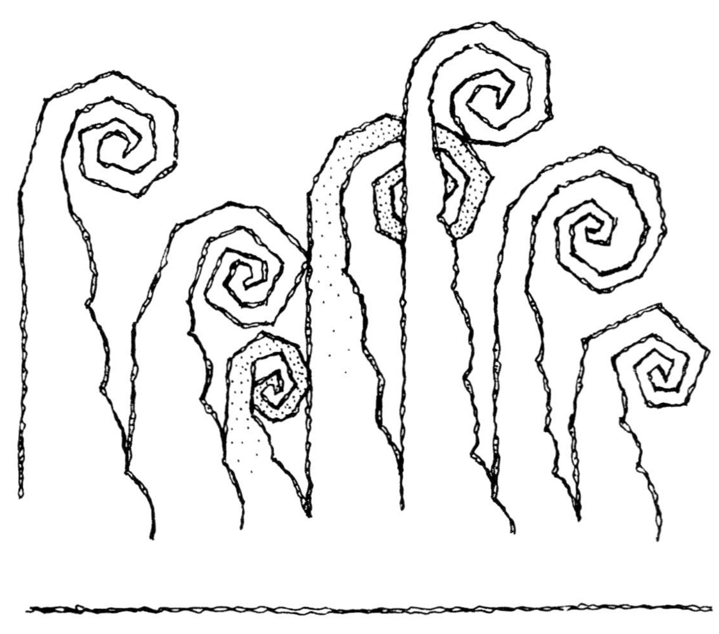

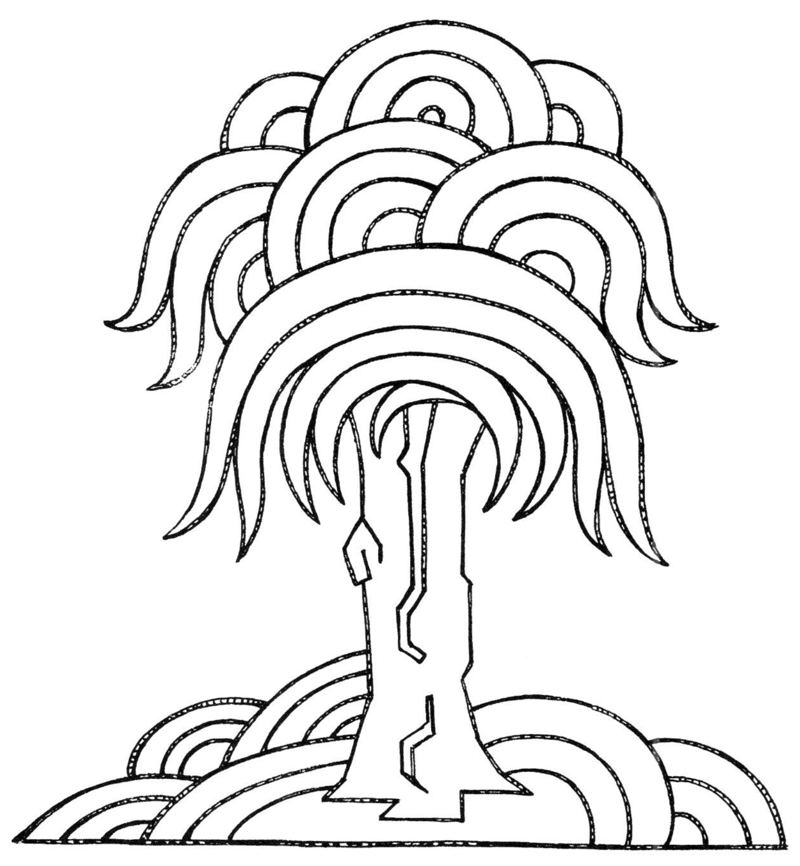

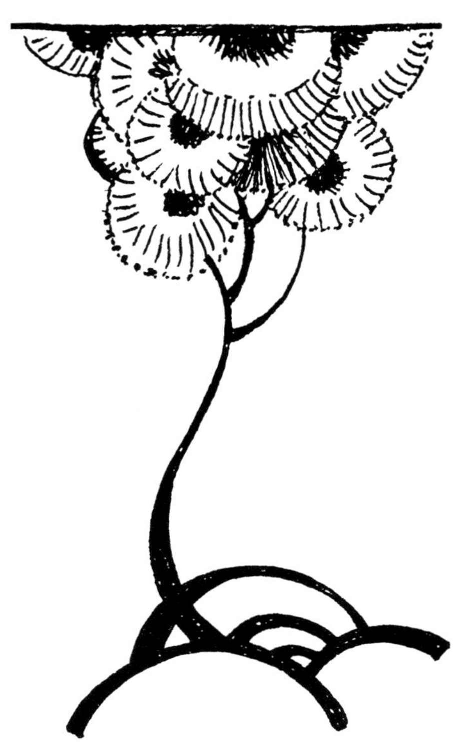

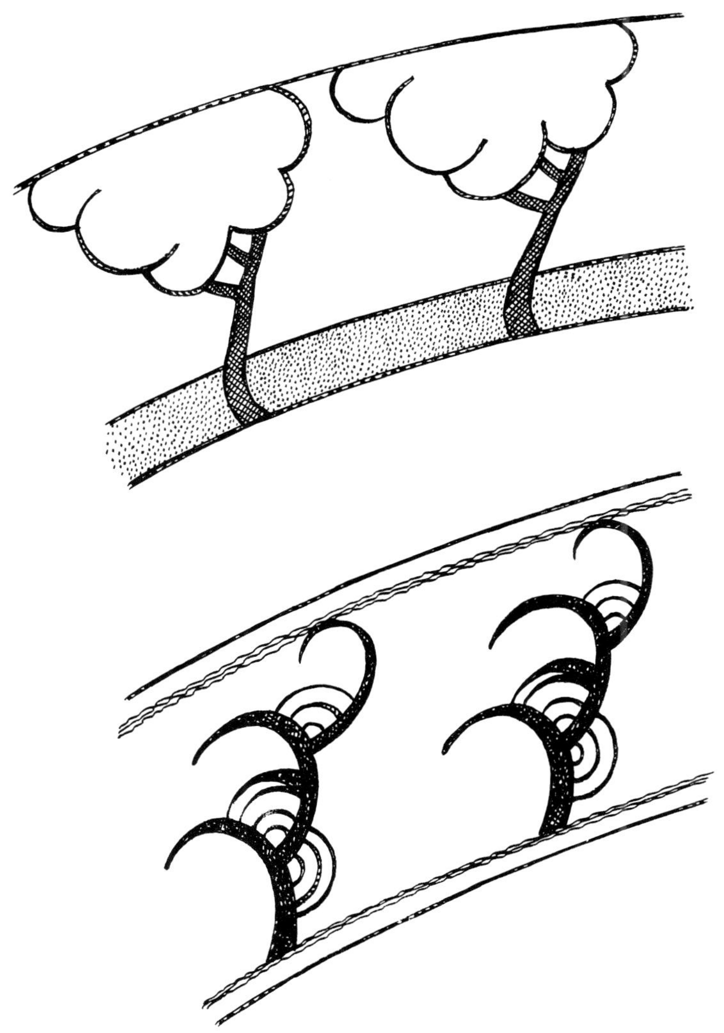

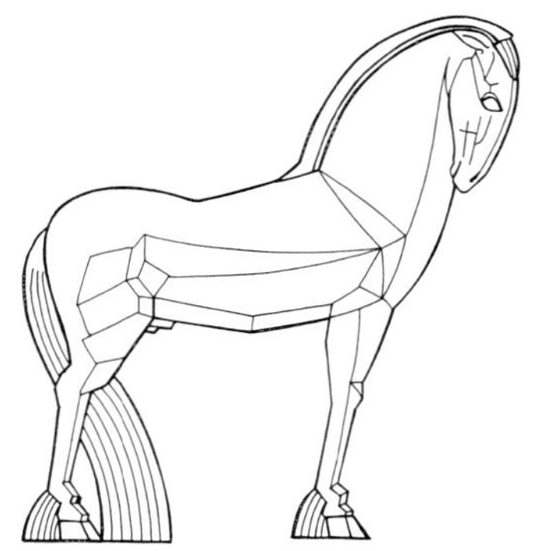
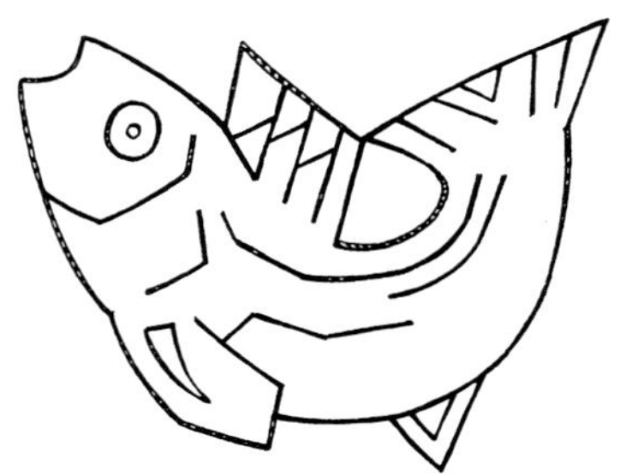
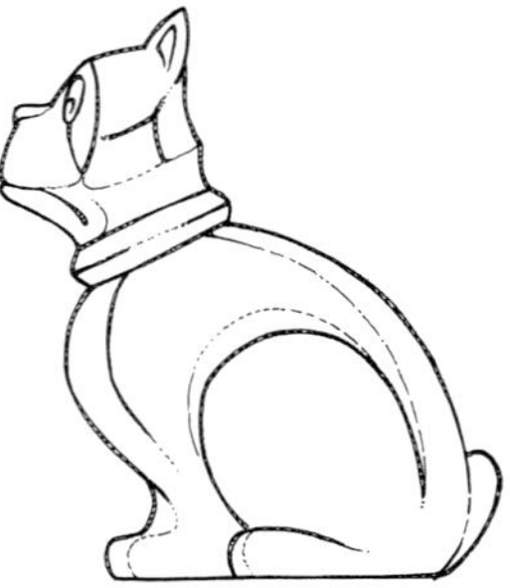

ANIMALS

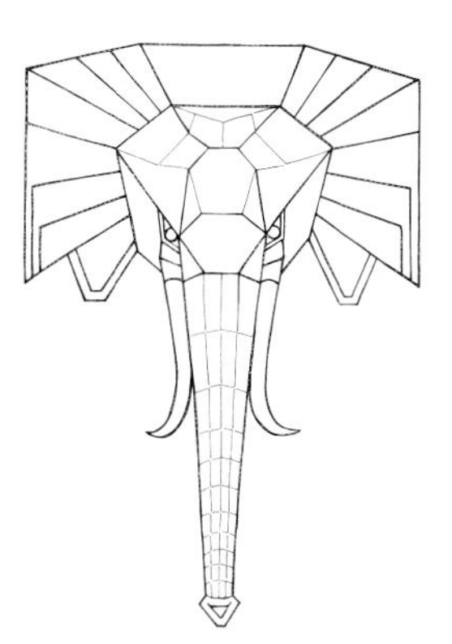

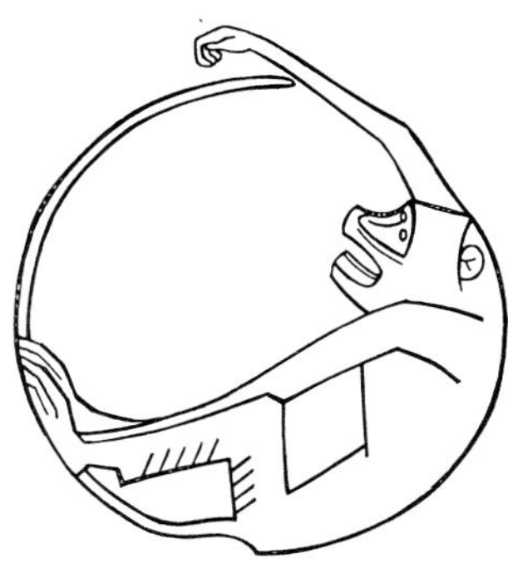

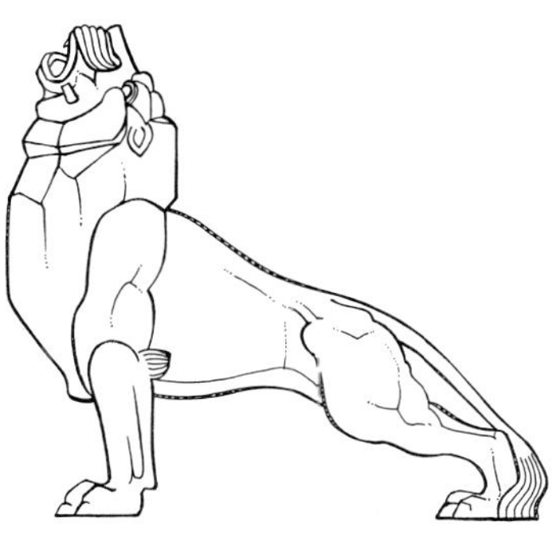

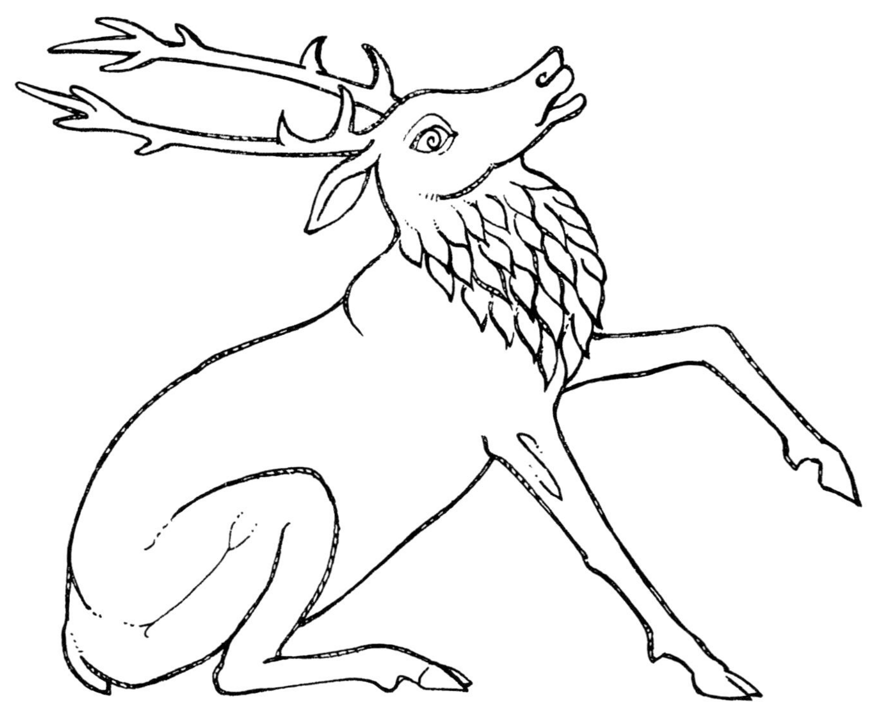

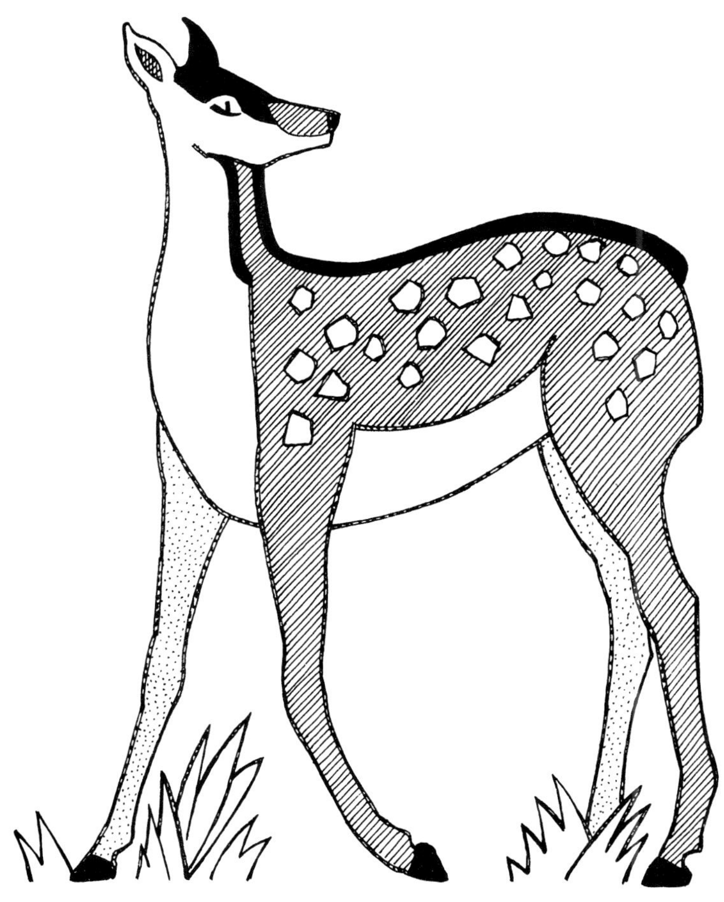

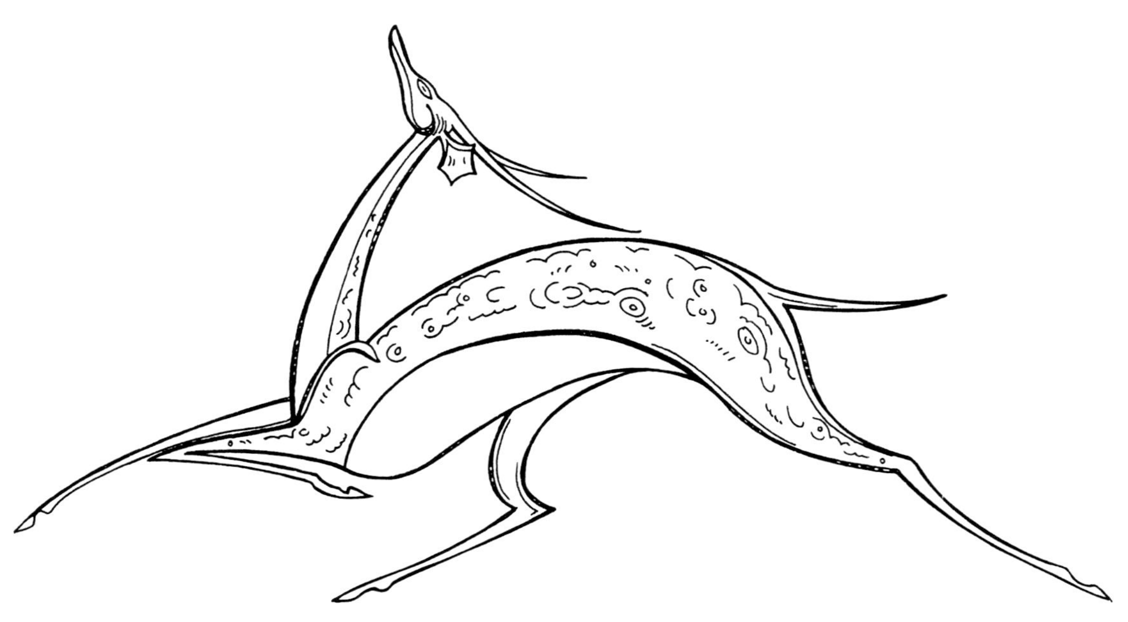

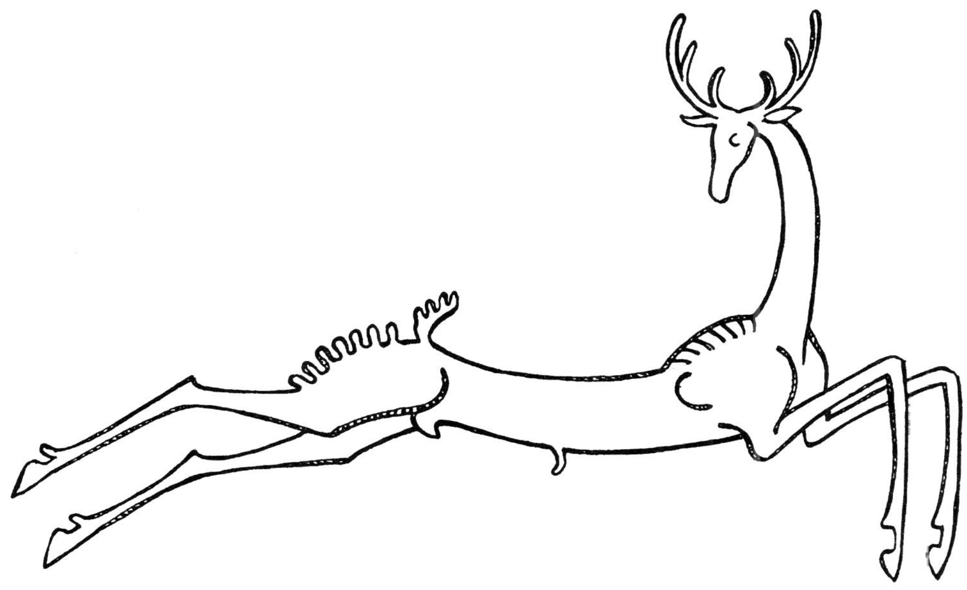

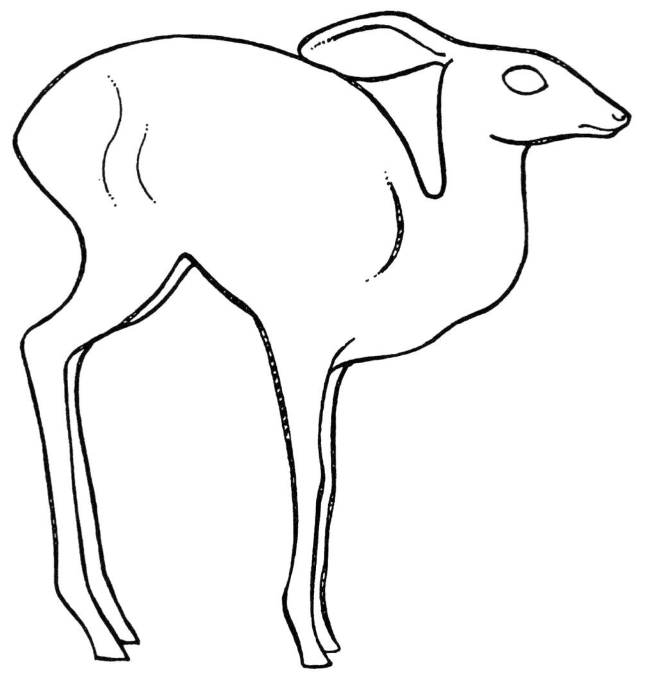

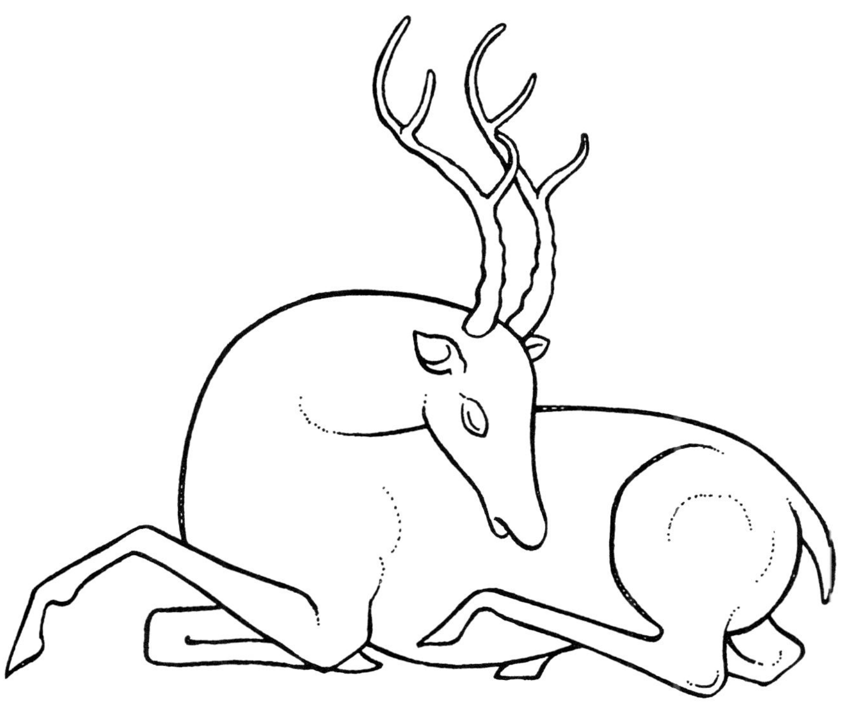

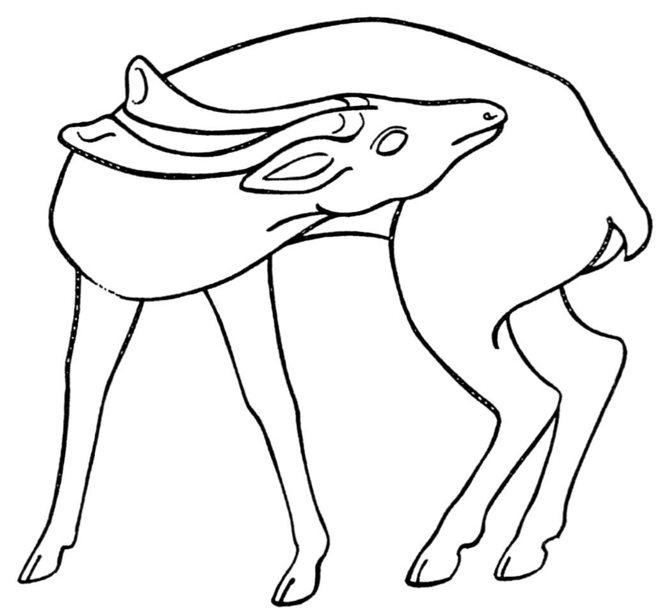

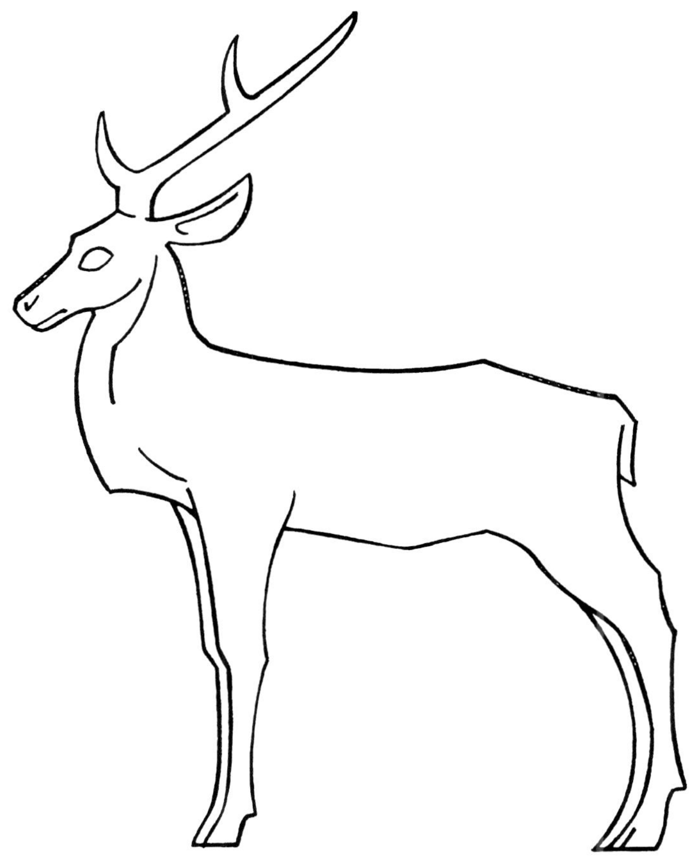

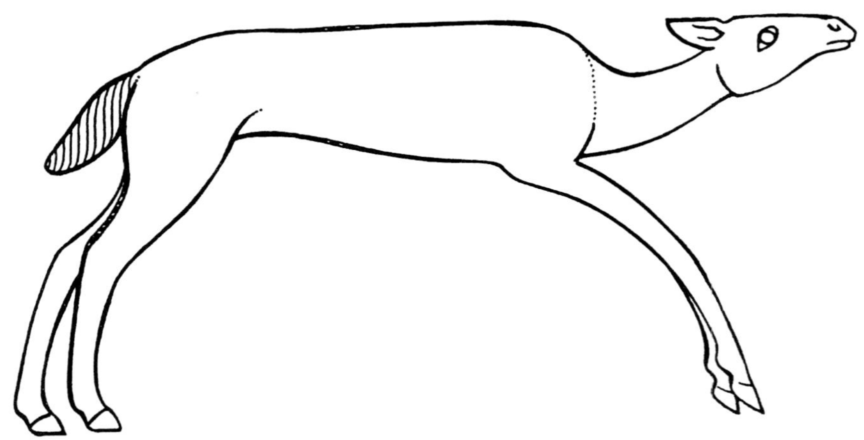

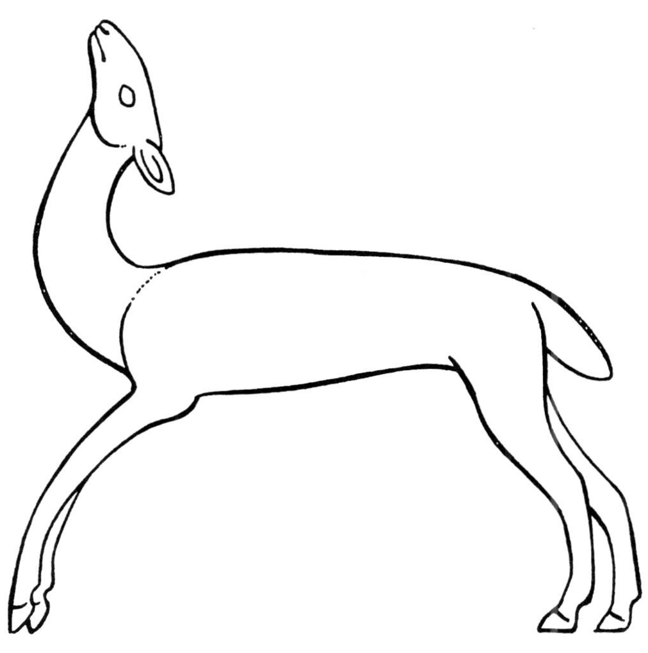

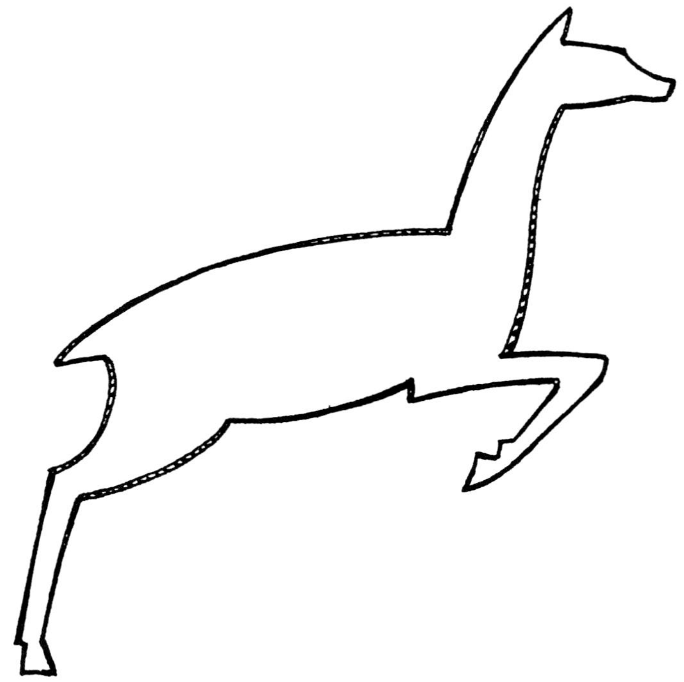

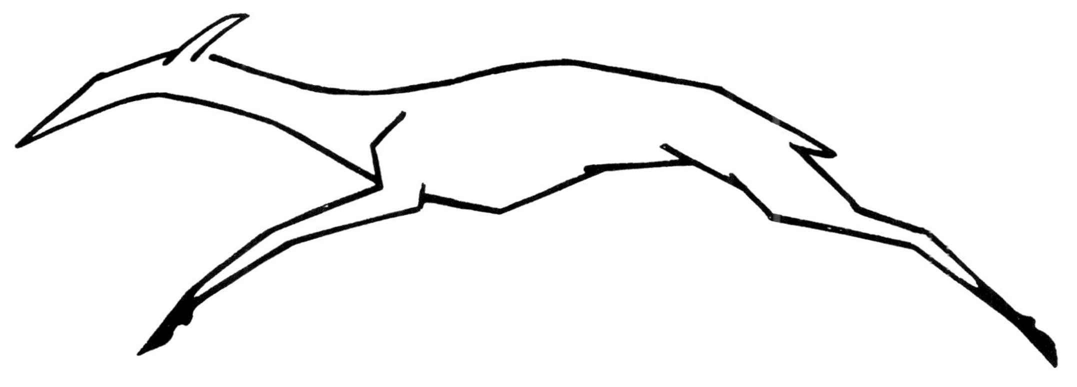

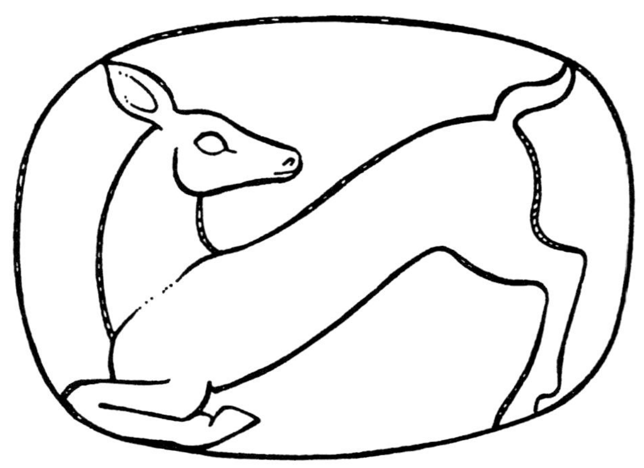

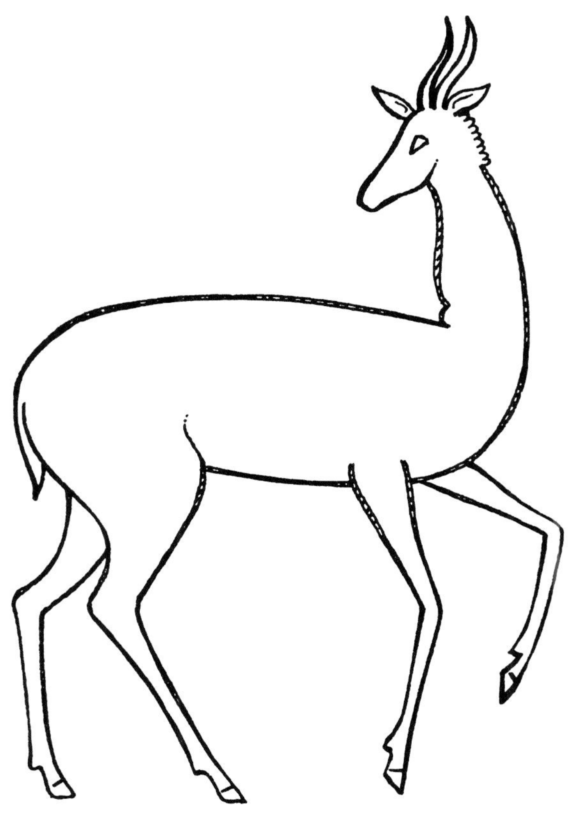

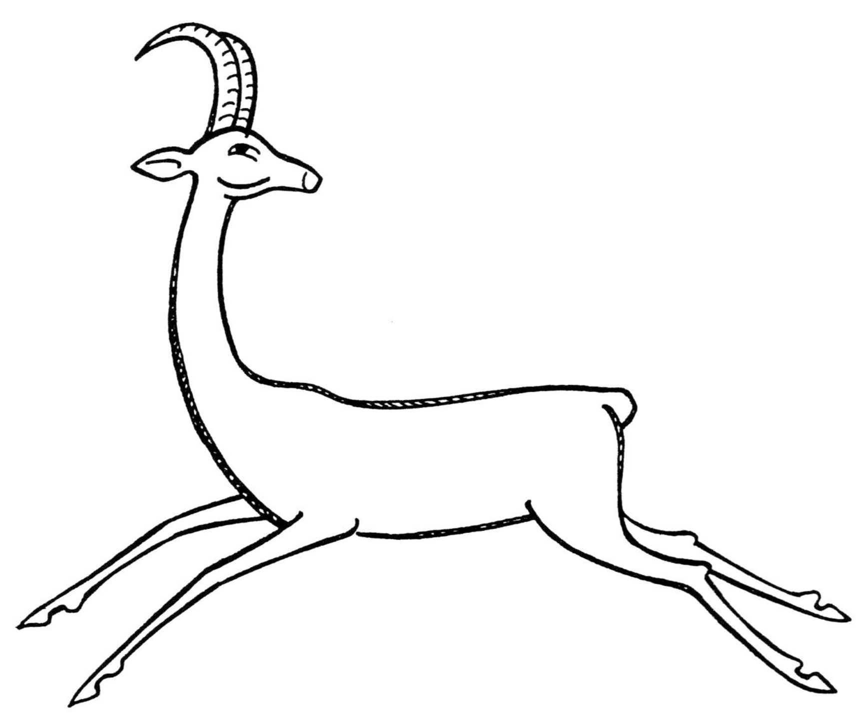

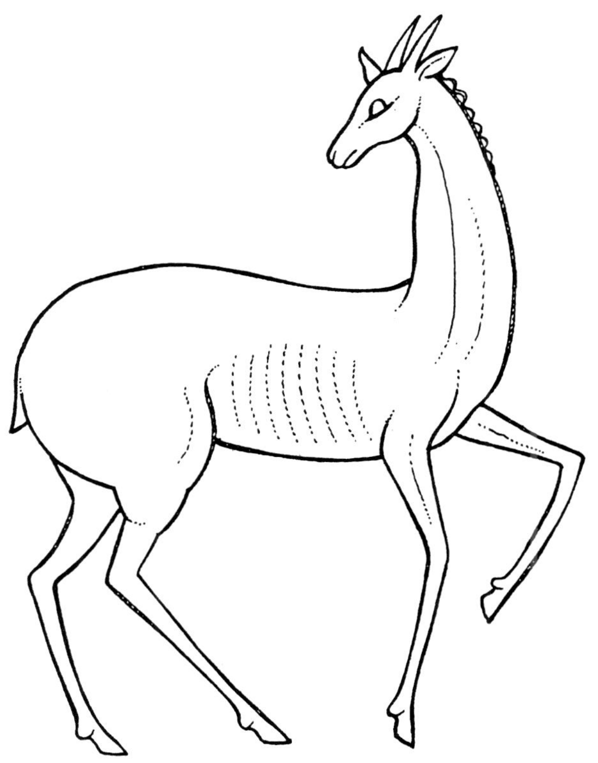

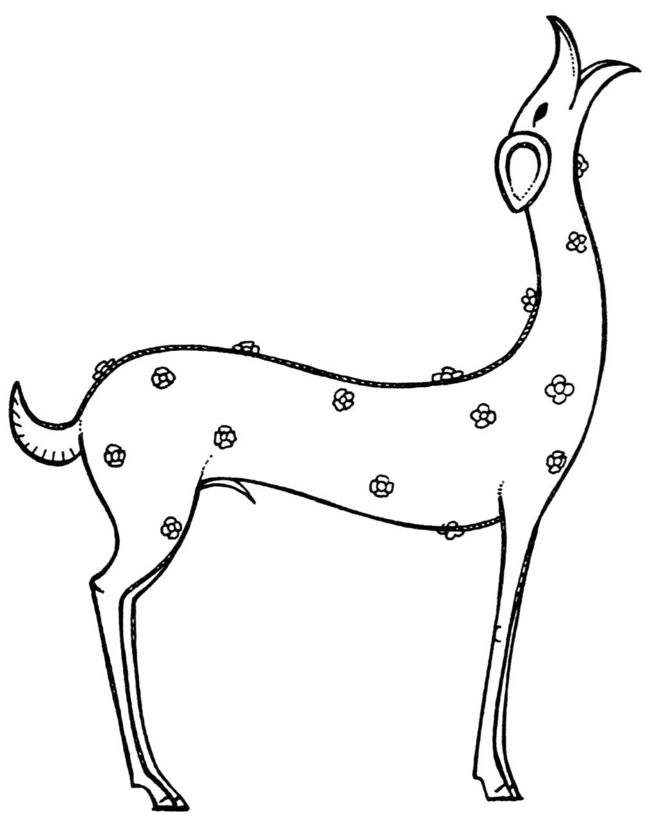

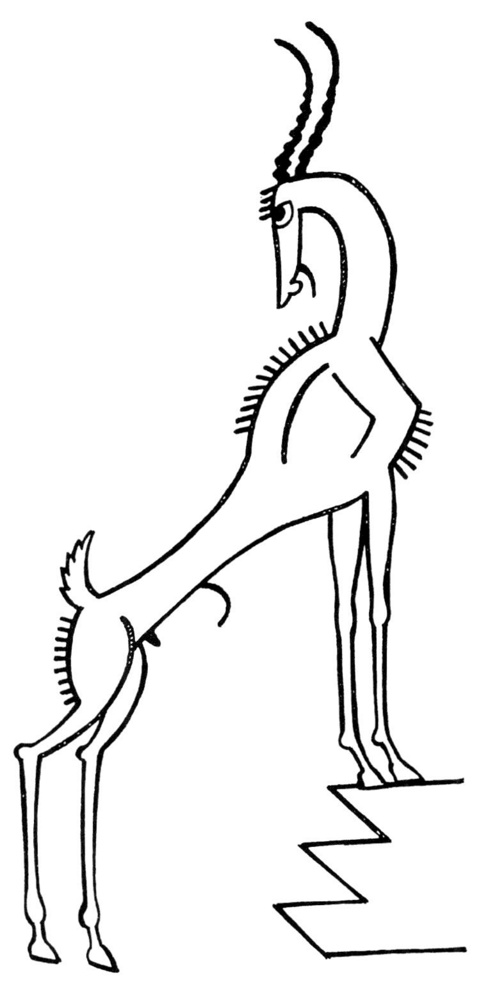

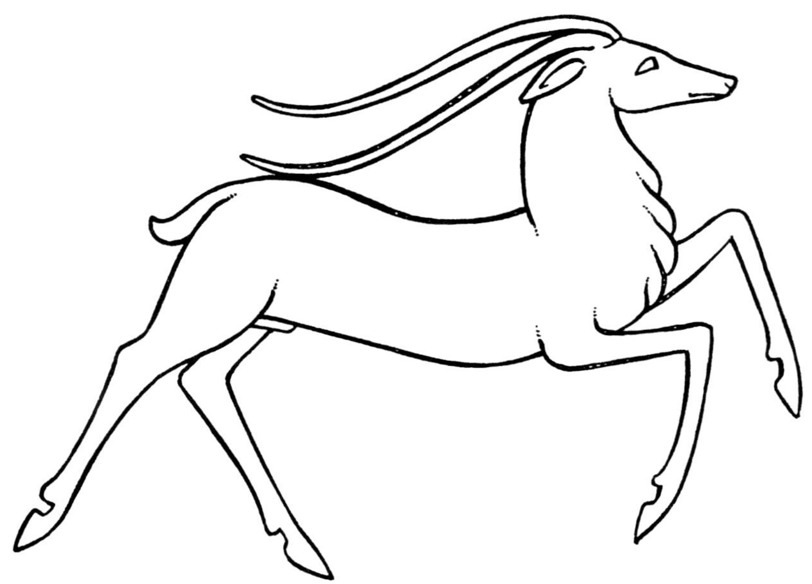

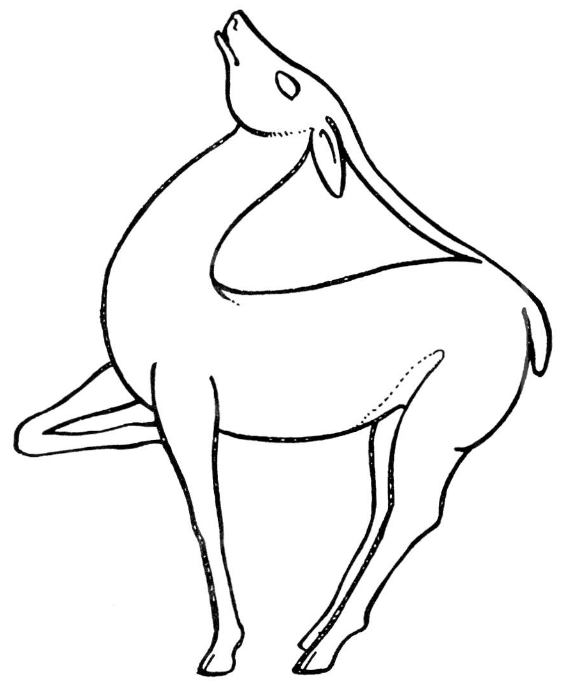

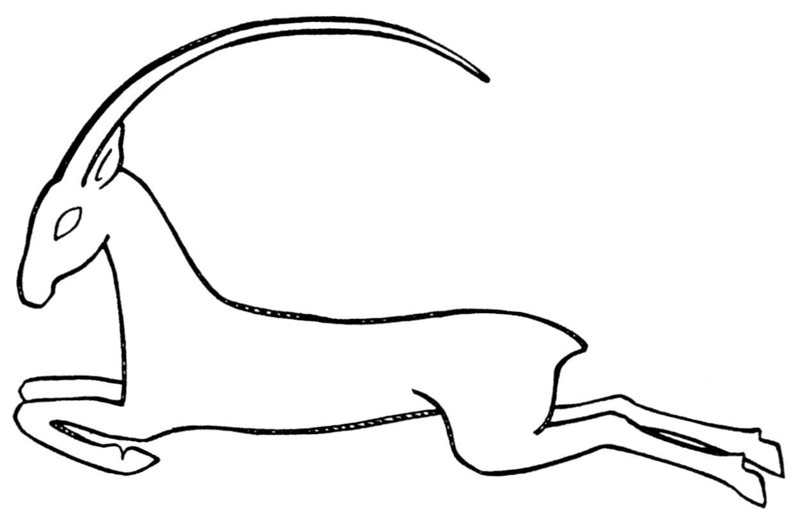

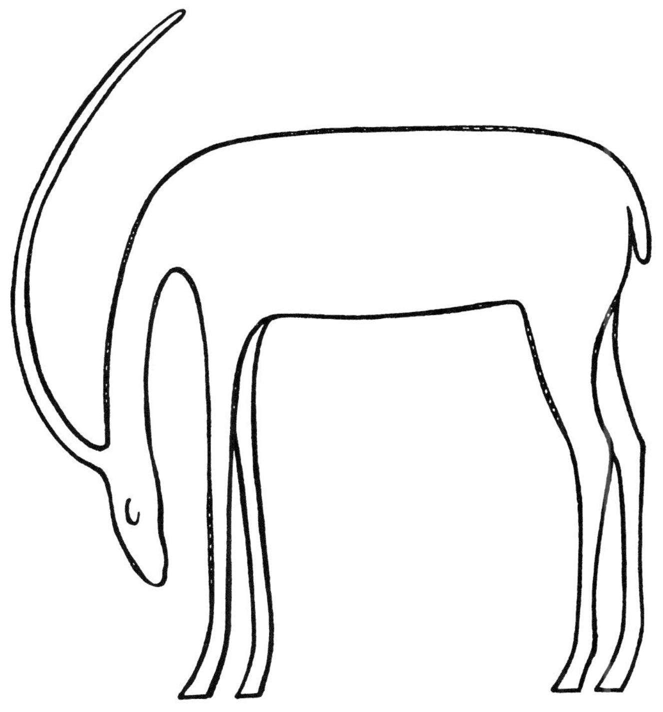

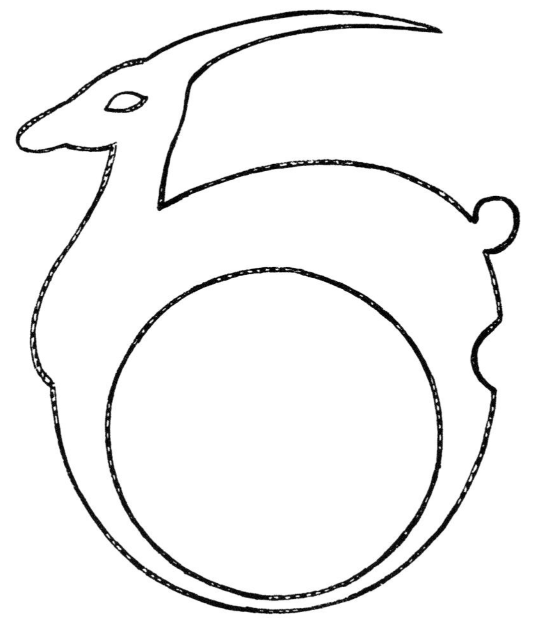

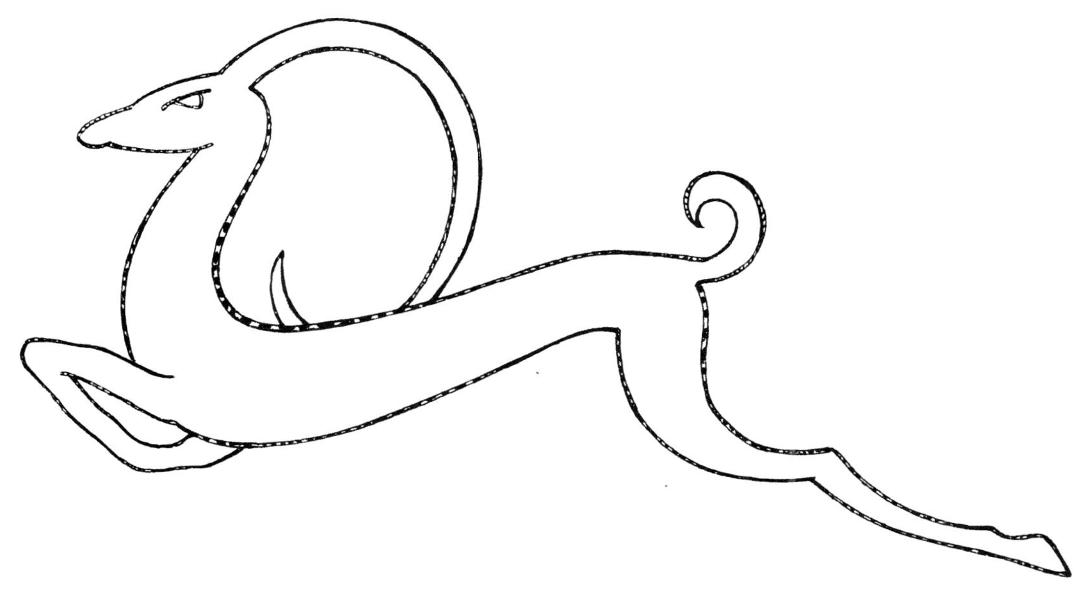

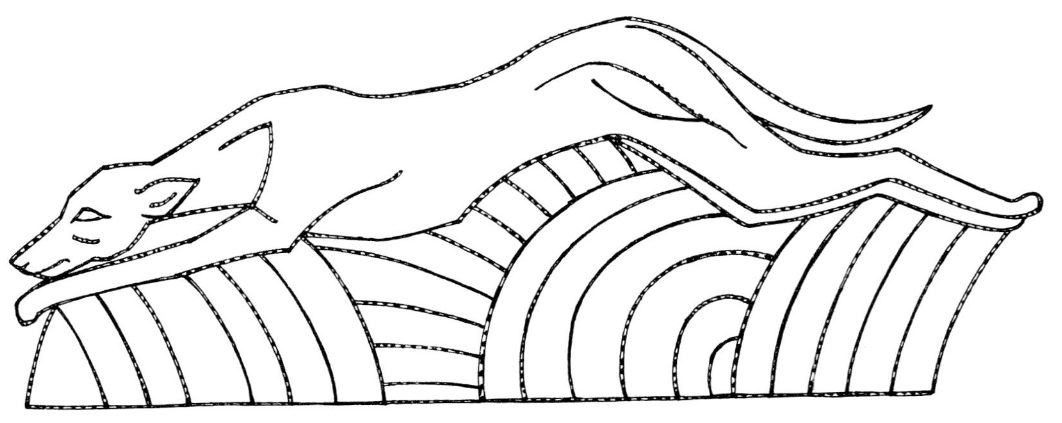

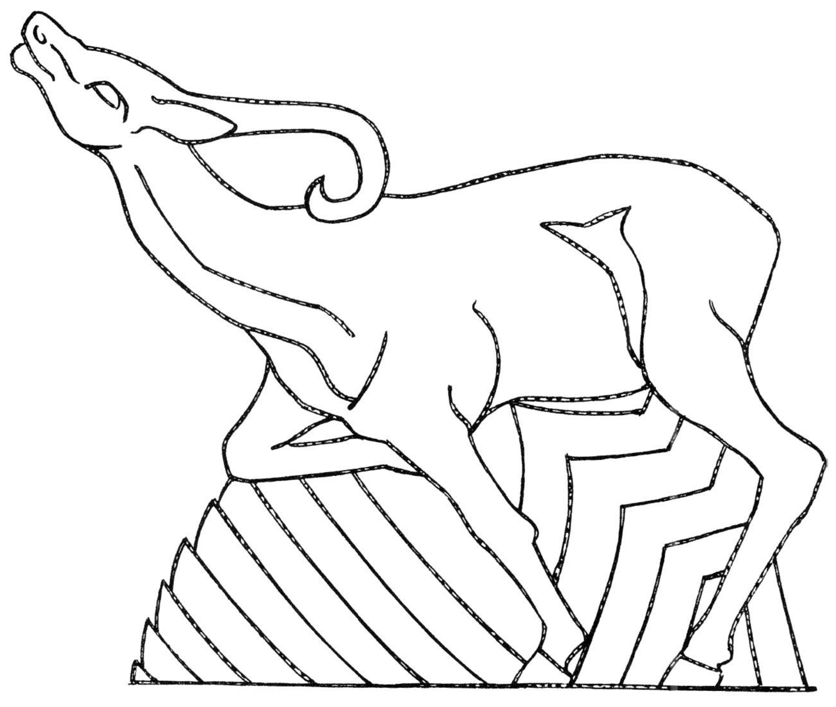

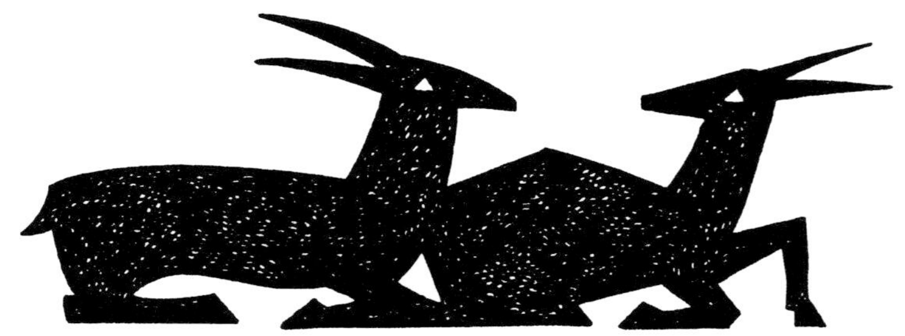

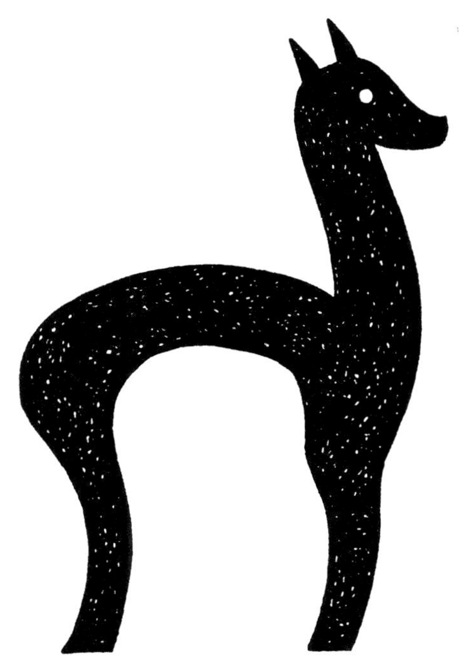

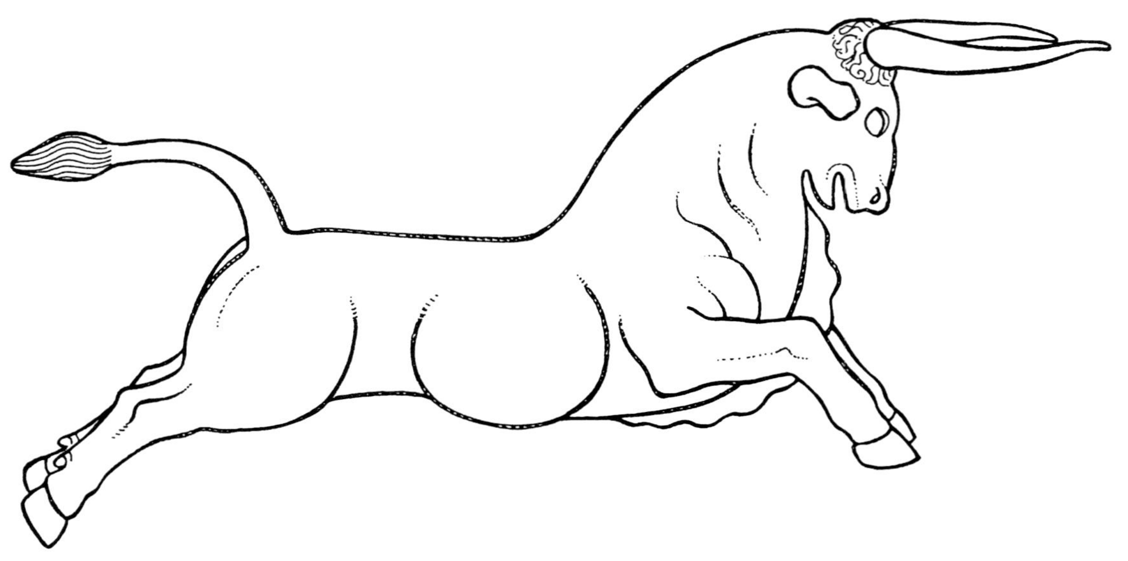

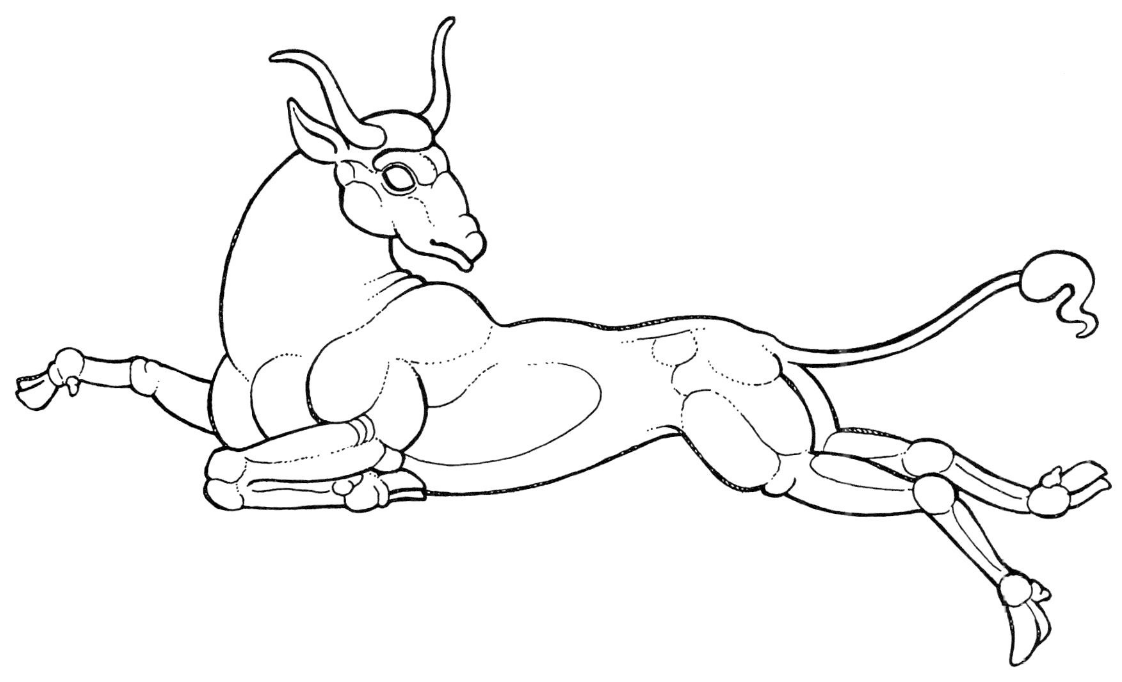

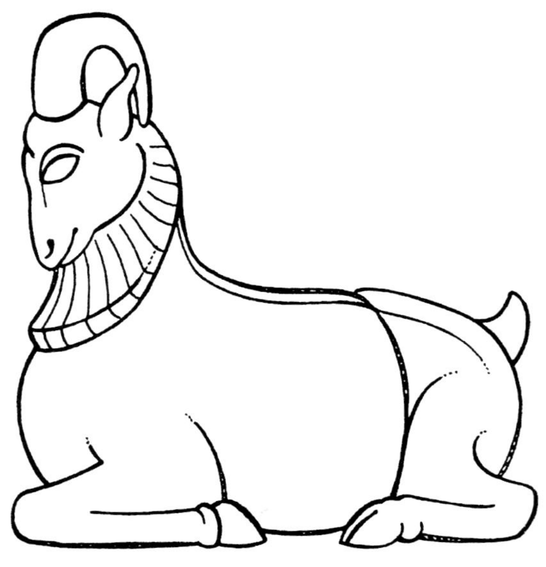

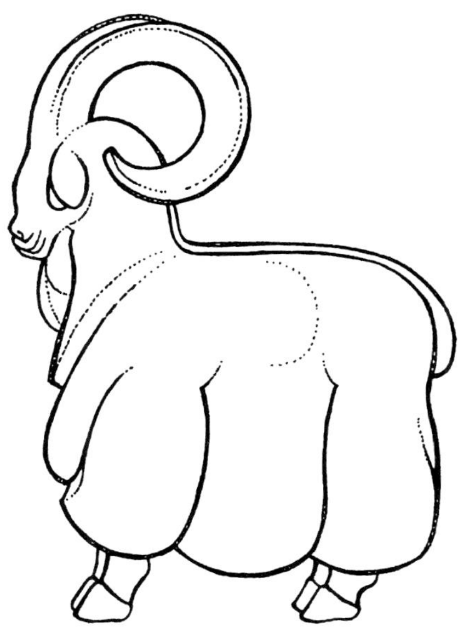

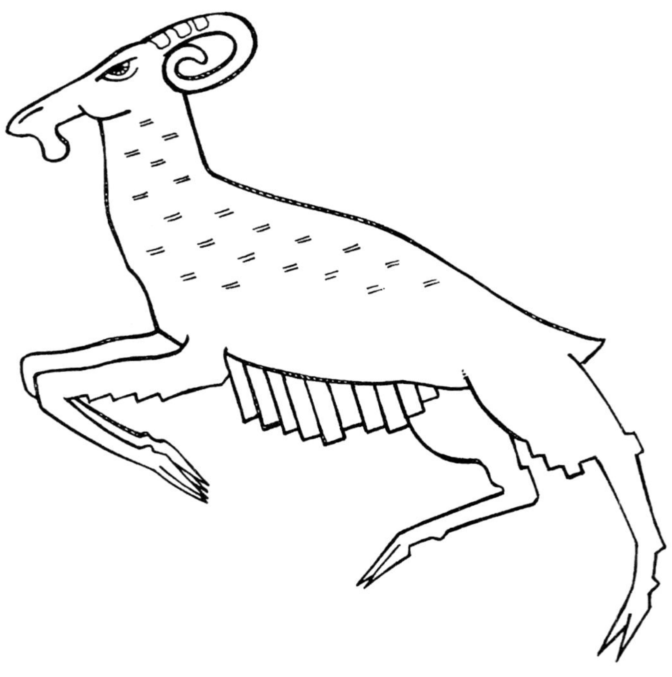

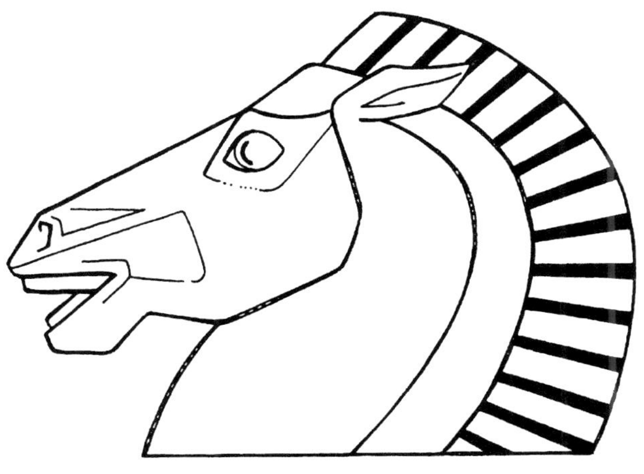

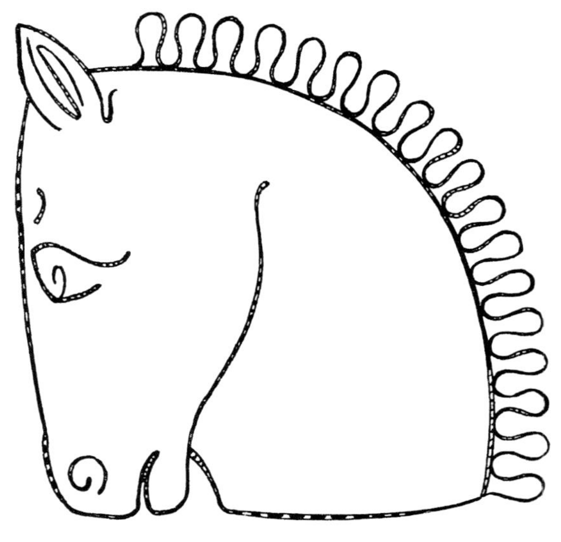

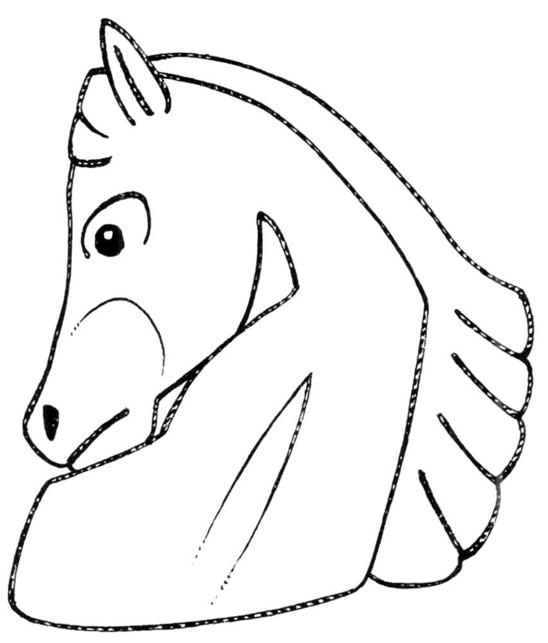

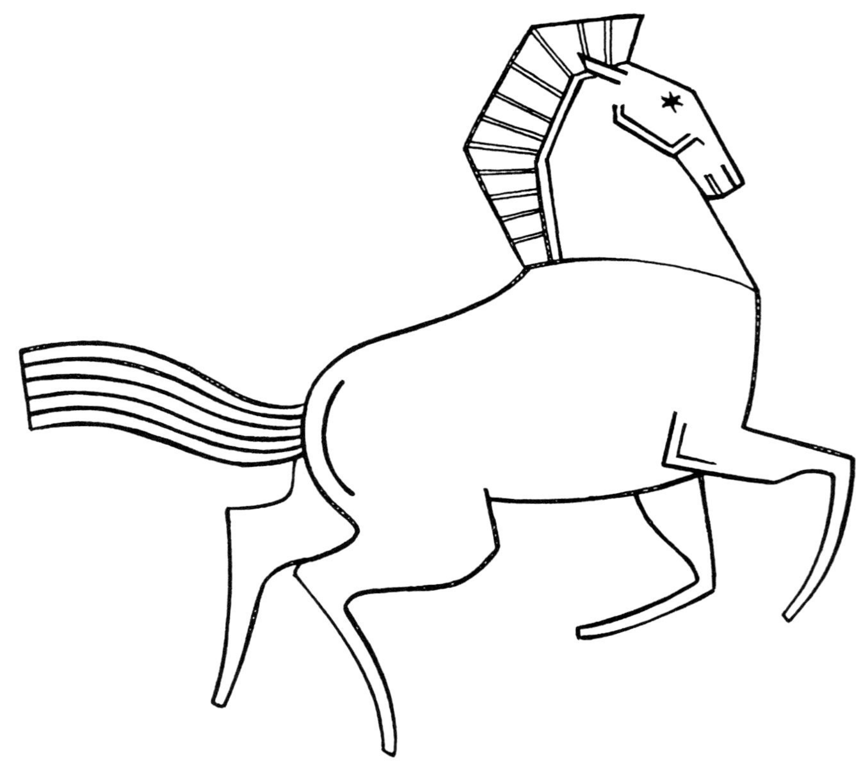

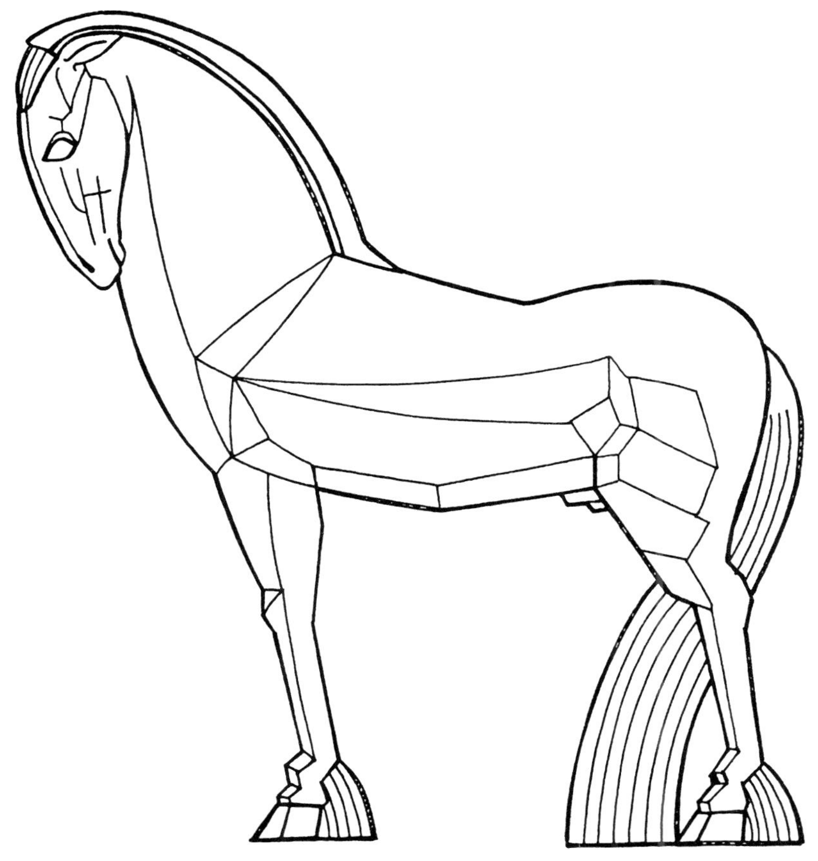

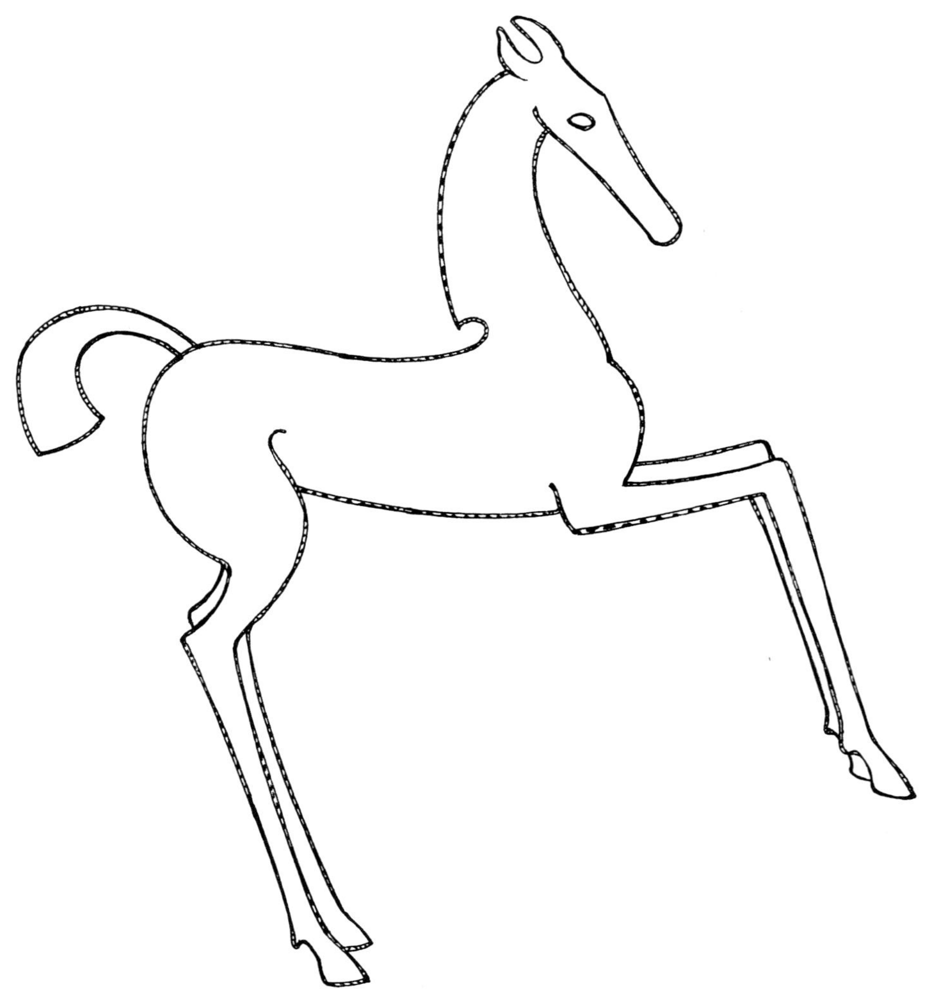

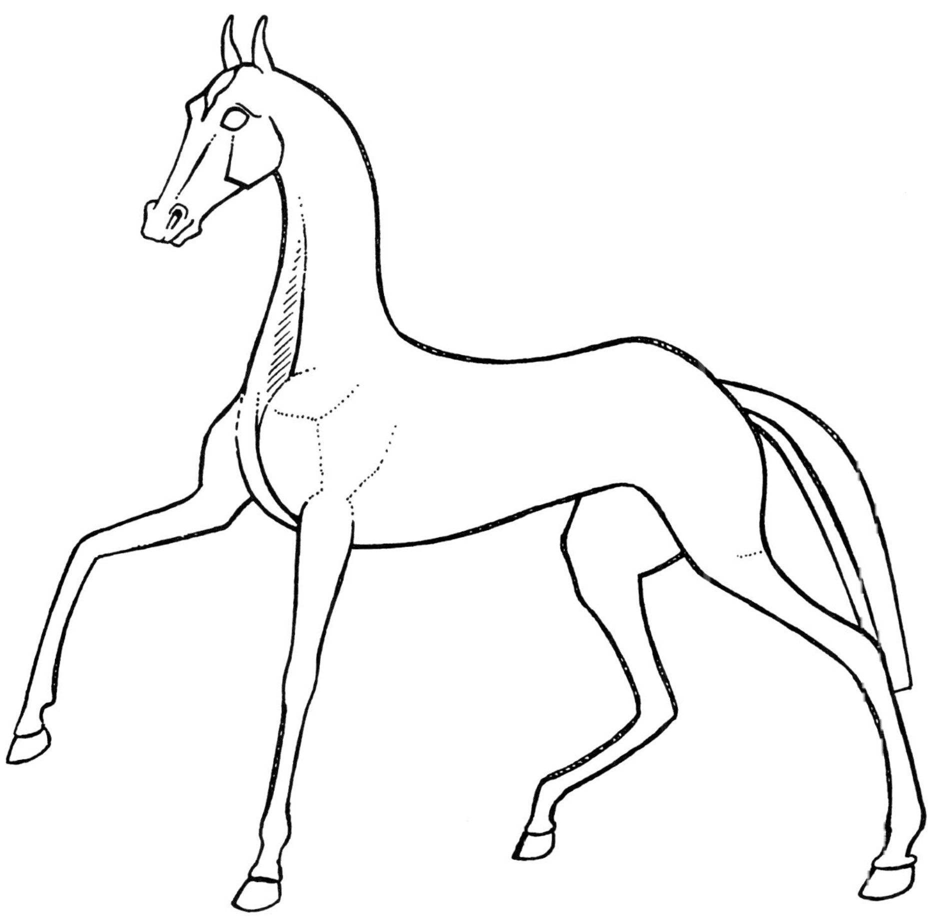

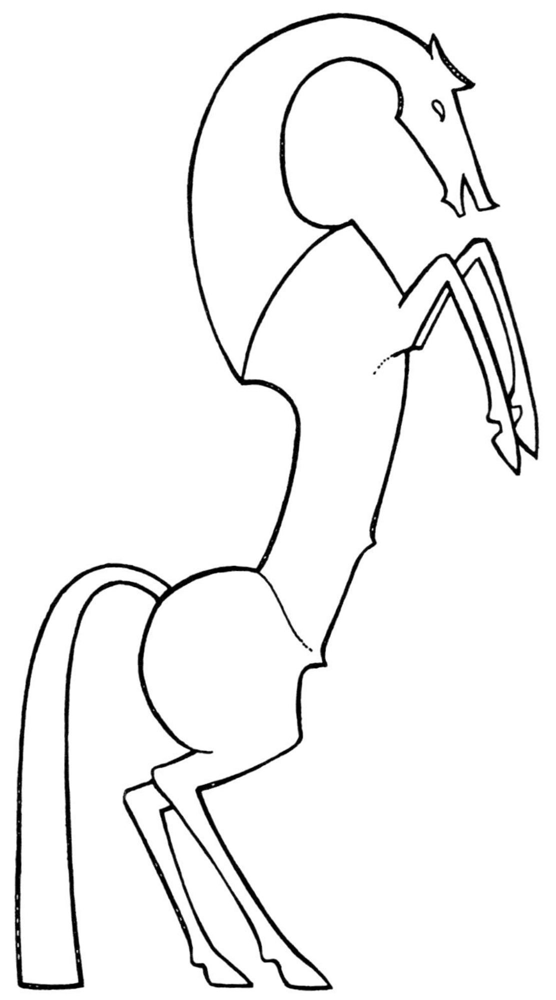

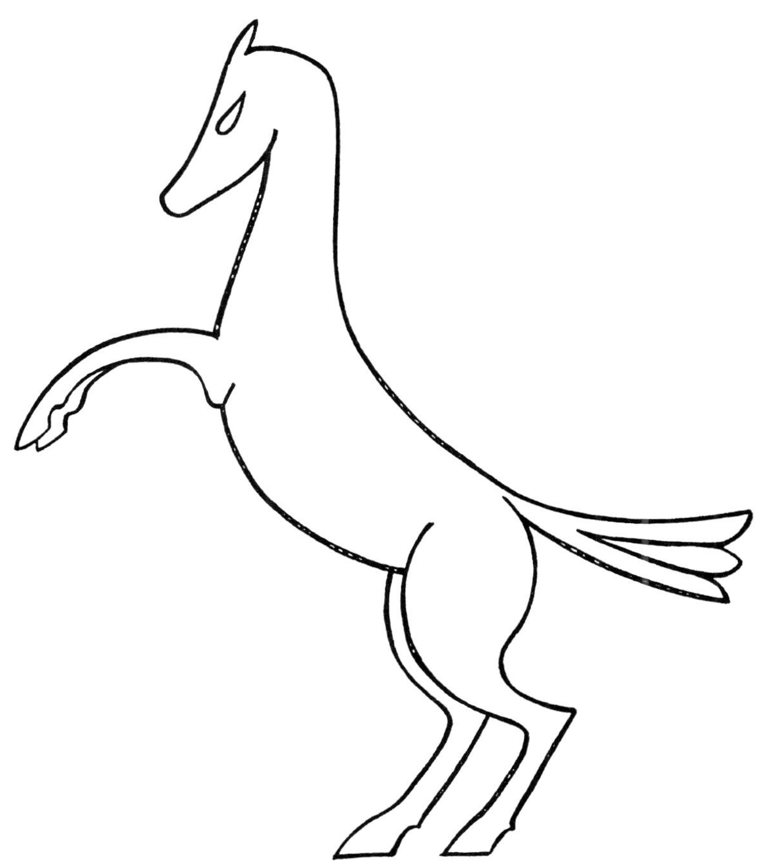

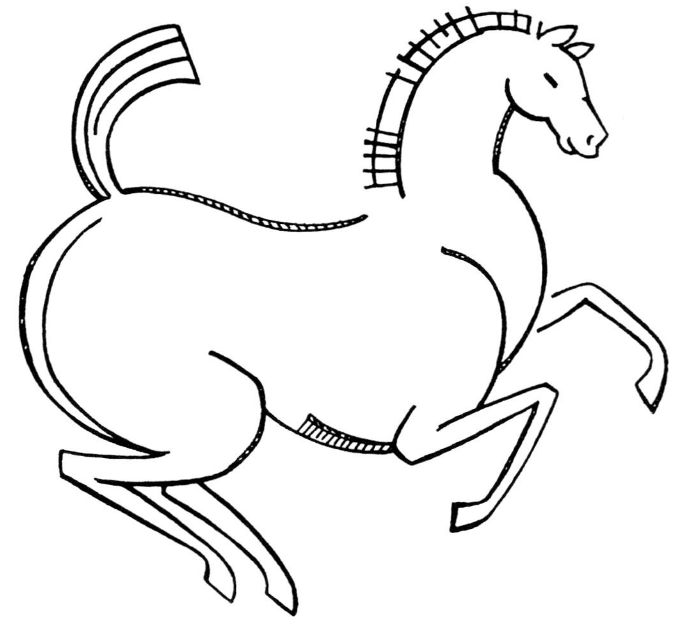

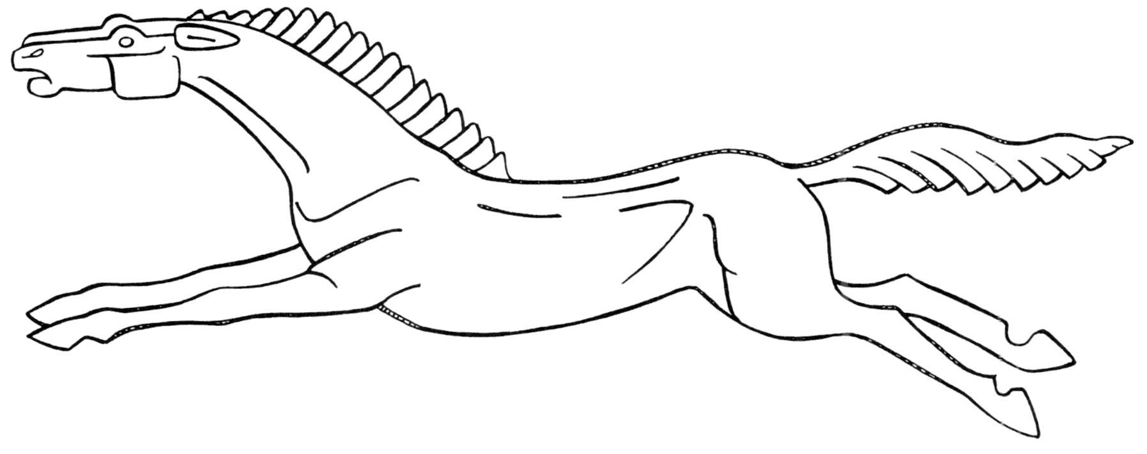

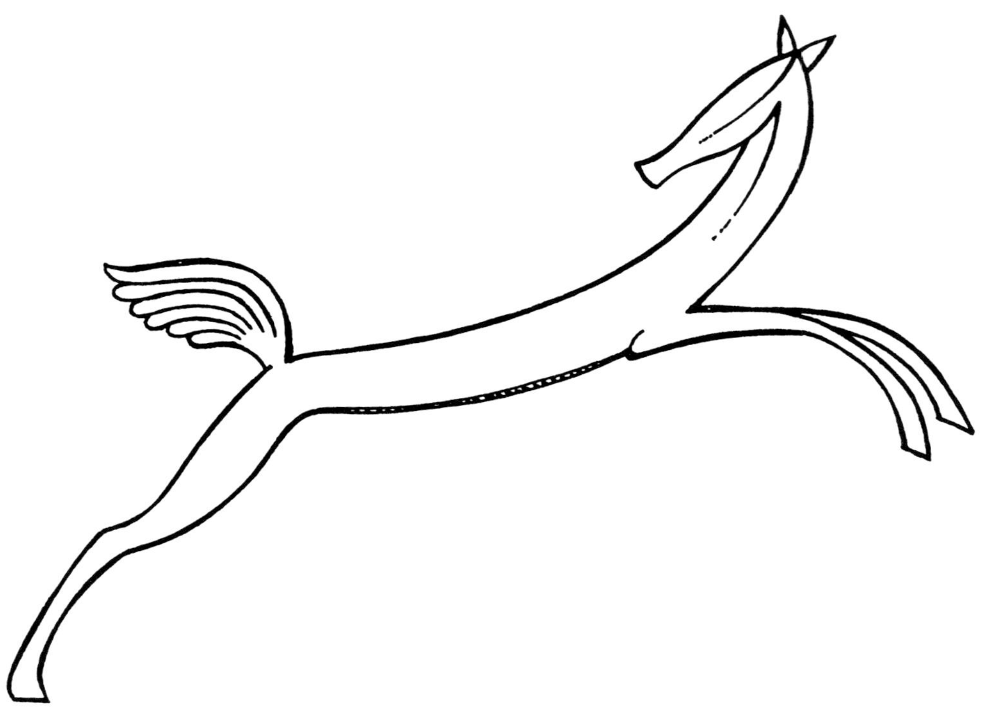

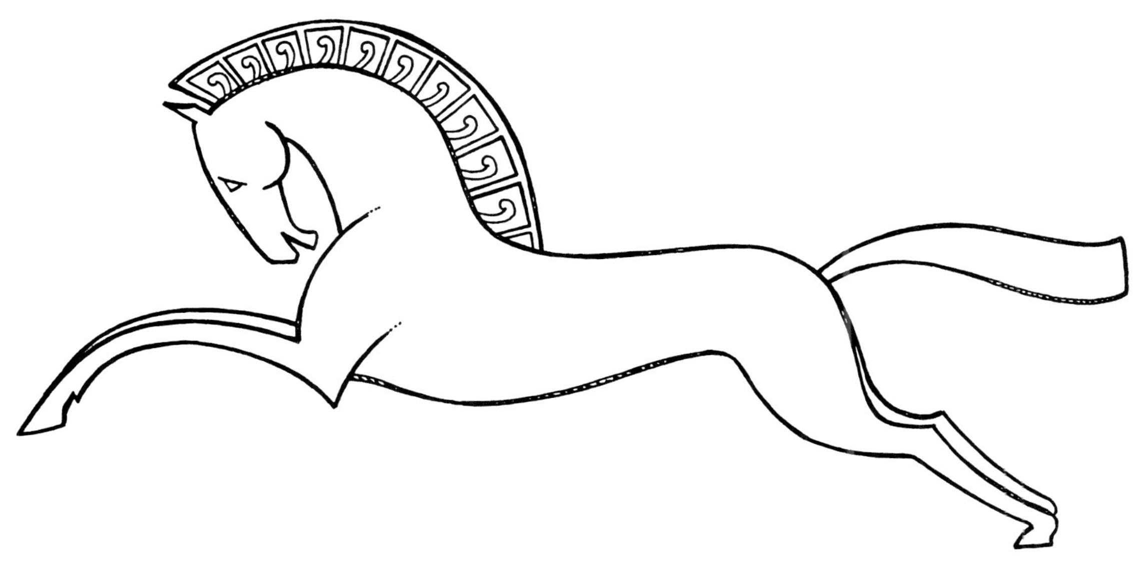

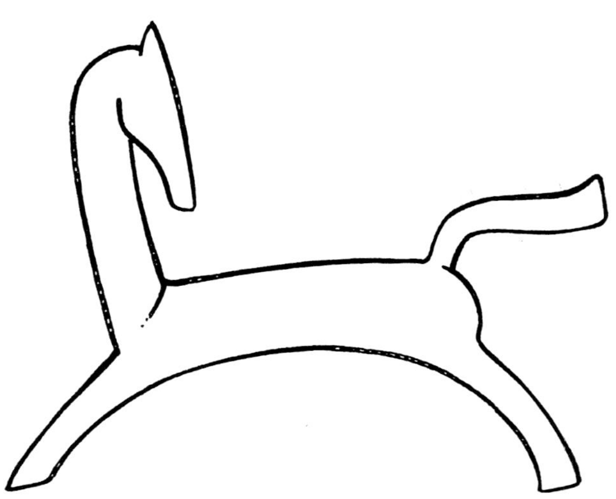

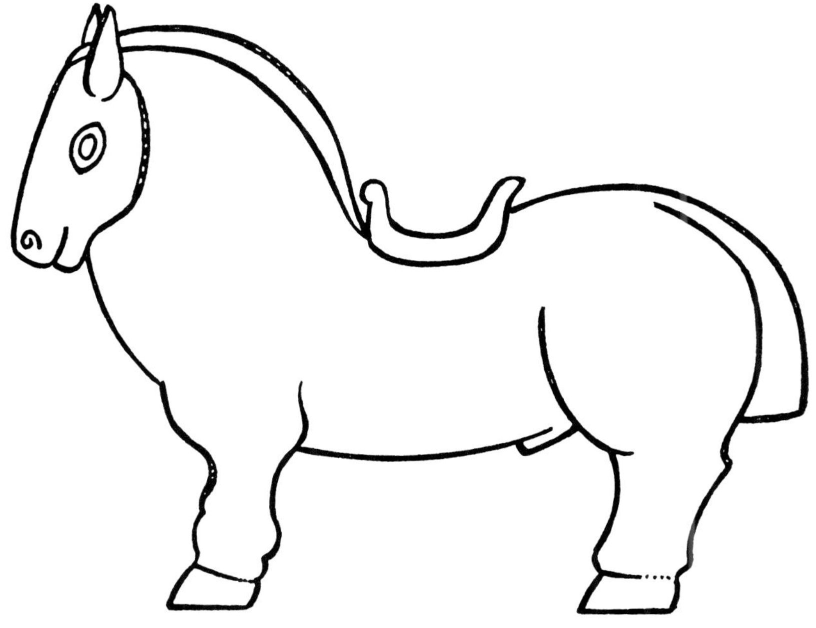

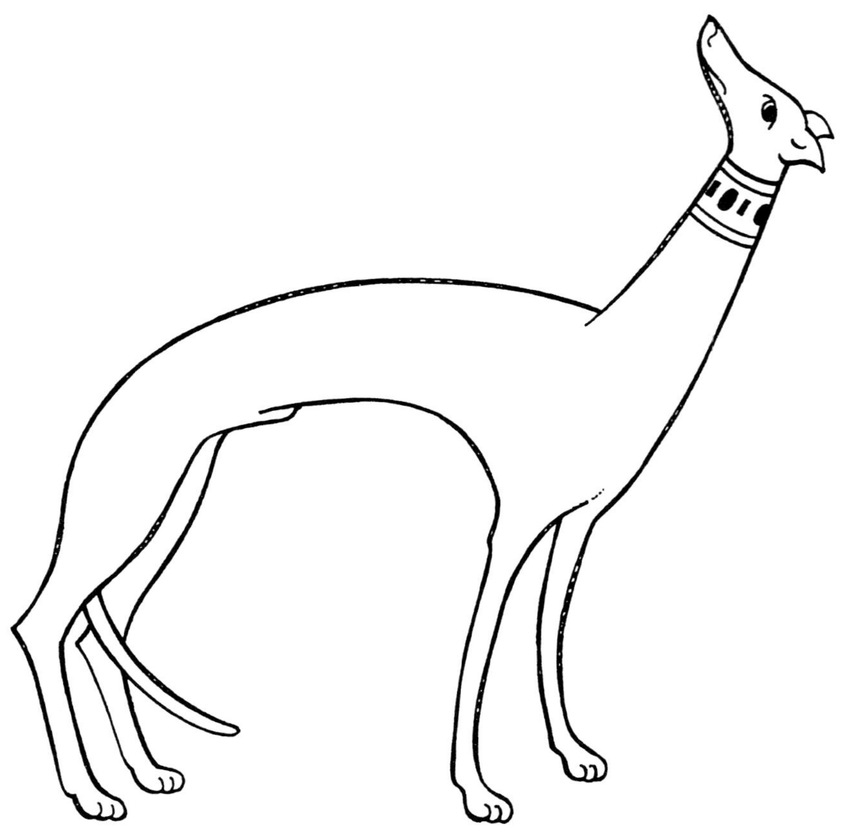

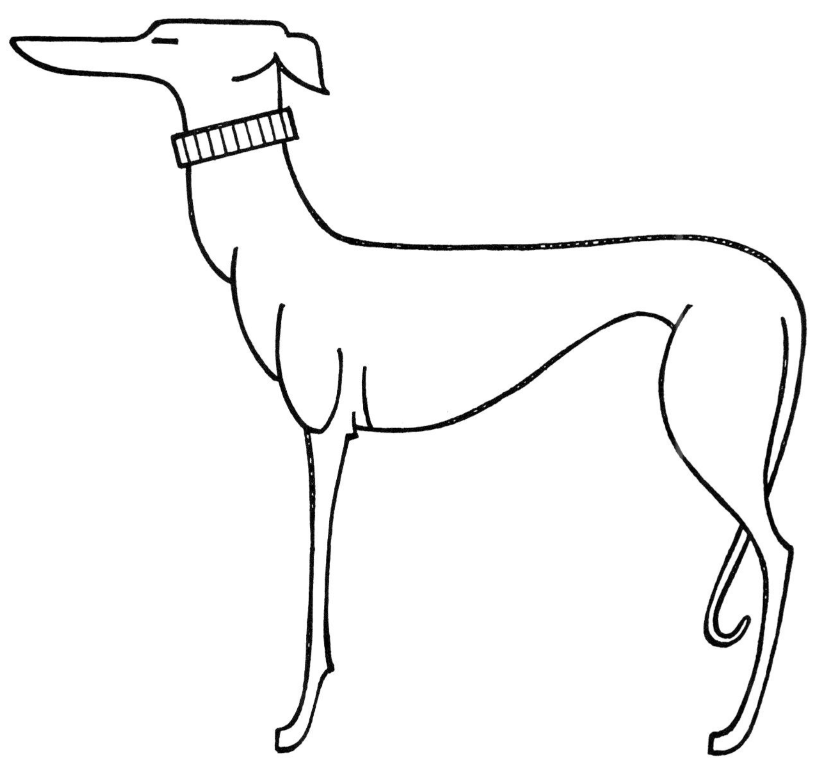

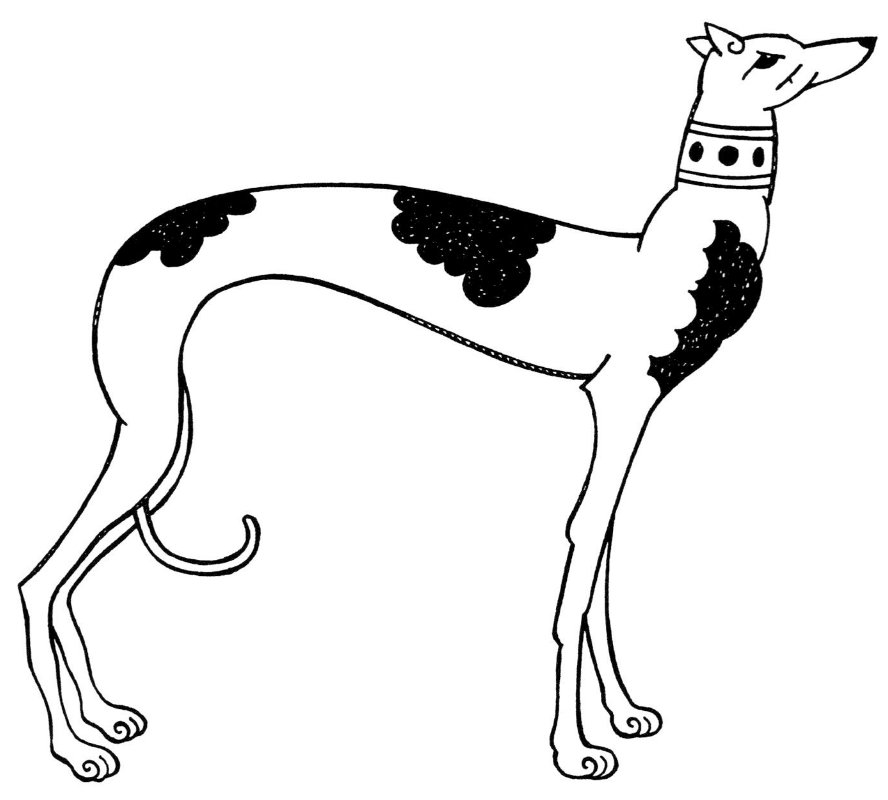

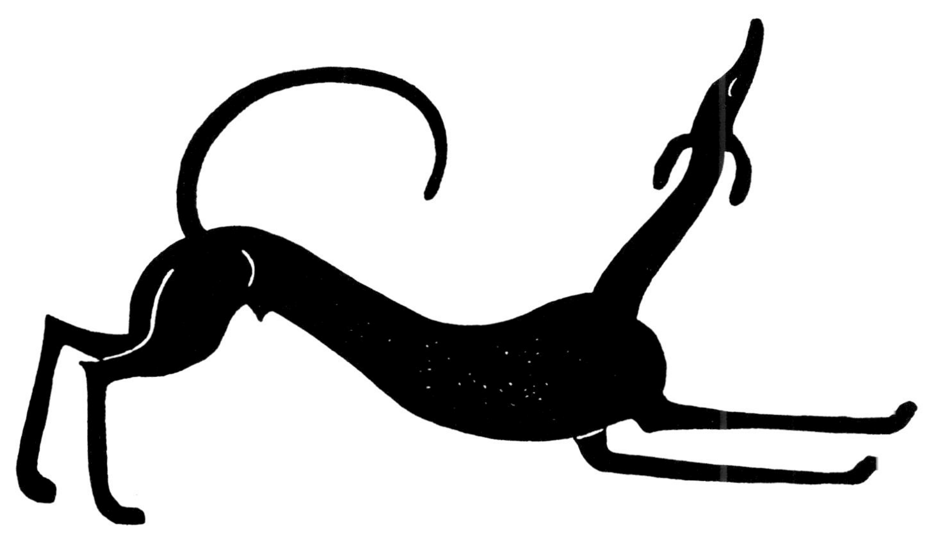

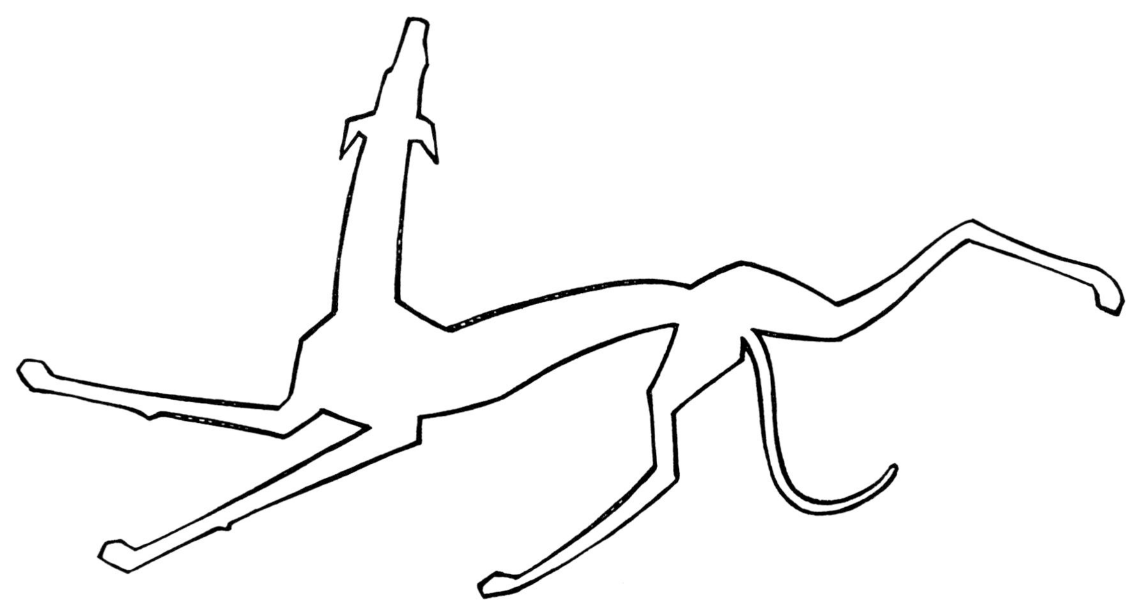

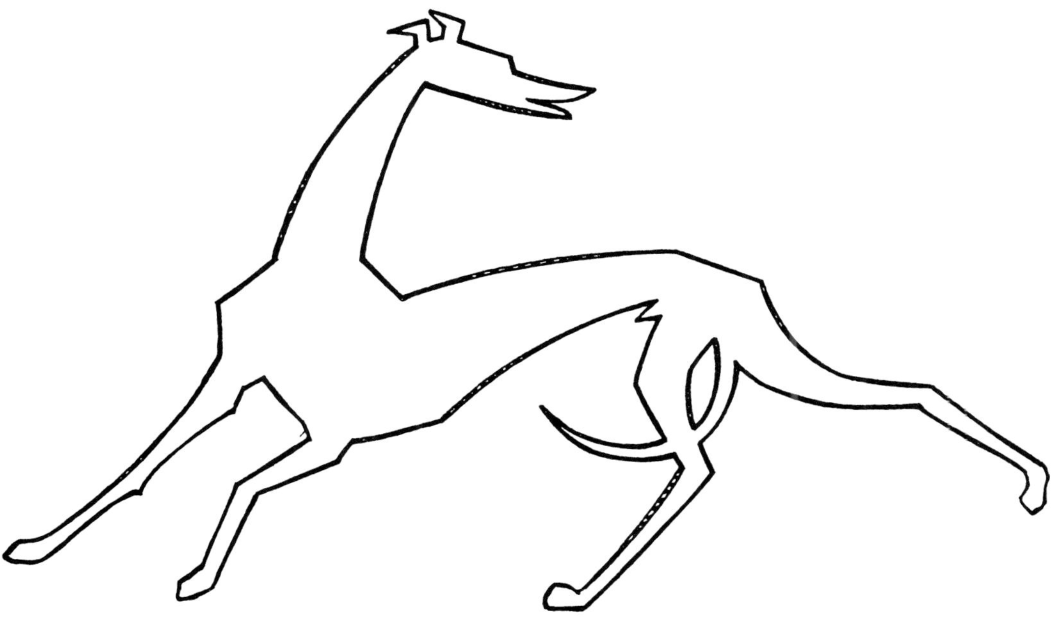

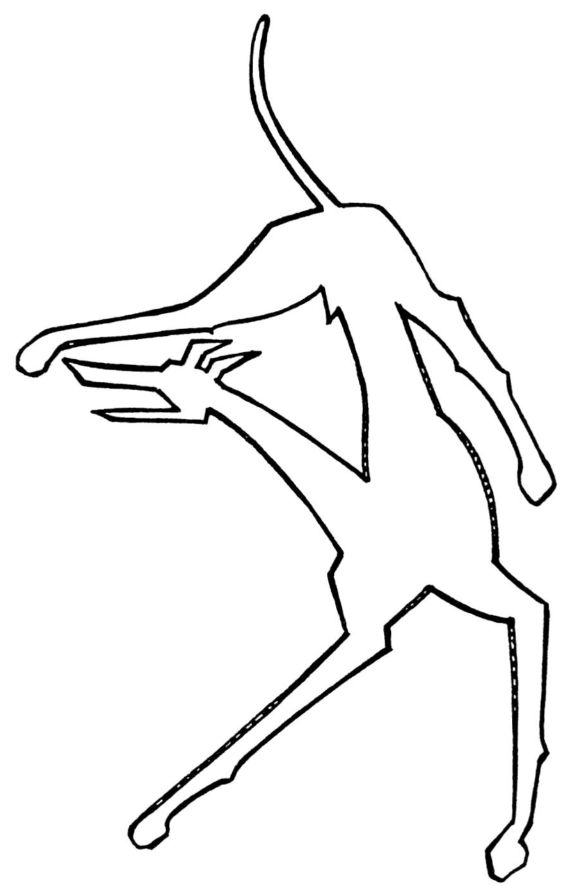

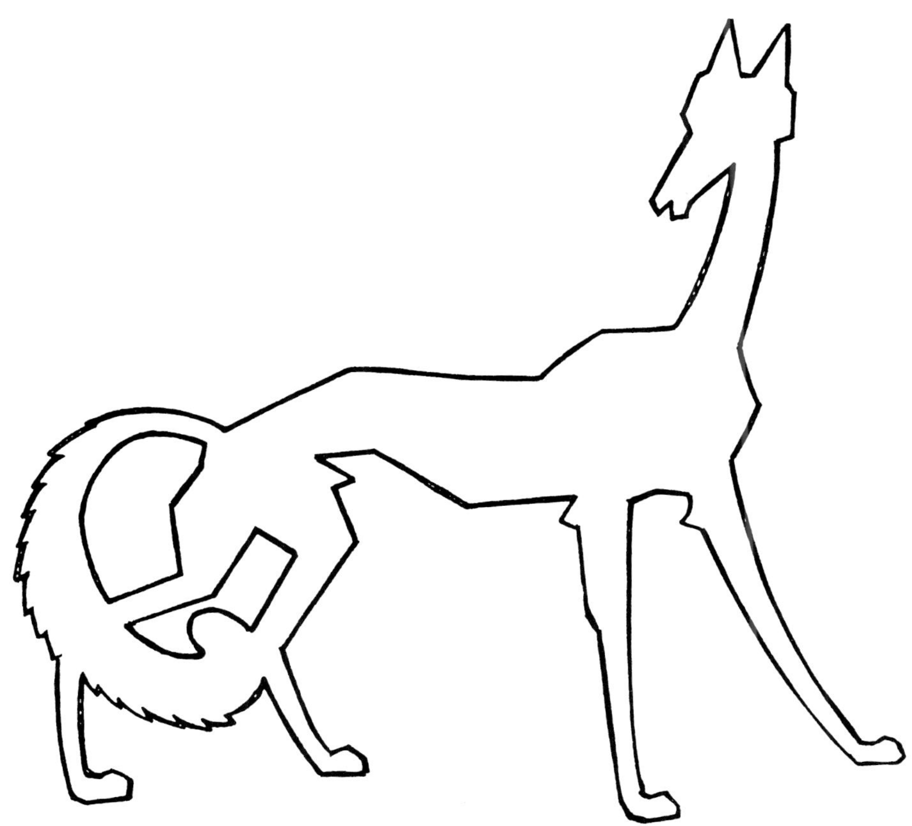

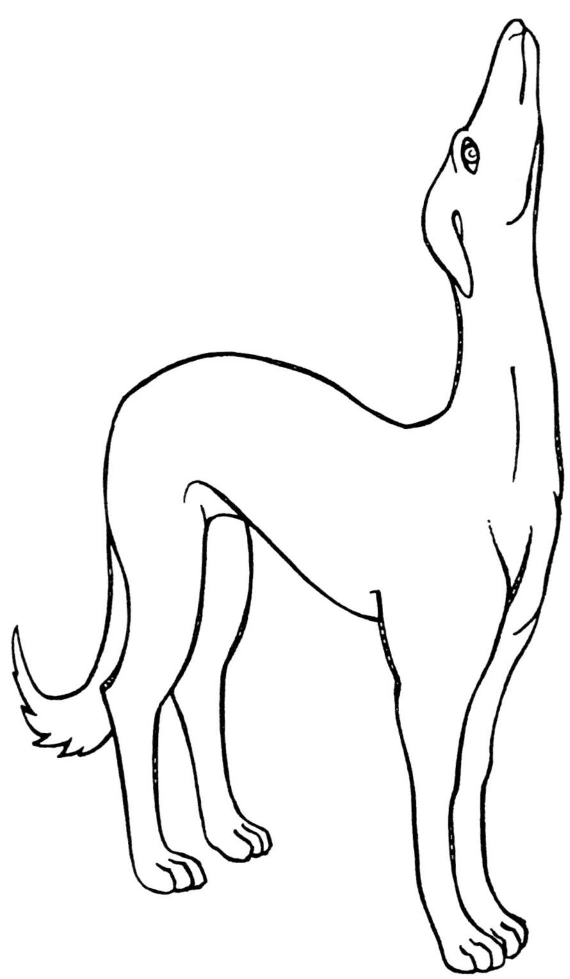

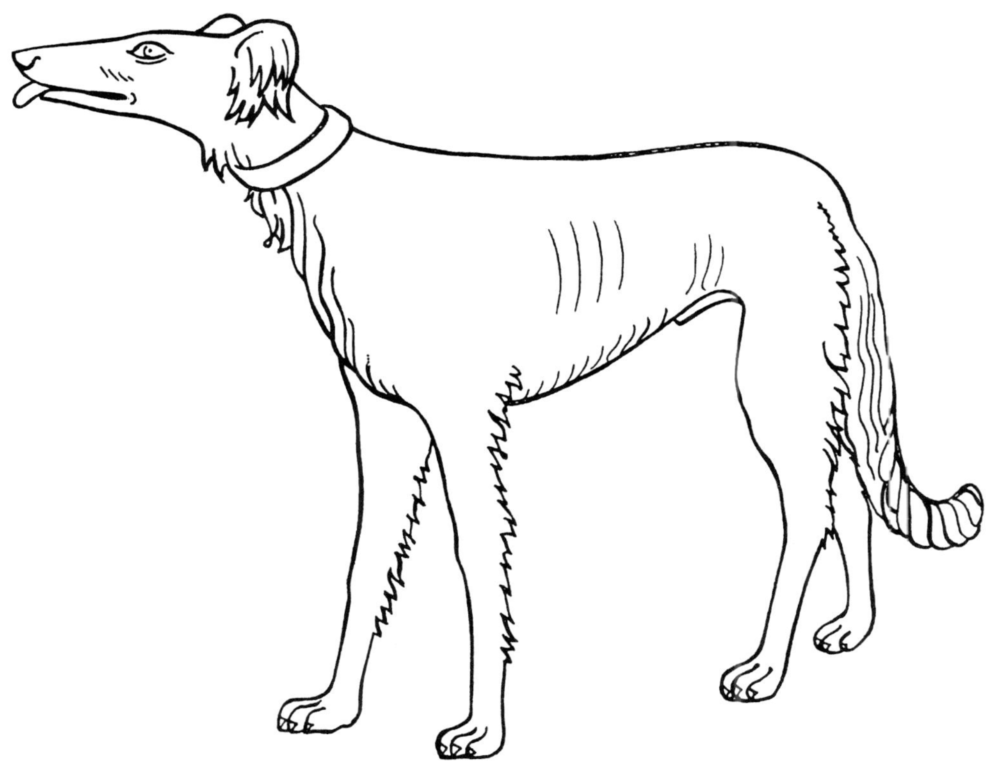

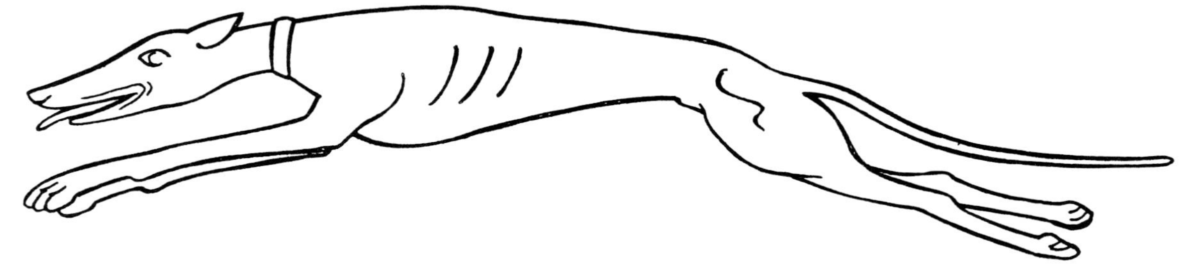

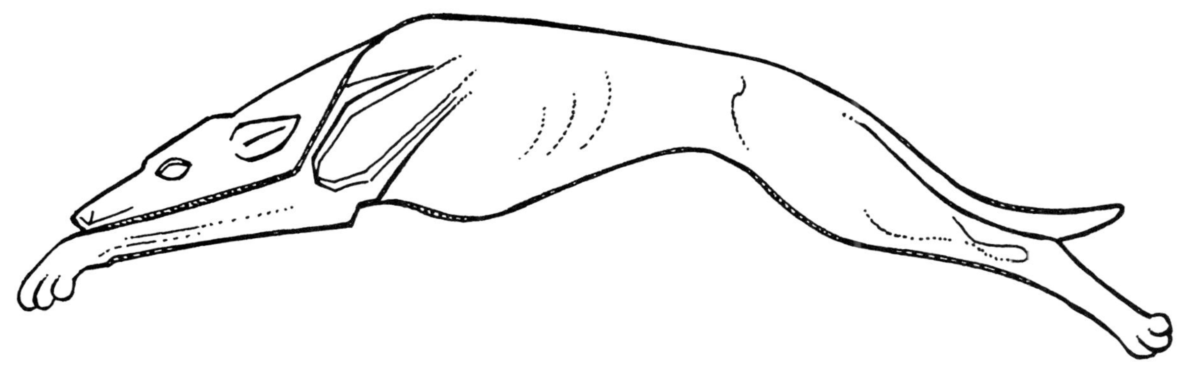

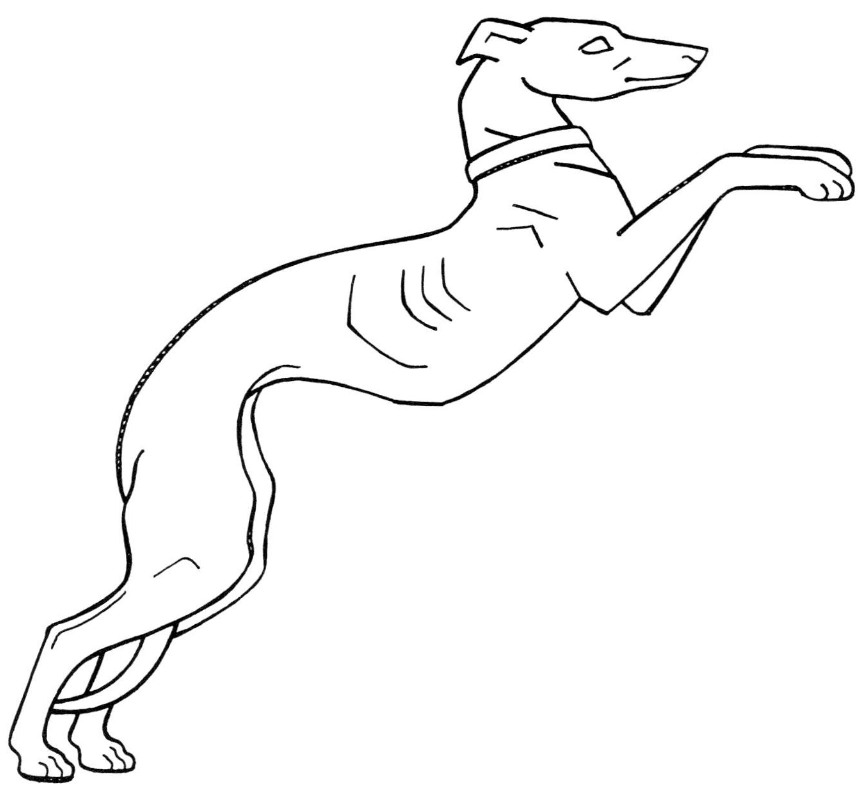

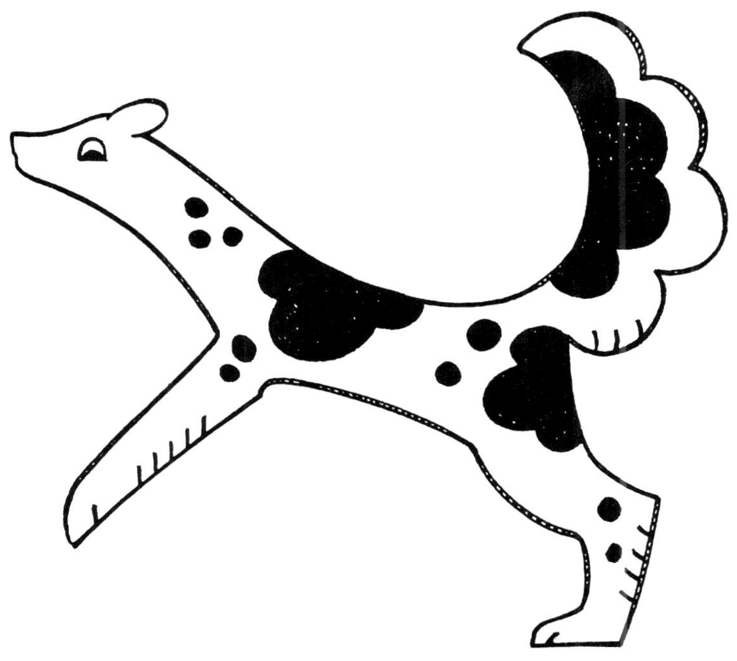

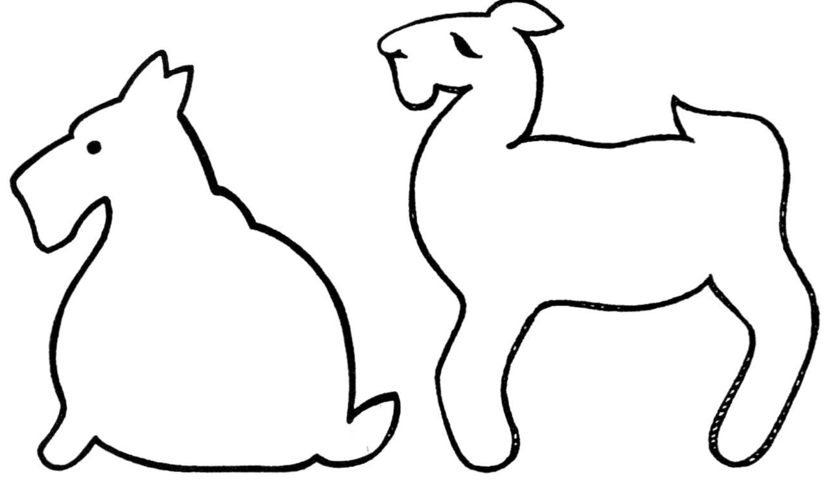

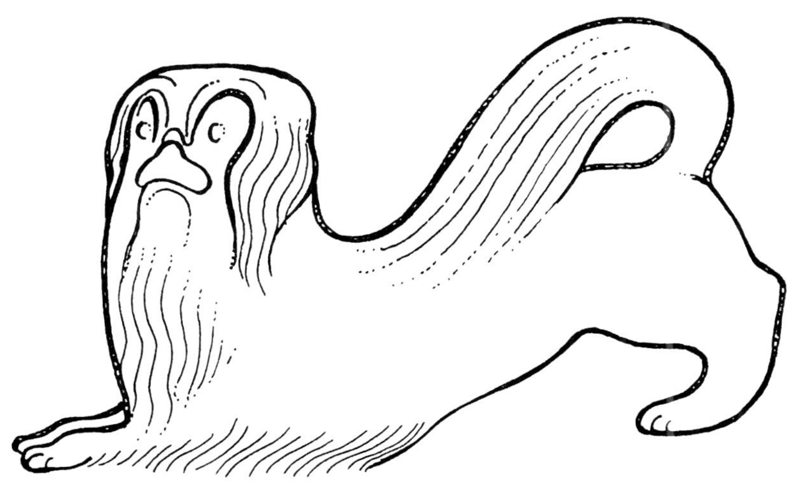

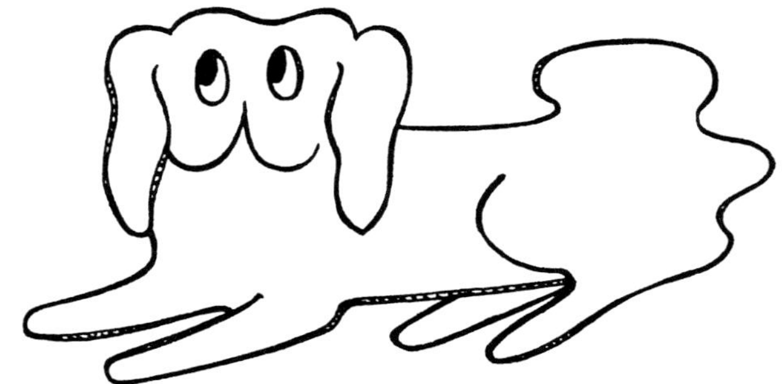

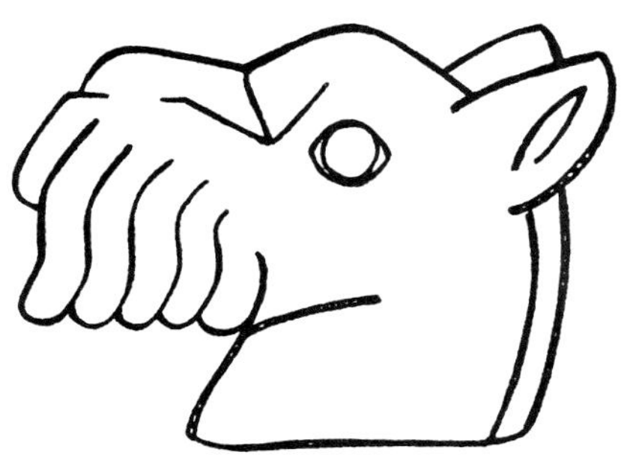

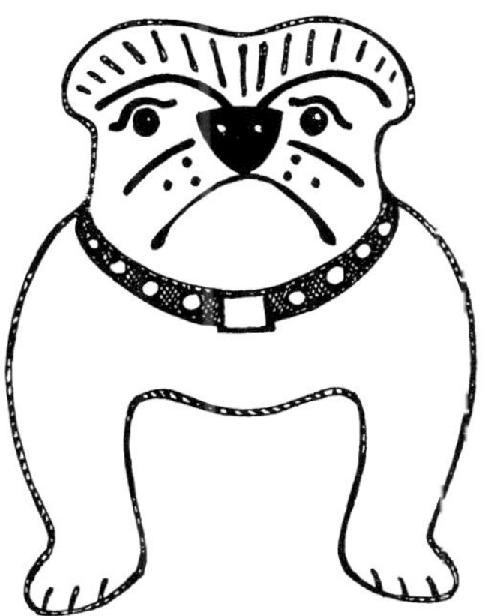

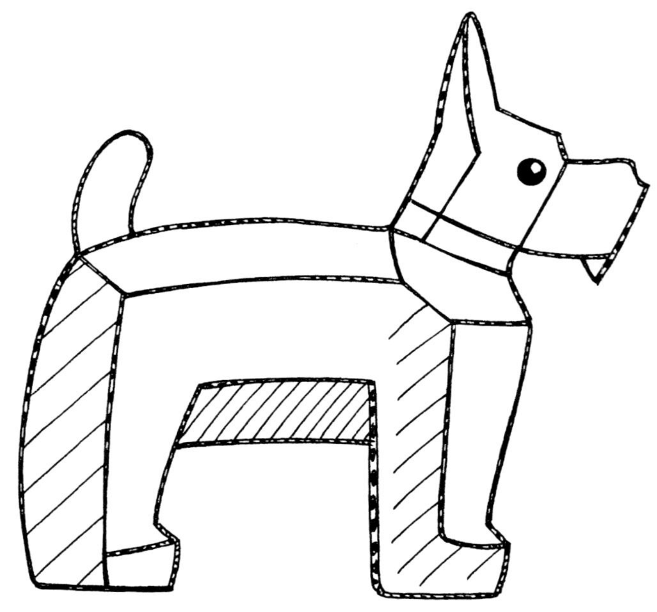

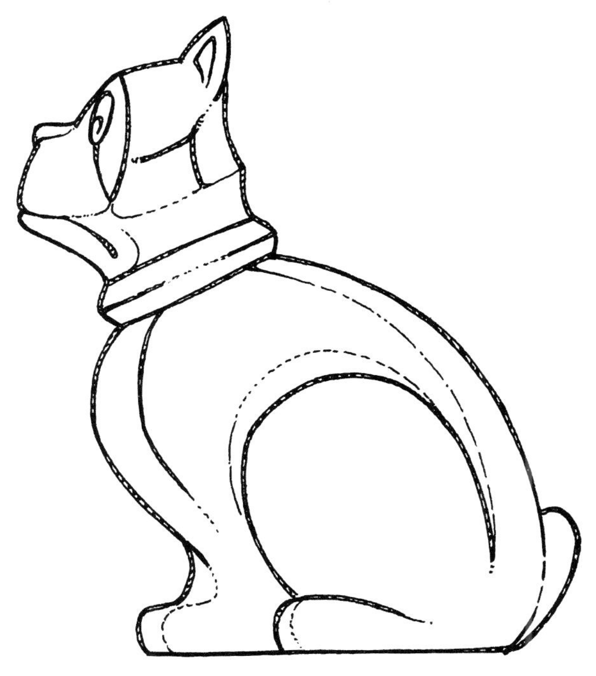

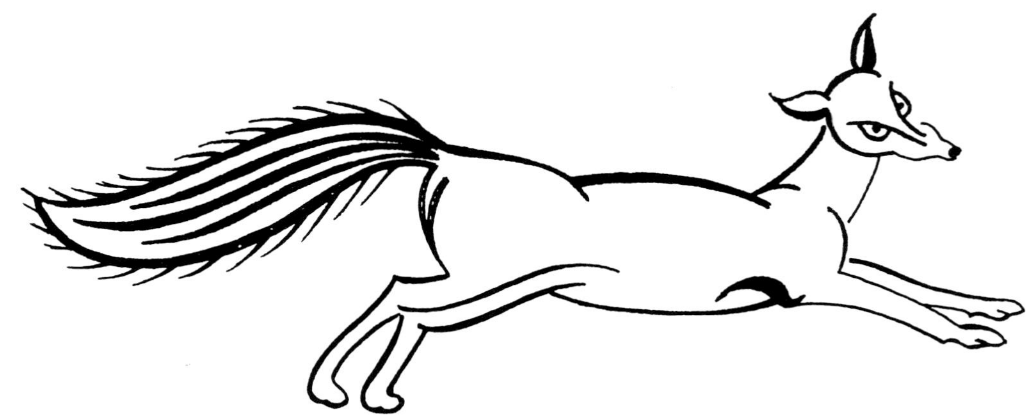

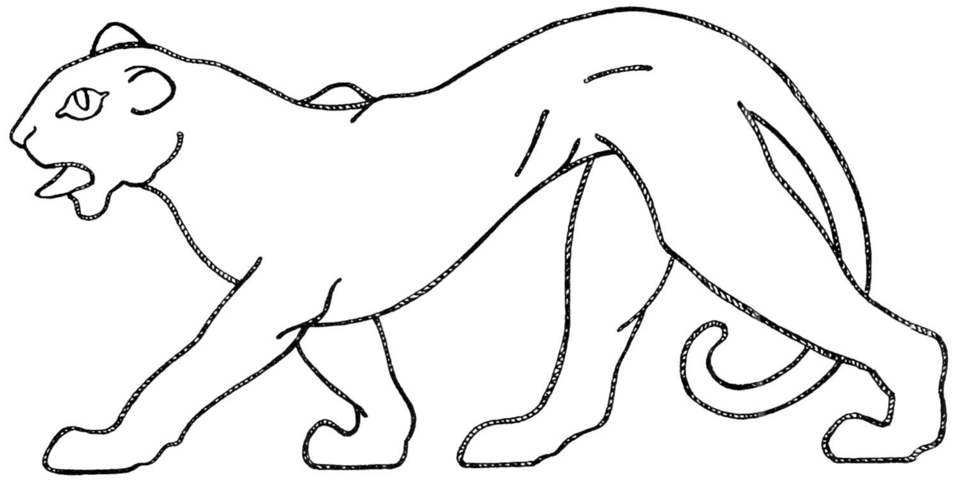

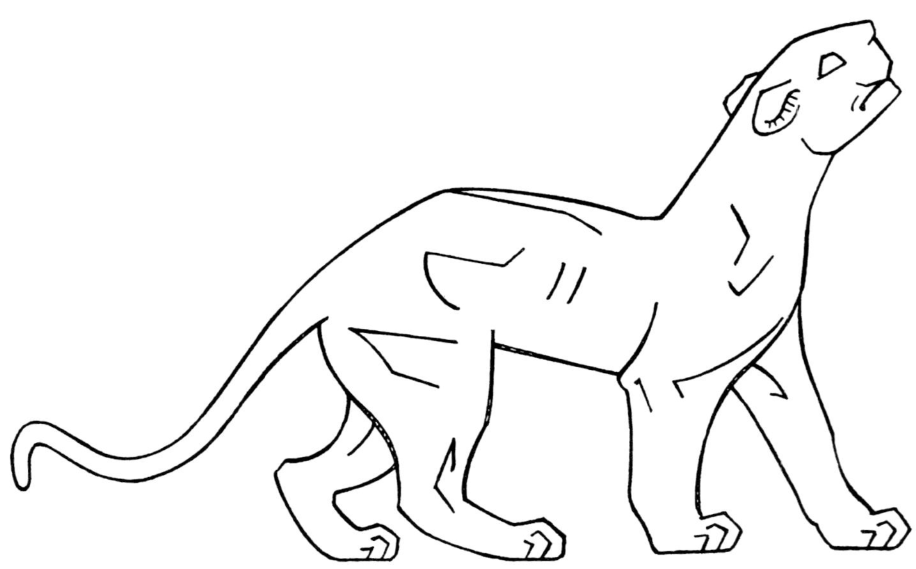

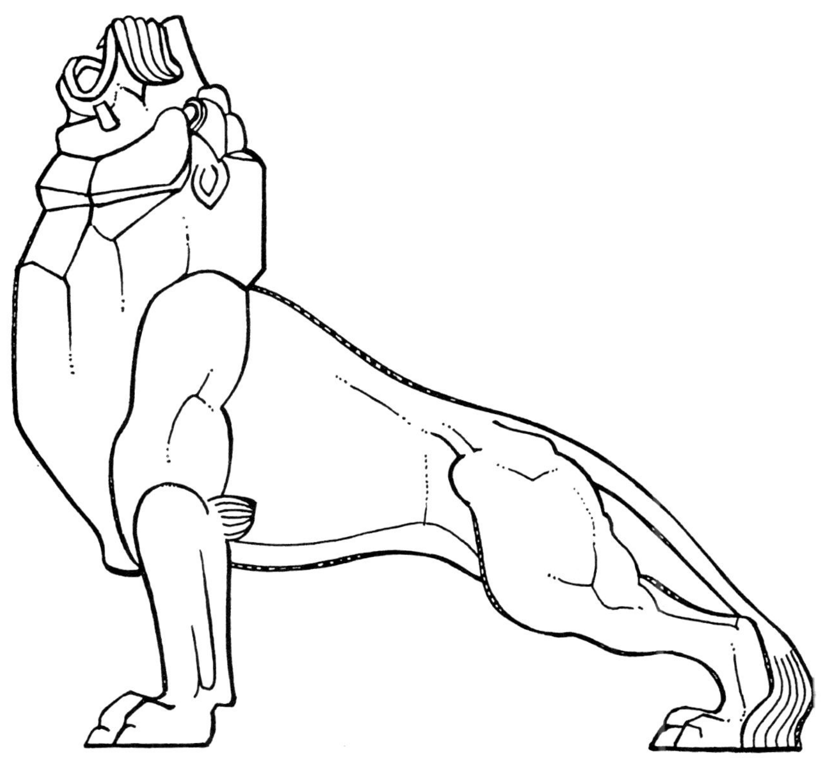

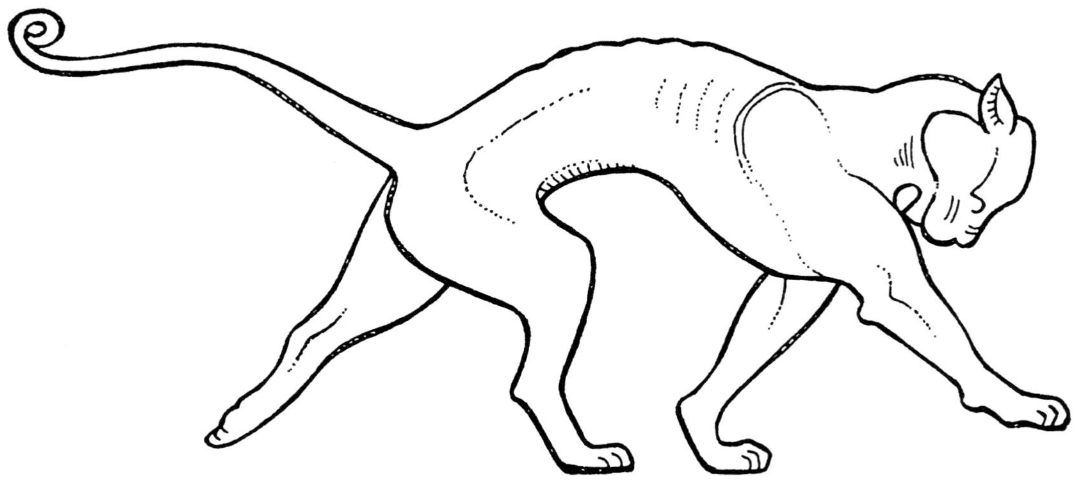

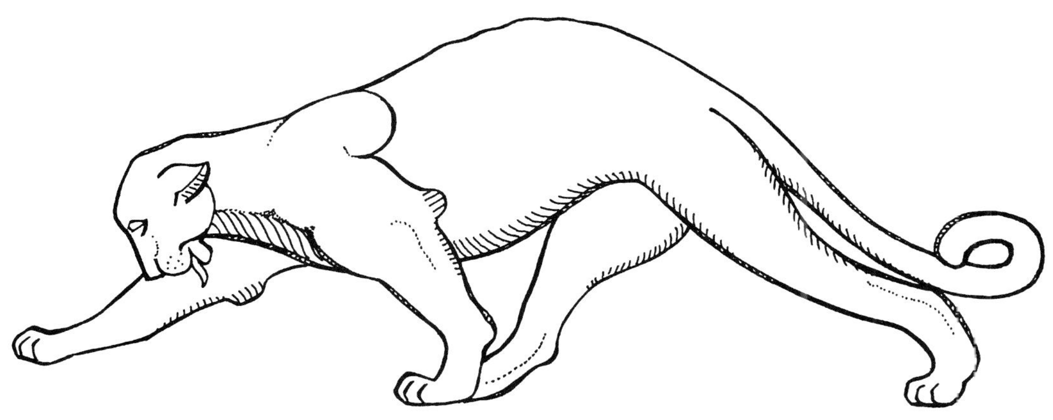

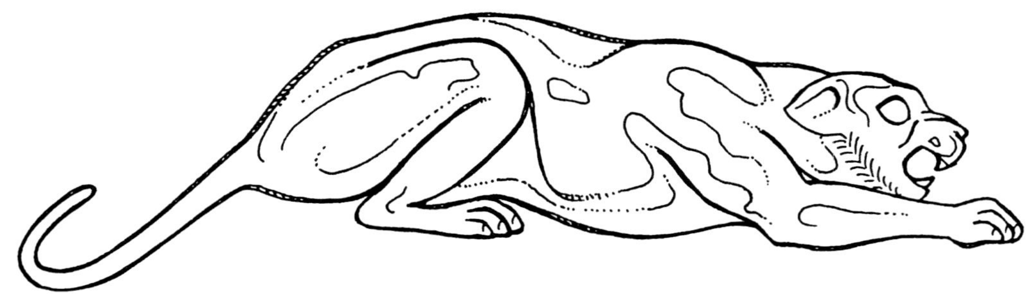

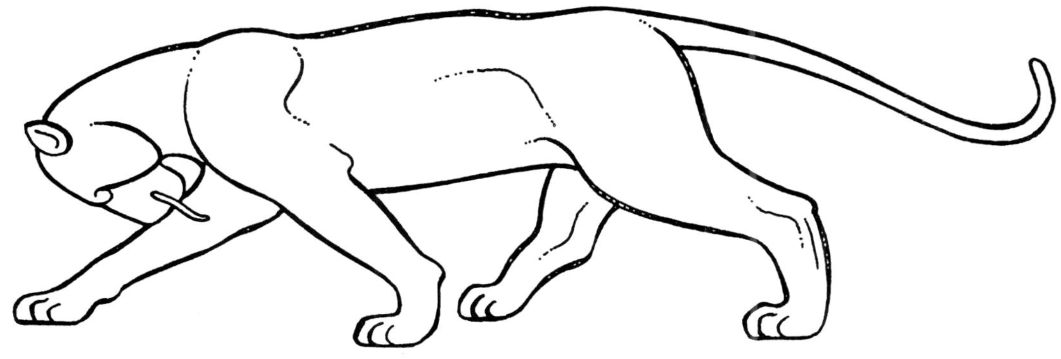

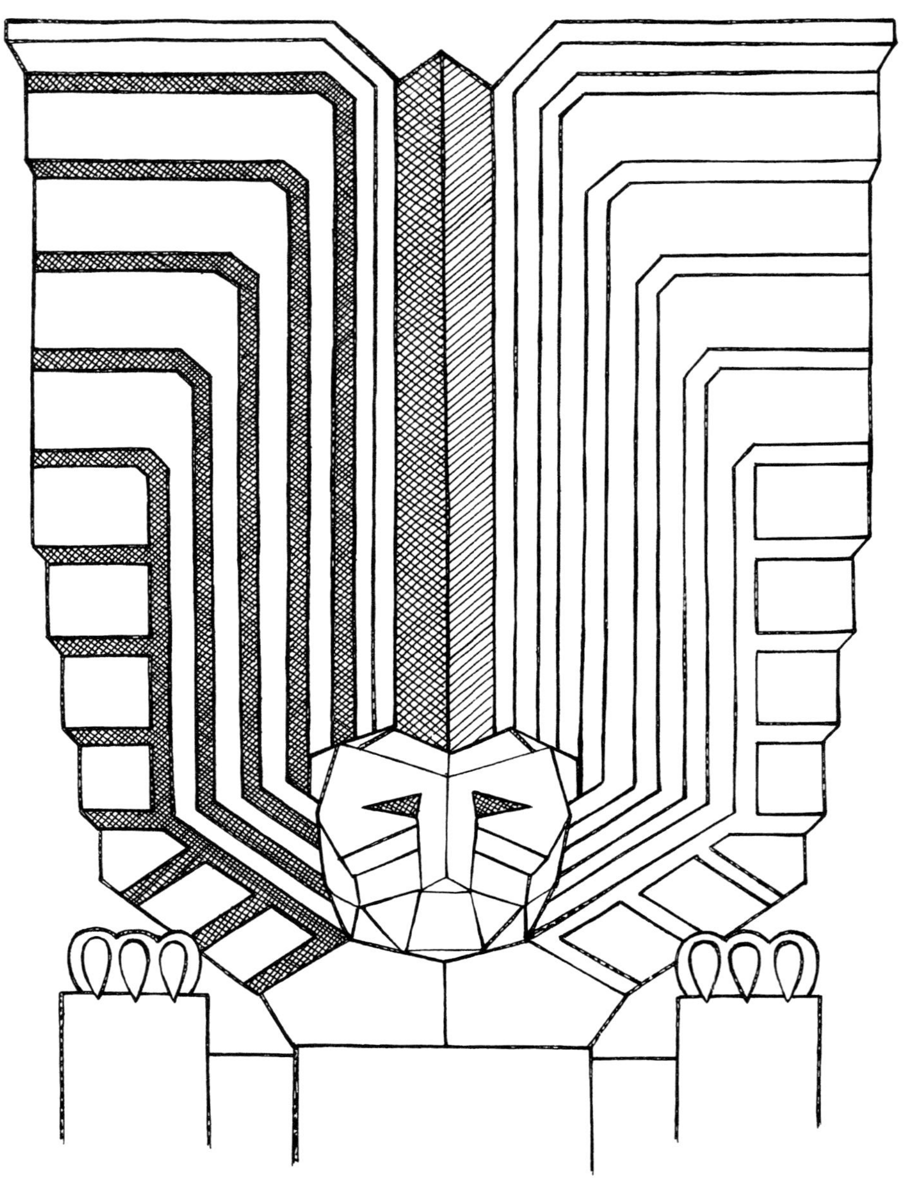

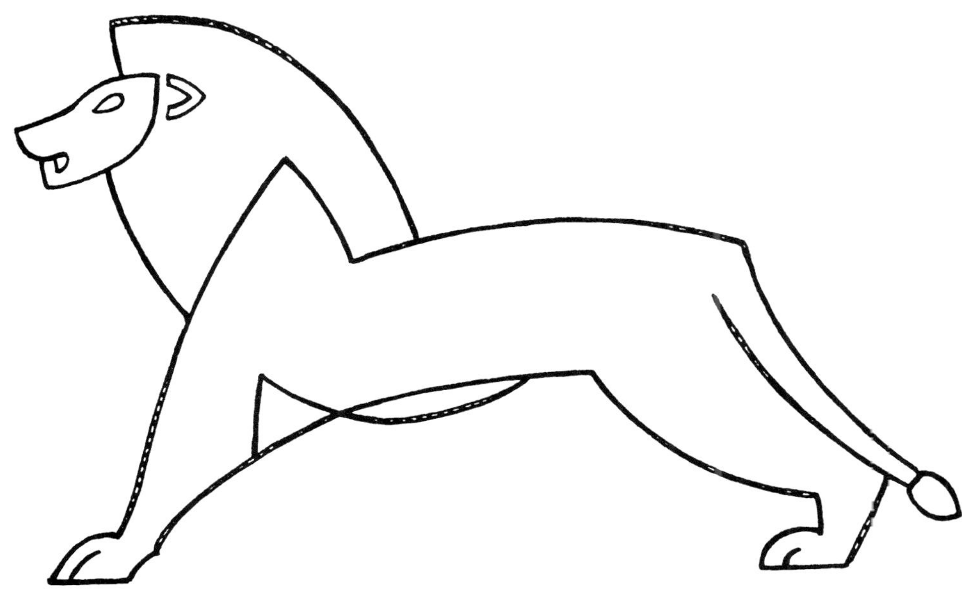

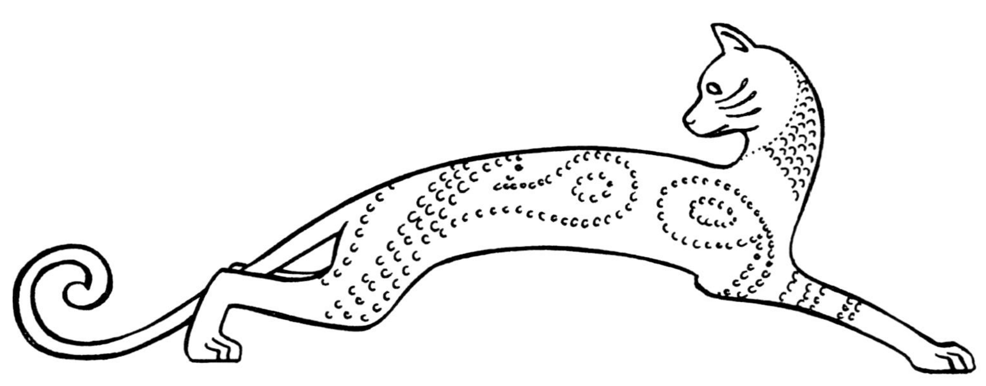

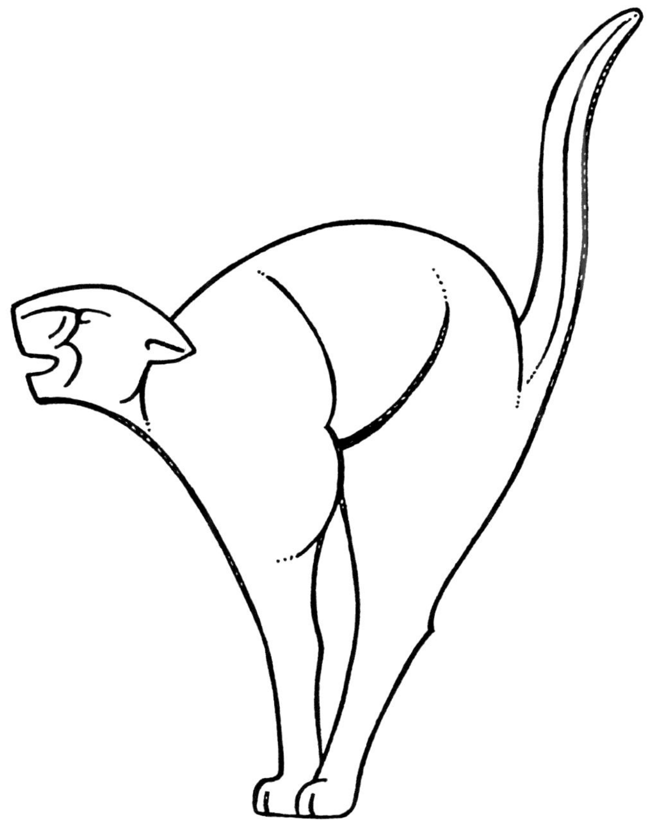

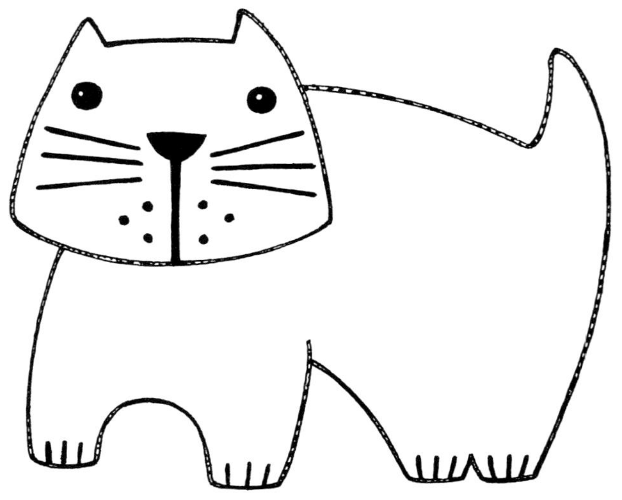

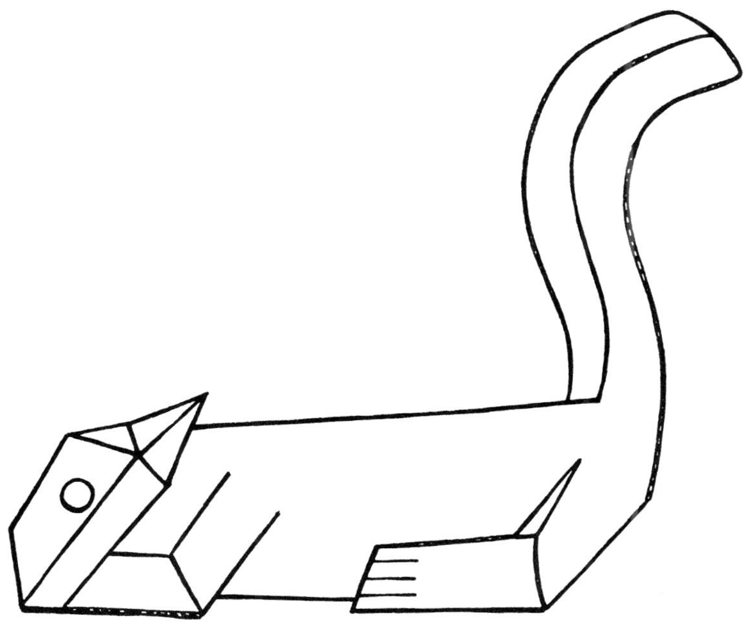

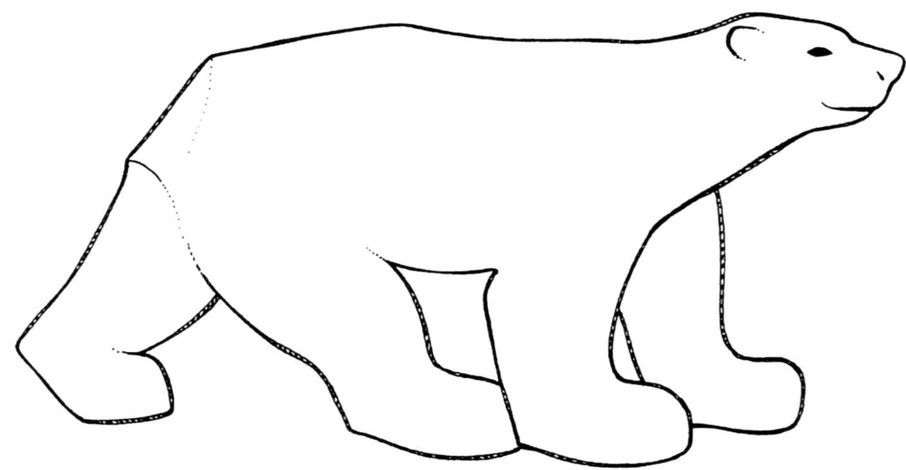

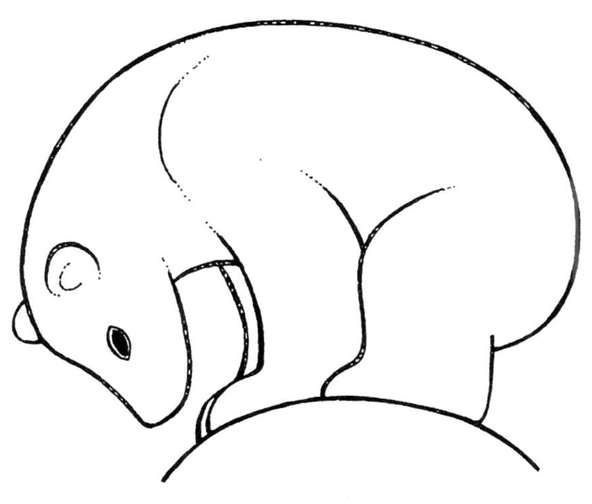

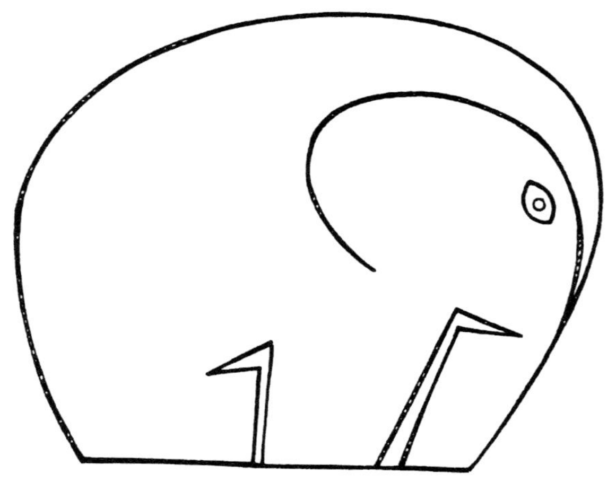

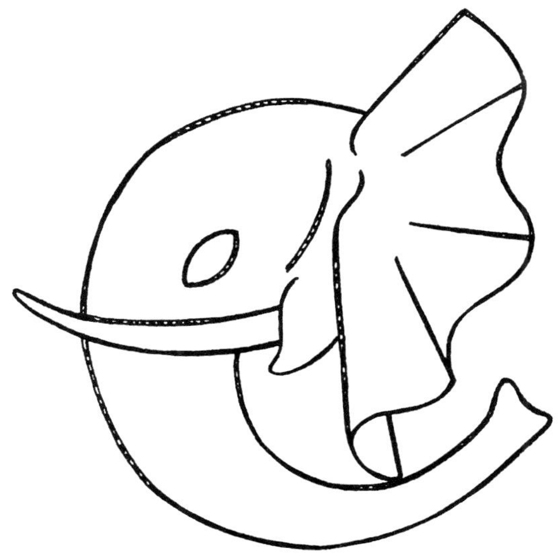

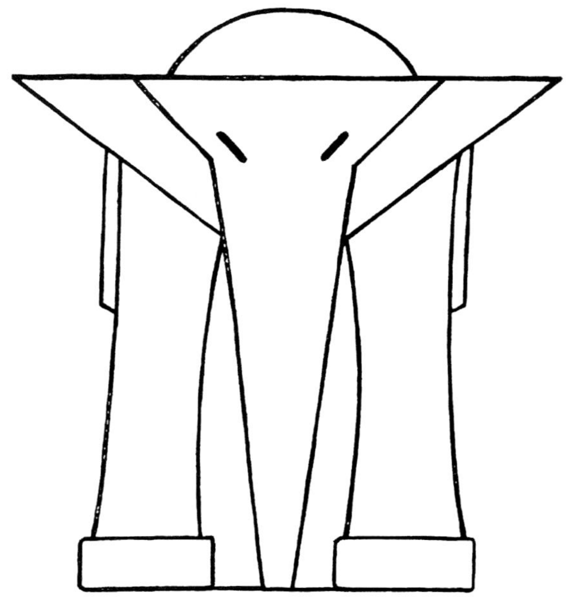

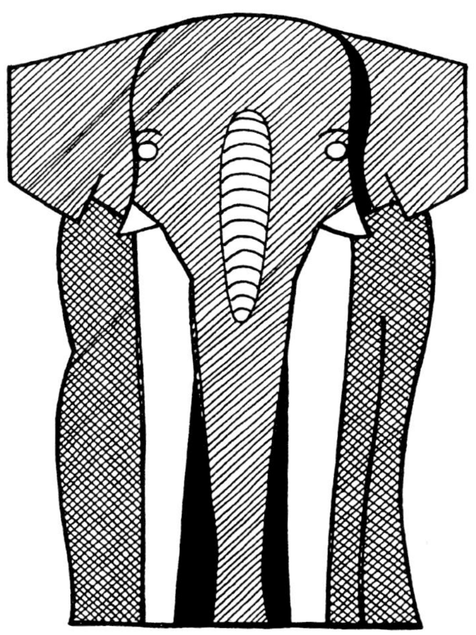

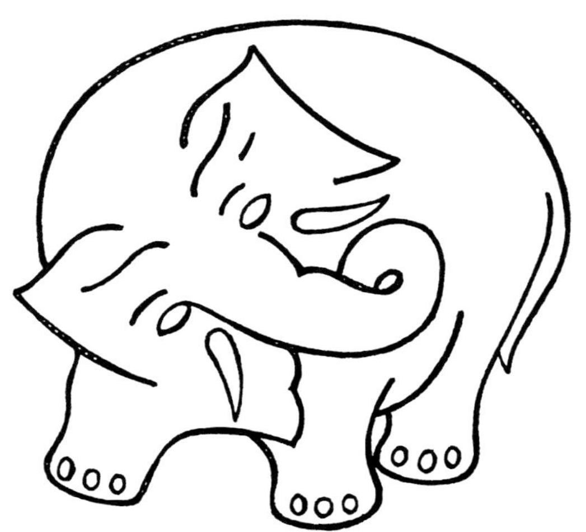

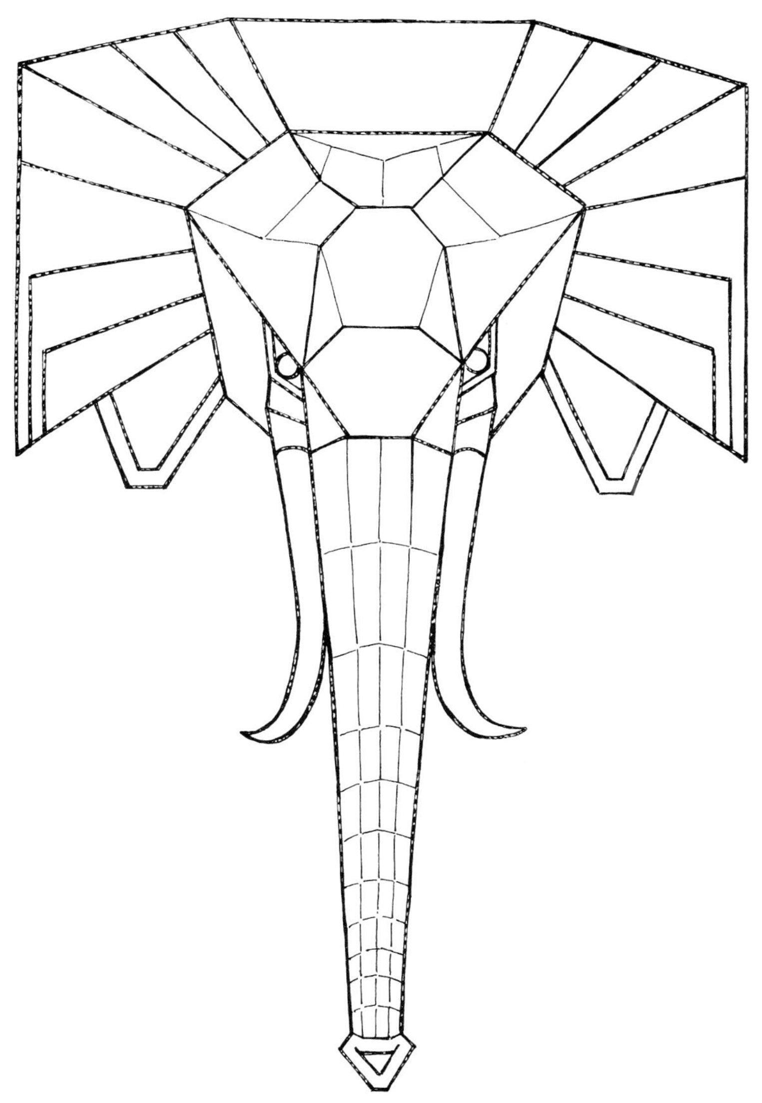

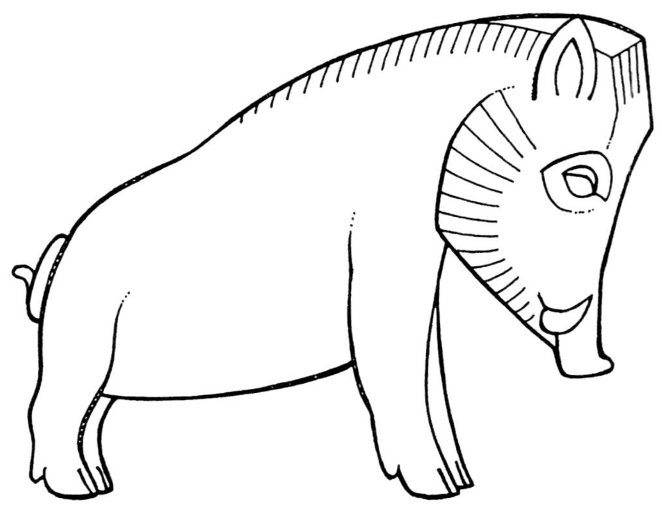

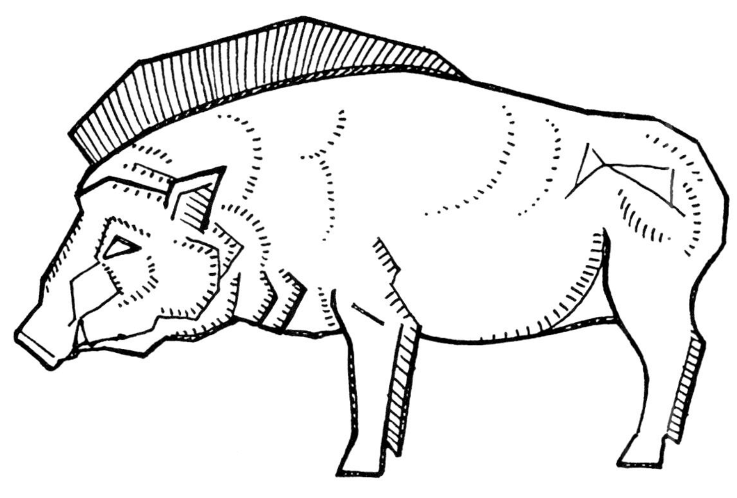

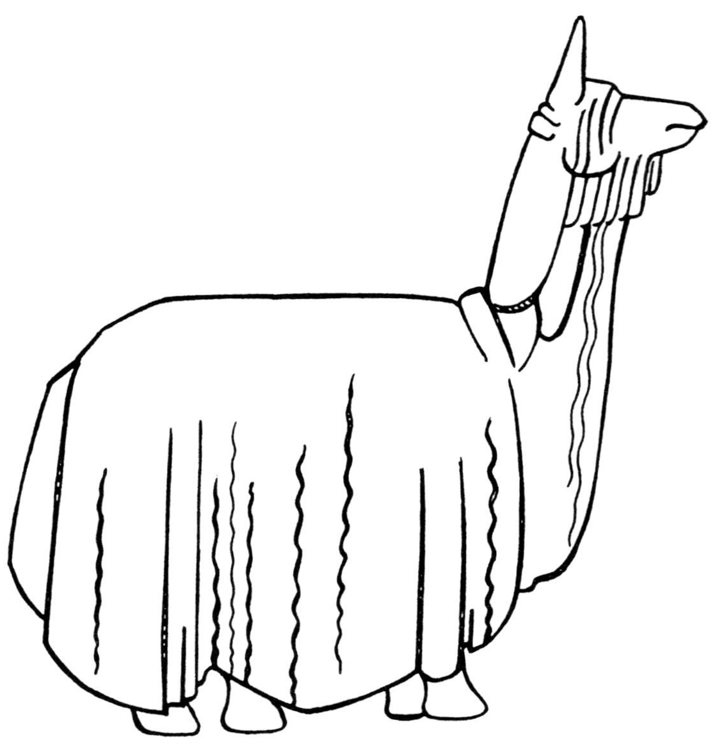

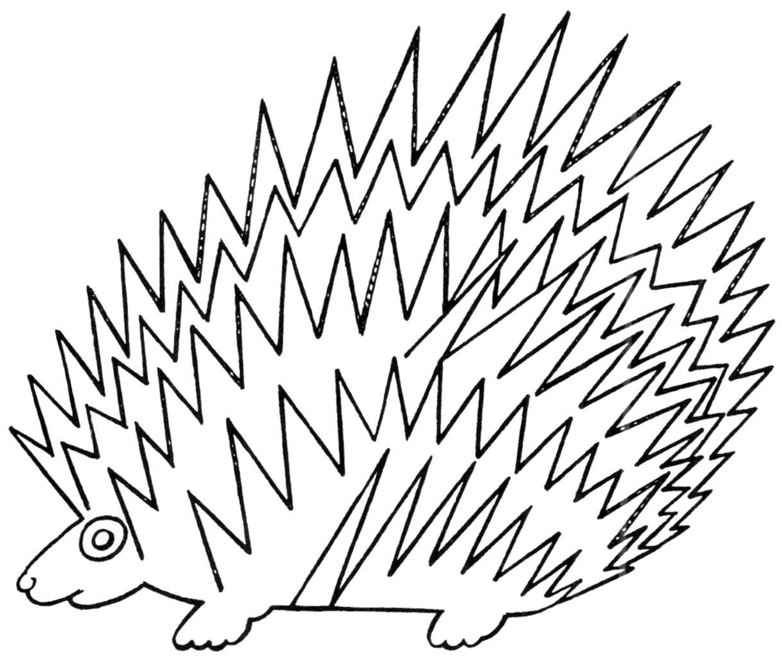

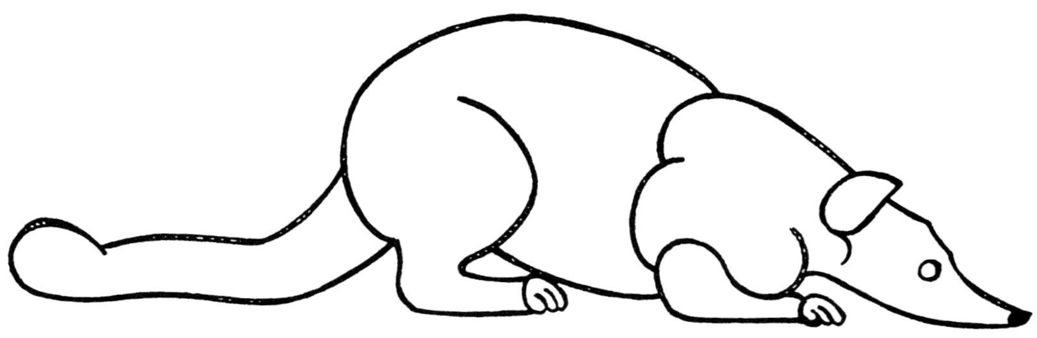

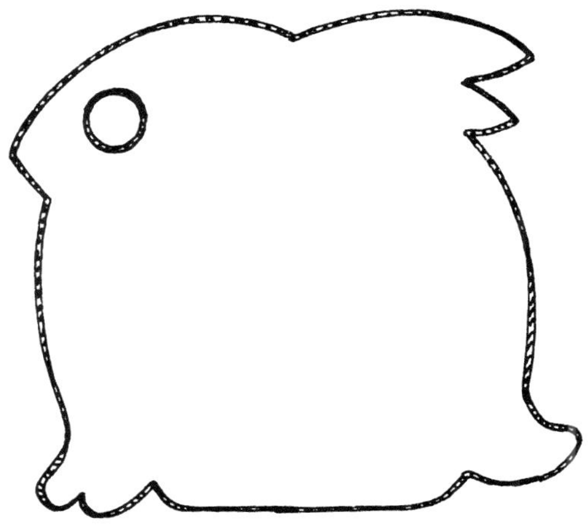

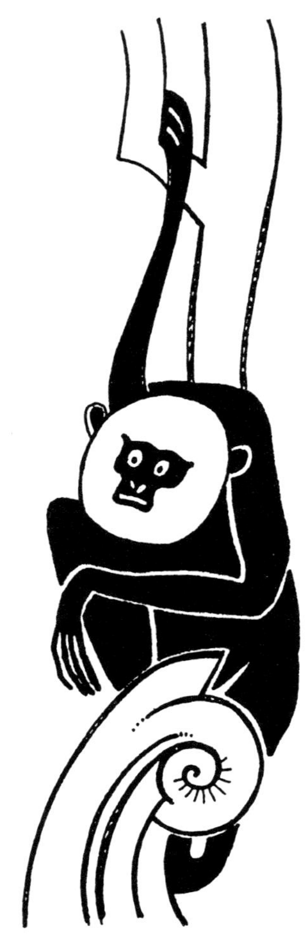

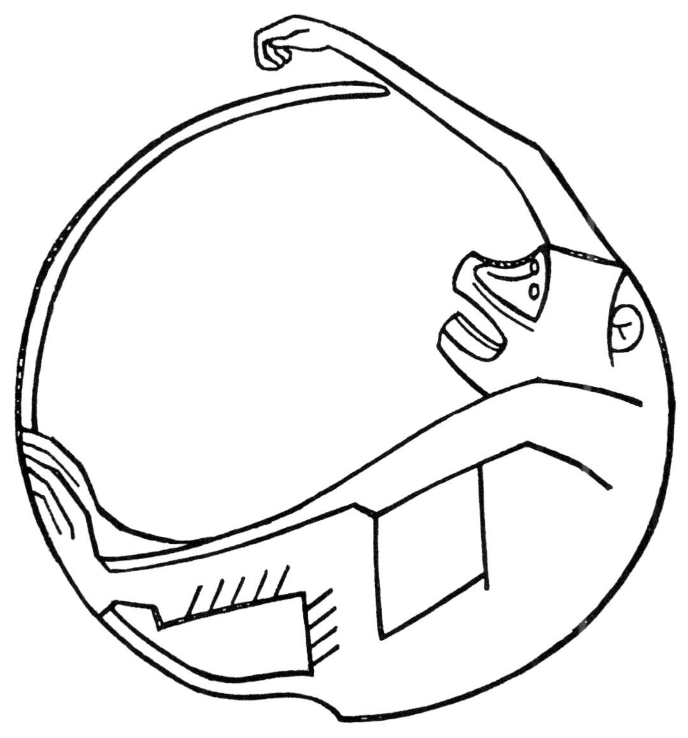

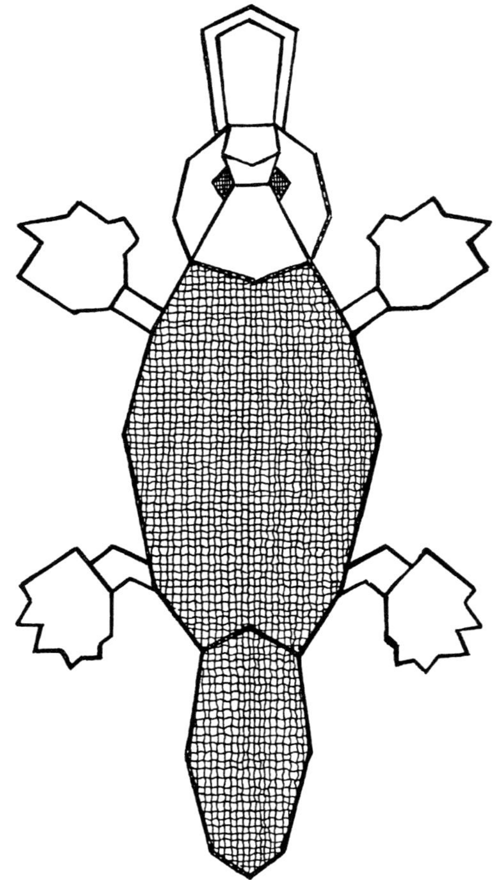

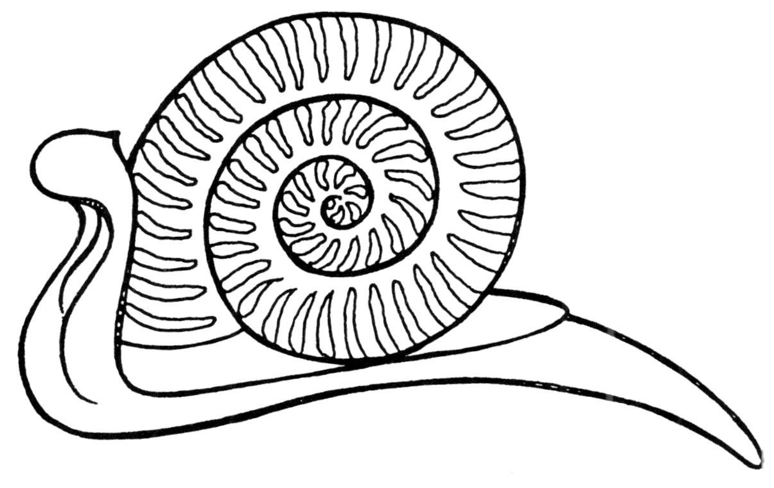

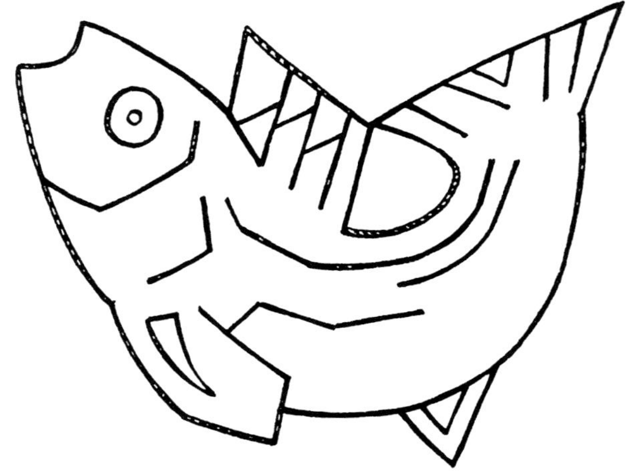

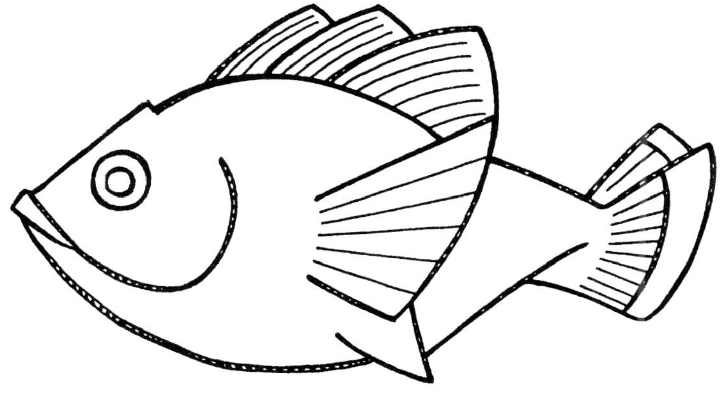

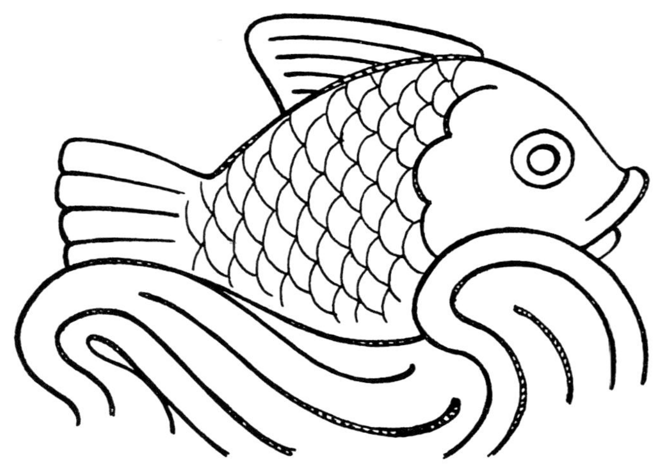

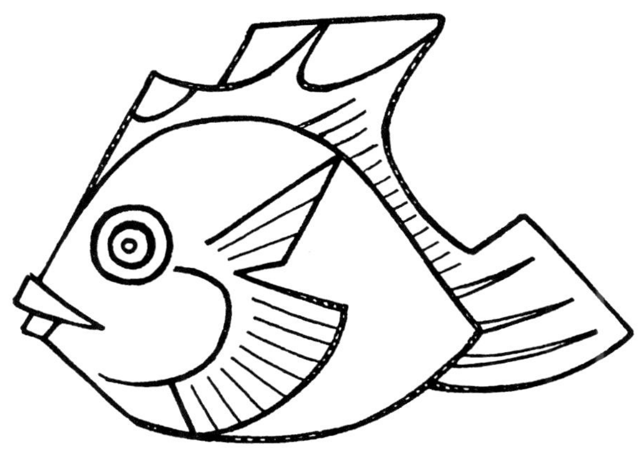

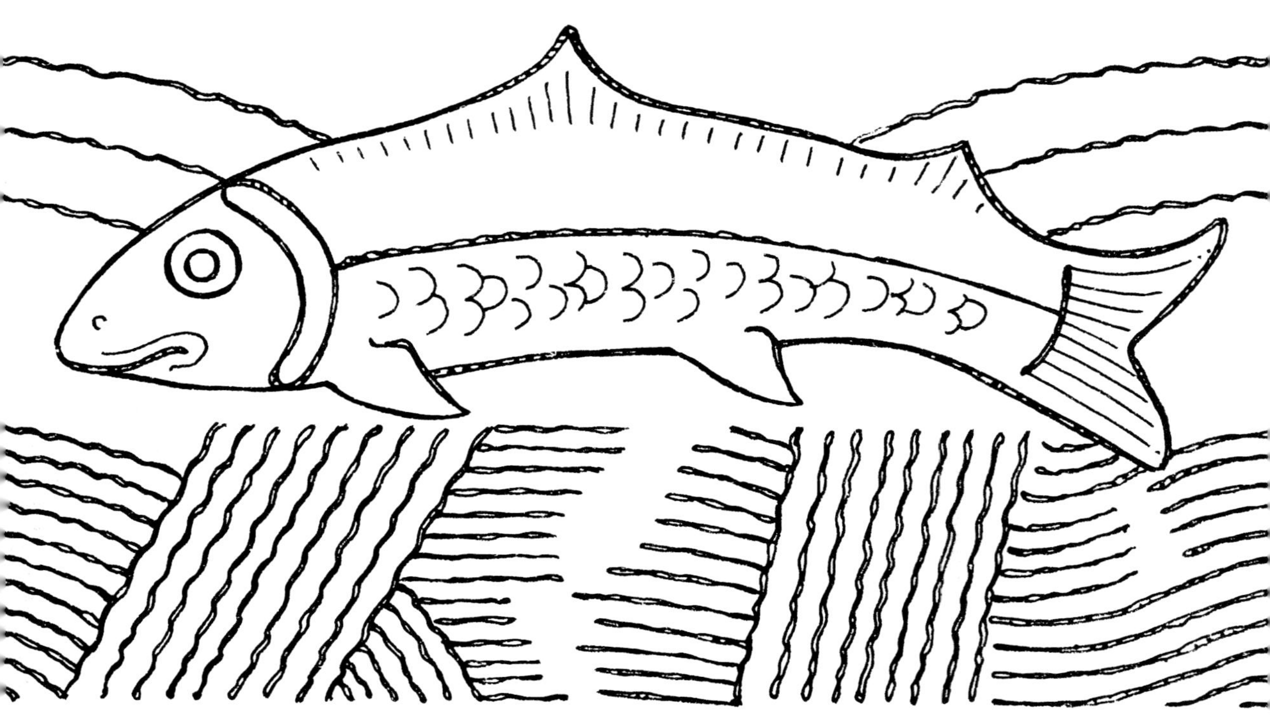

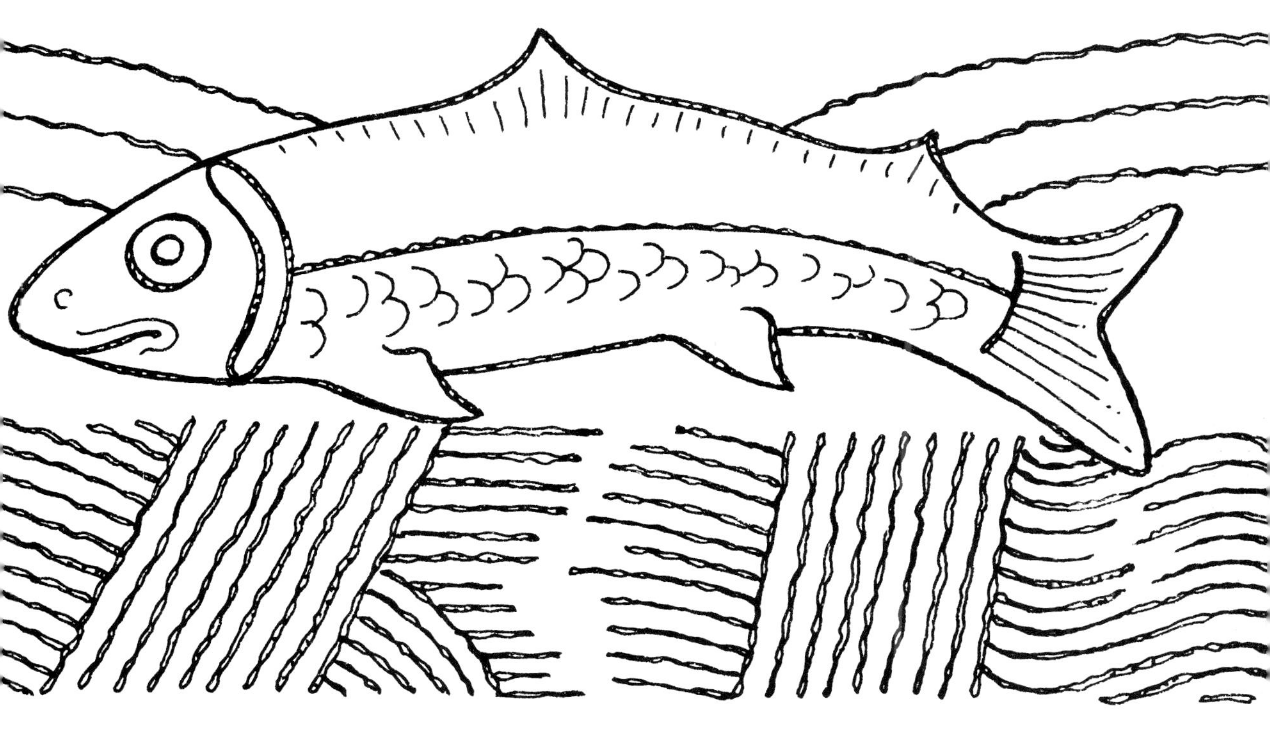

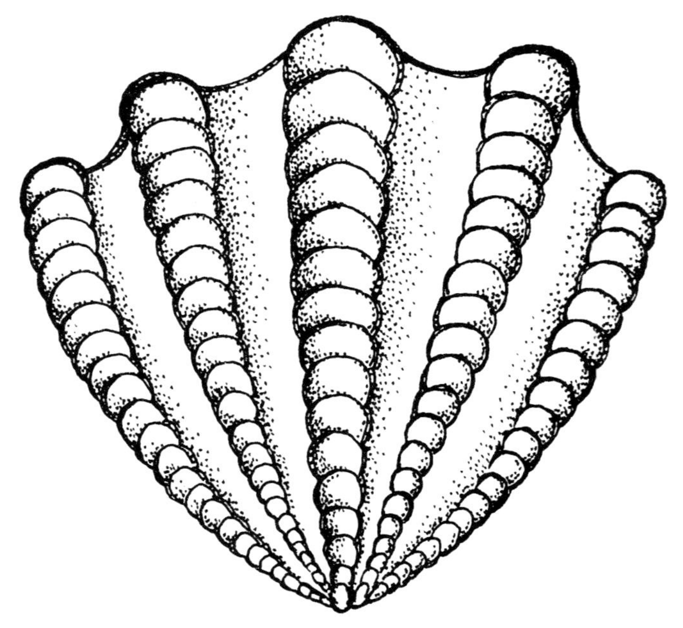

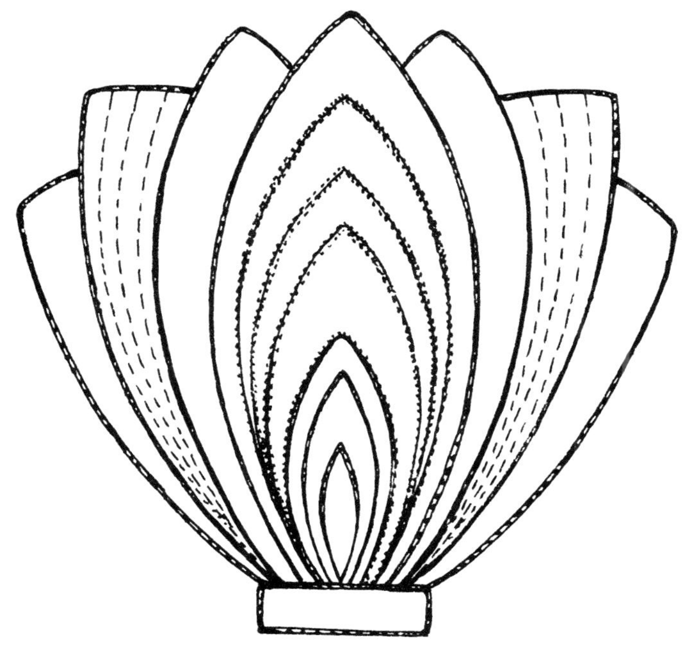

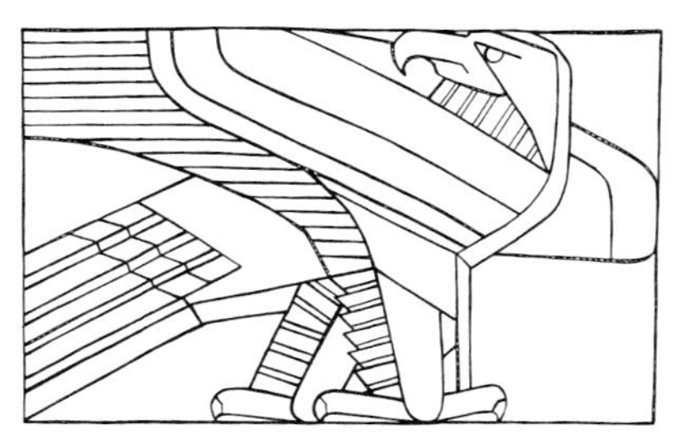
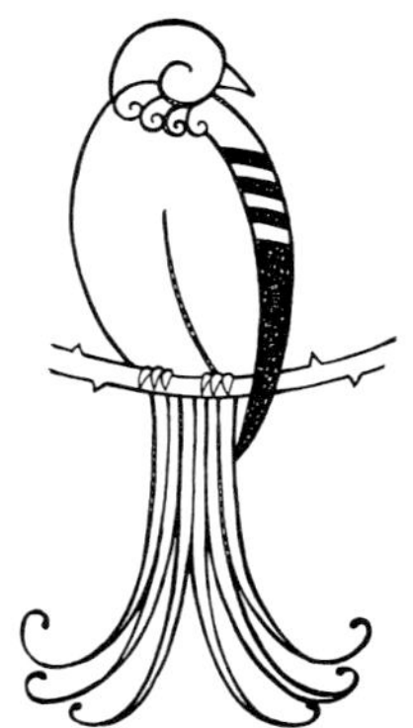
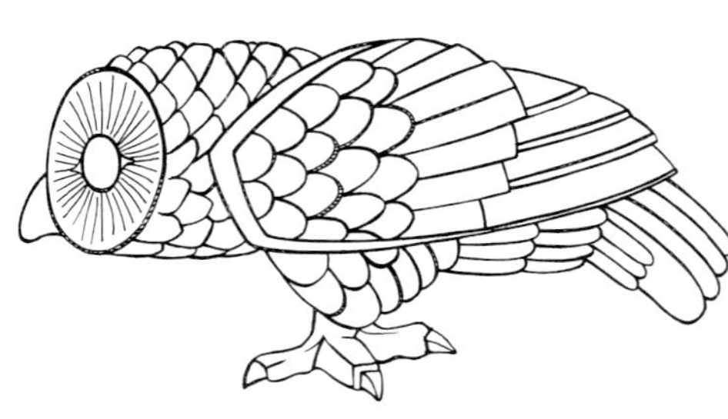

BIRDS

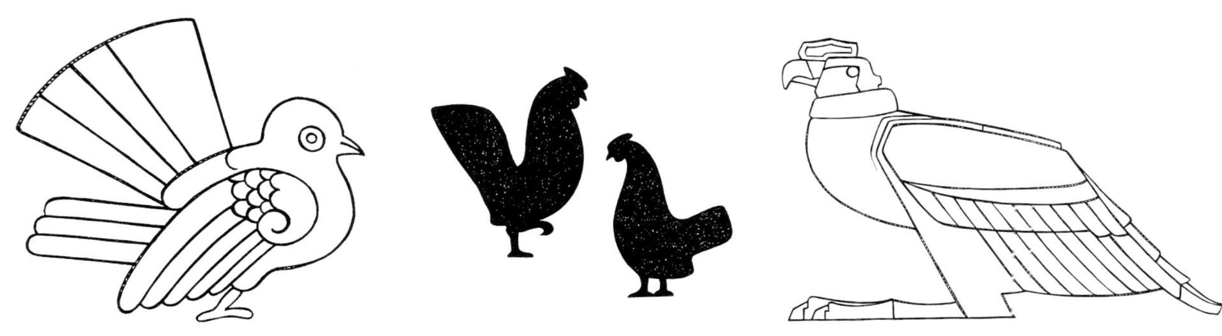

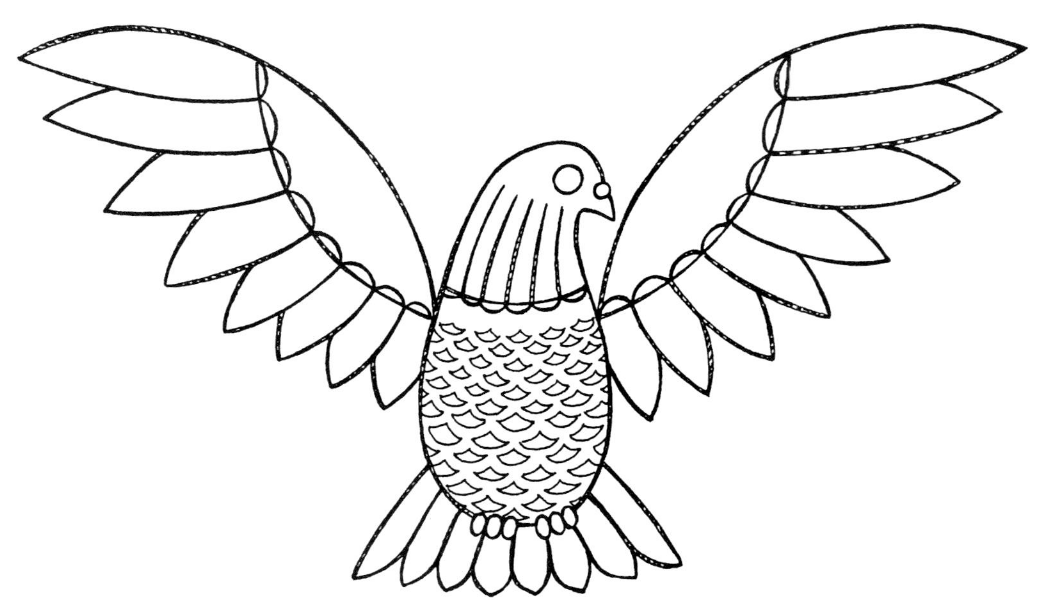

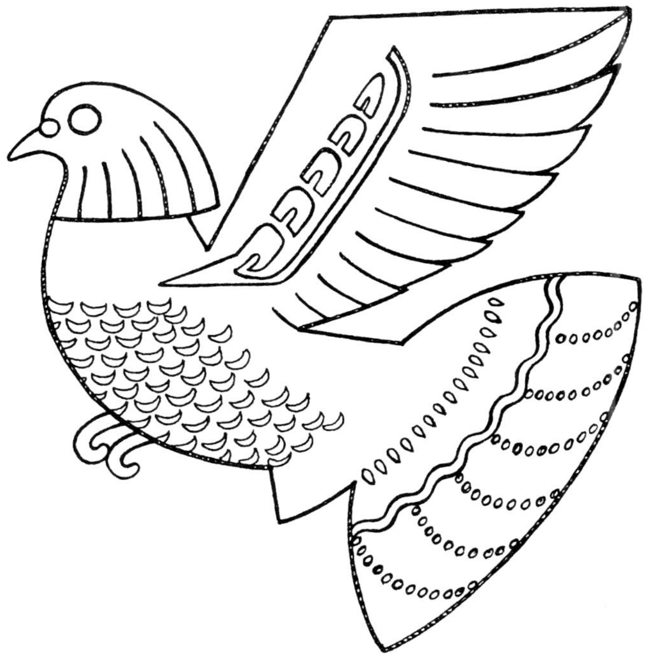

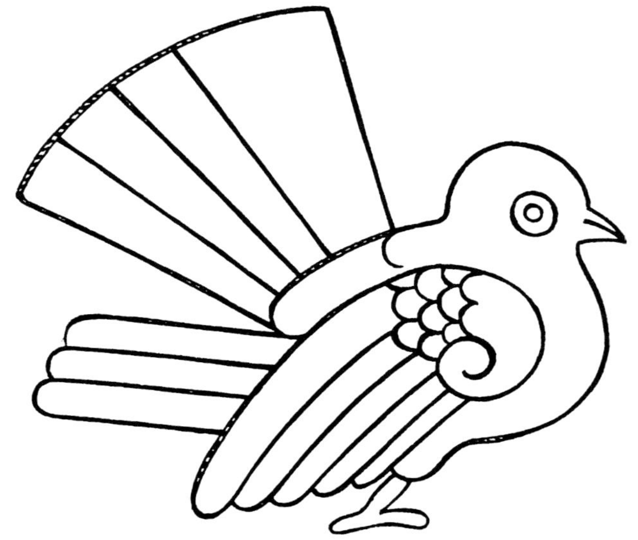

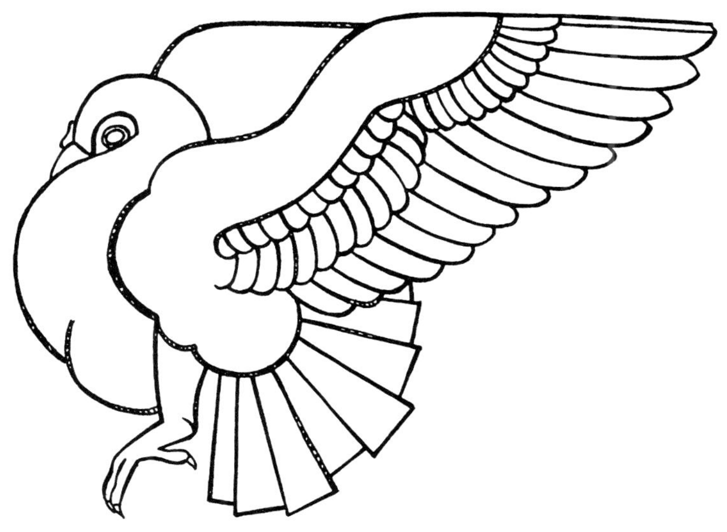

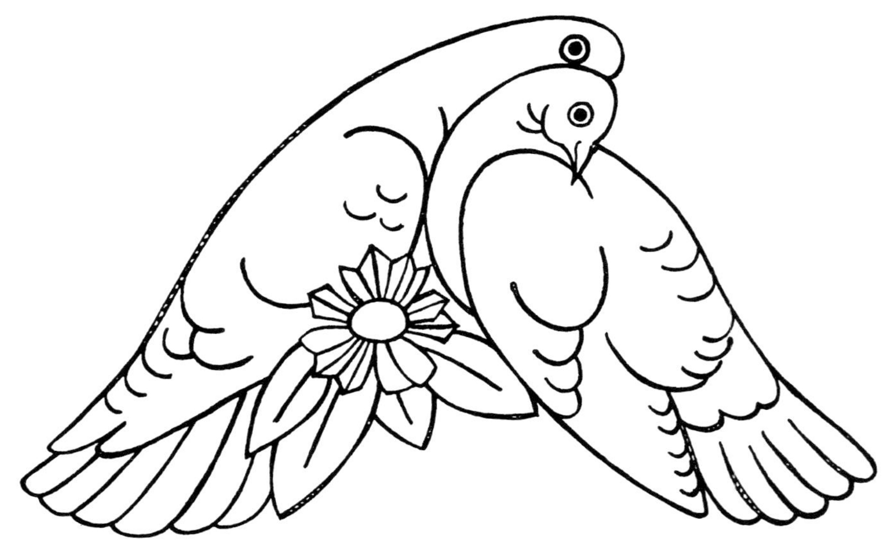

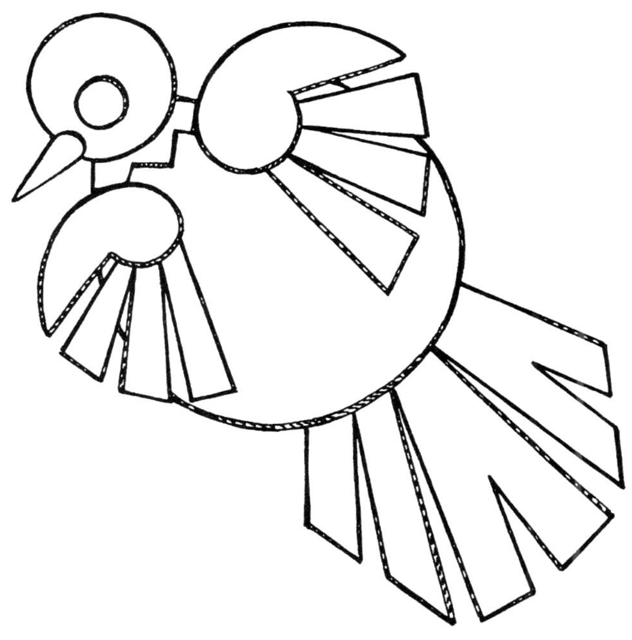

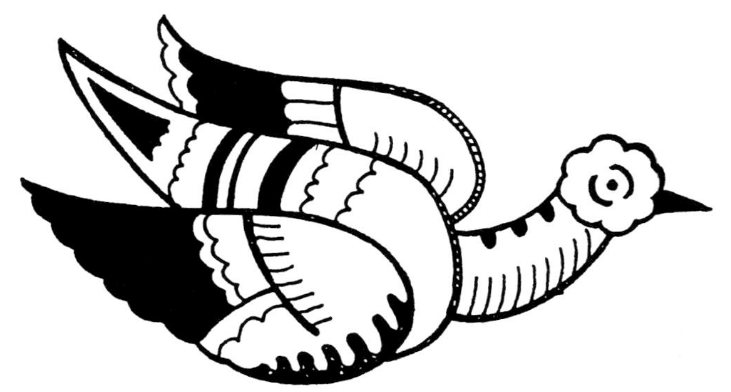

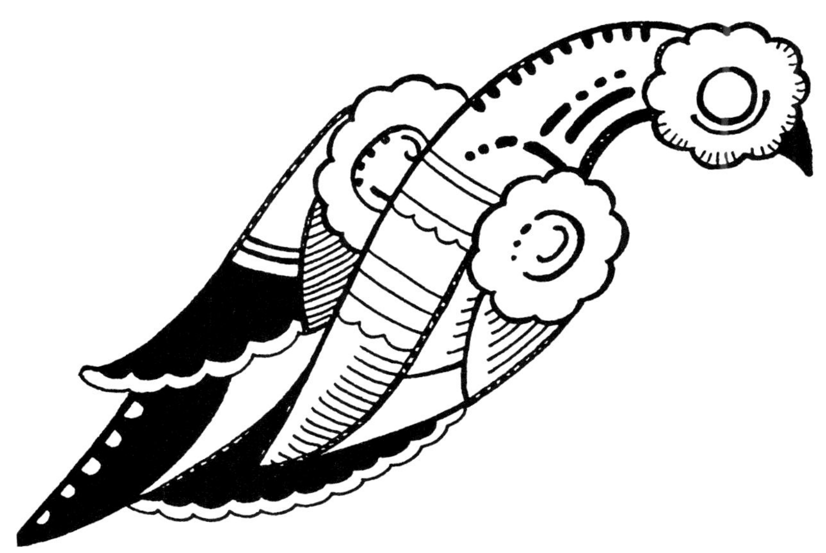

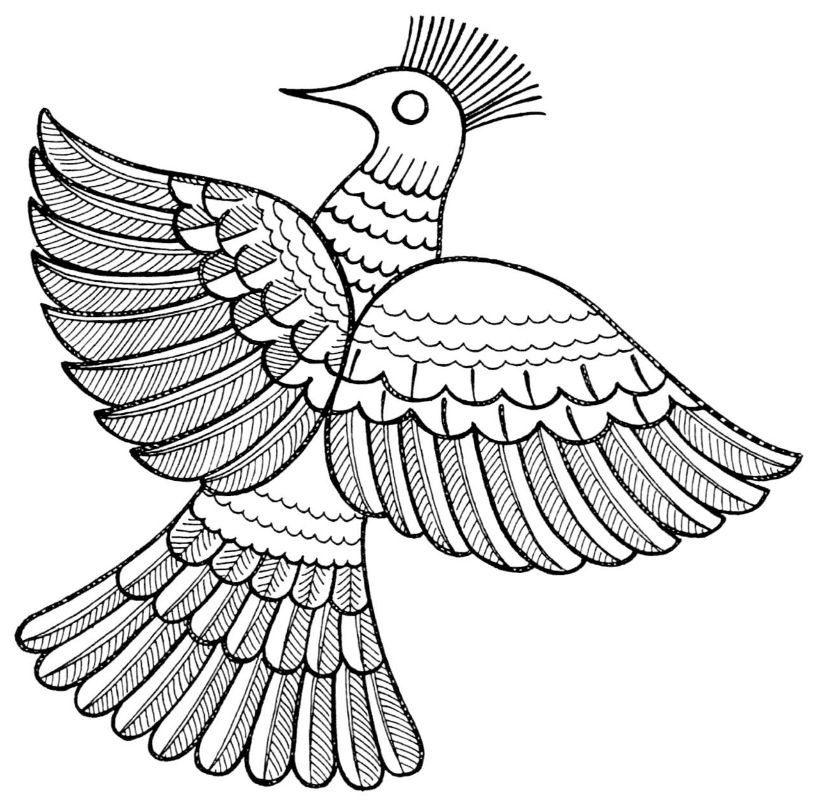

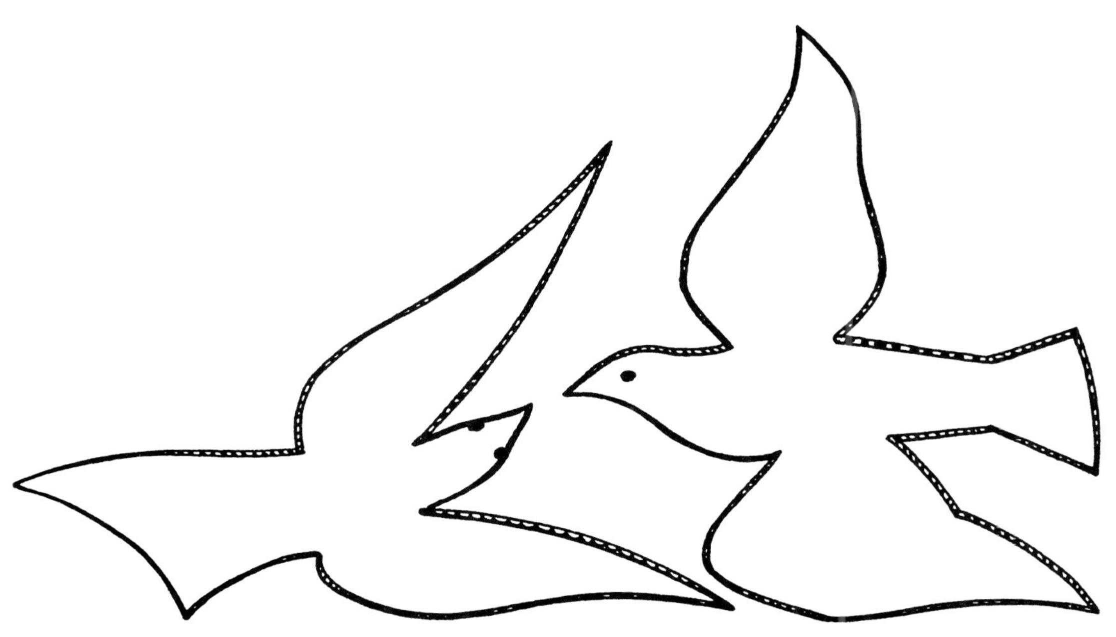

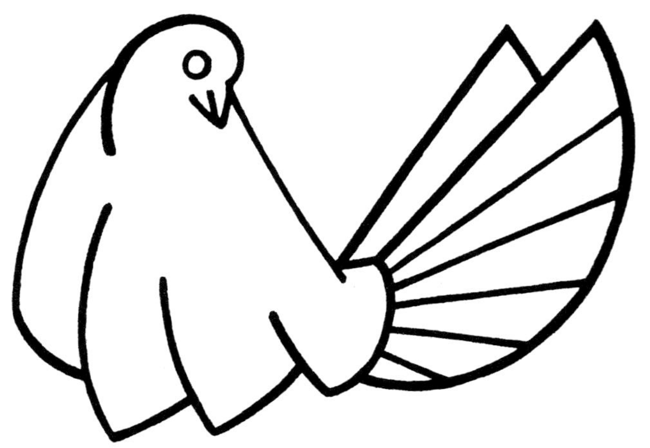

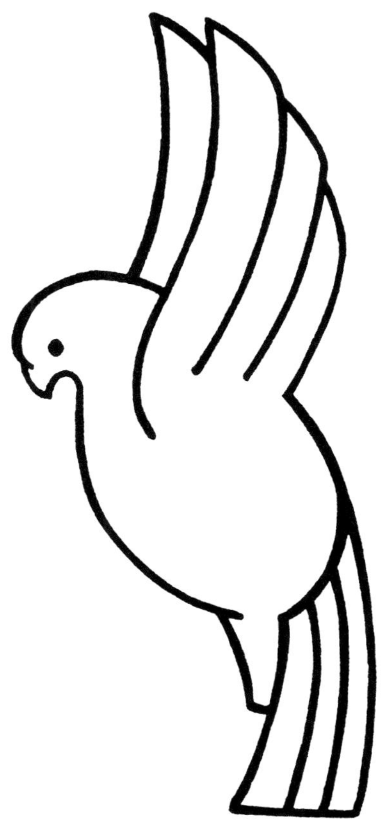

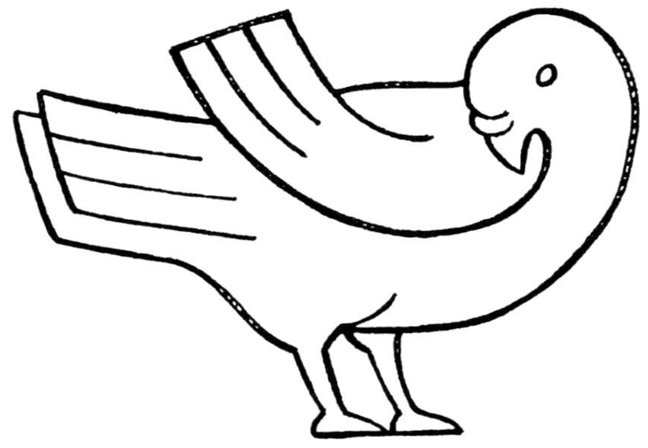

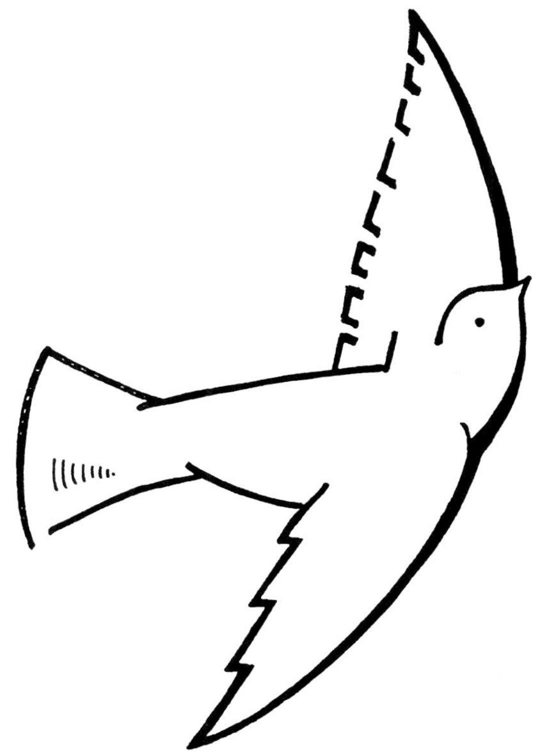

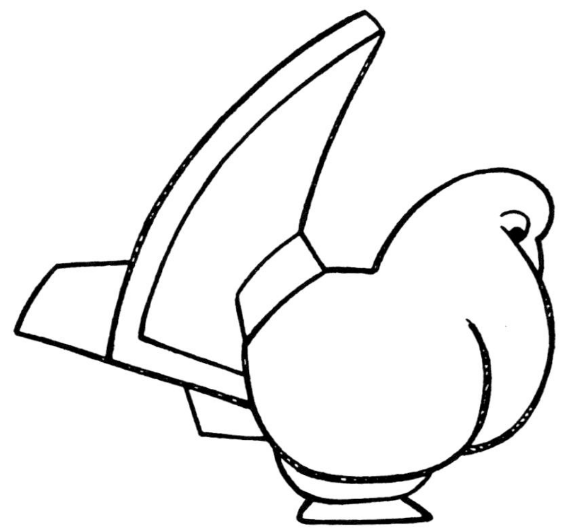

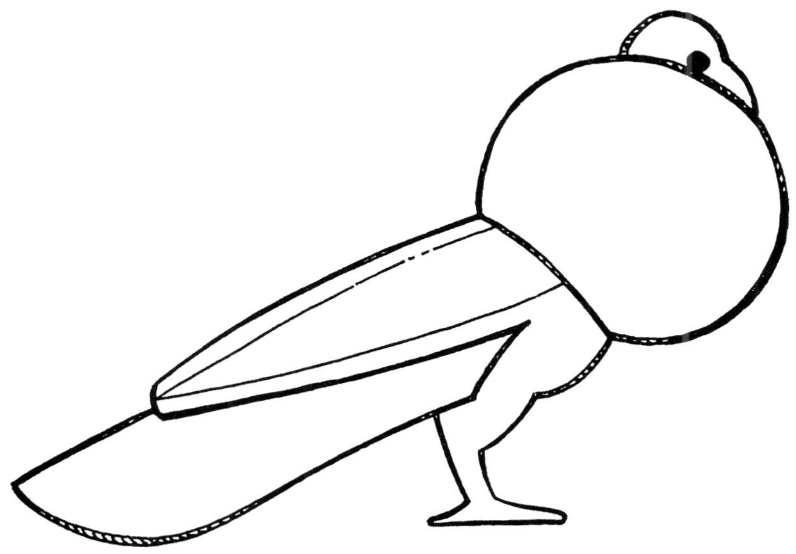

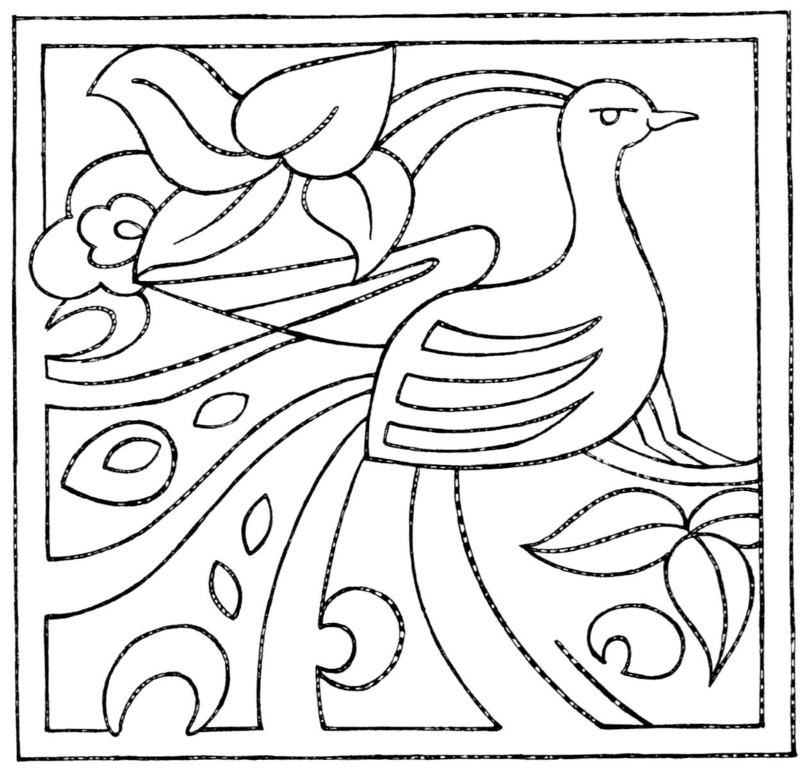

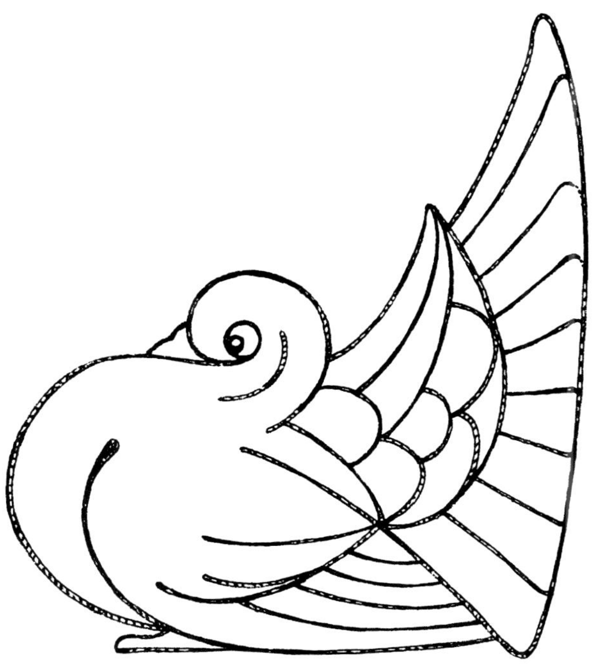

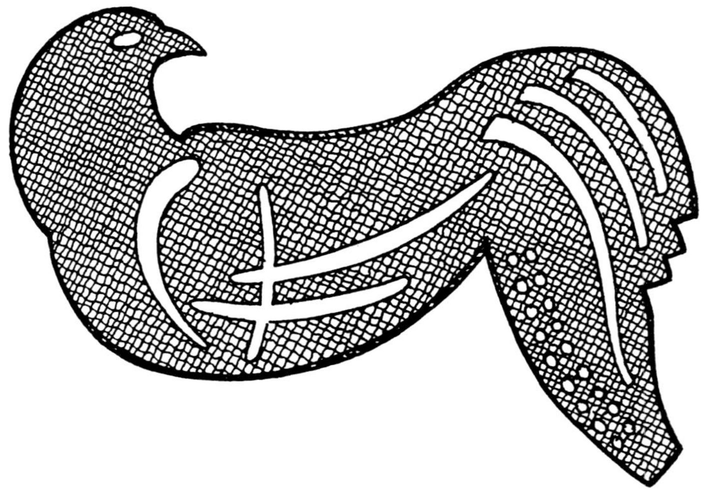

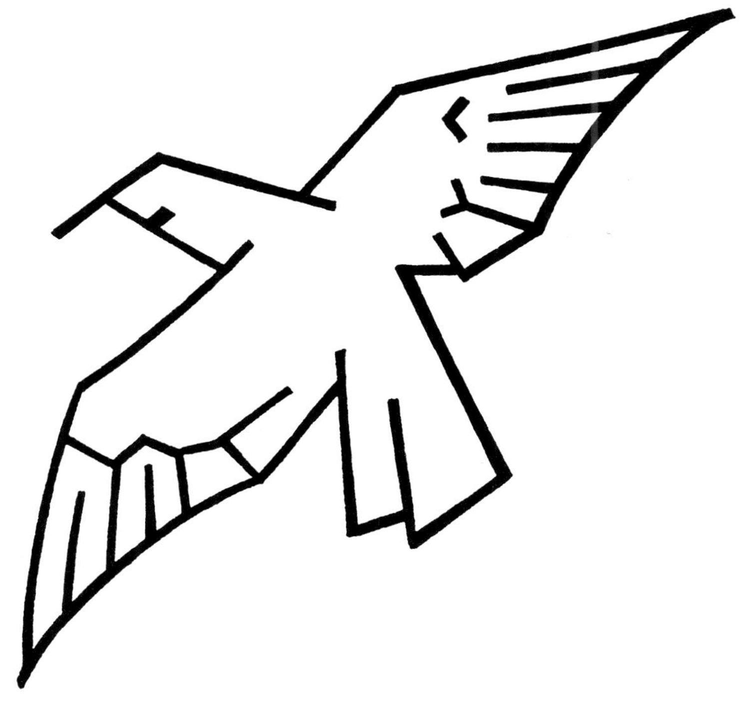

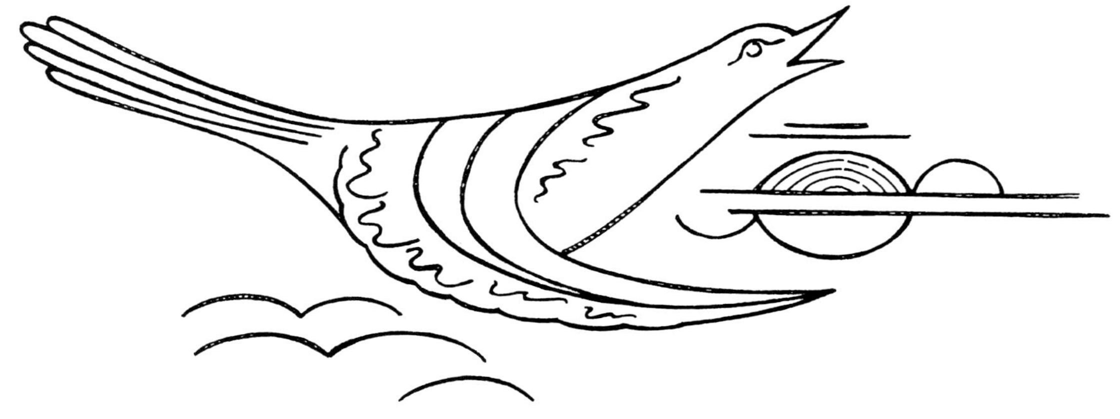

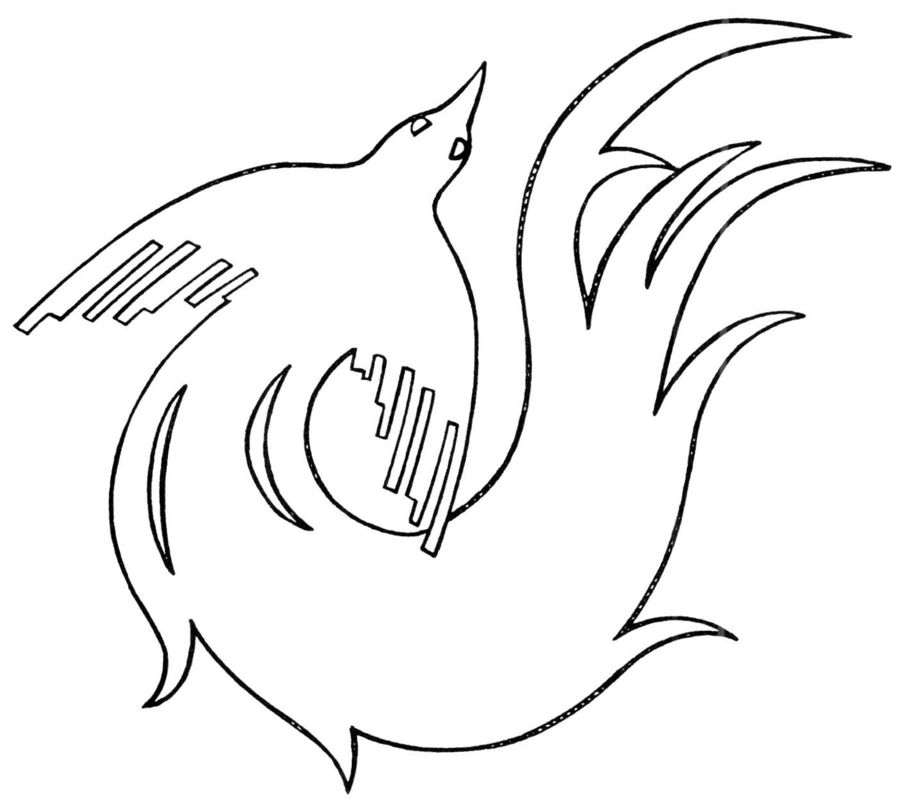

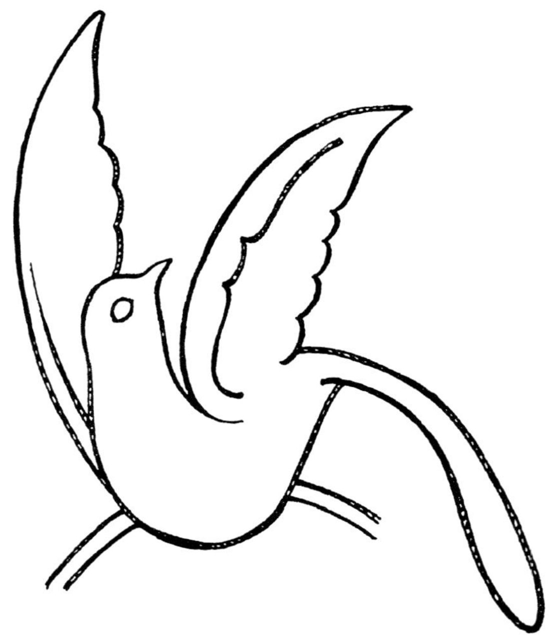

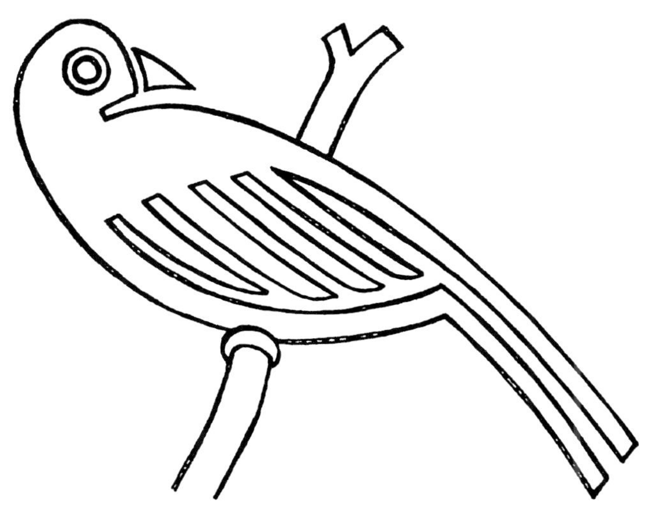

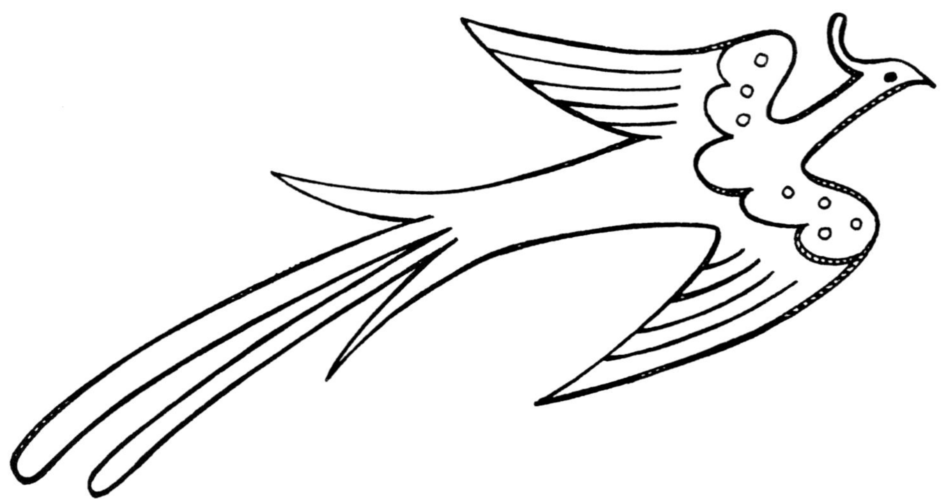

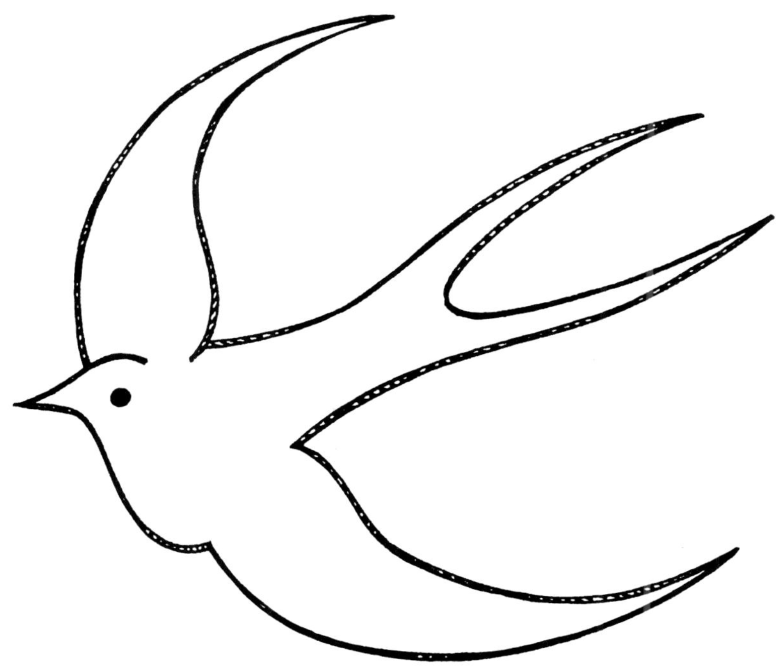

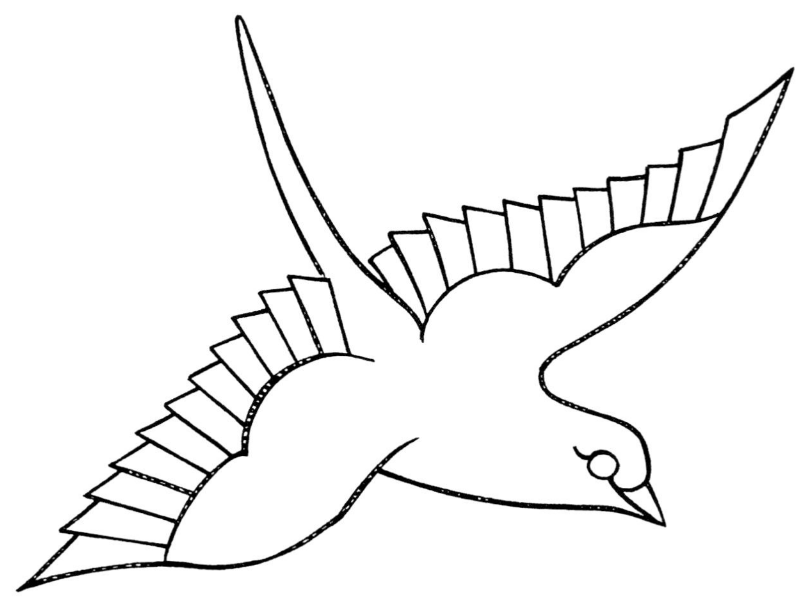

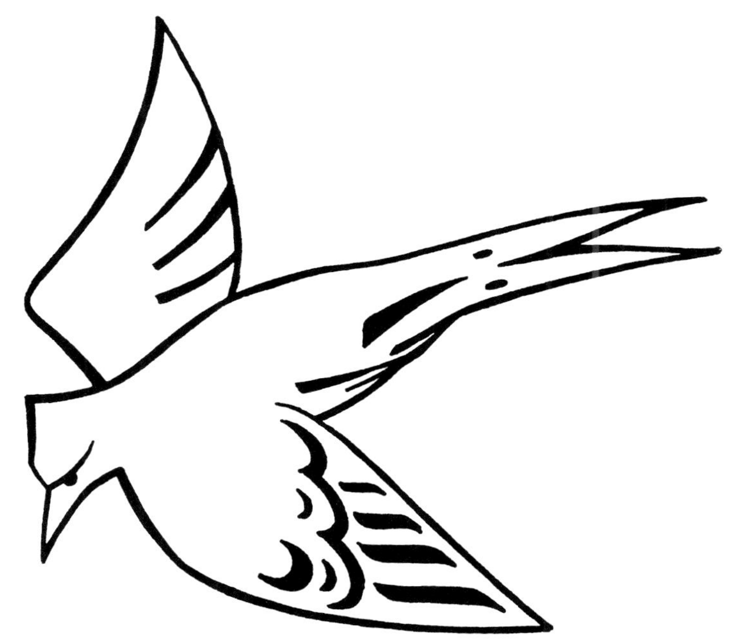

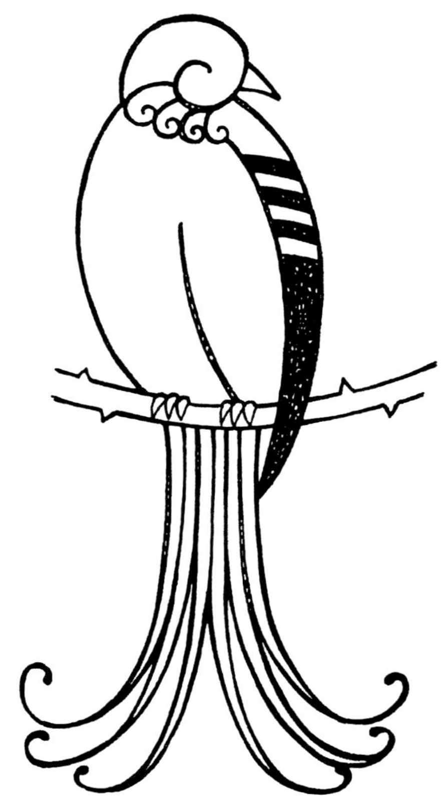

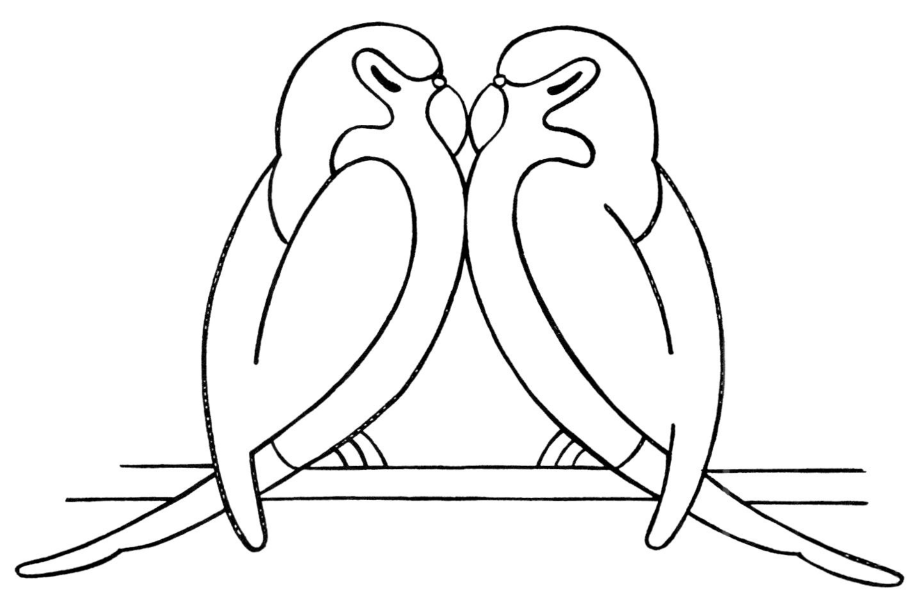

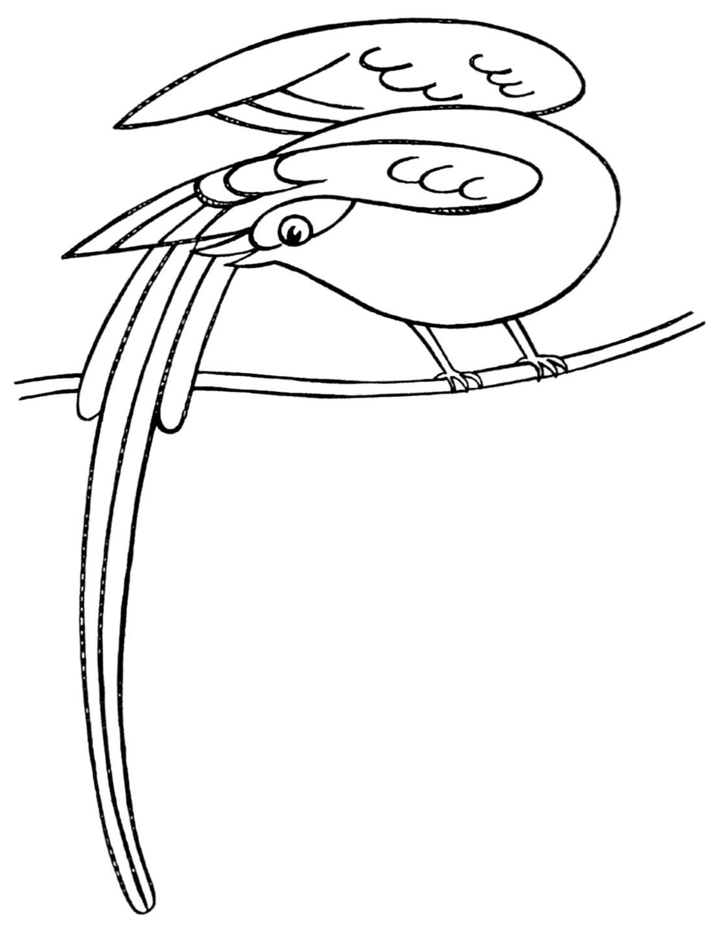

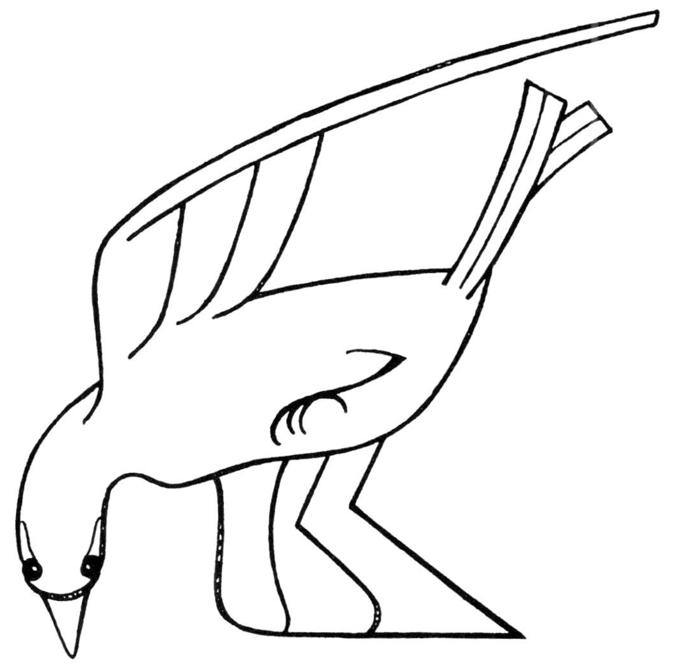

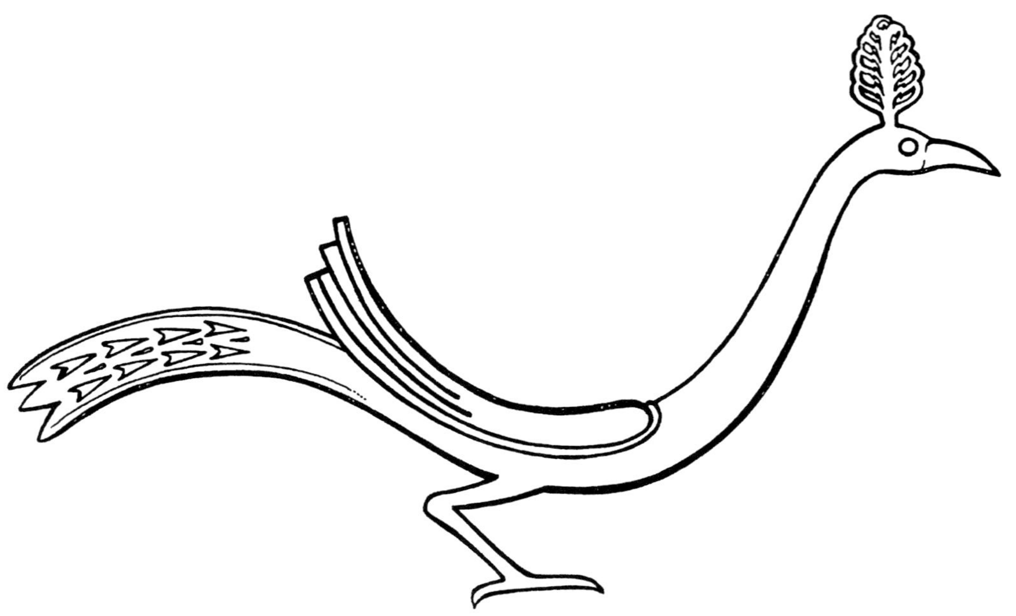

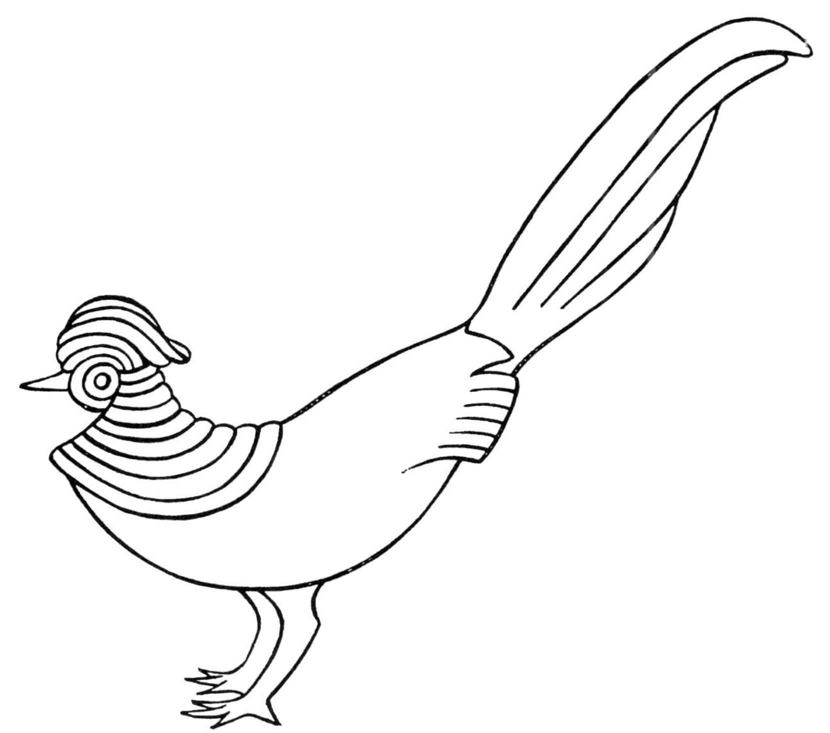

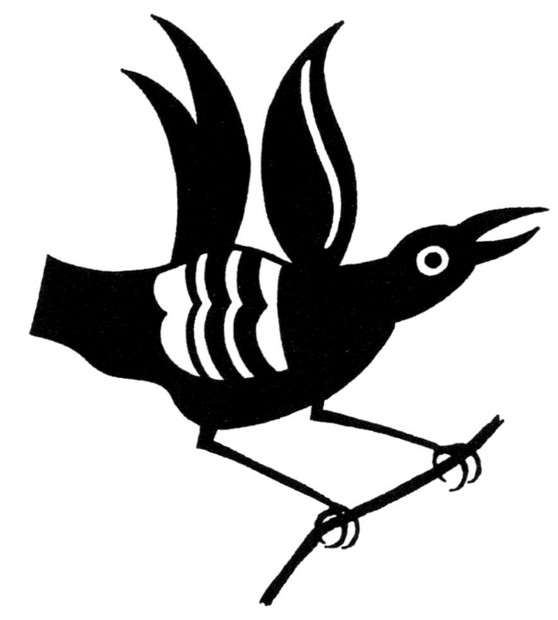

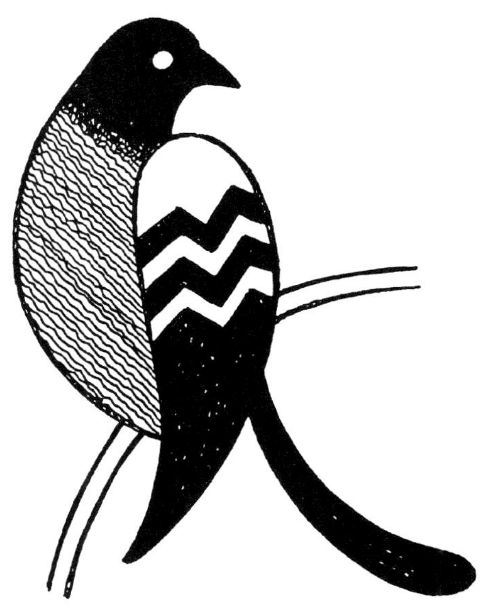

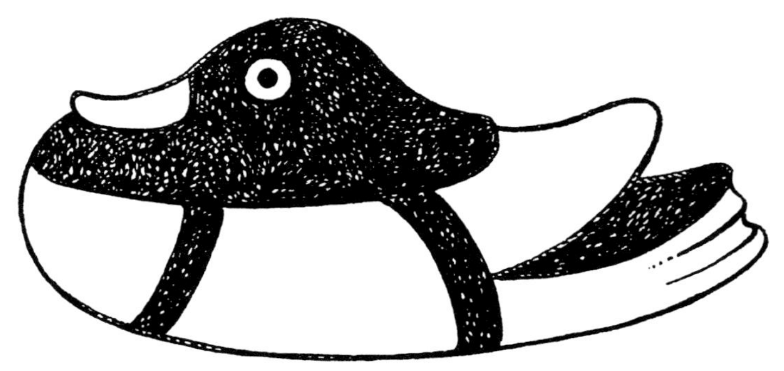

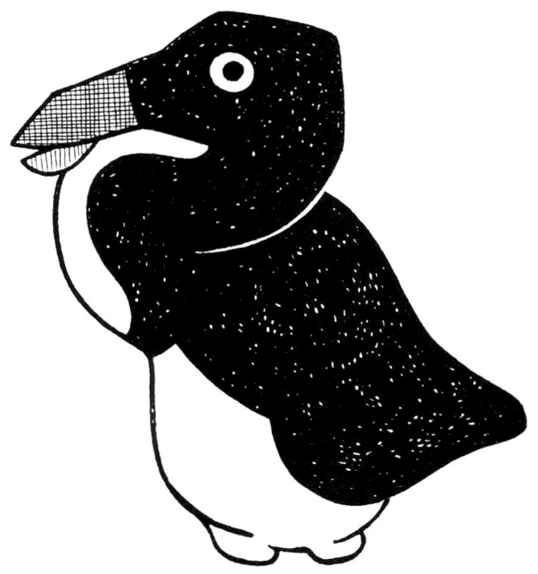

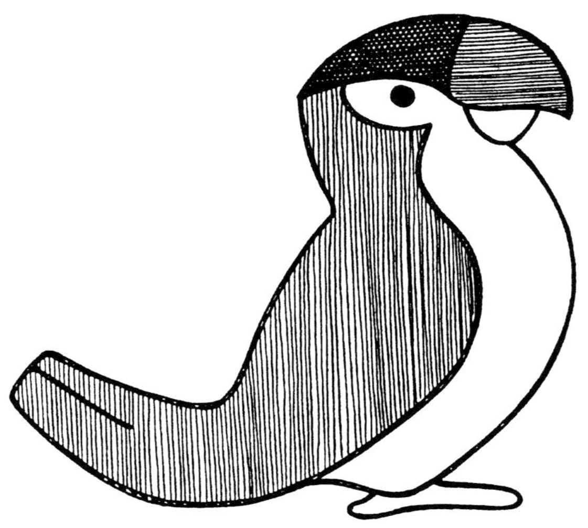

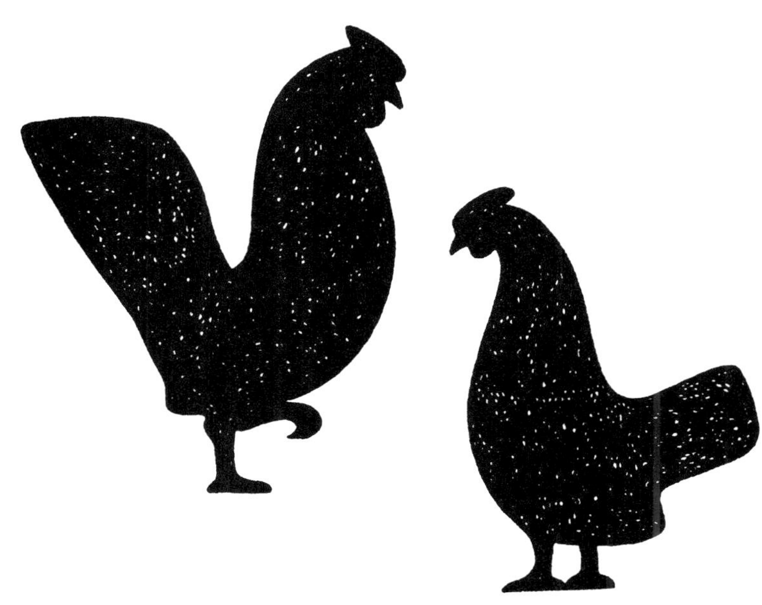

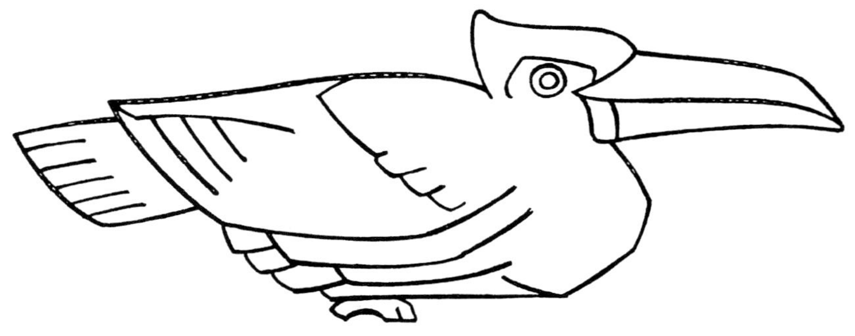

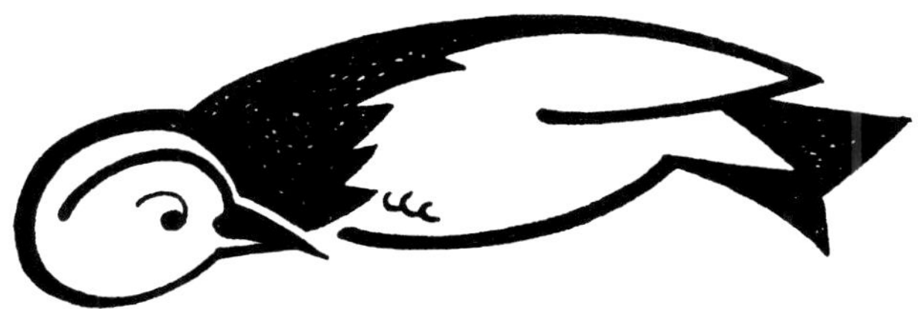

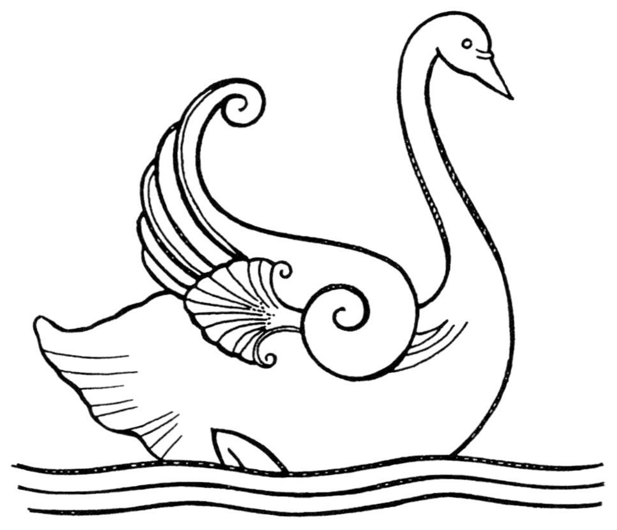

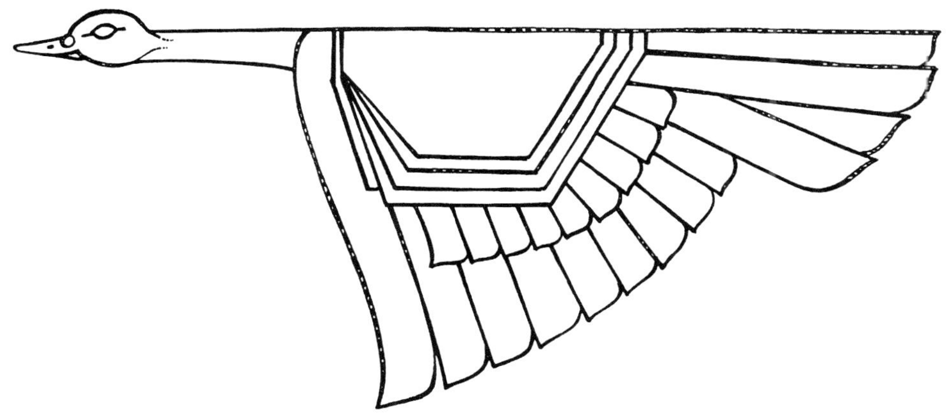

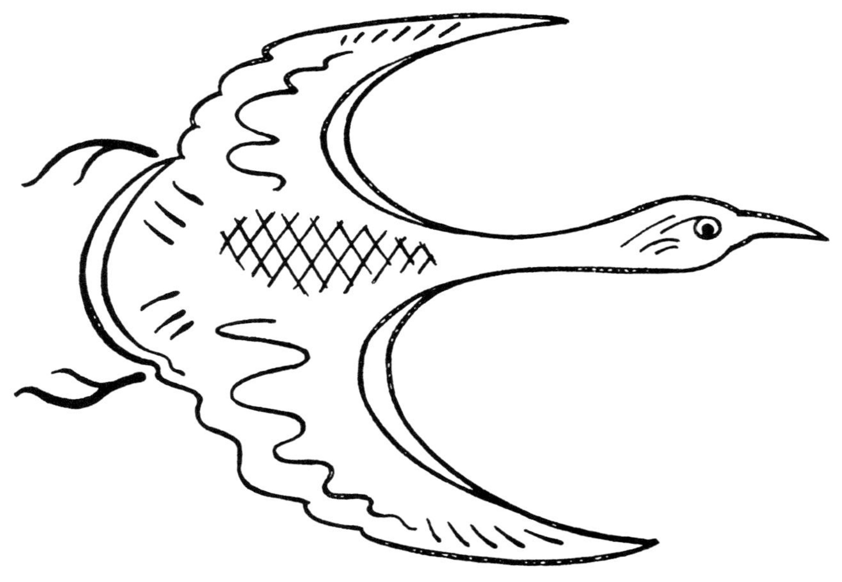

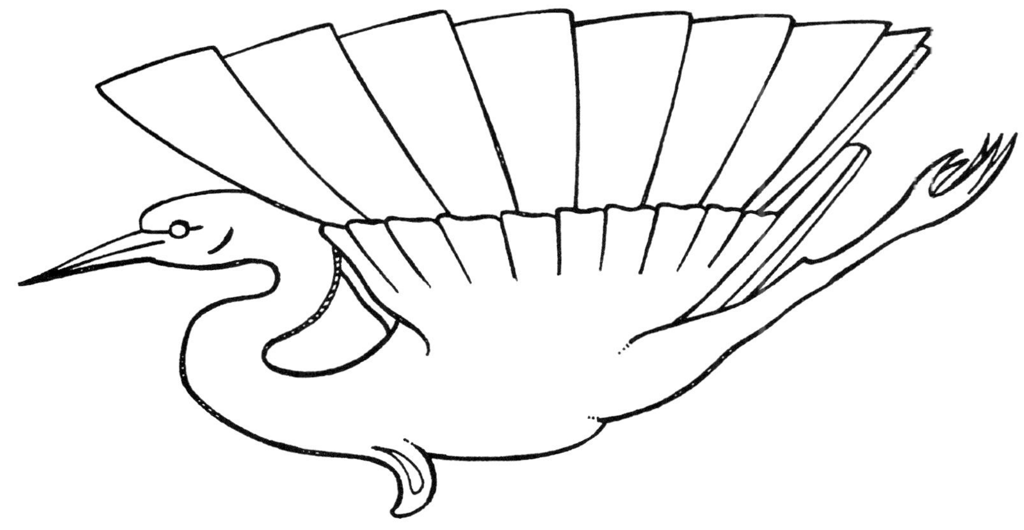

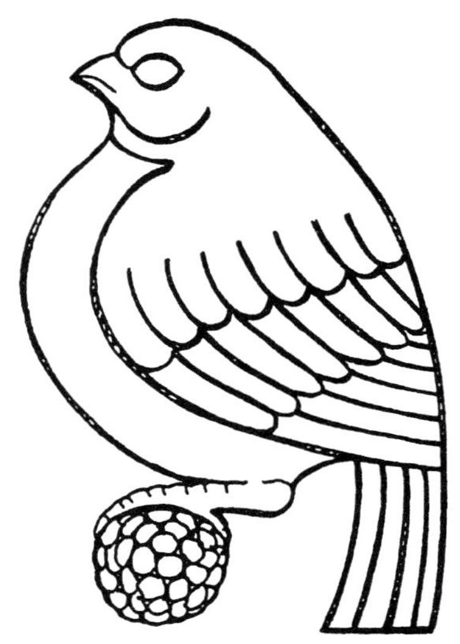

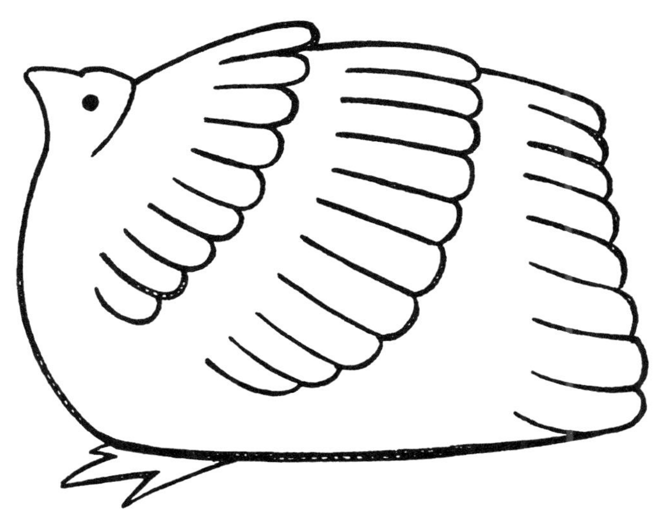

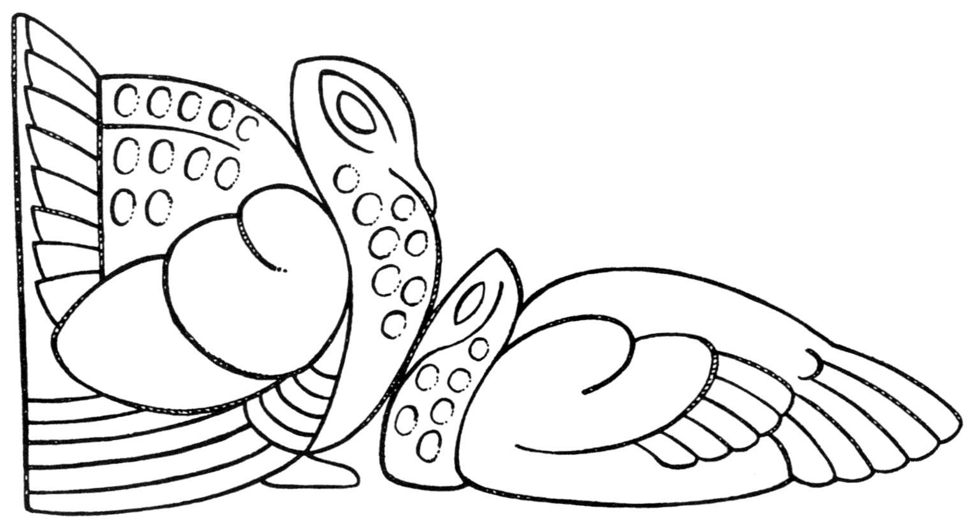

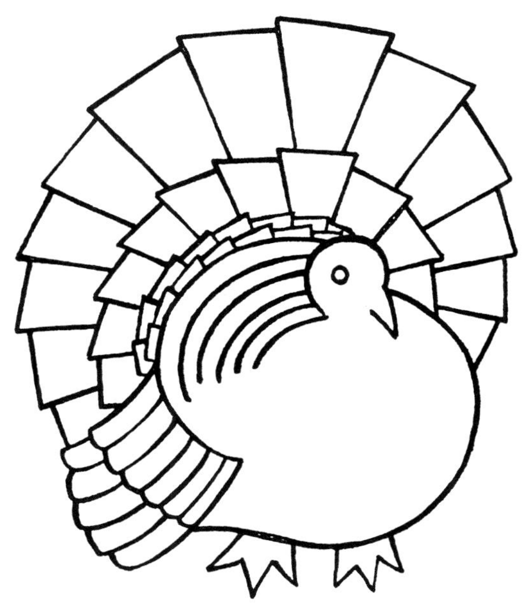

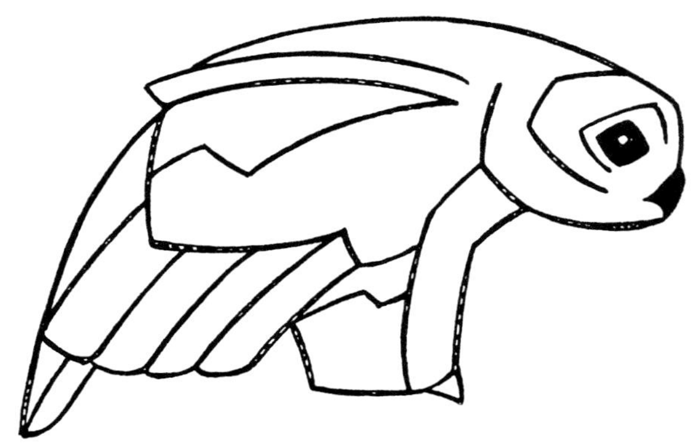

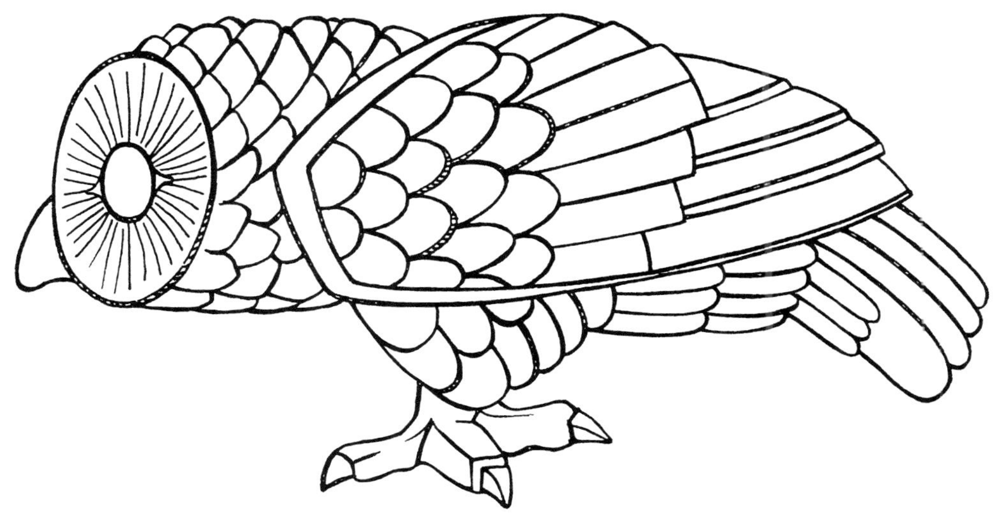

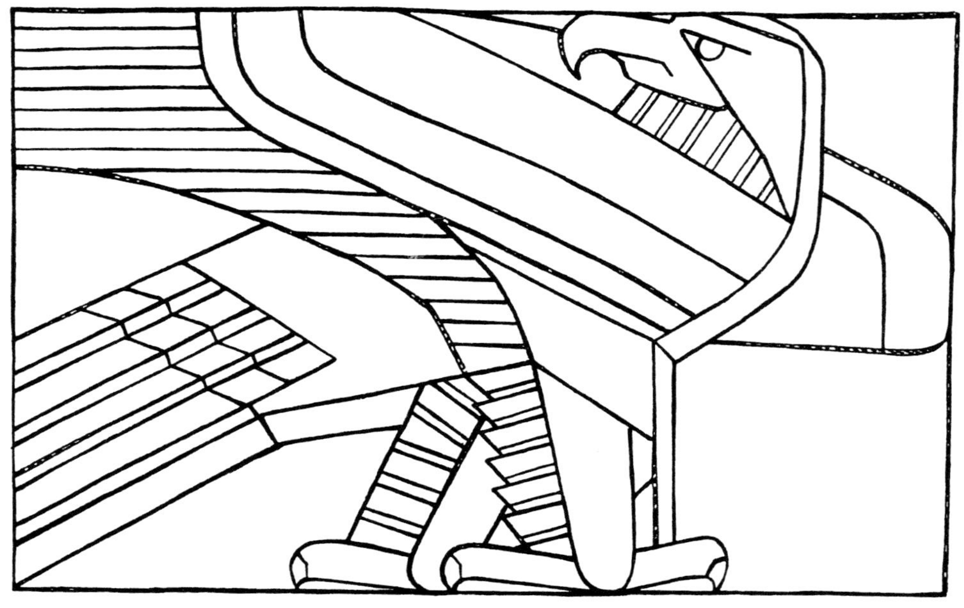

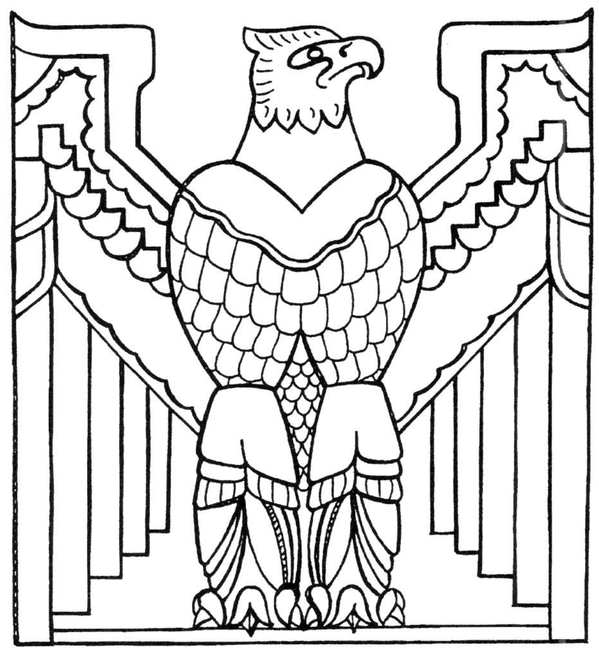

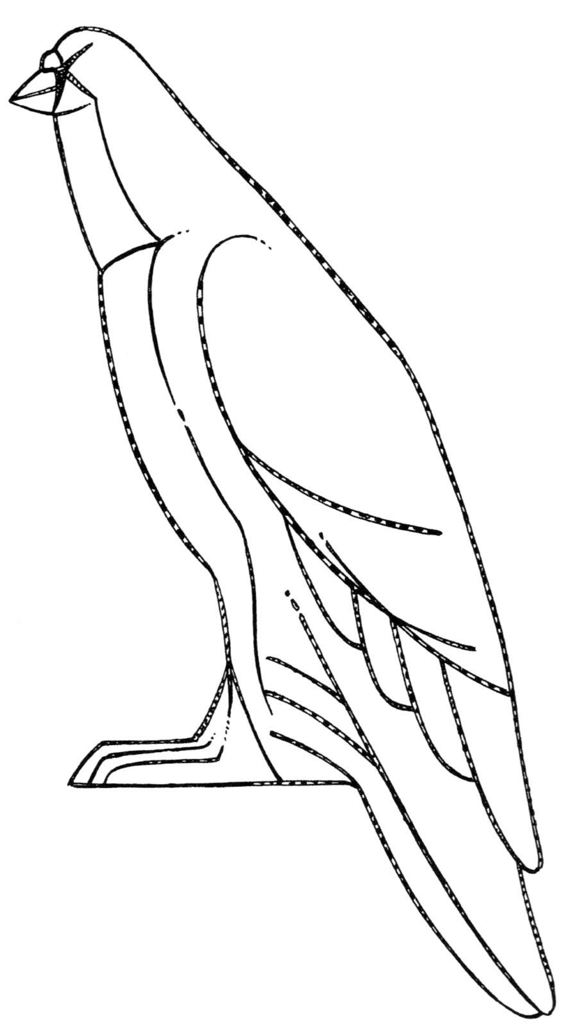

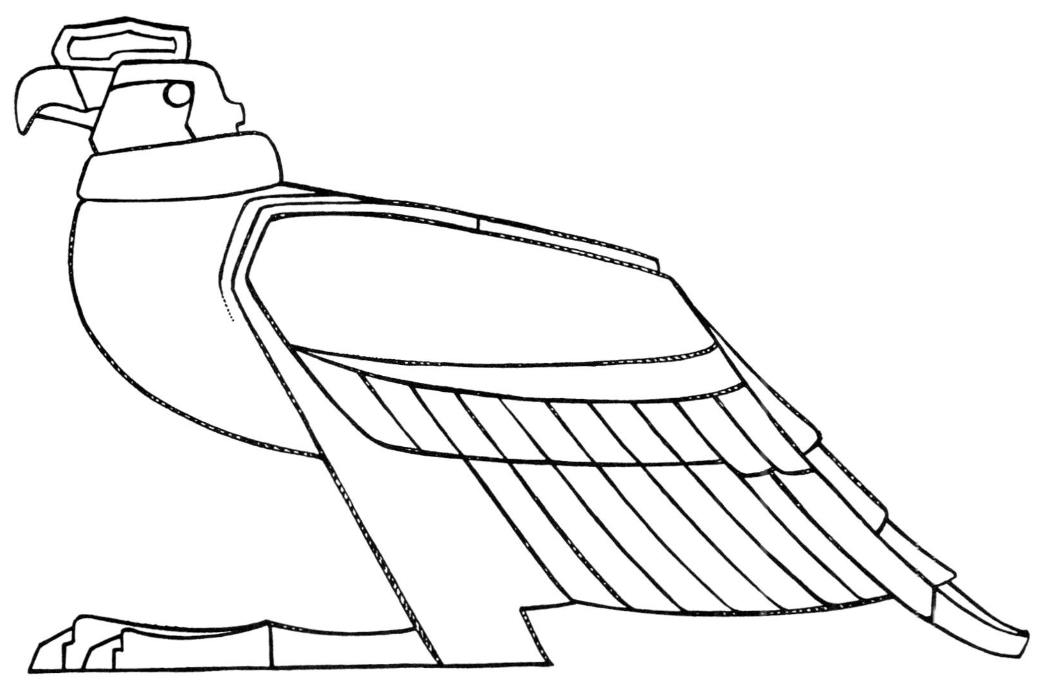

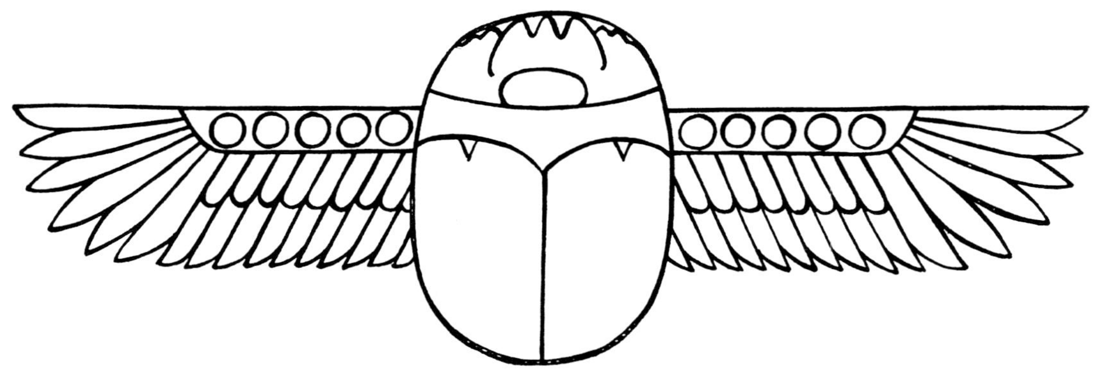

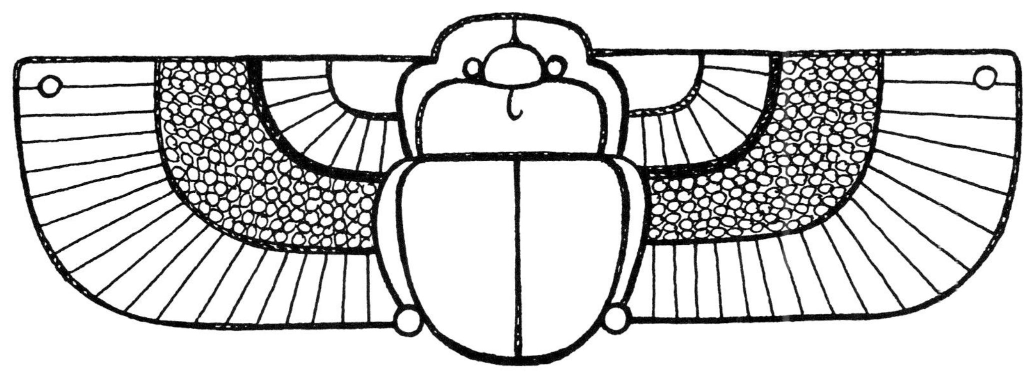

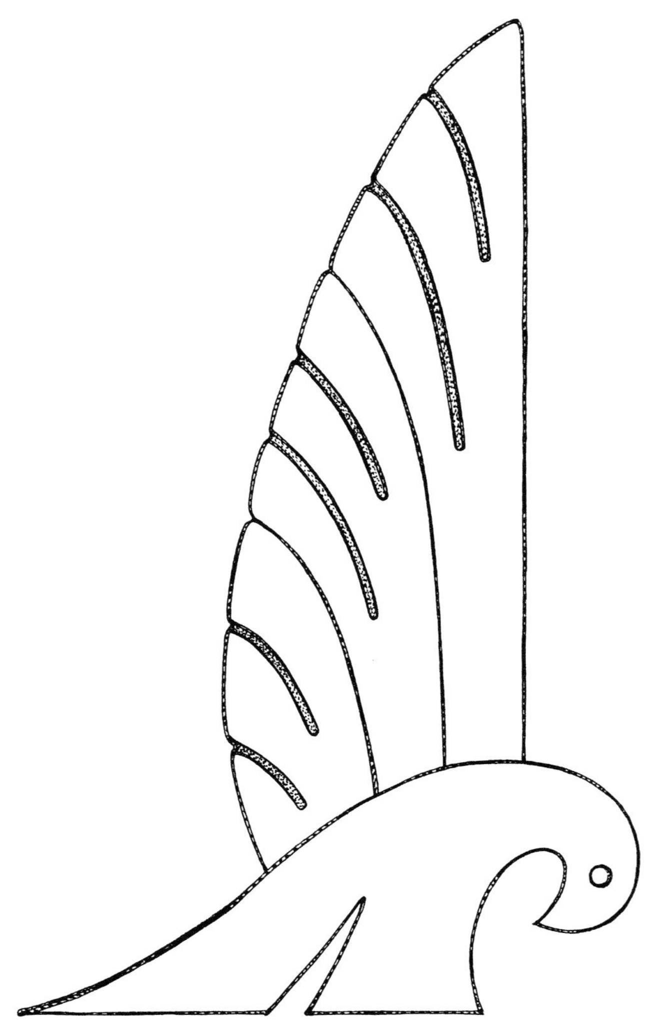

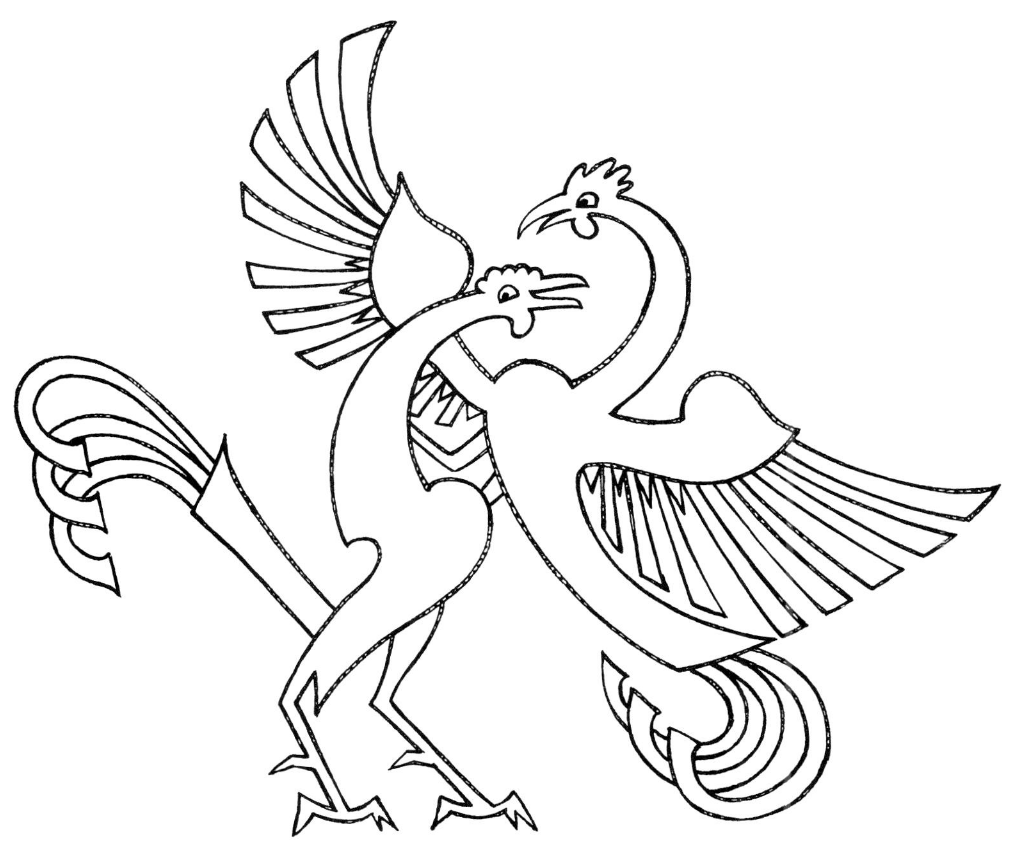

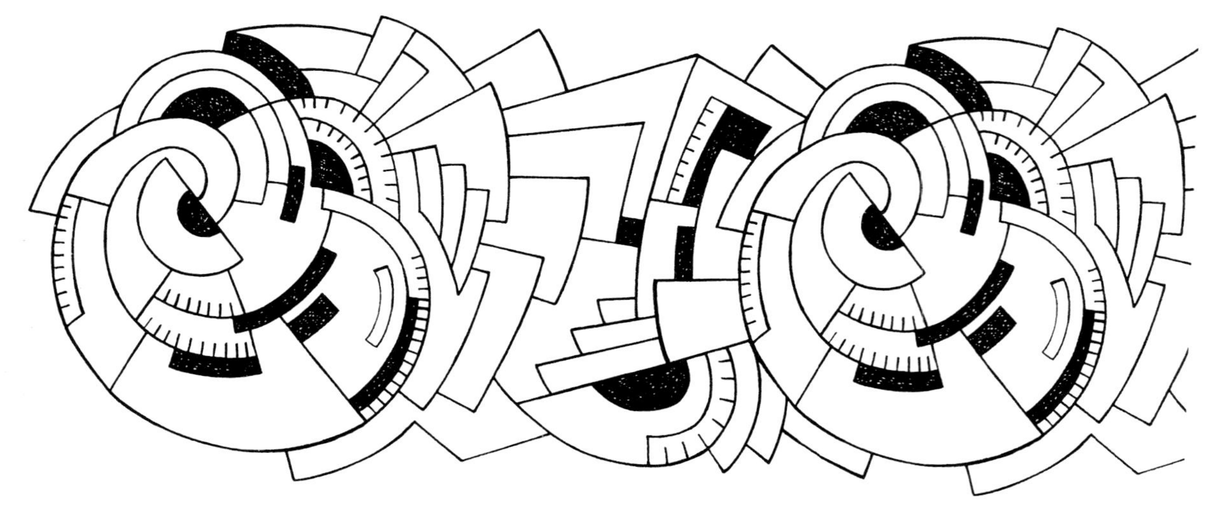

BORDERS AND PATTERNS

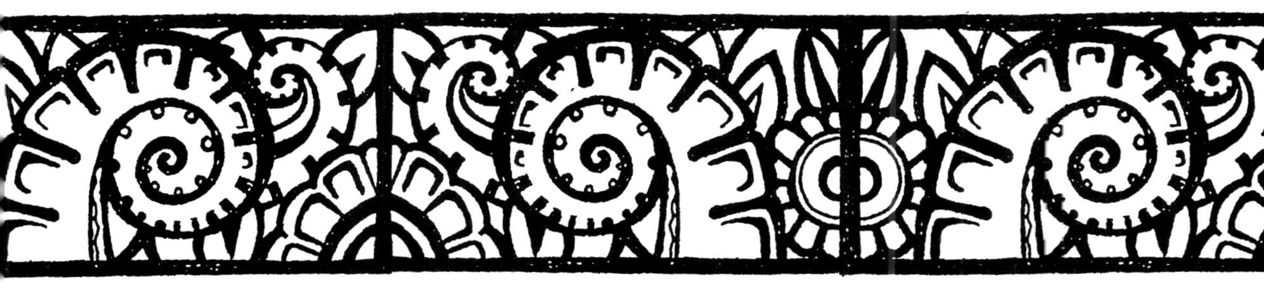

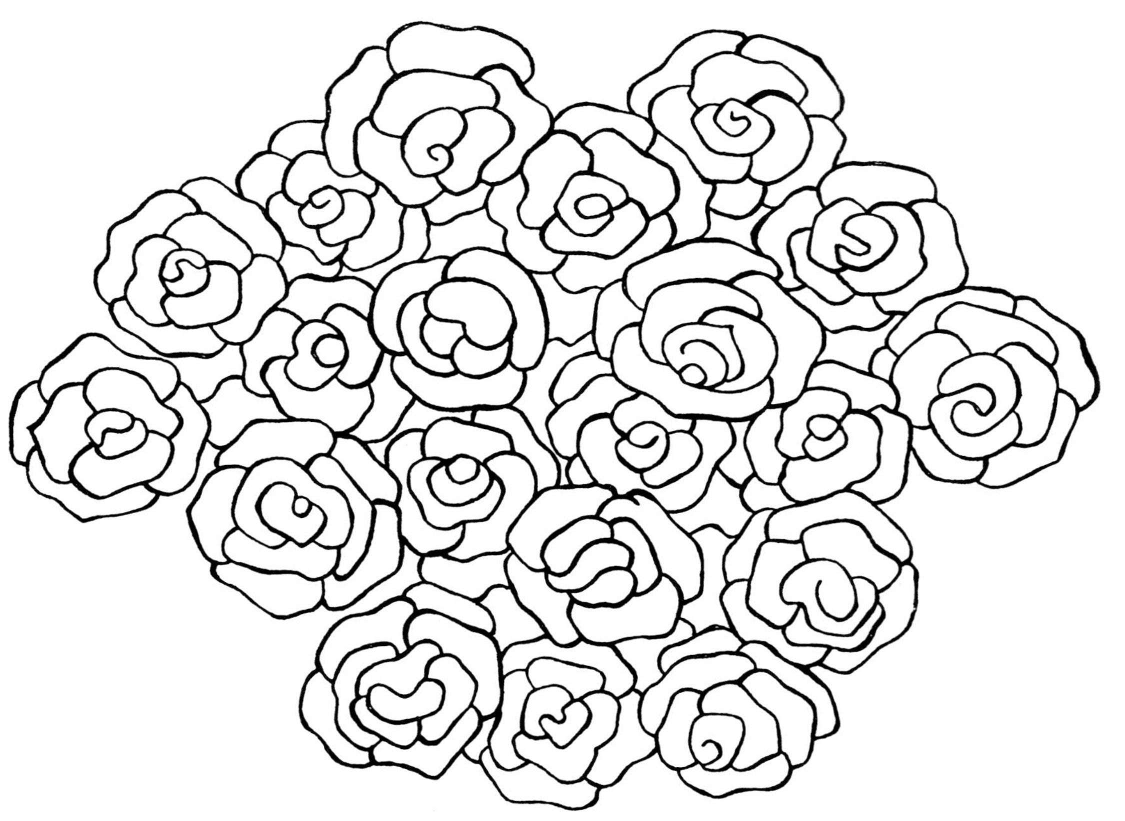

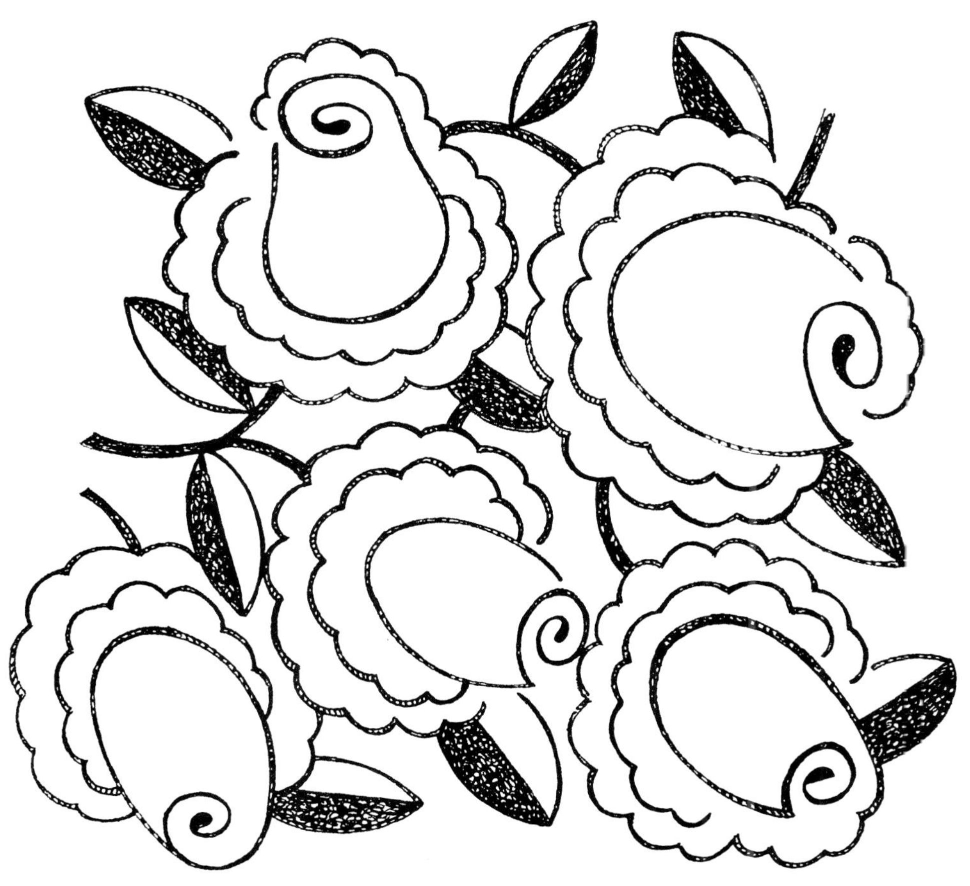

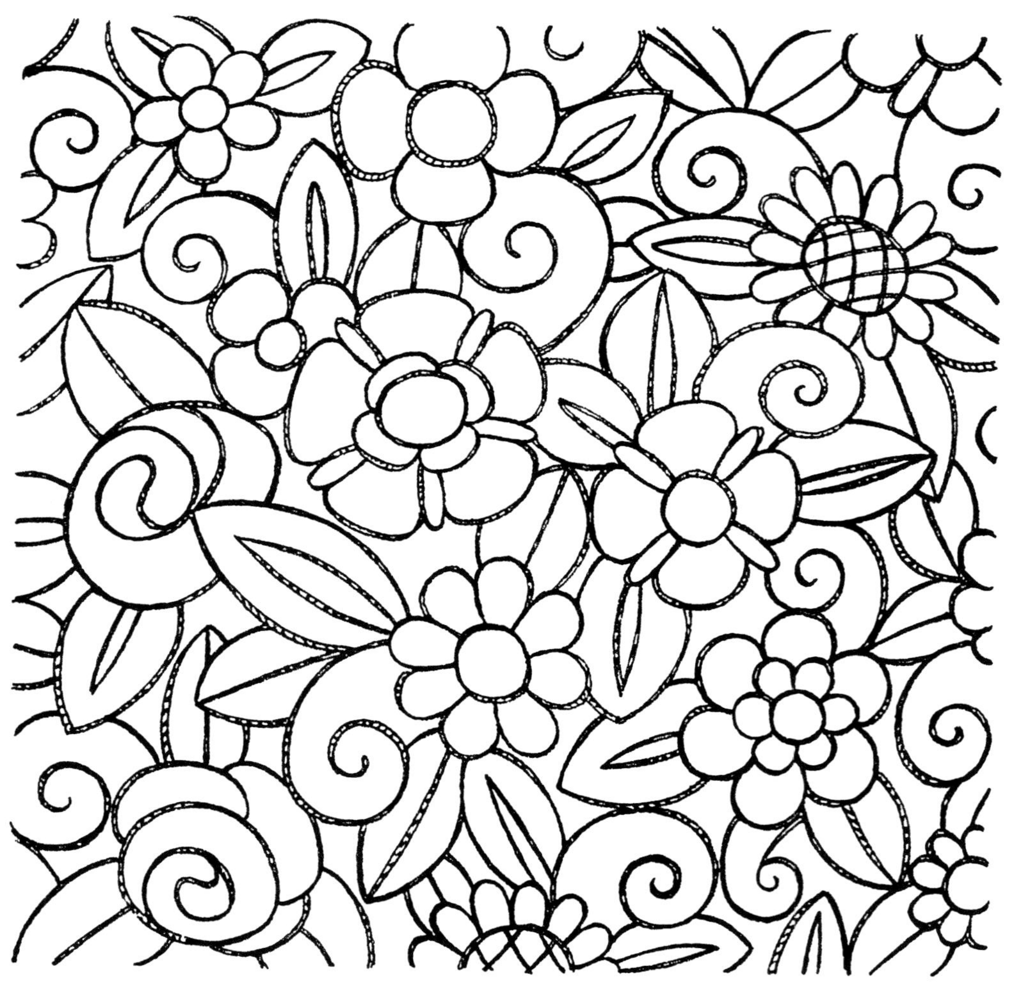

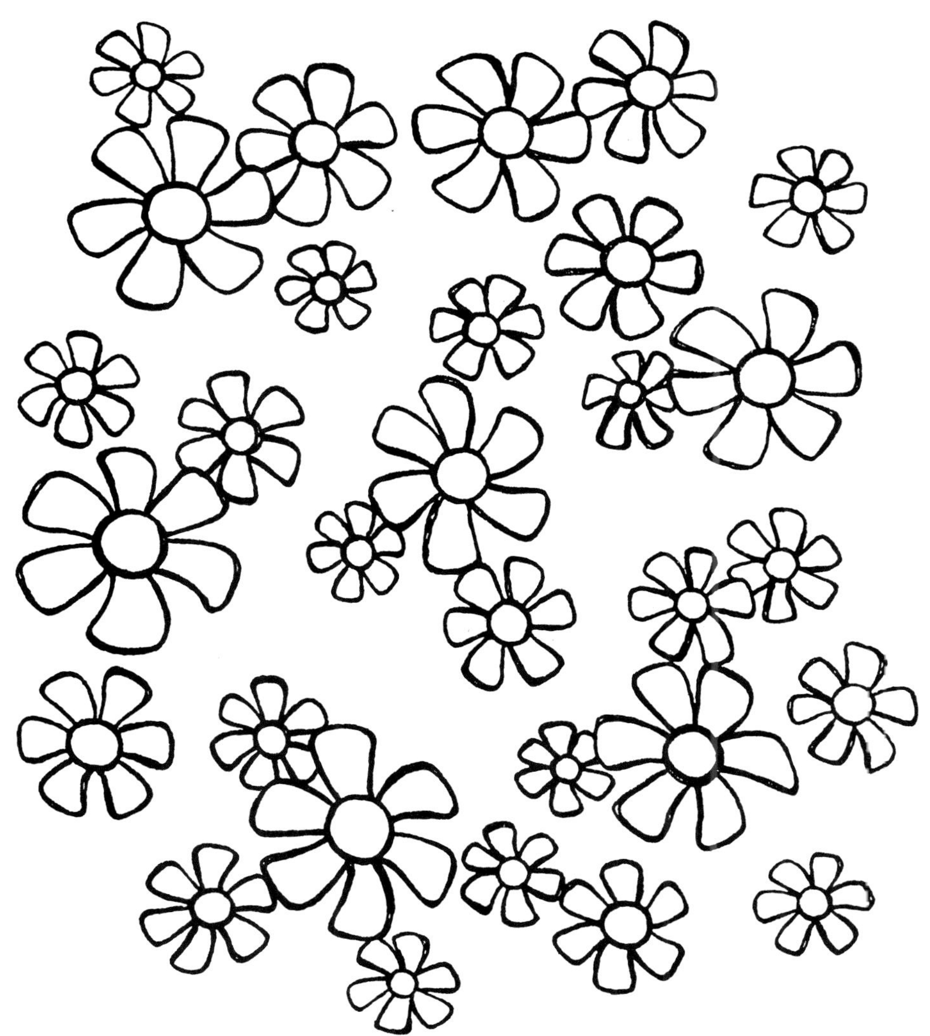

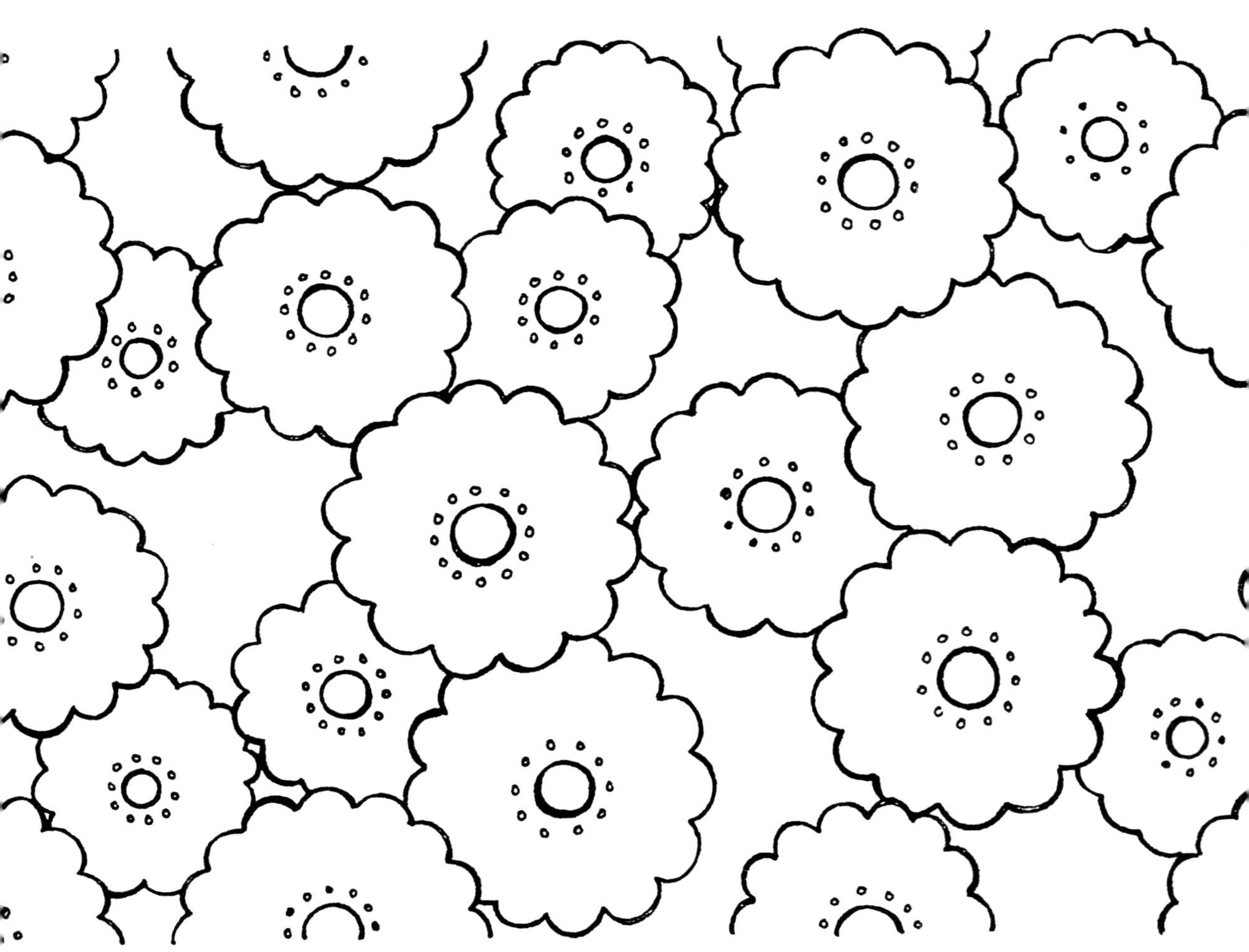

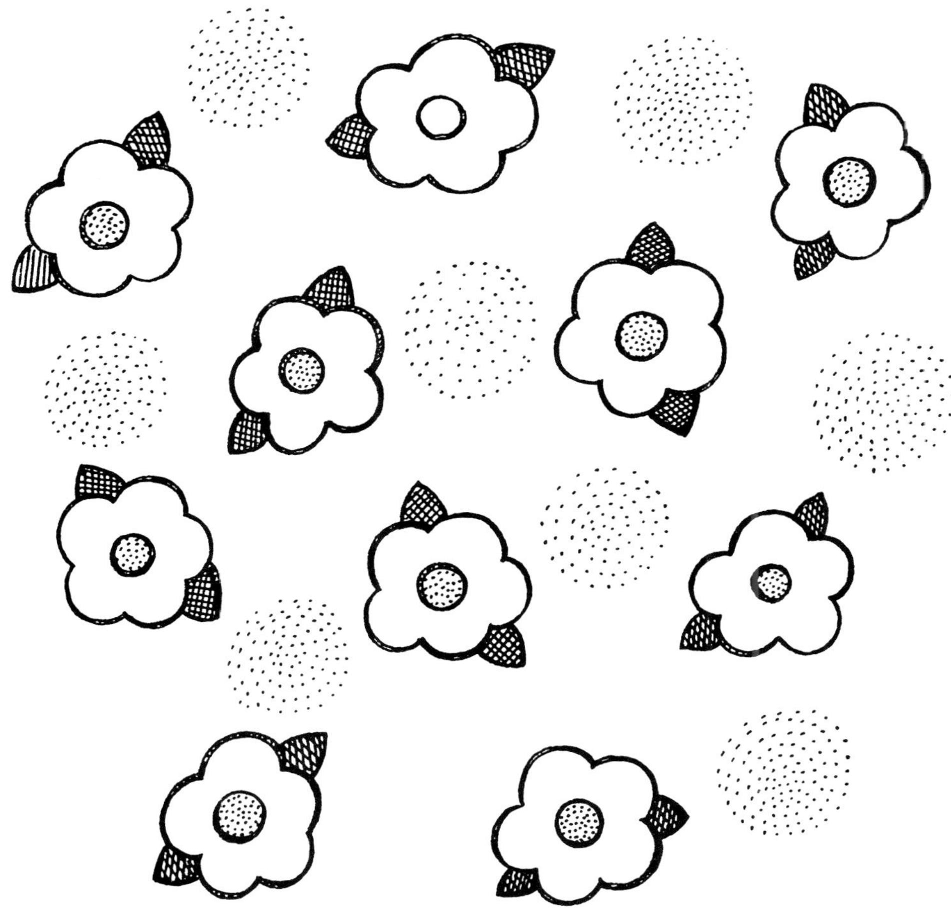

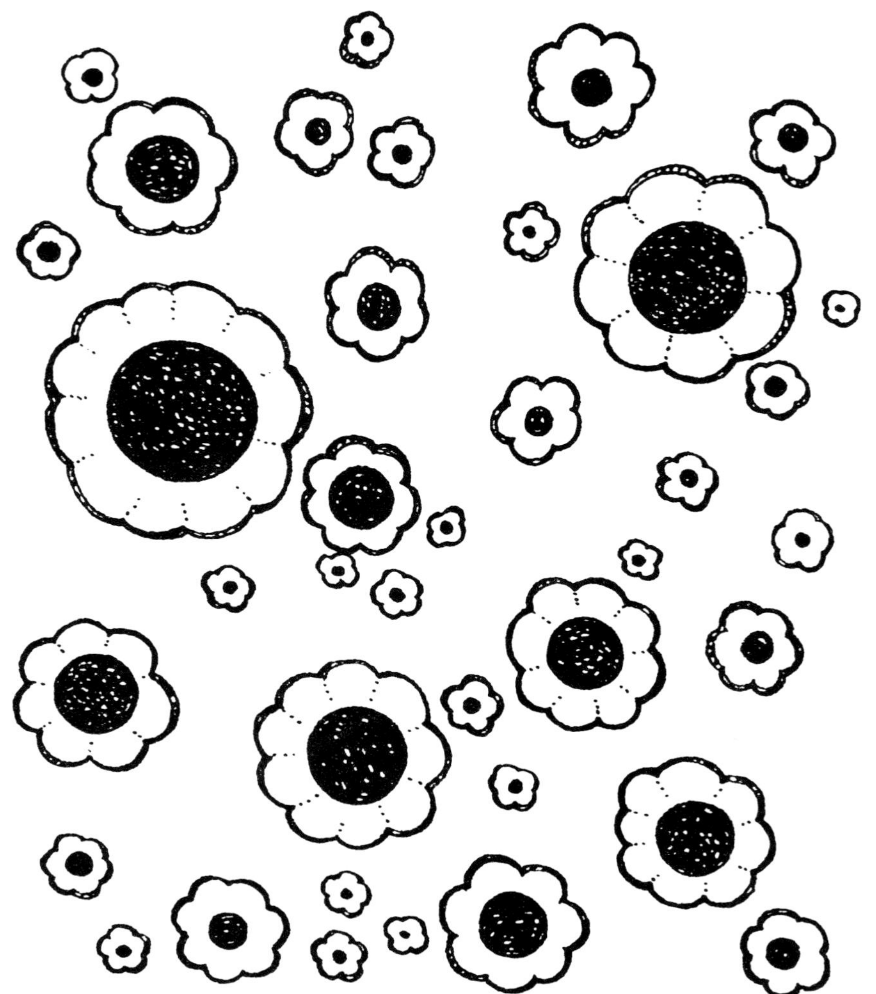

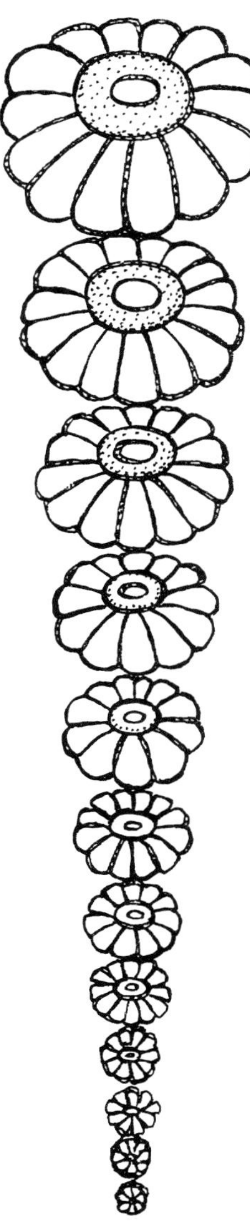

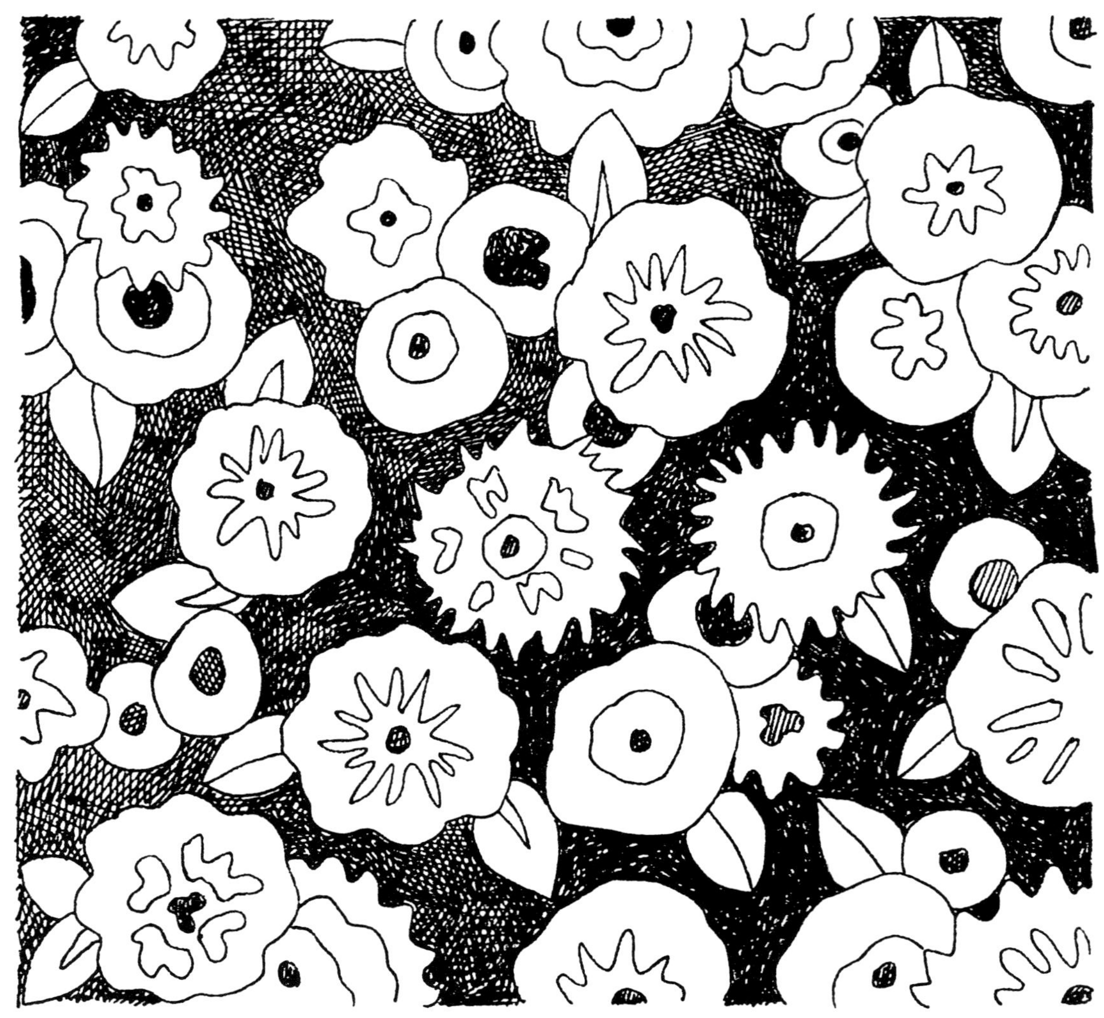

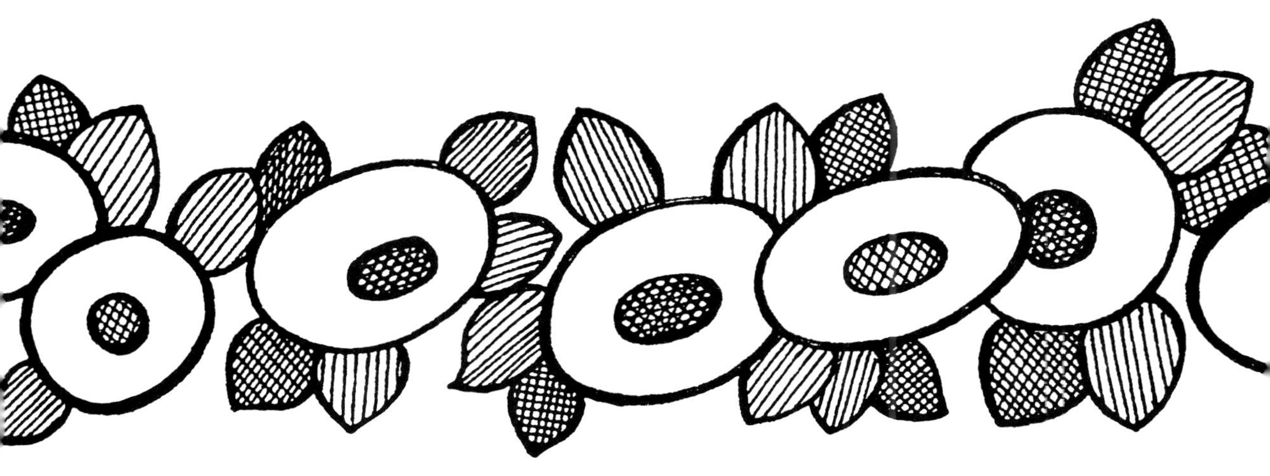

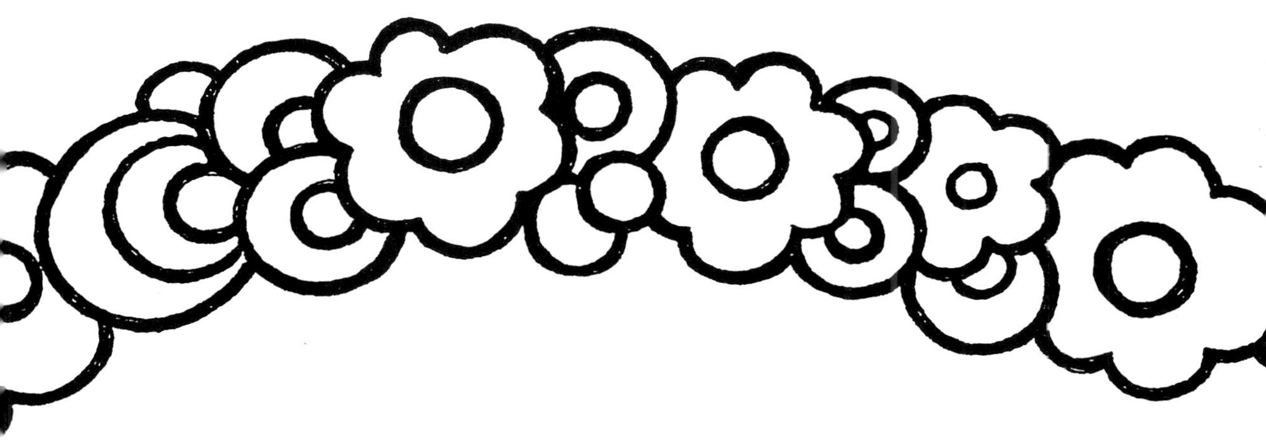

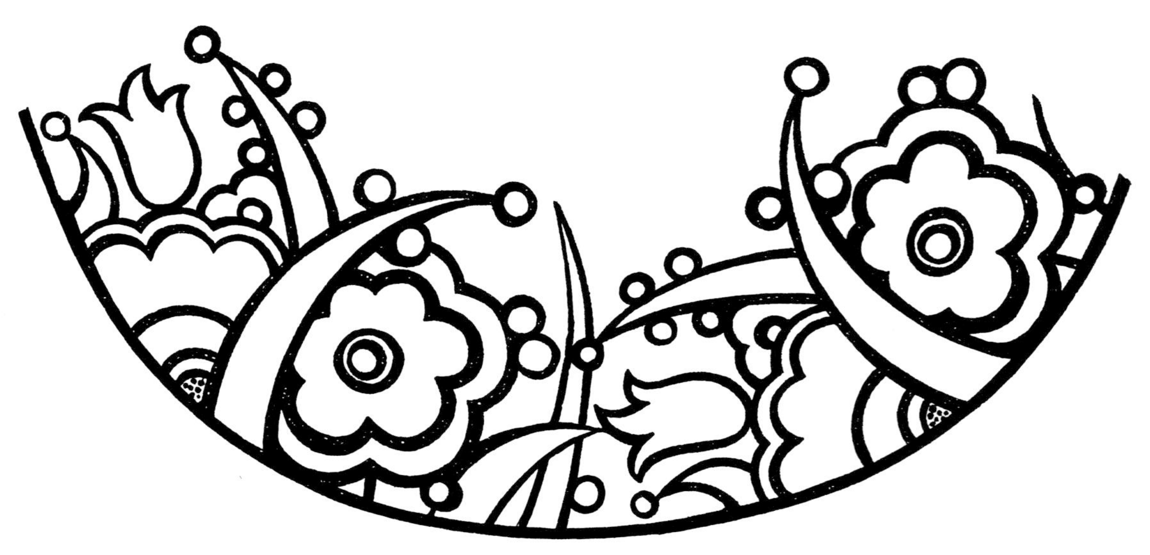

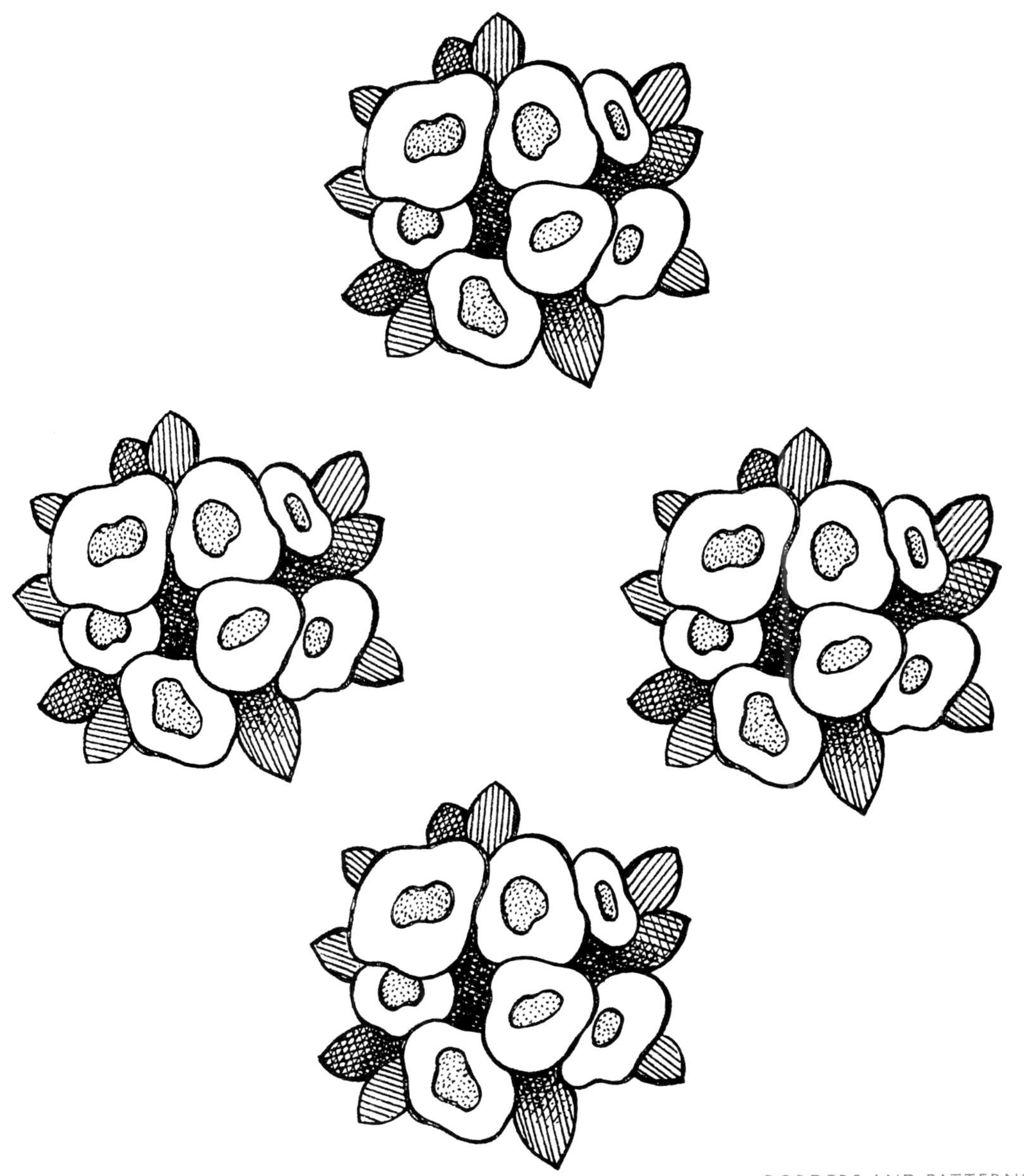

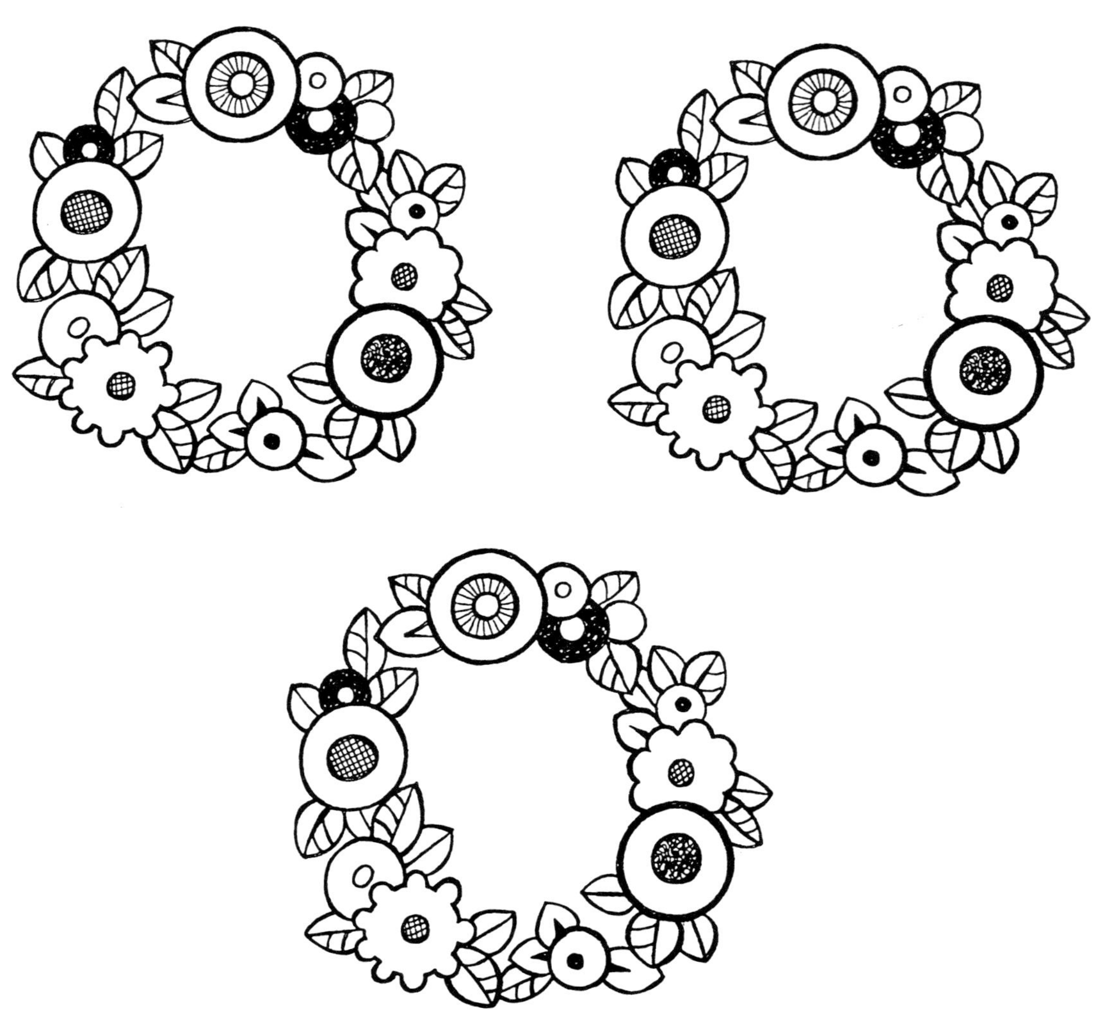

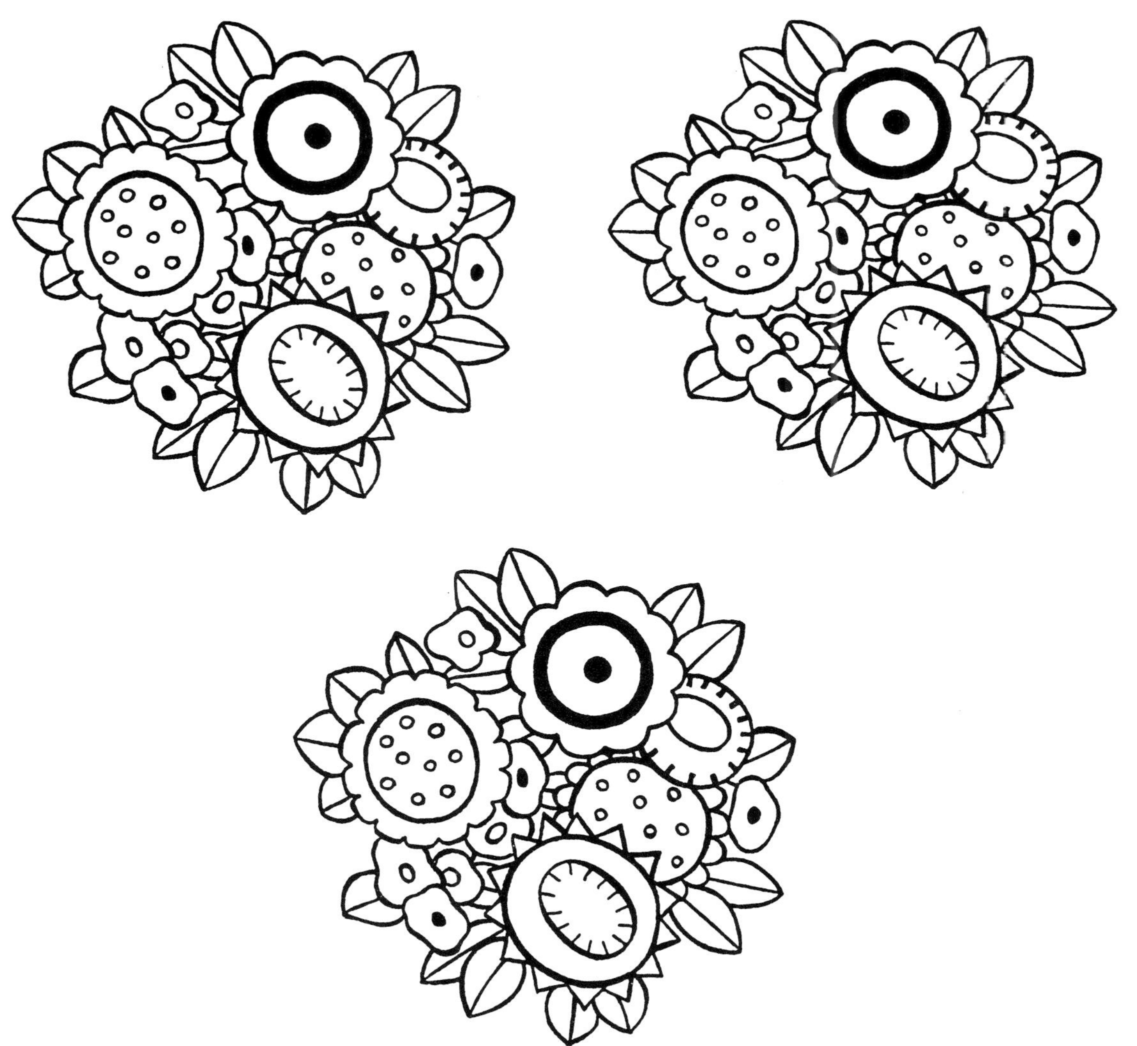

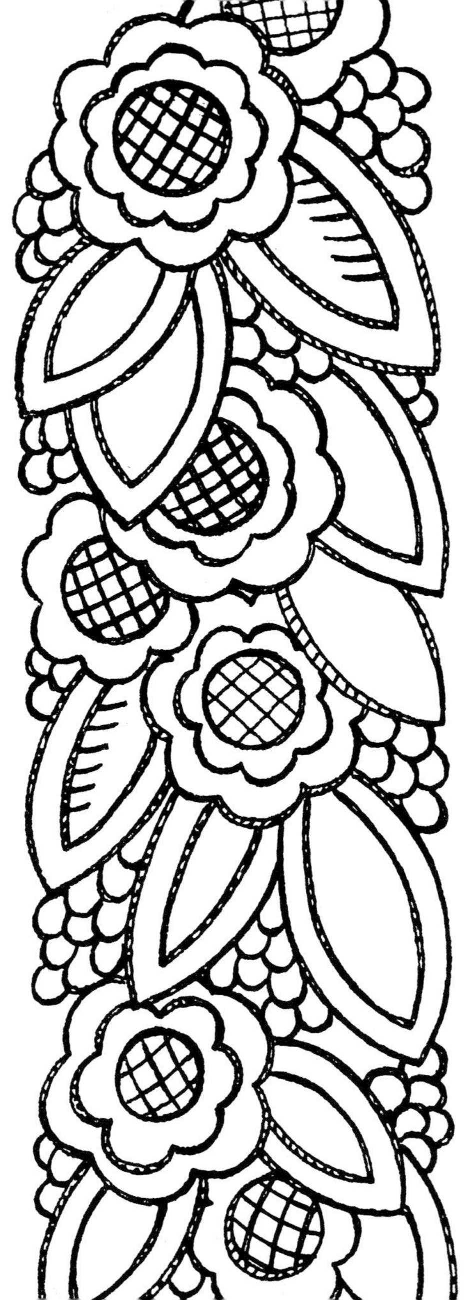

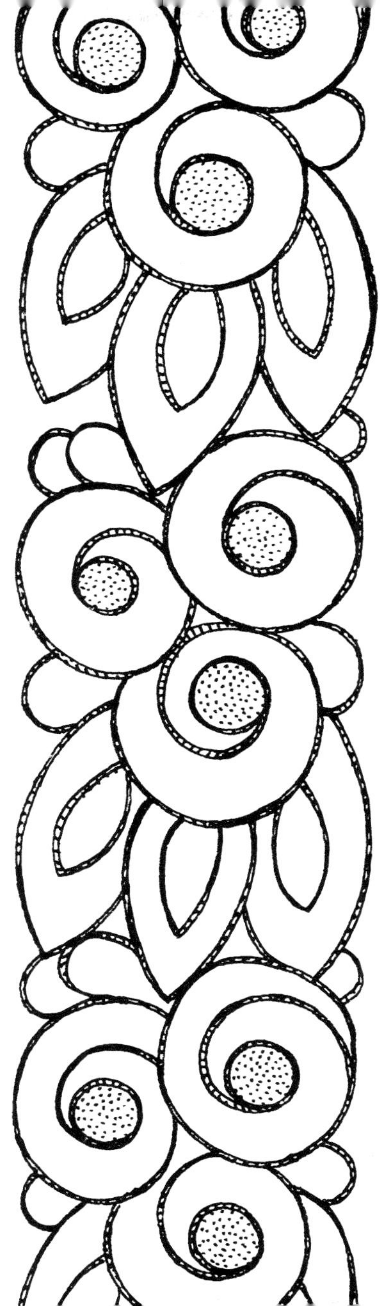

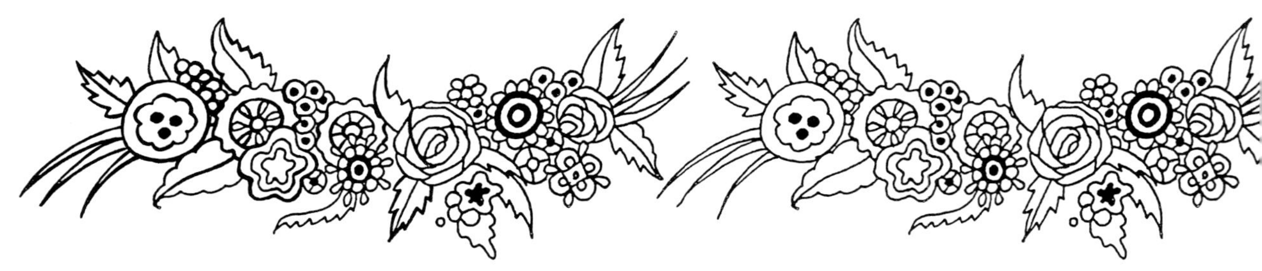

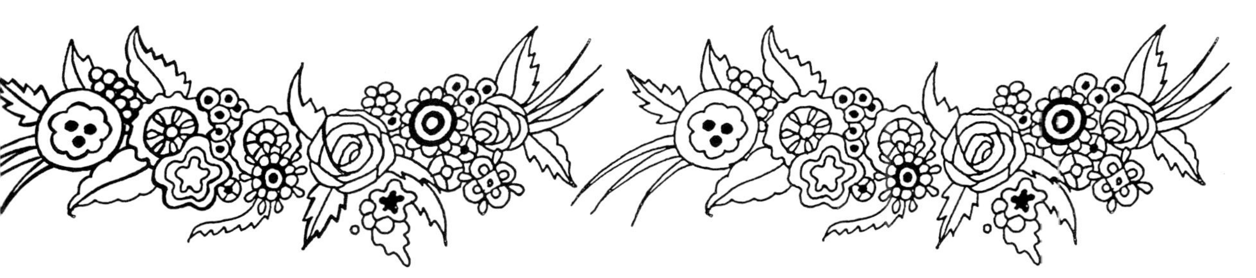

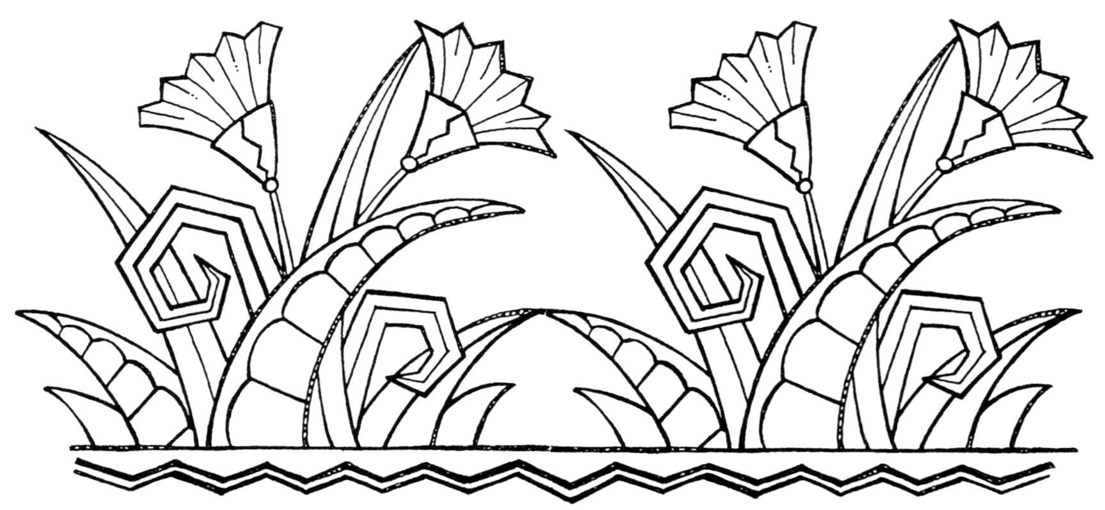

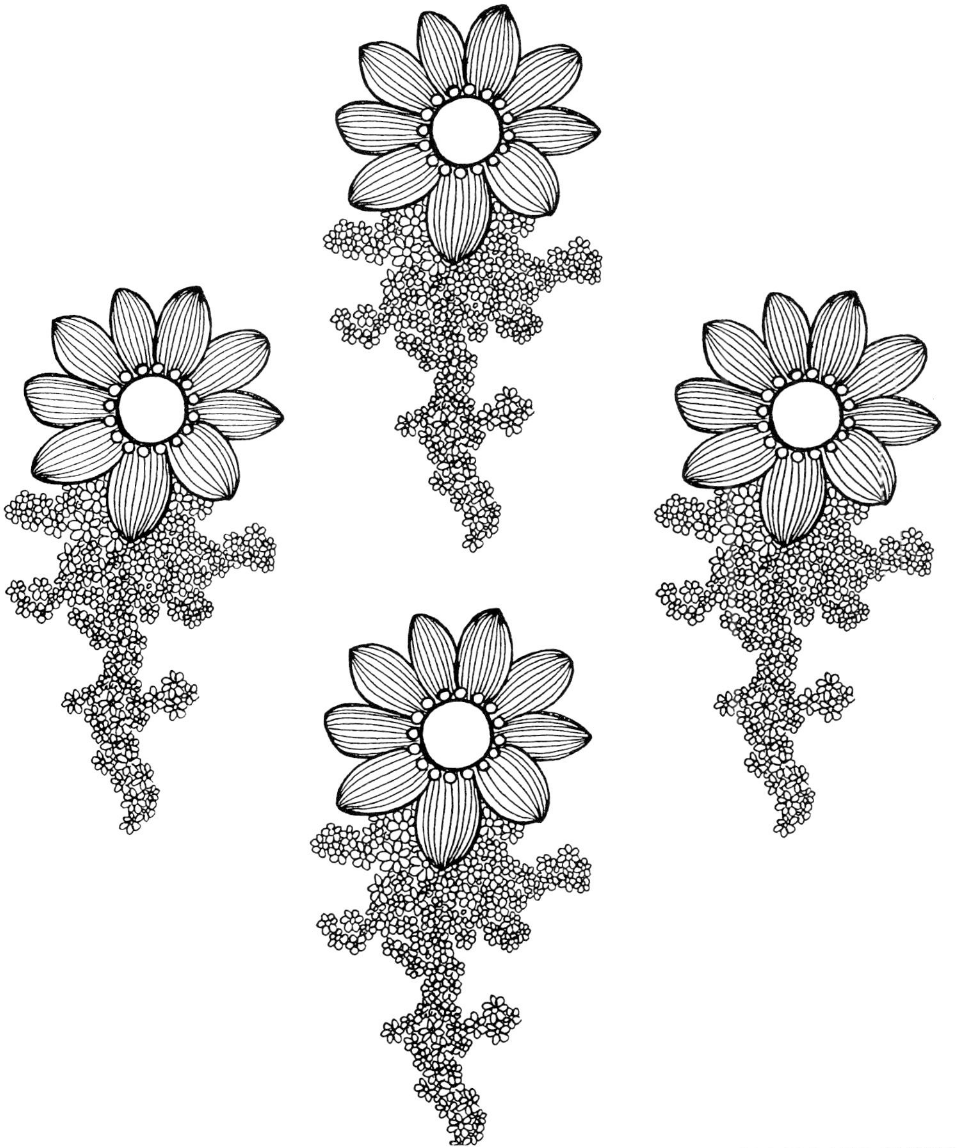

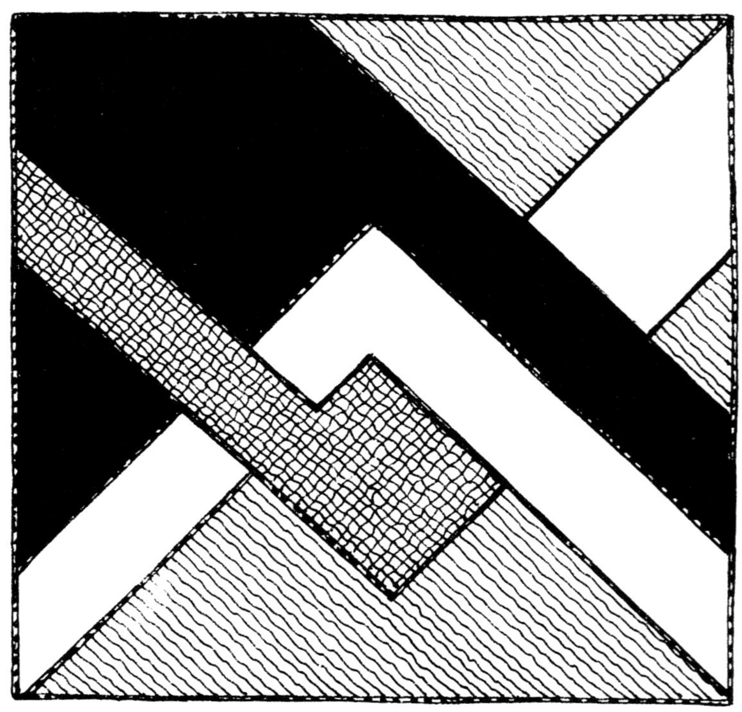

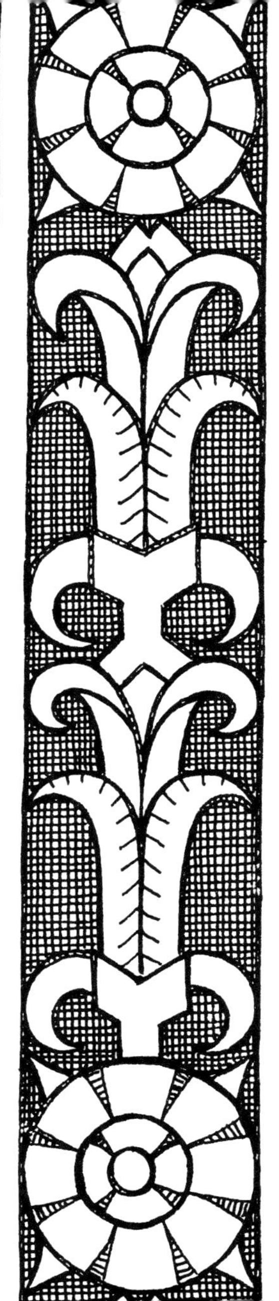

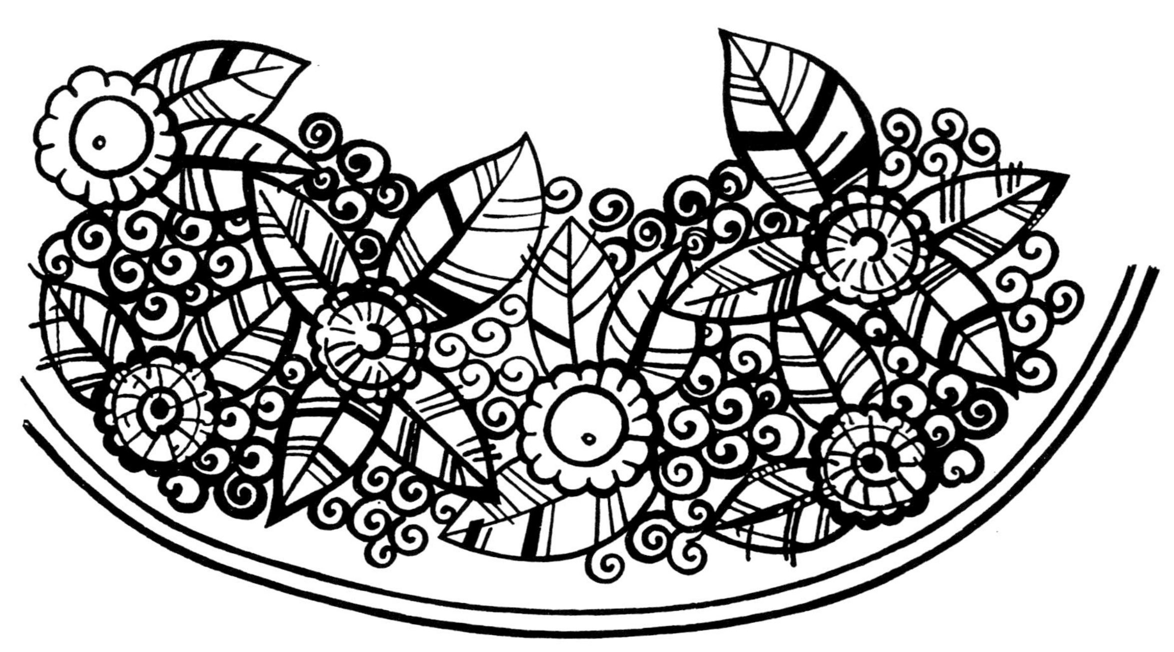

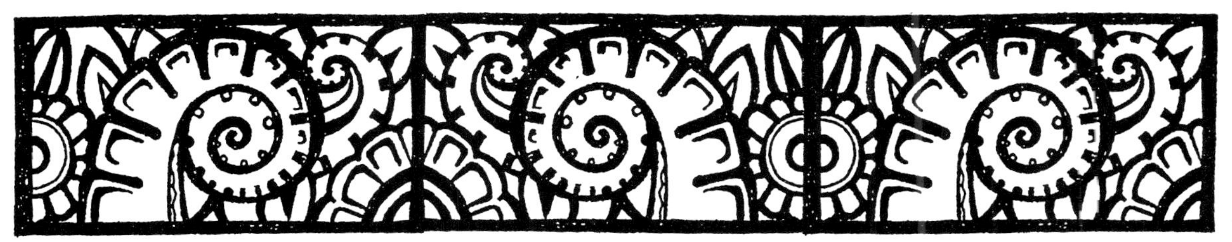

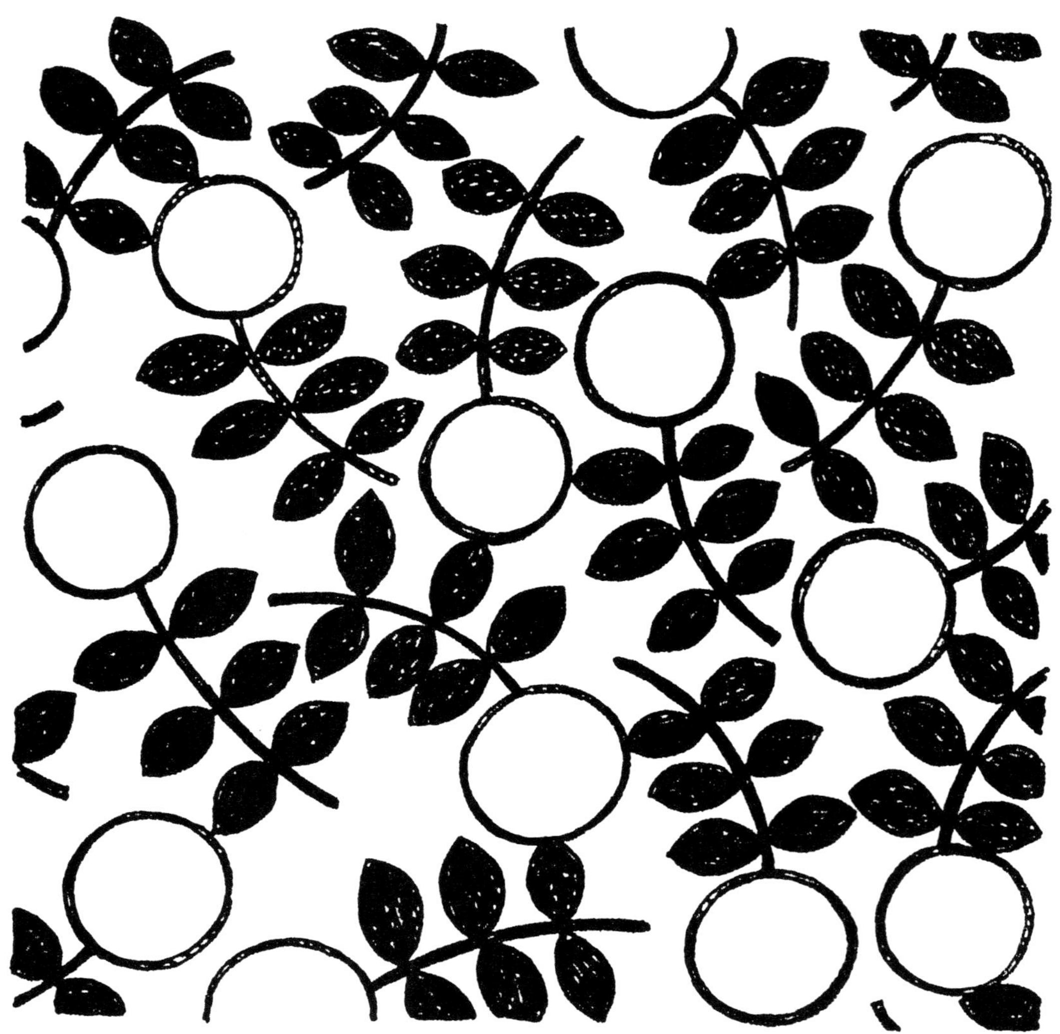

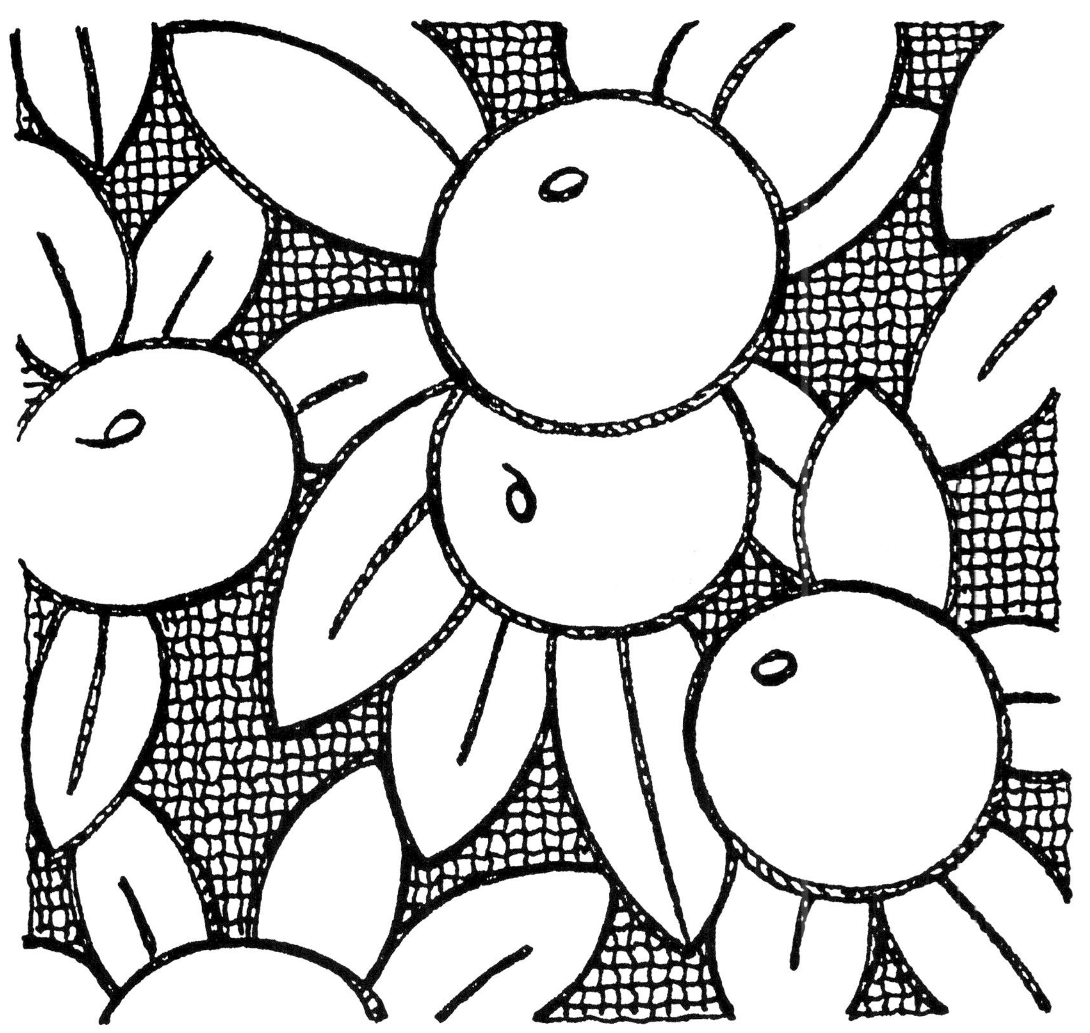

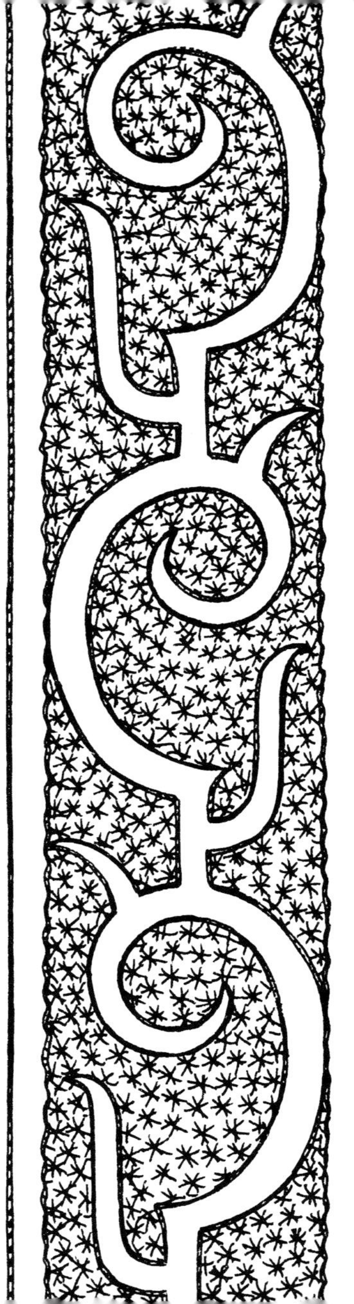

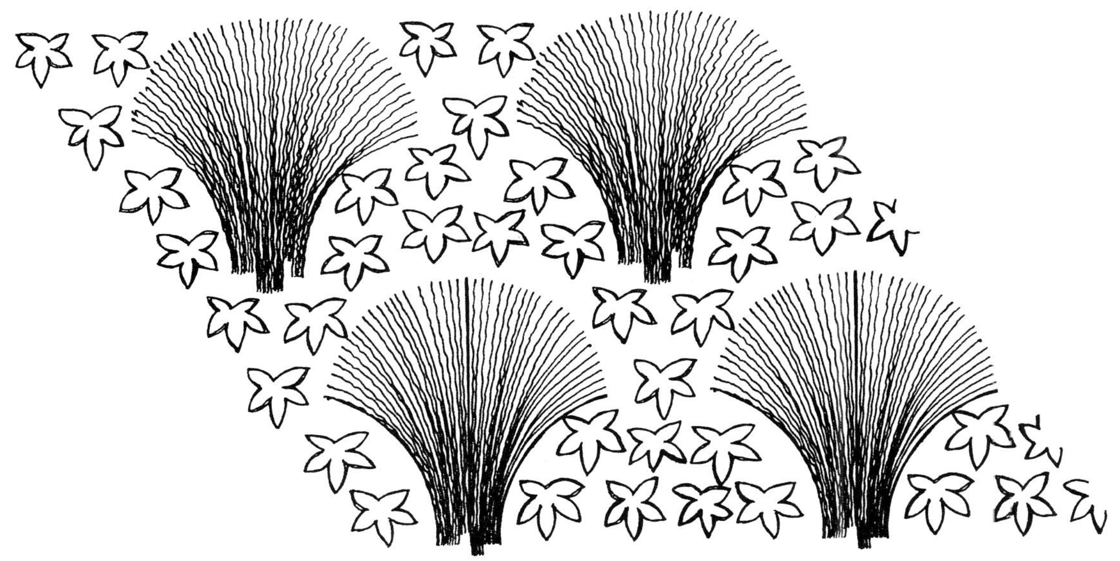

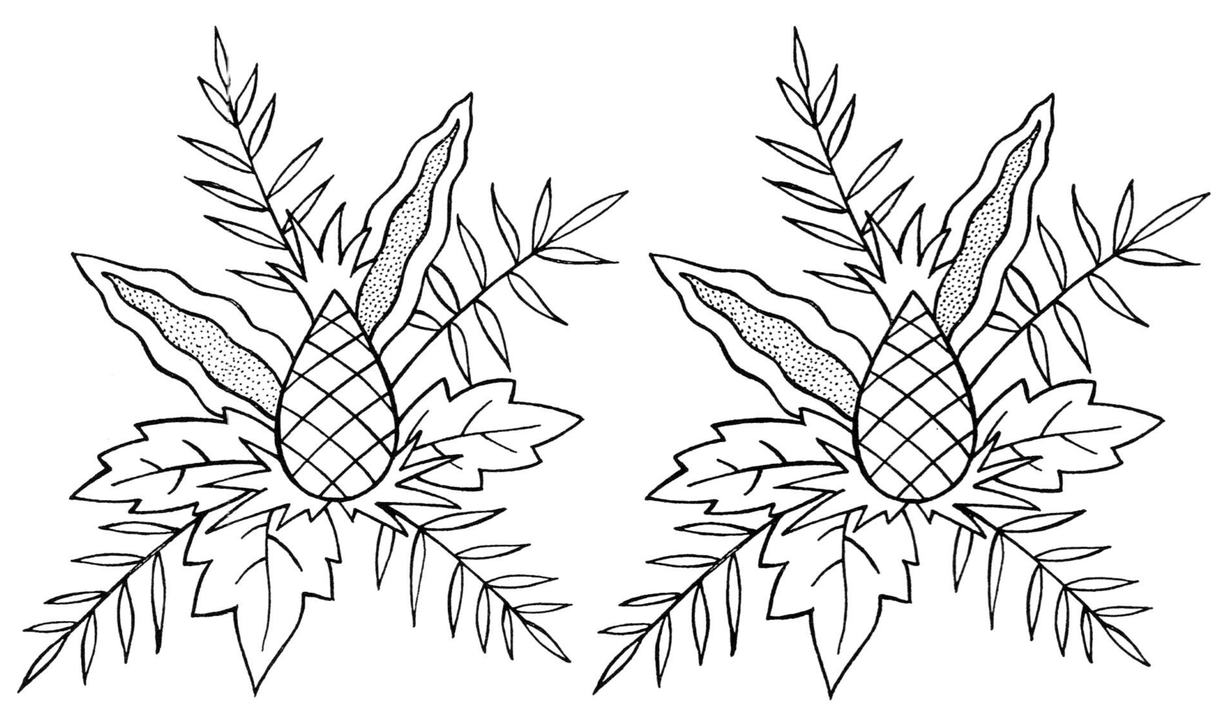

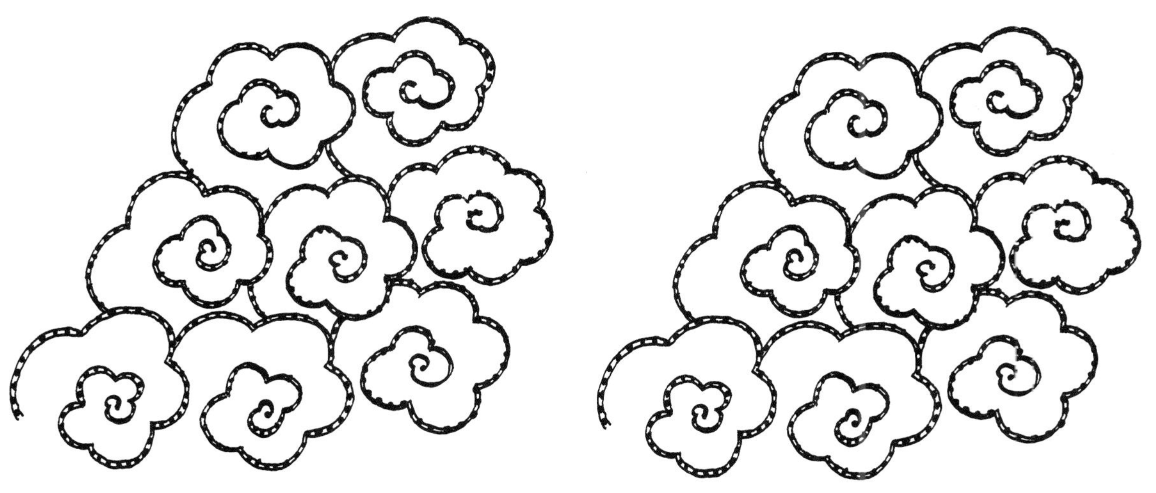

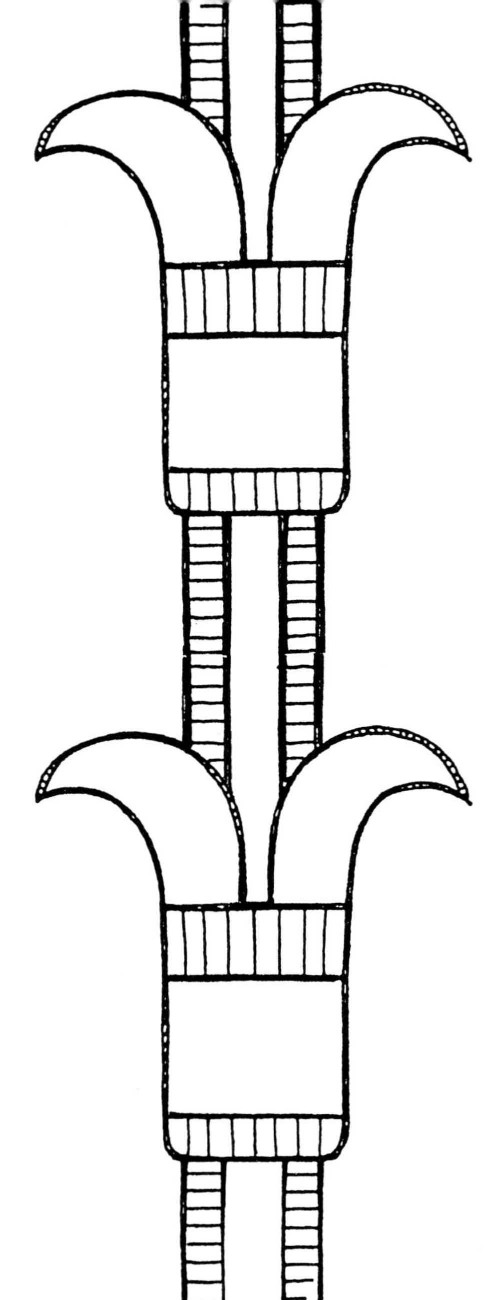

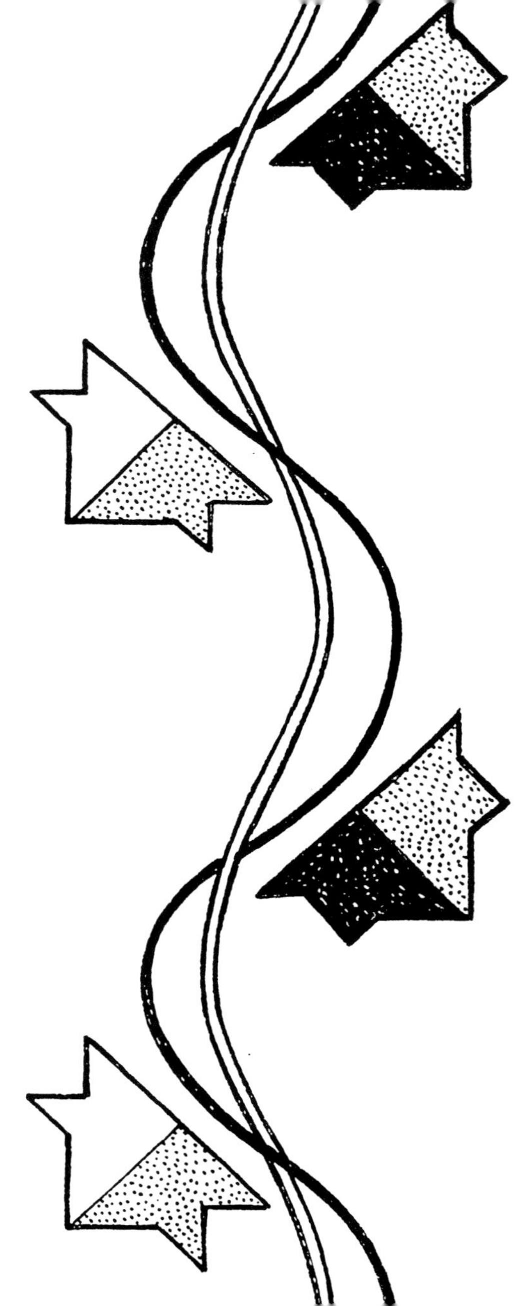

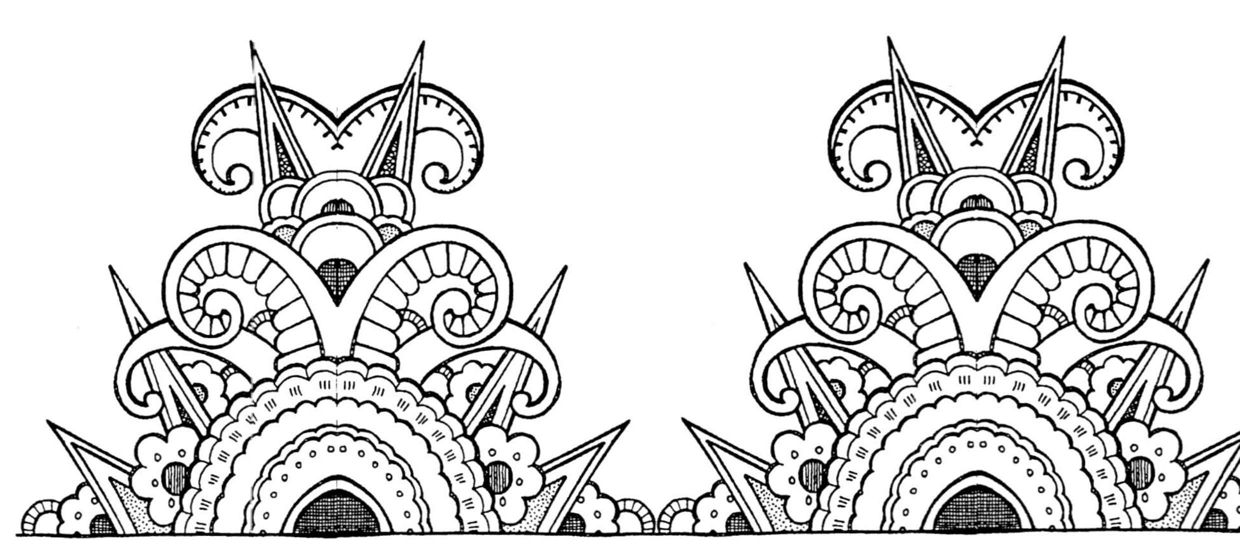

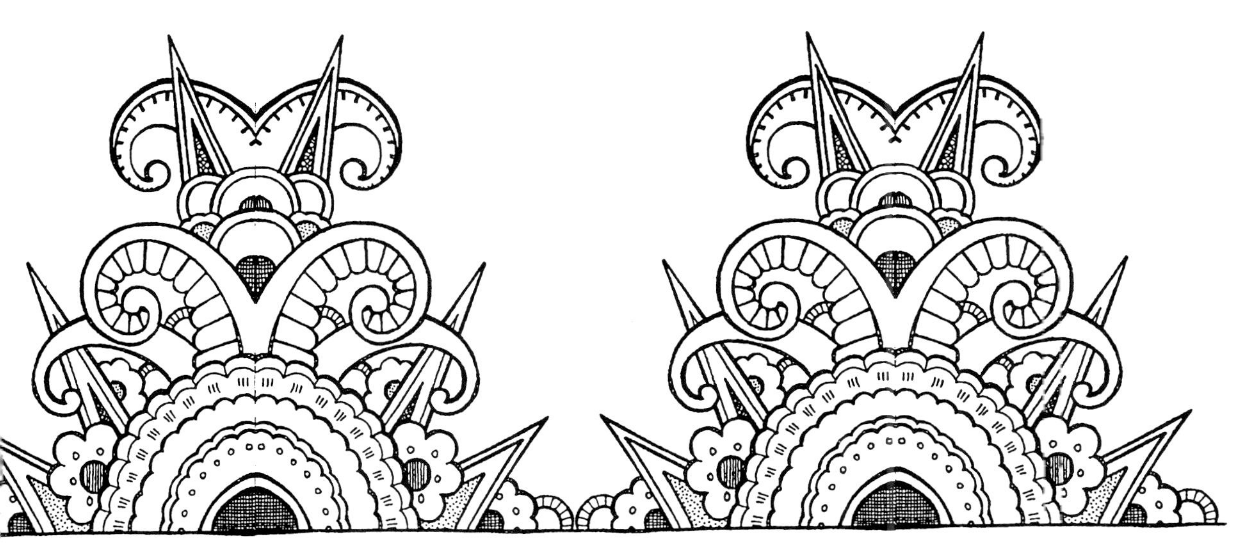

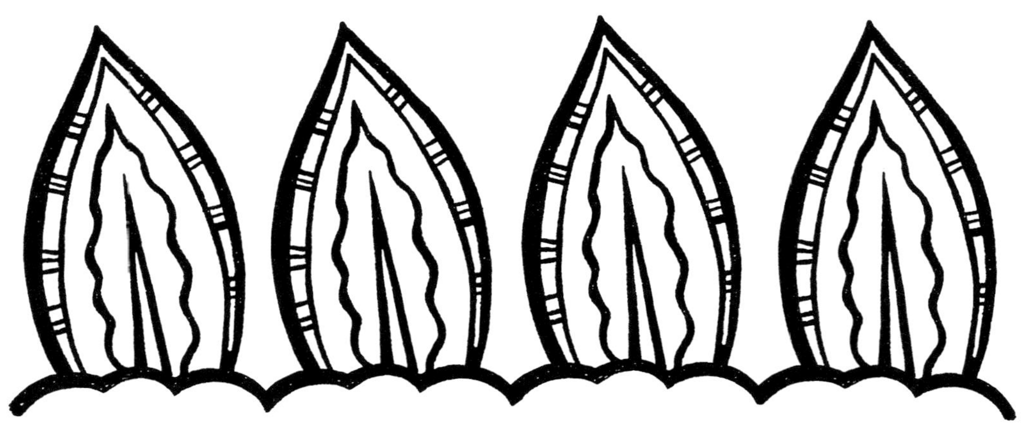

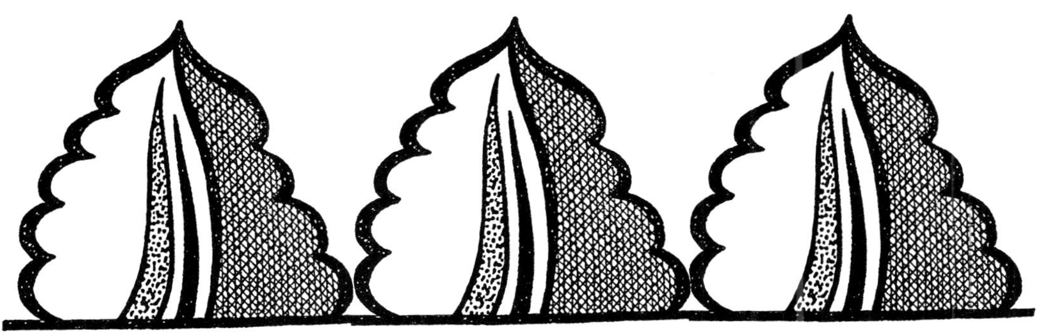

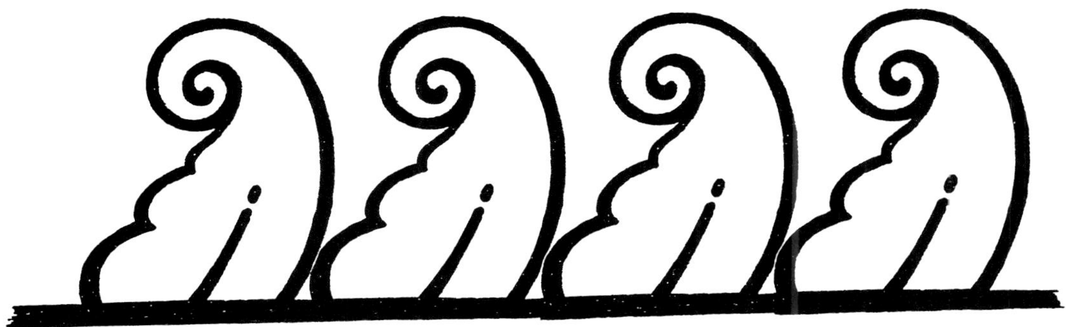

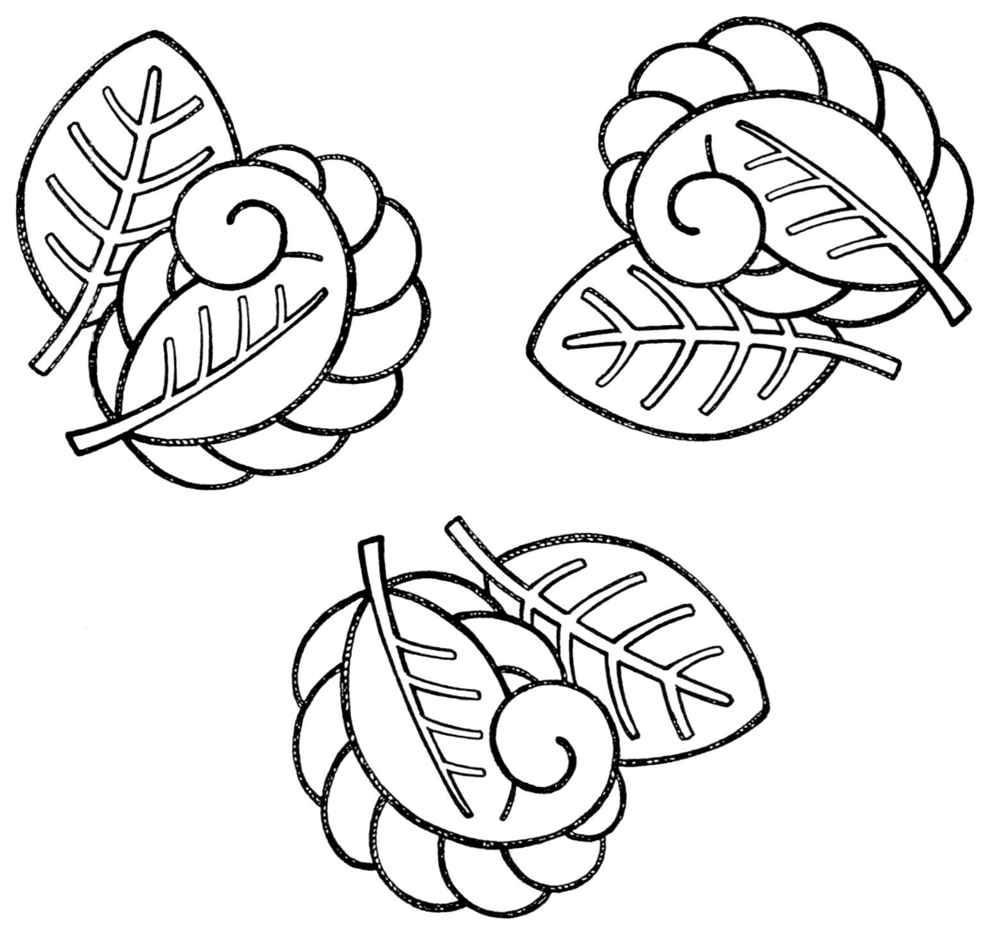

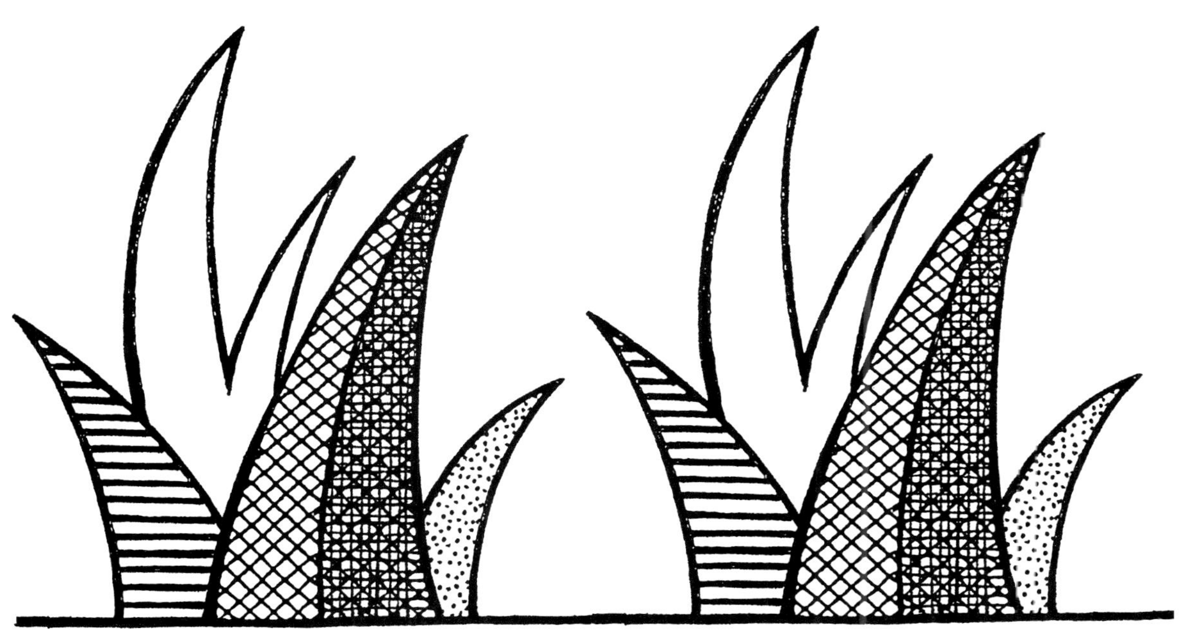

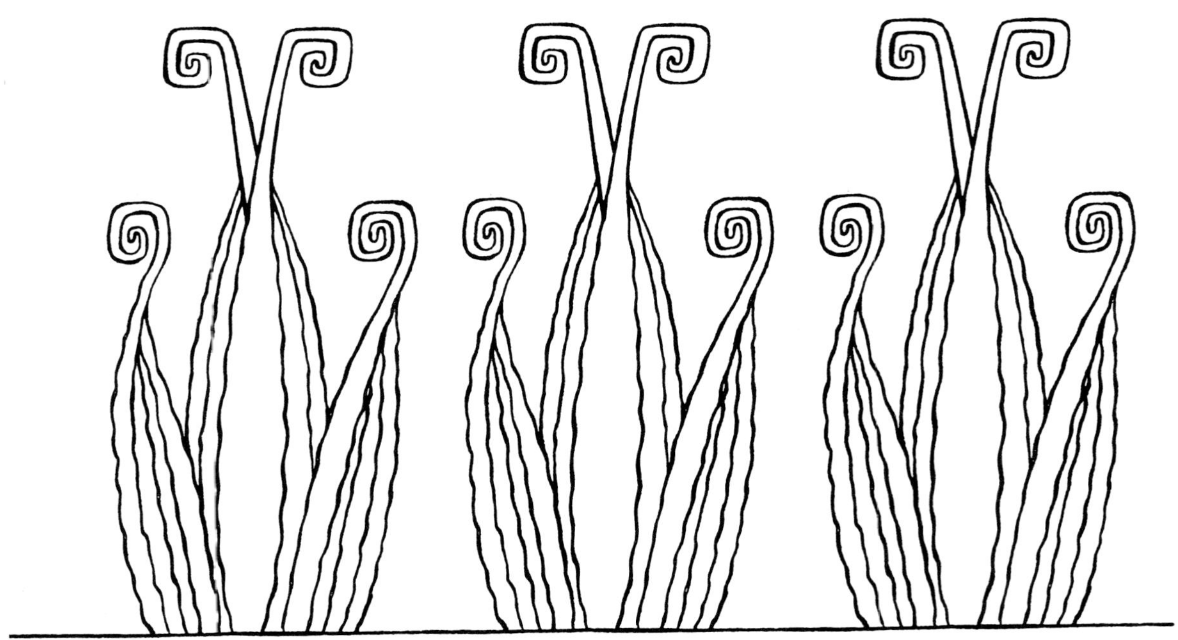

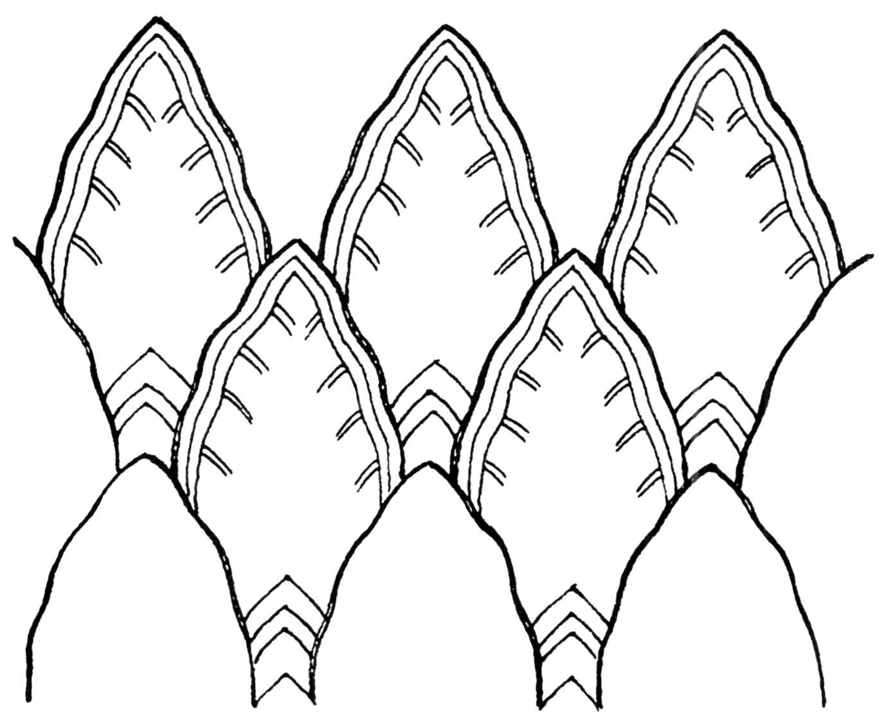

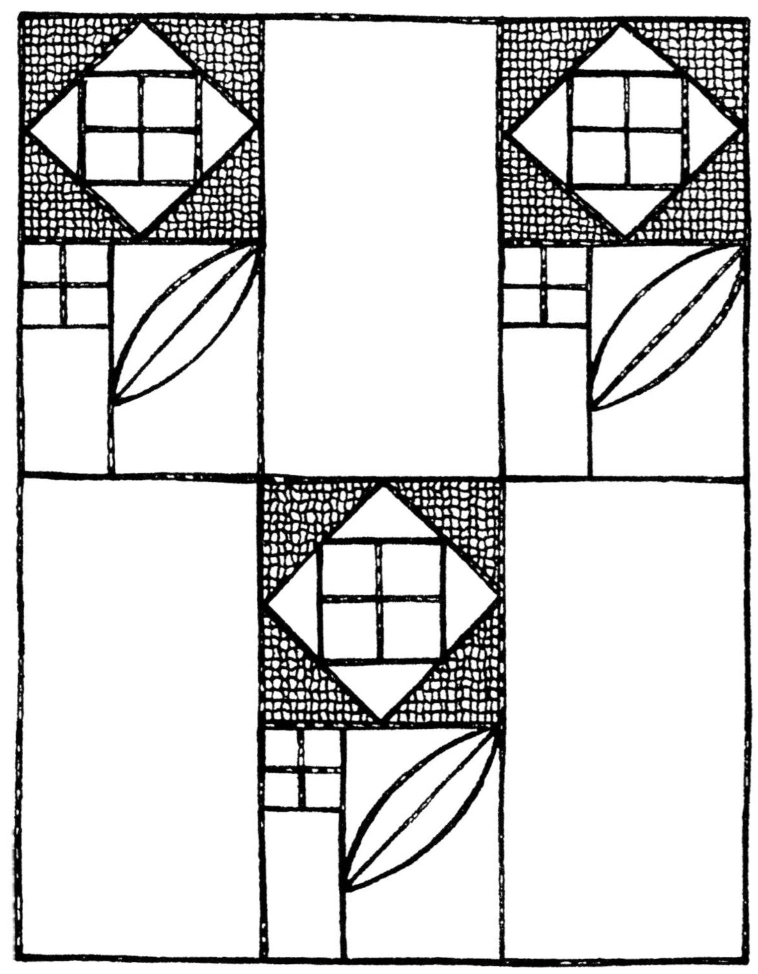

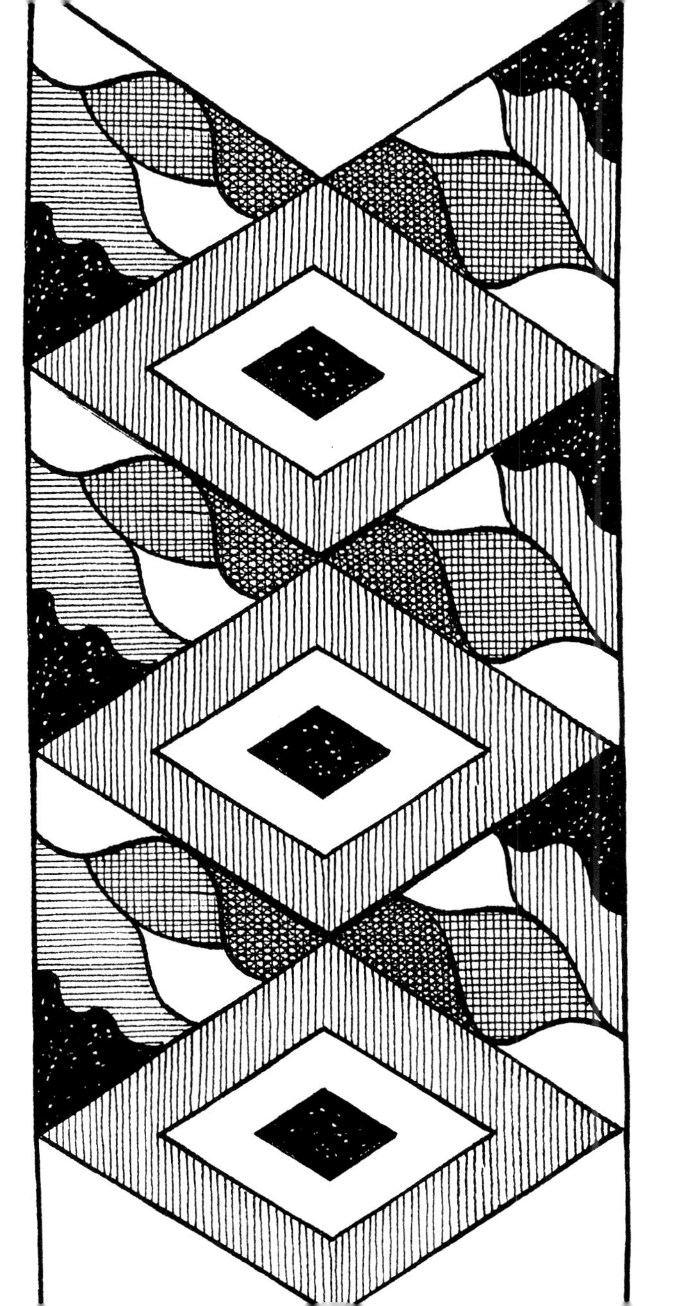

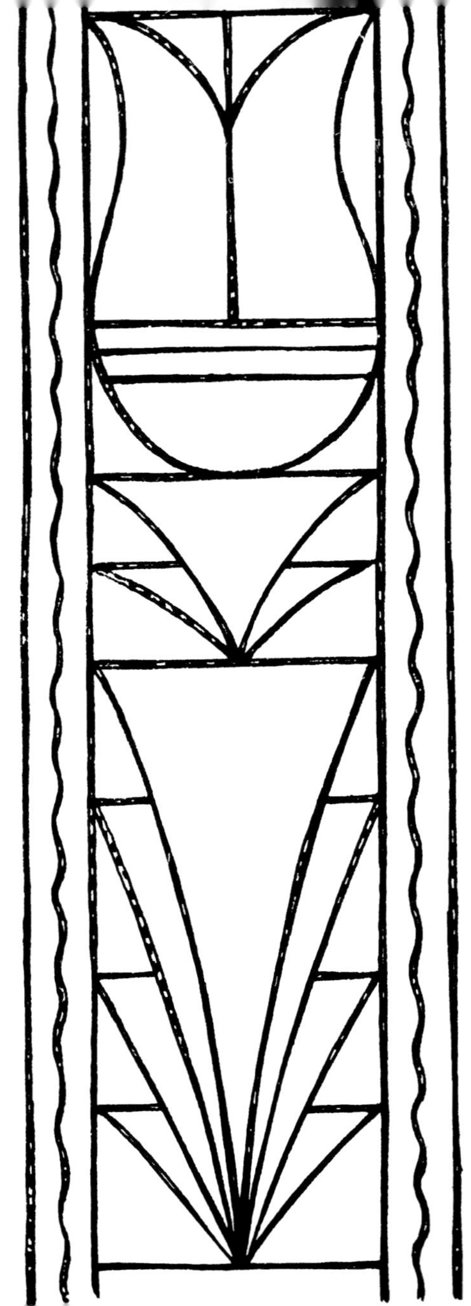

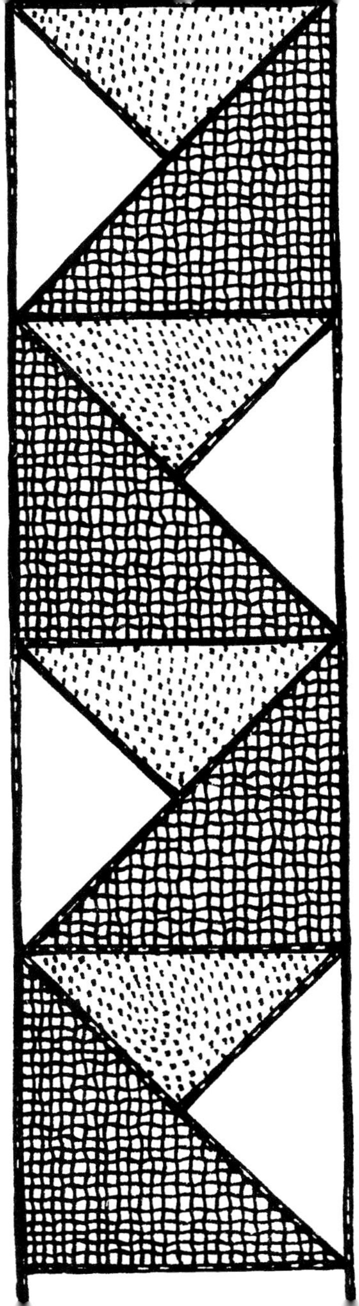

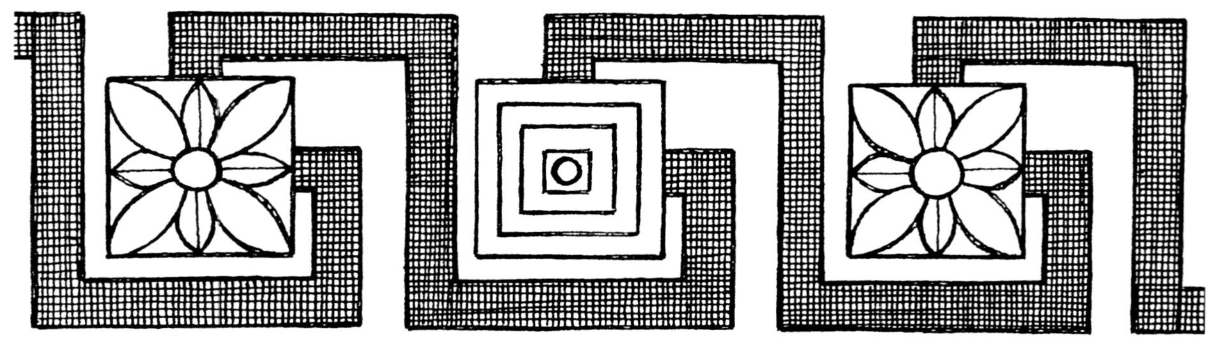

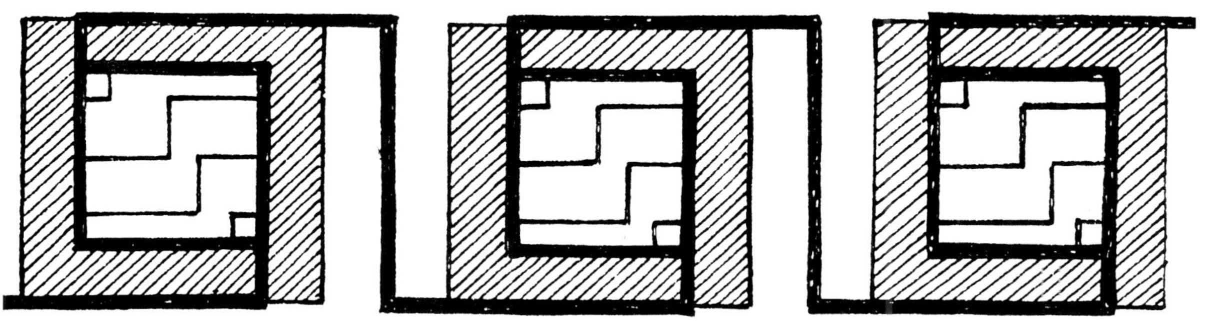

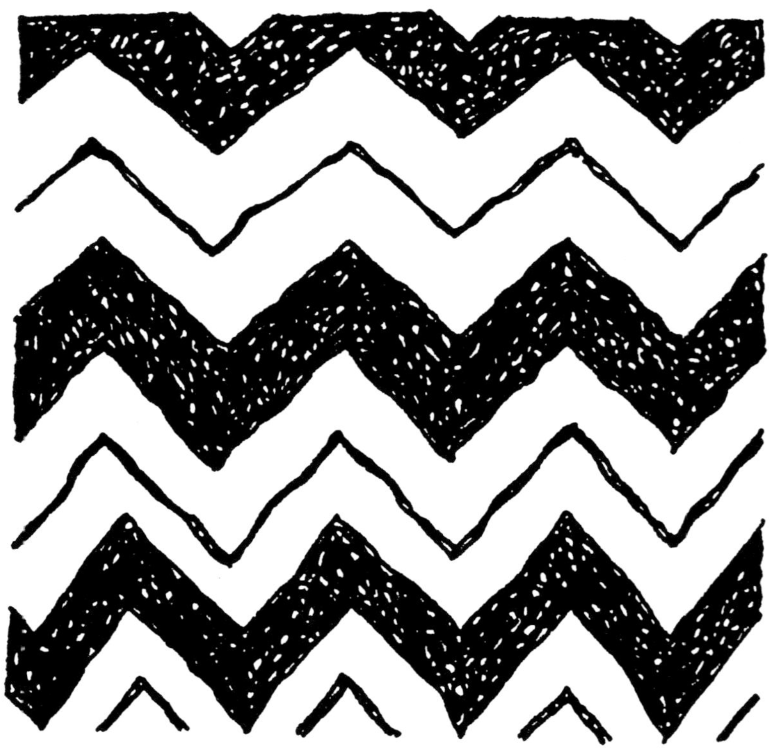

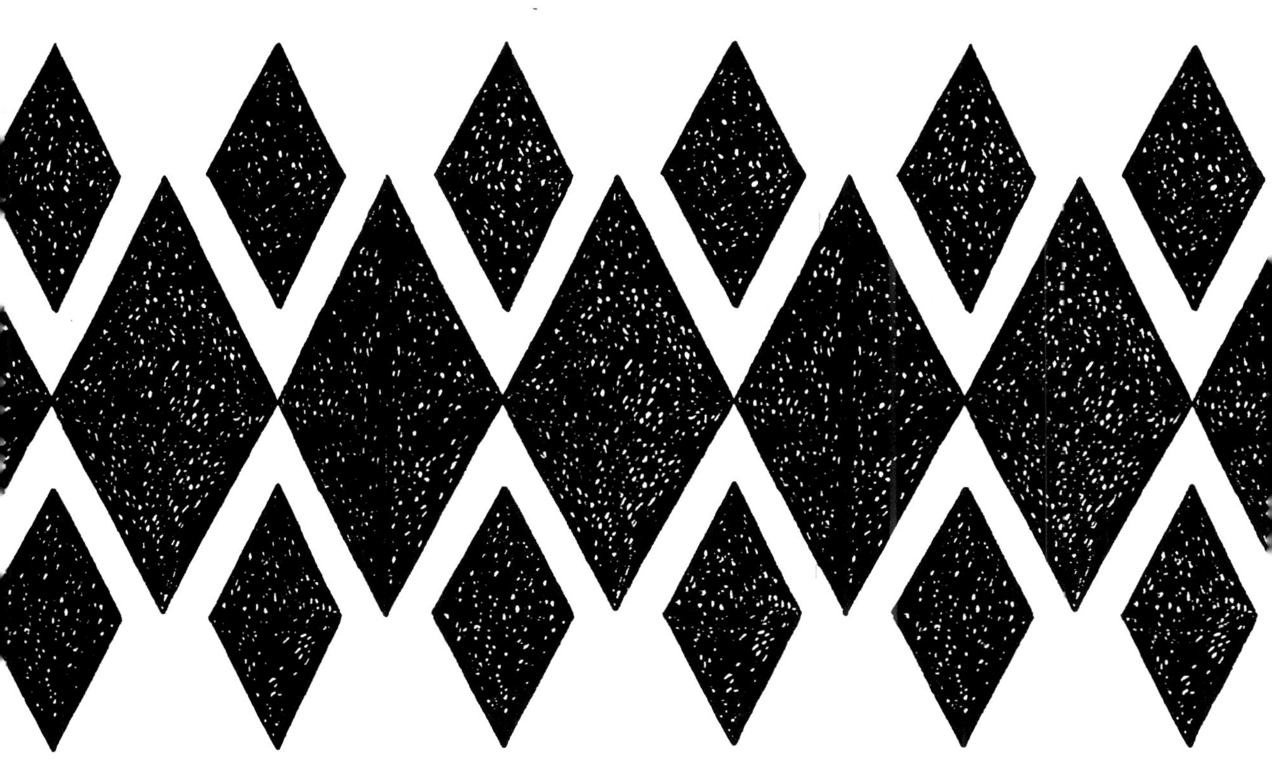

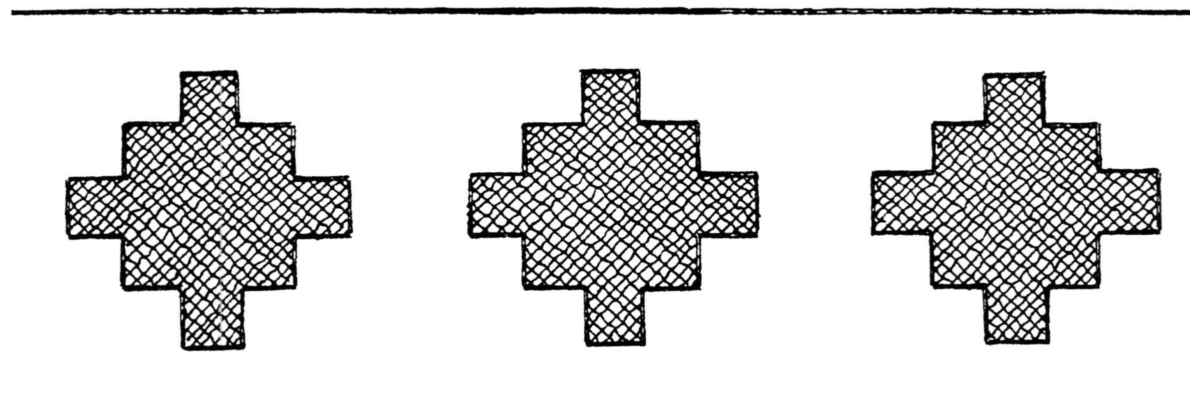

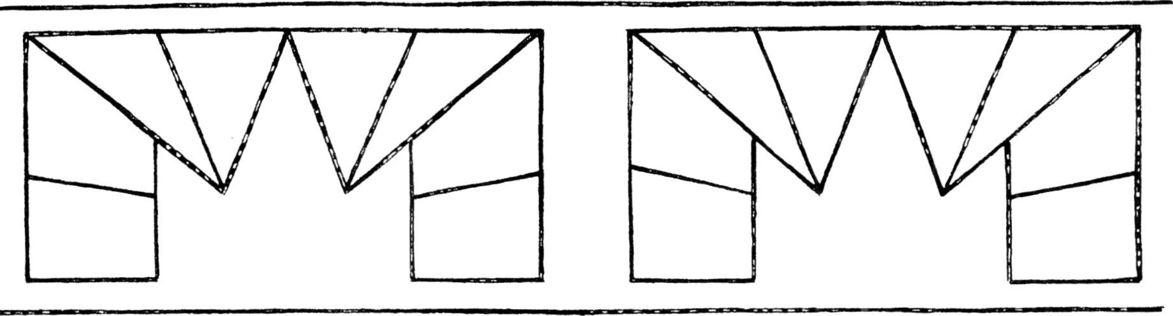

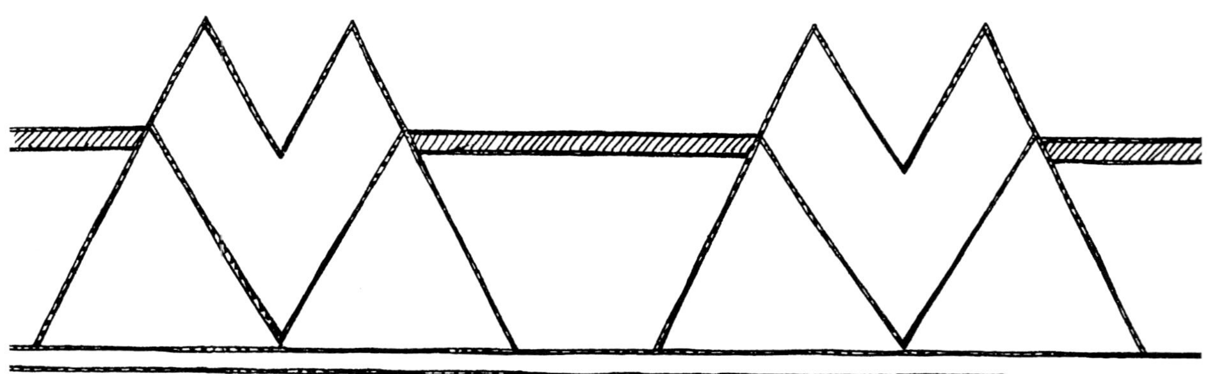

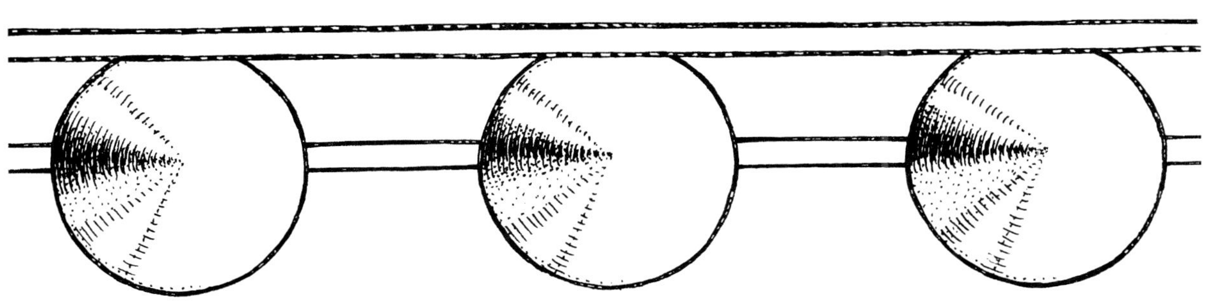

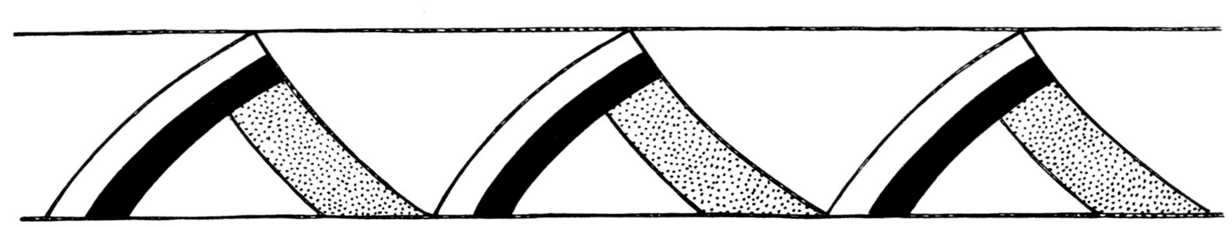

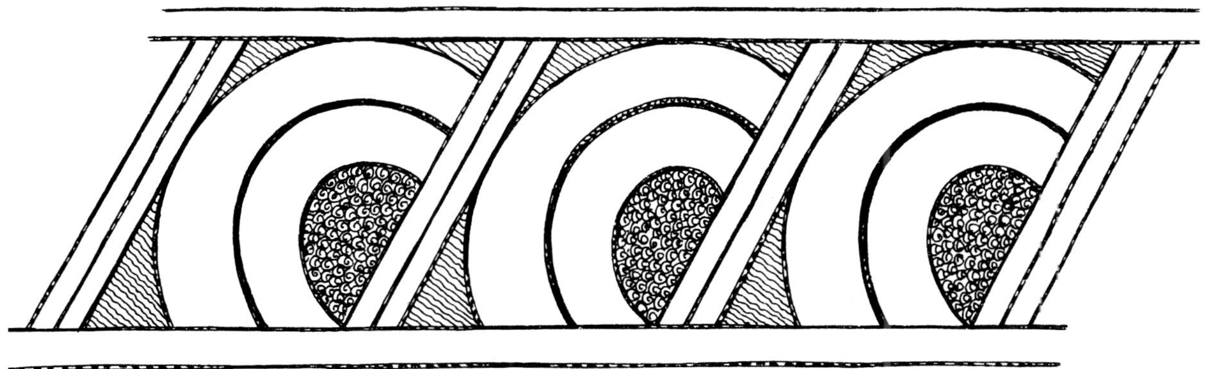

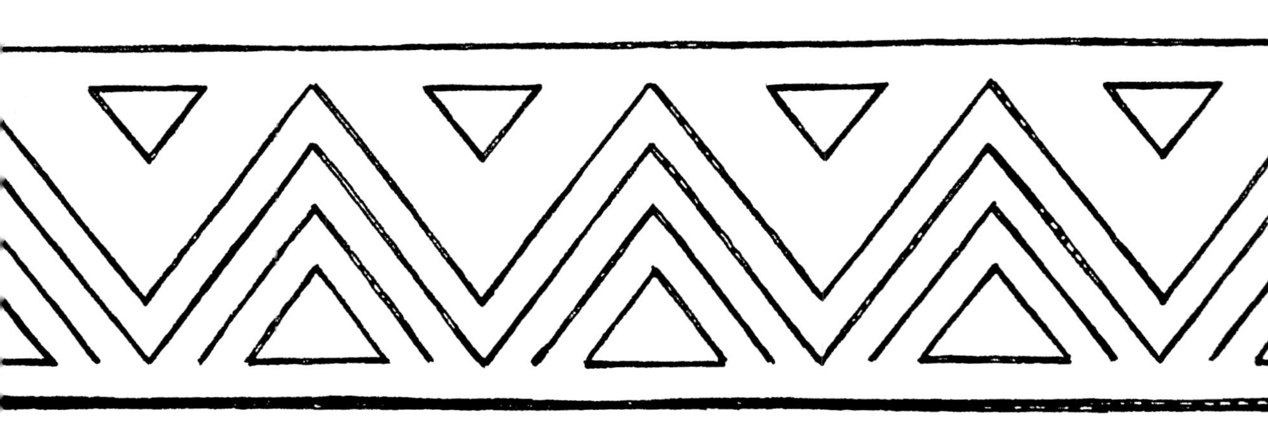

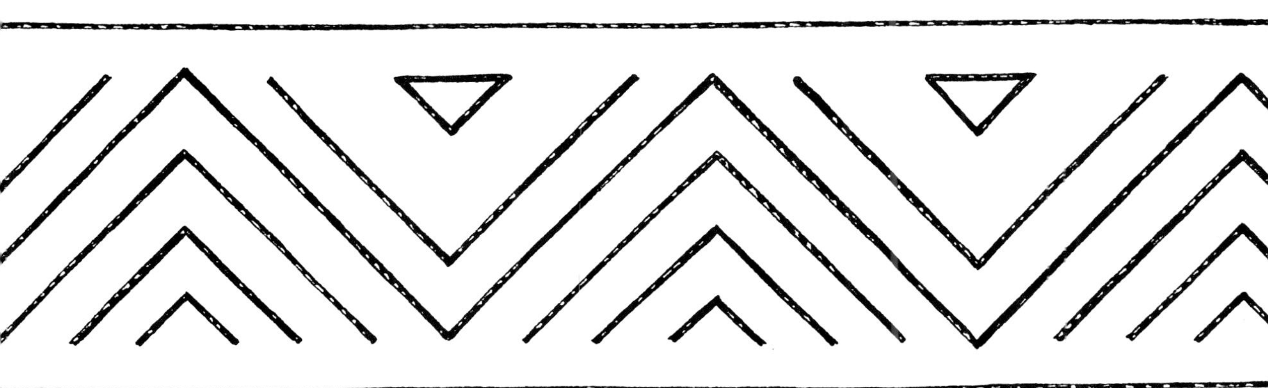

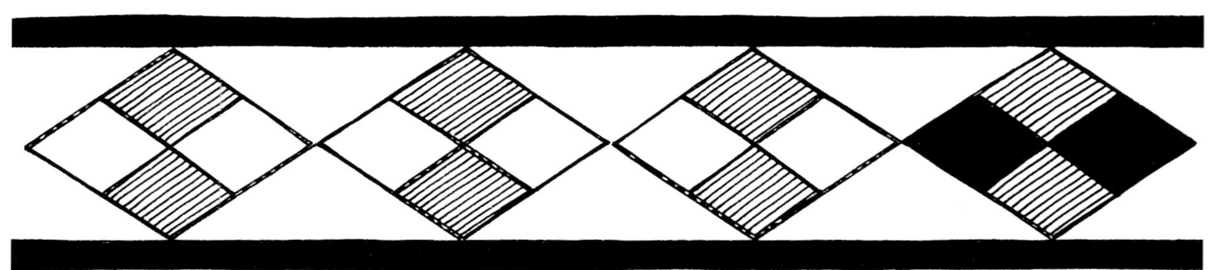

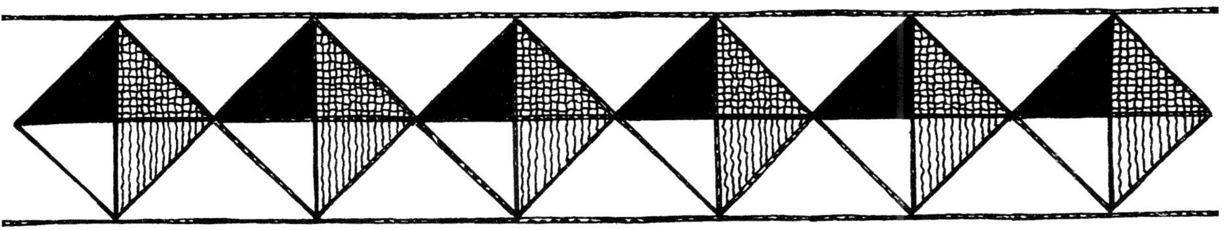

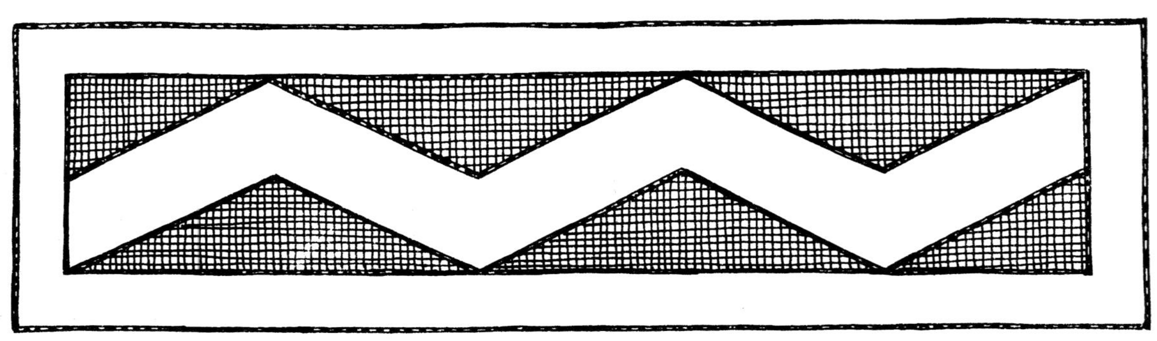

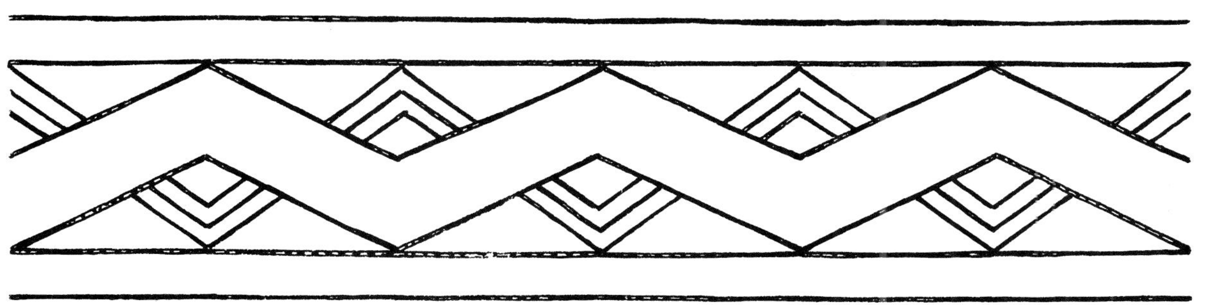

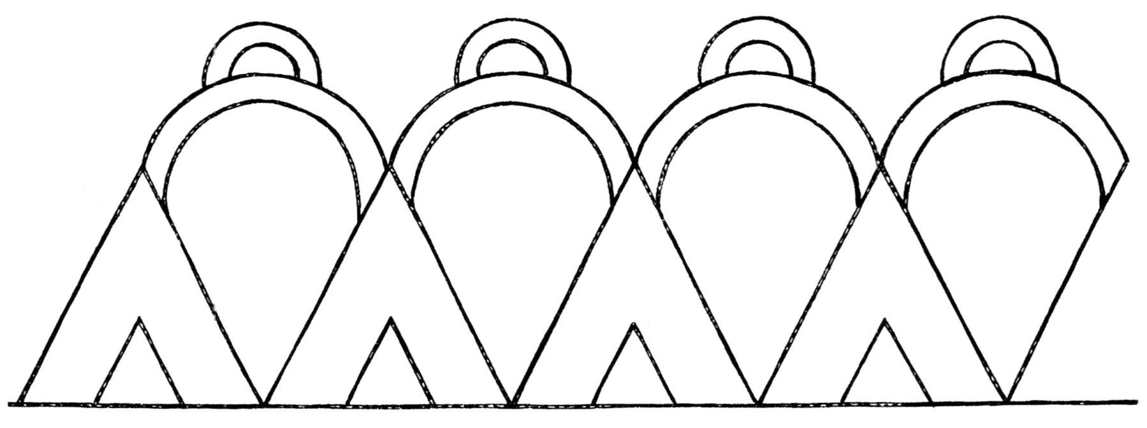

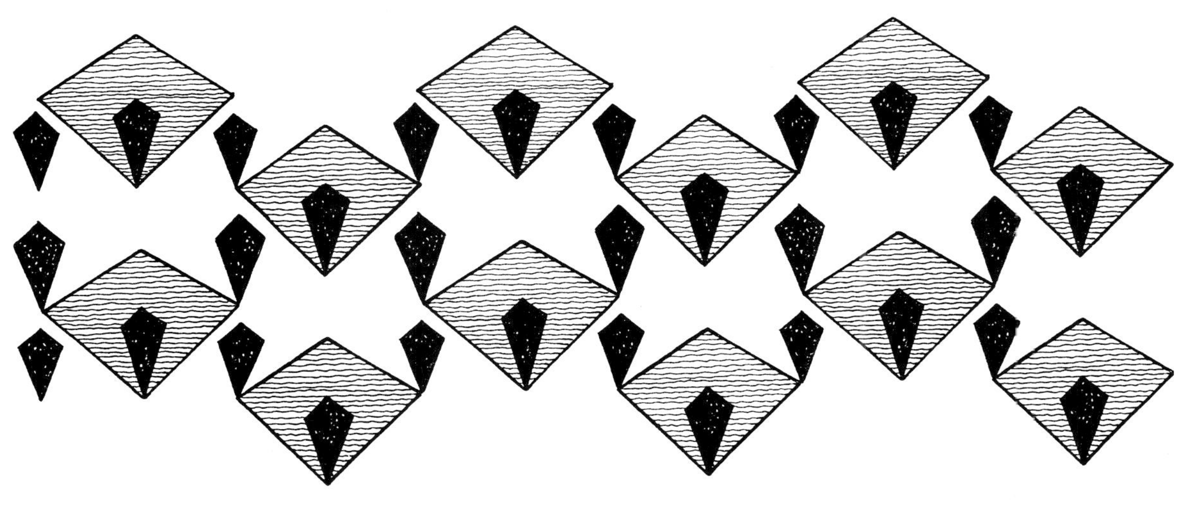

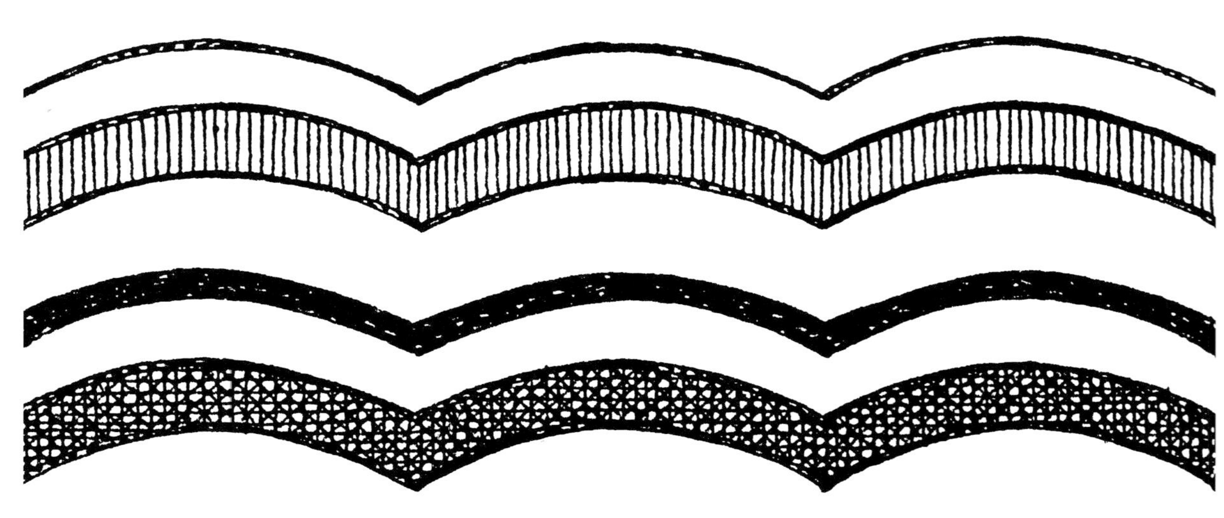

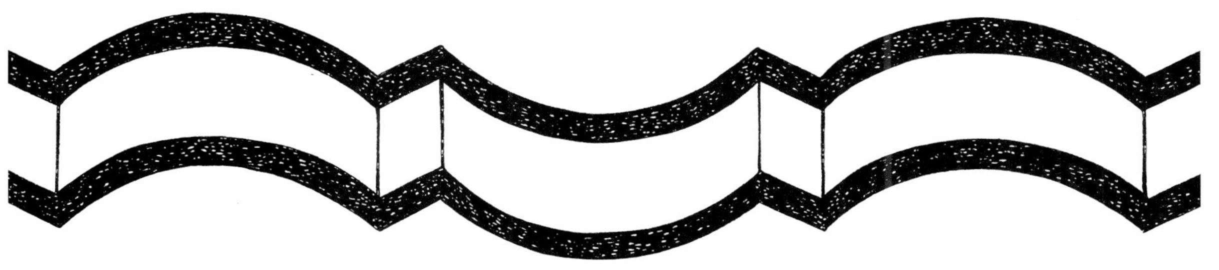

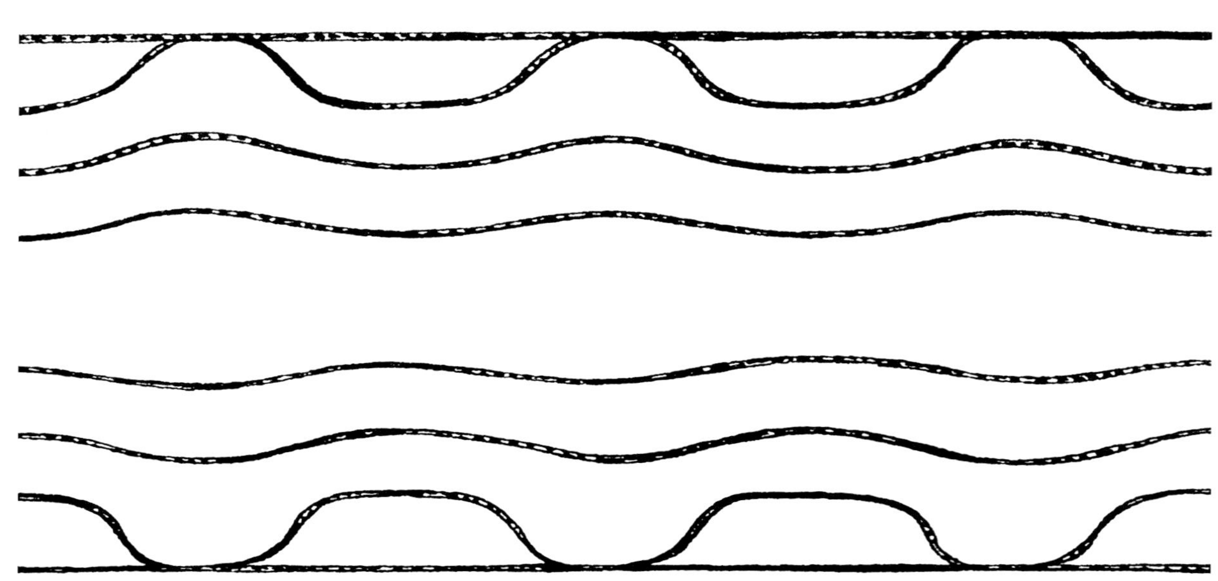

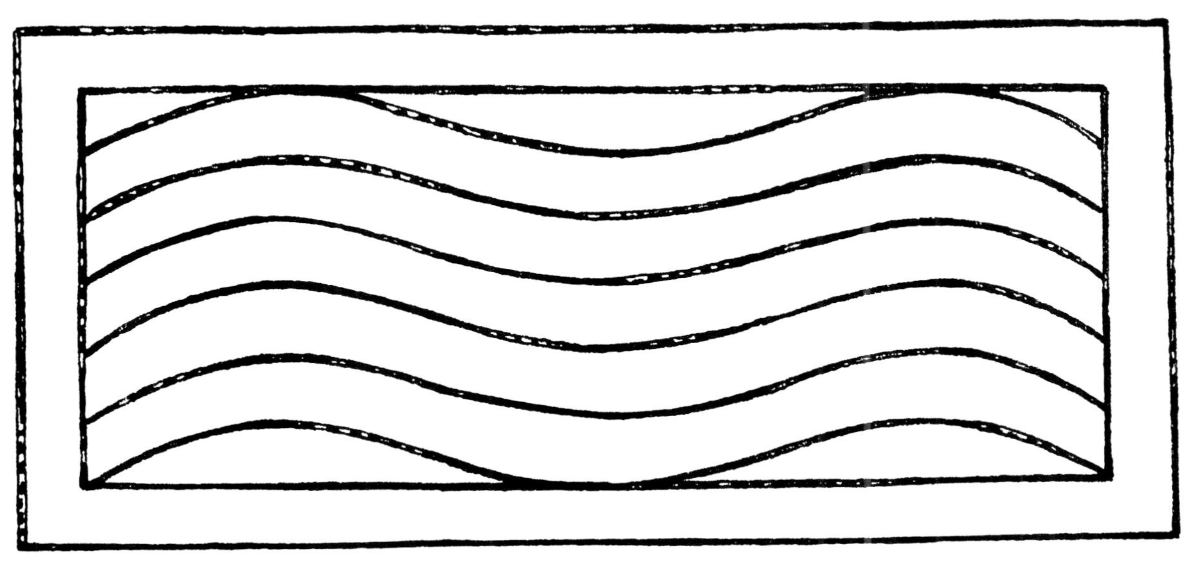

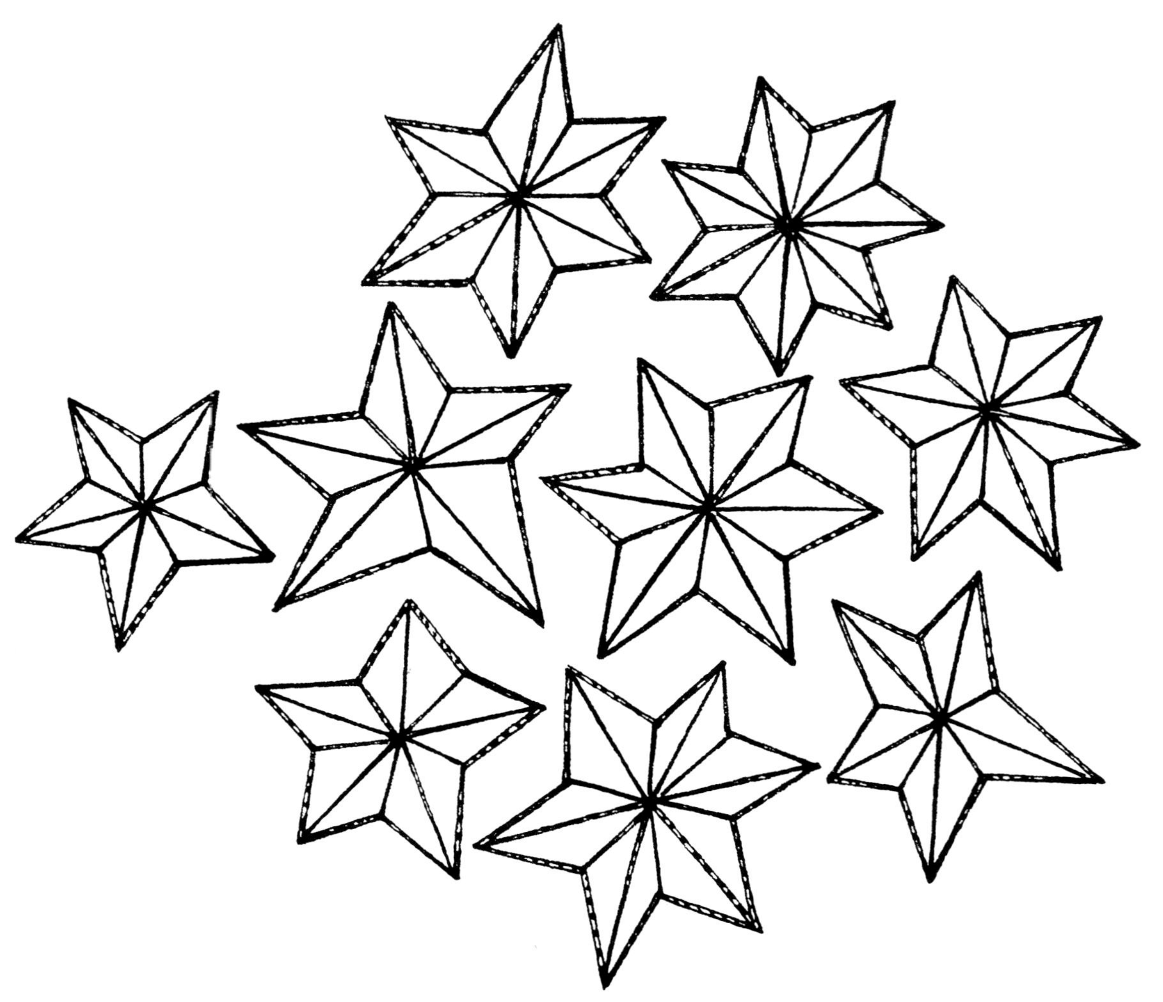

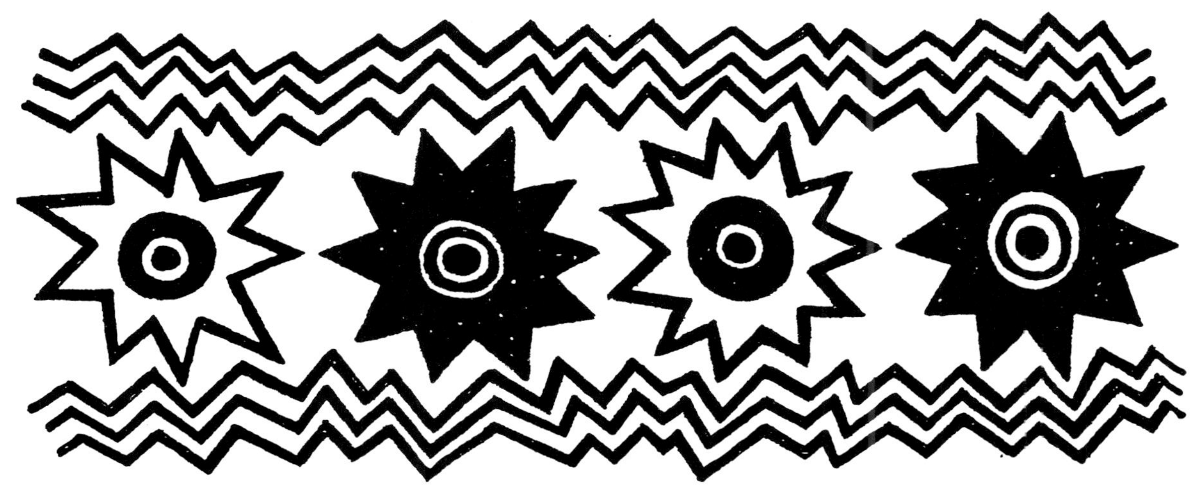

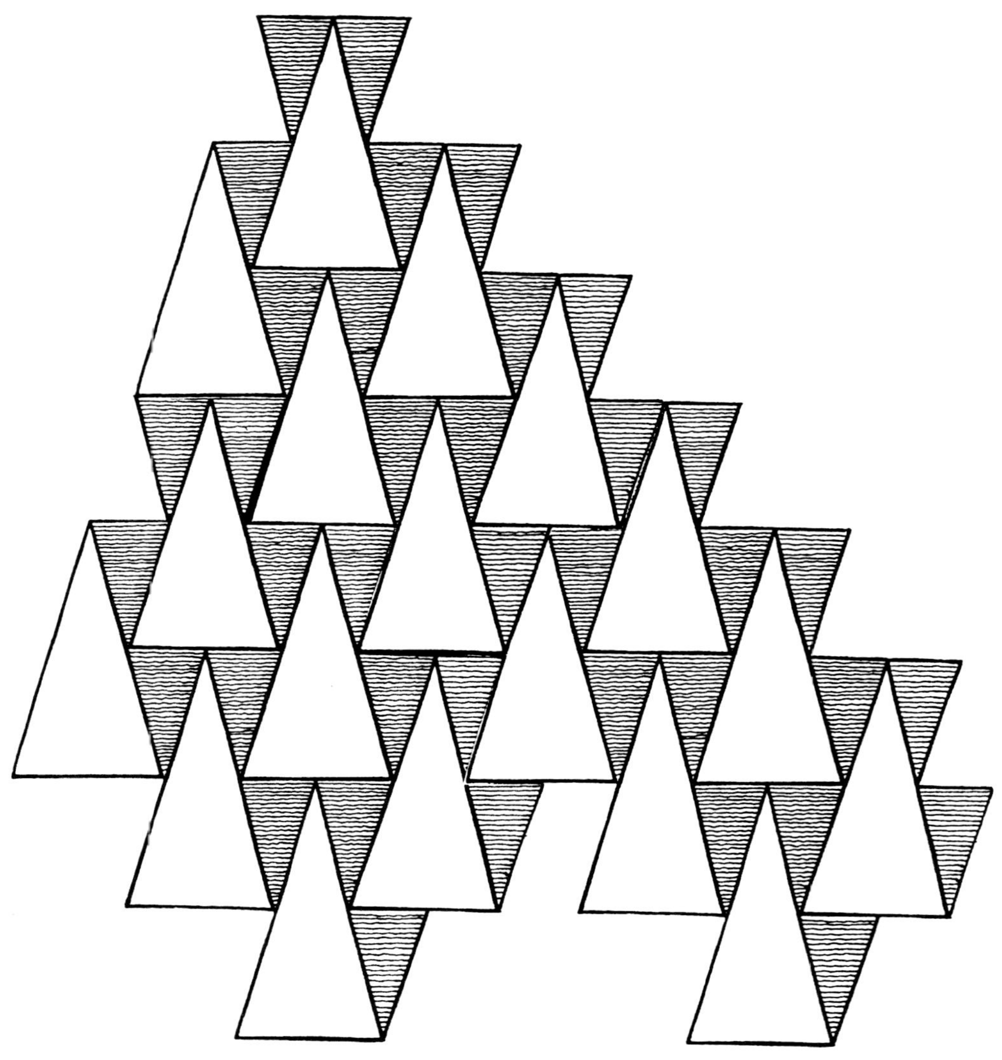

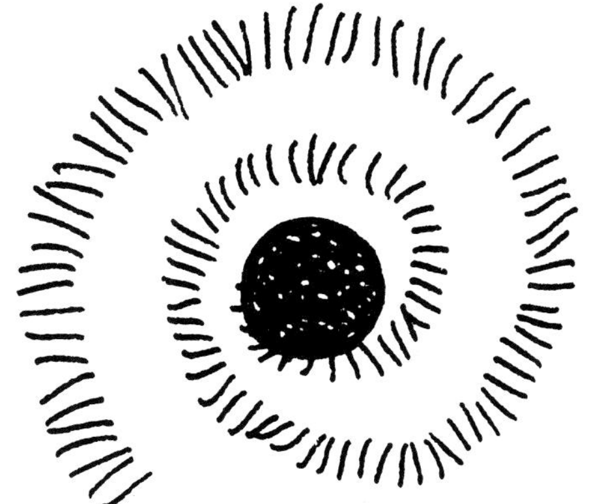

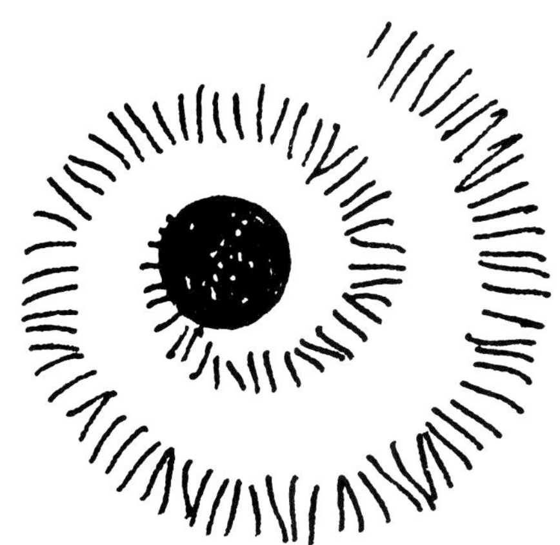

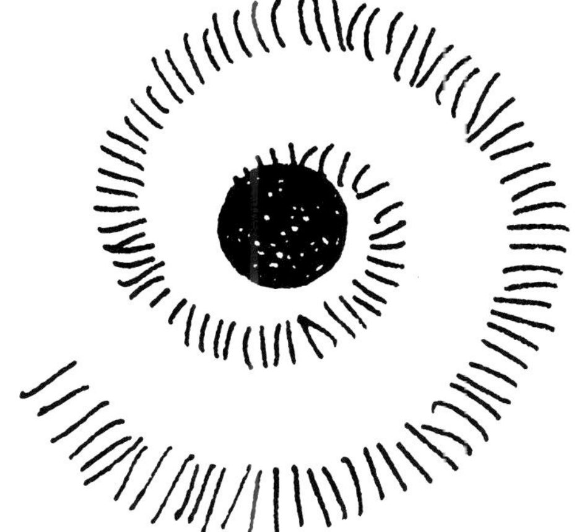

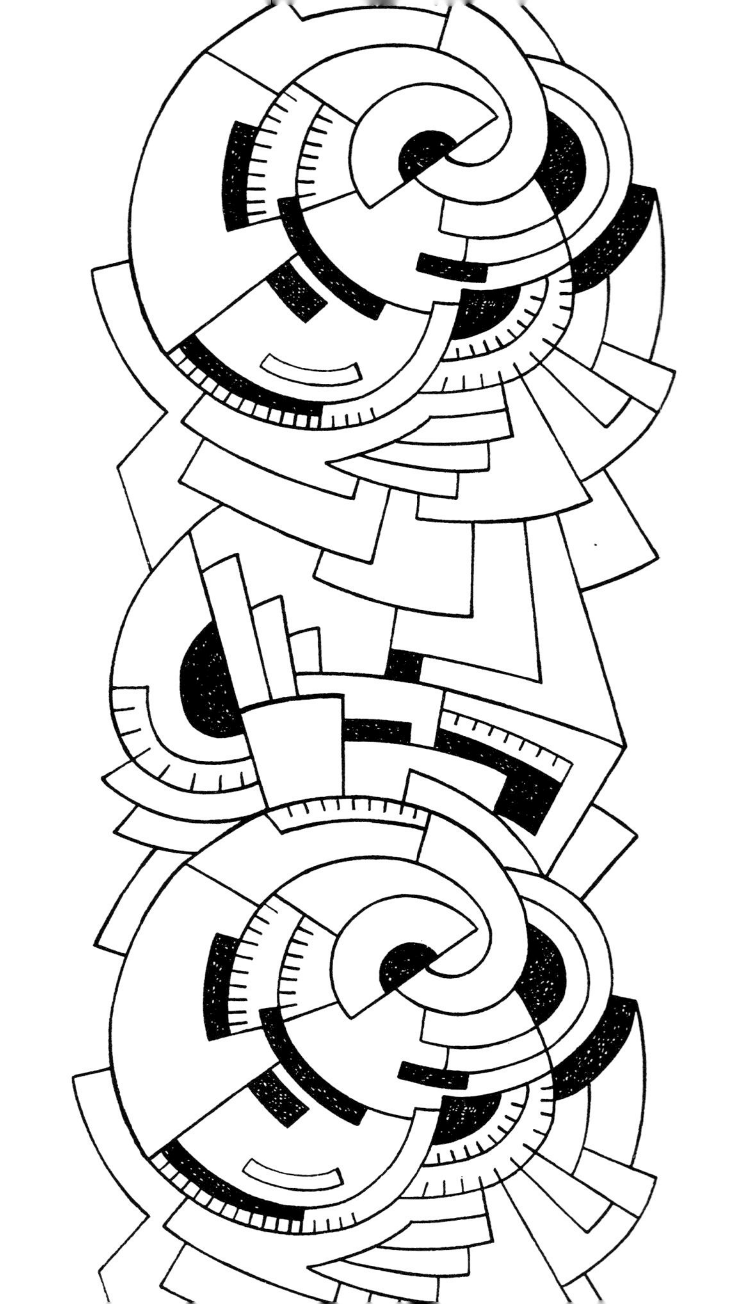

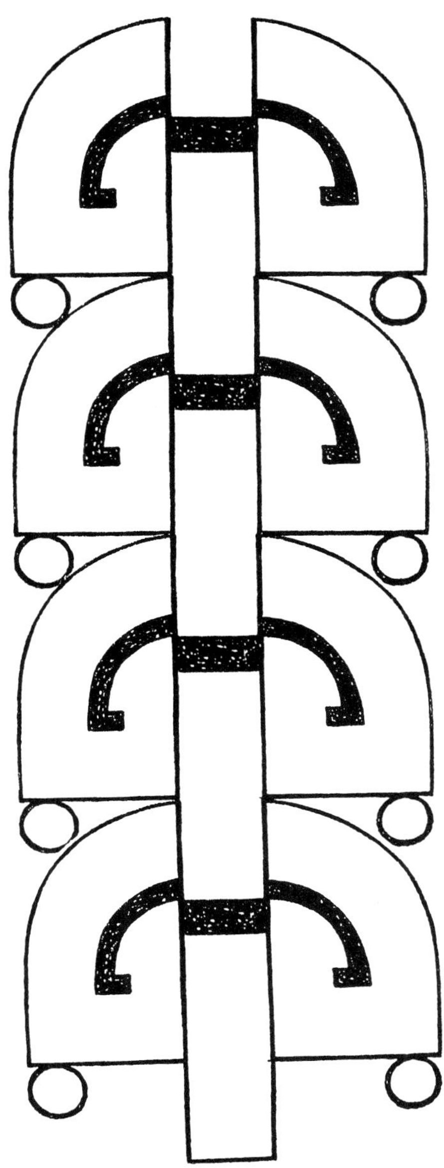

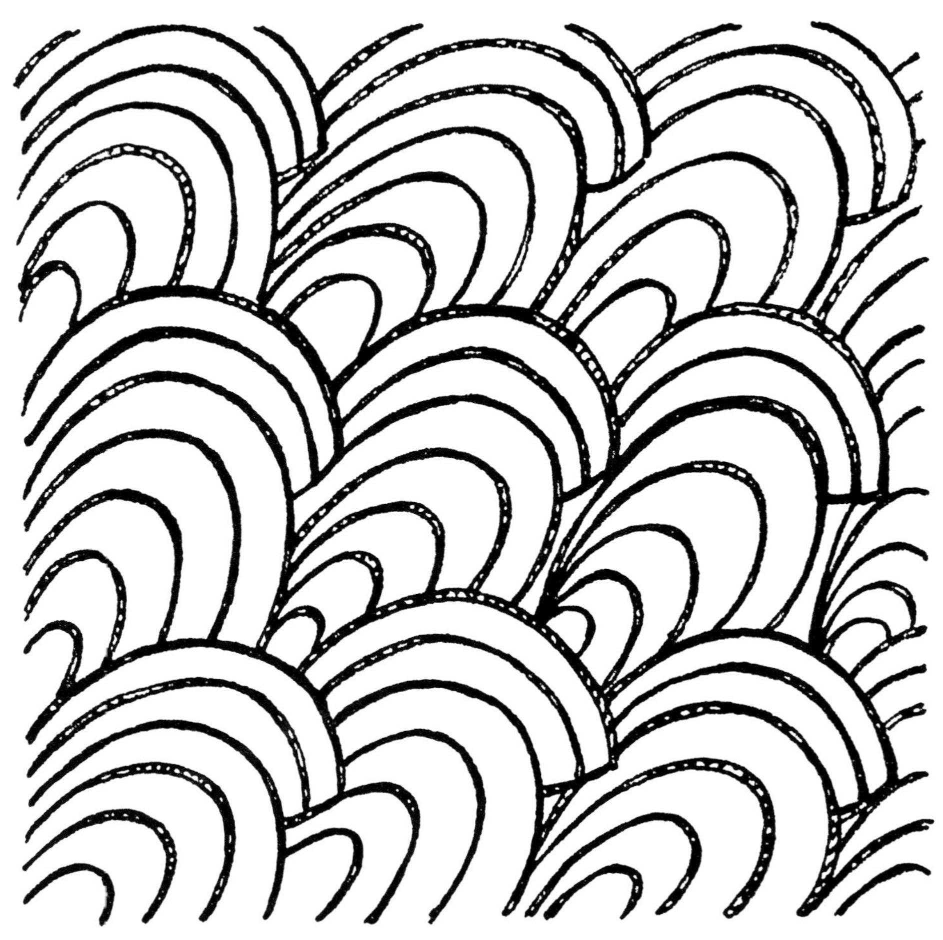

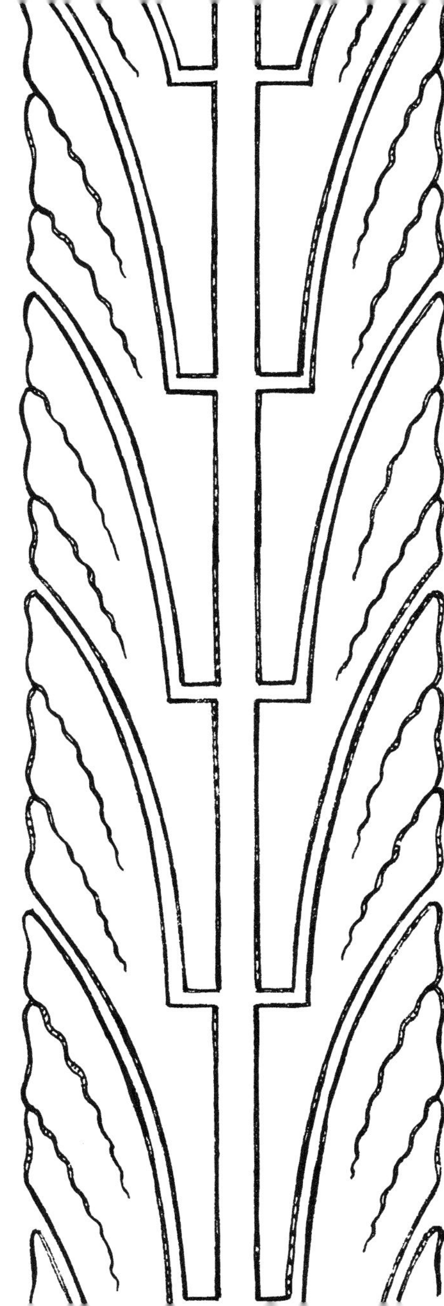

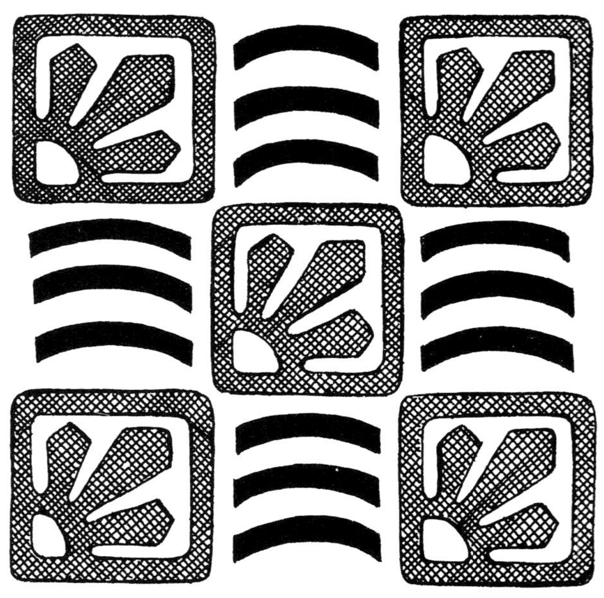

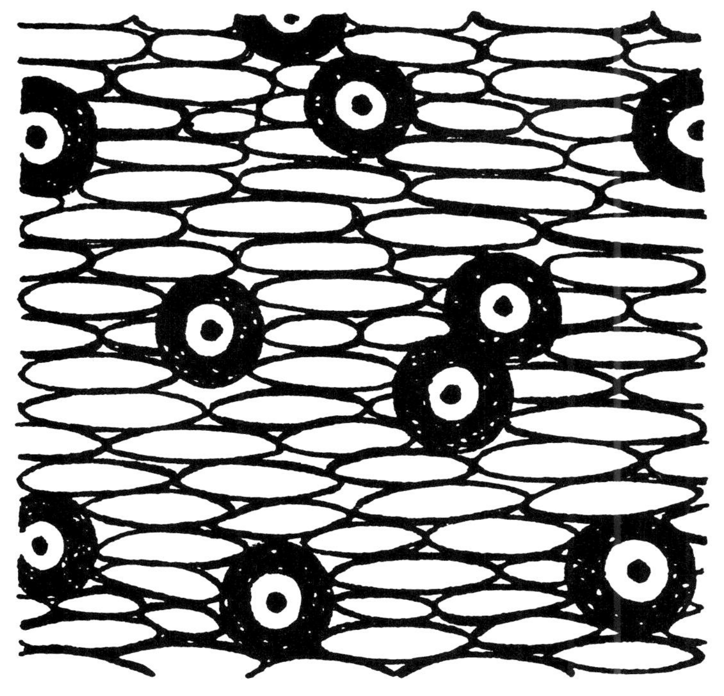

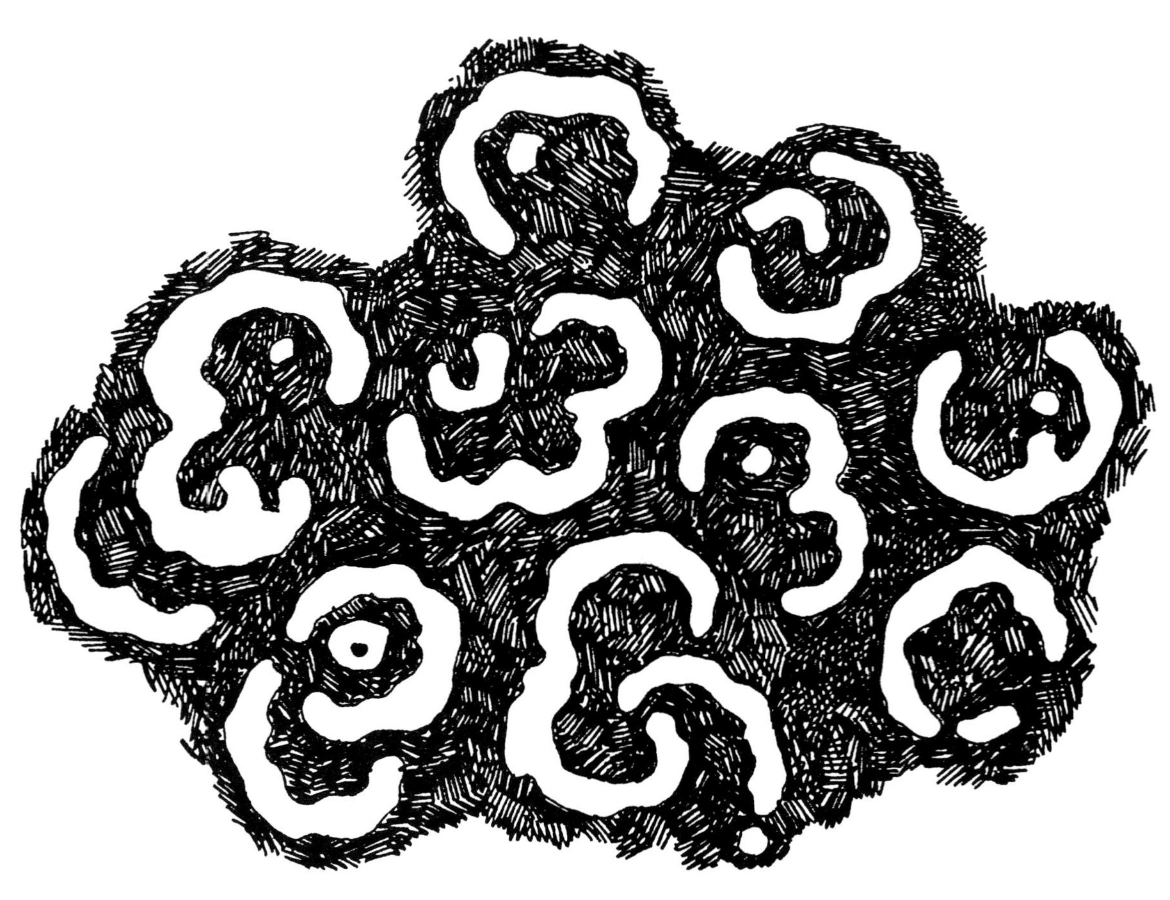

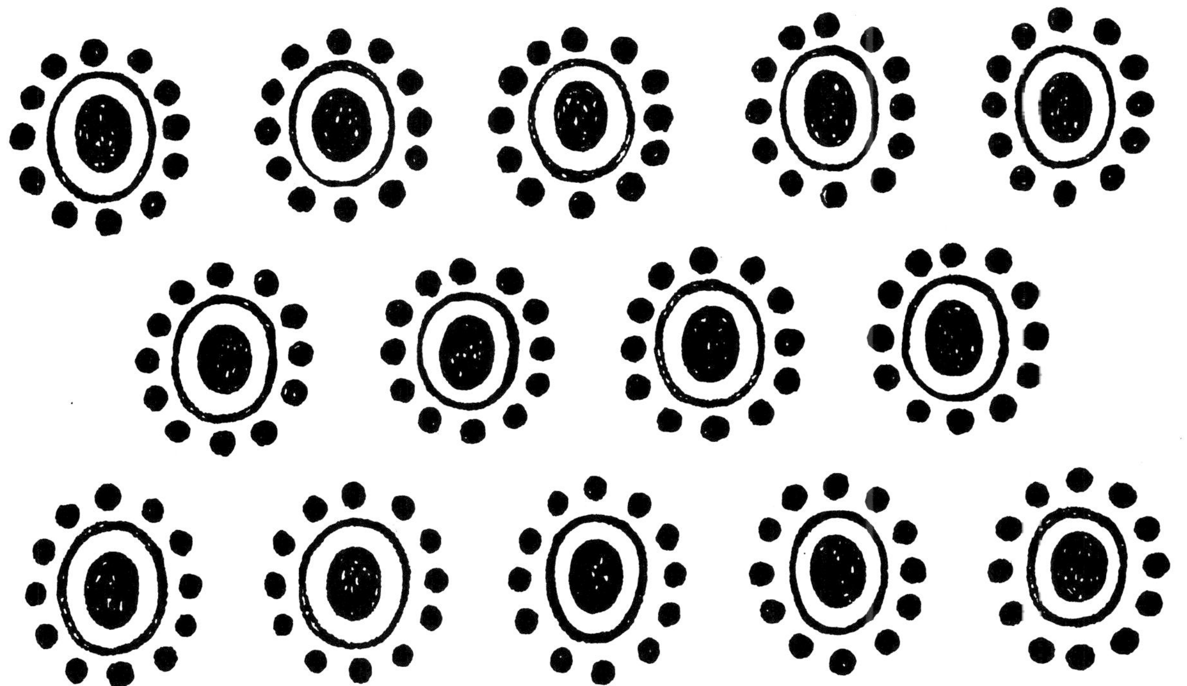

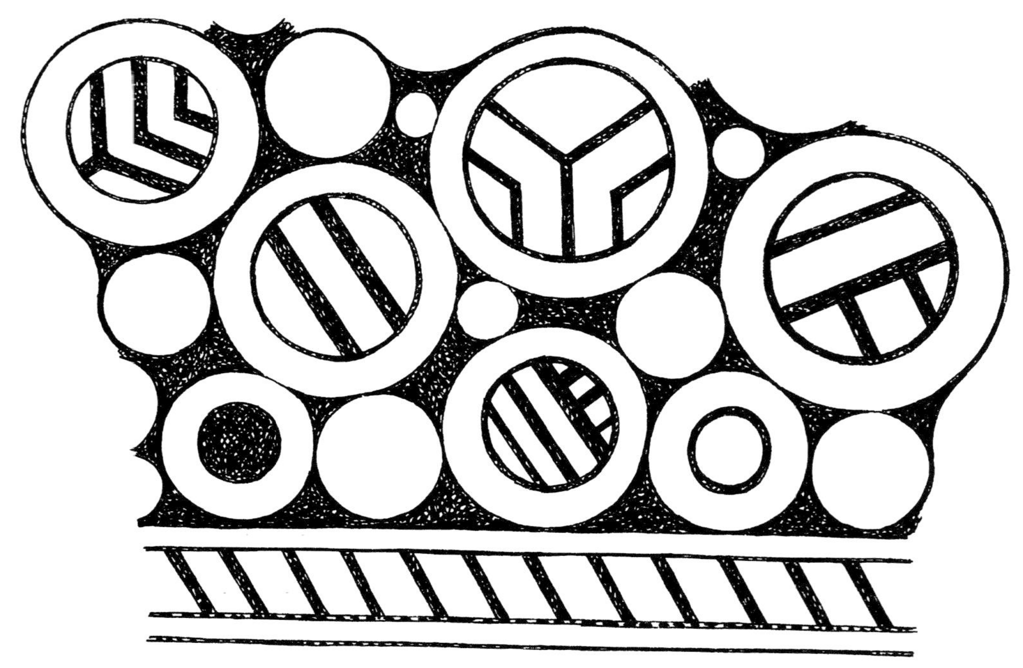

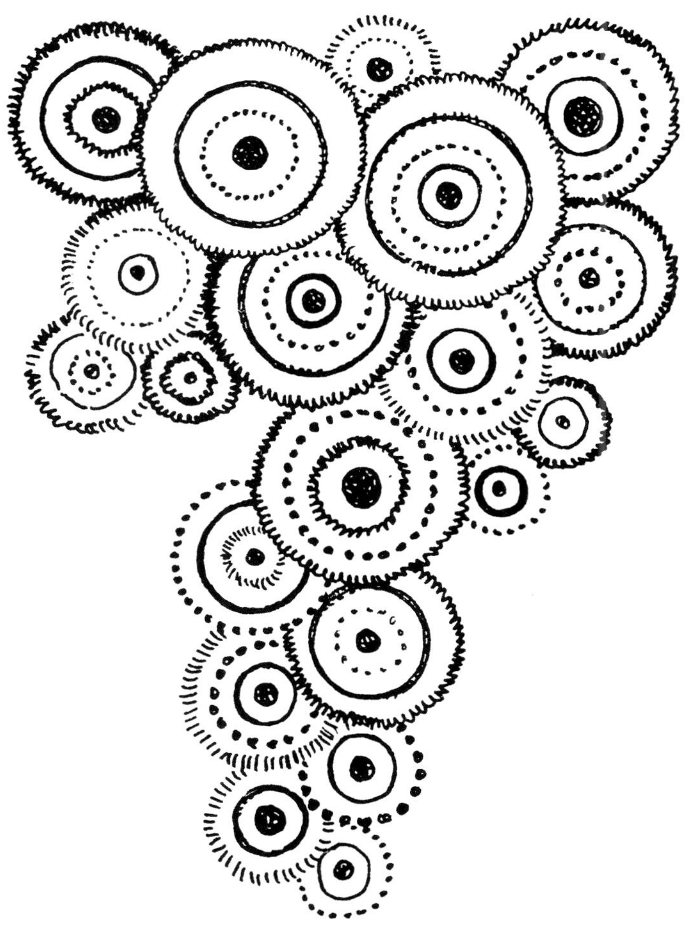

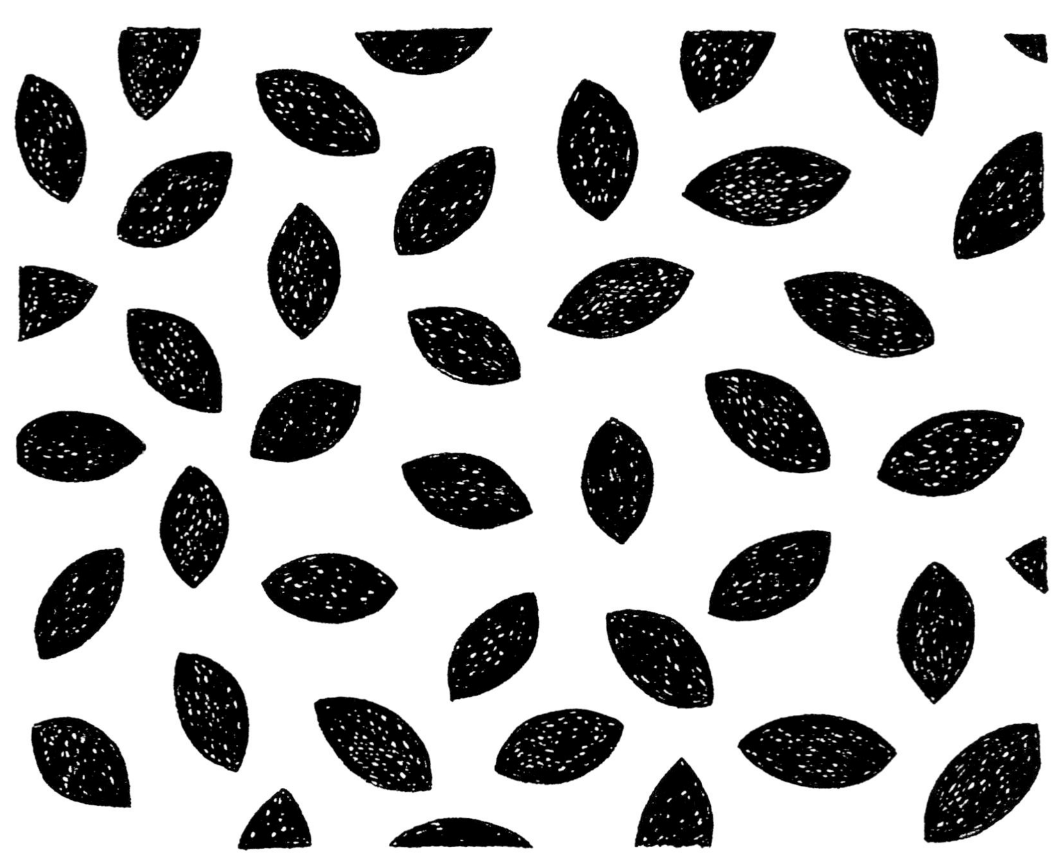

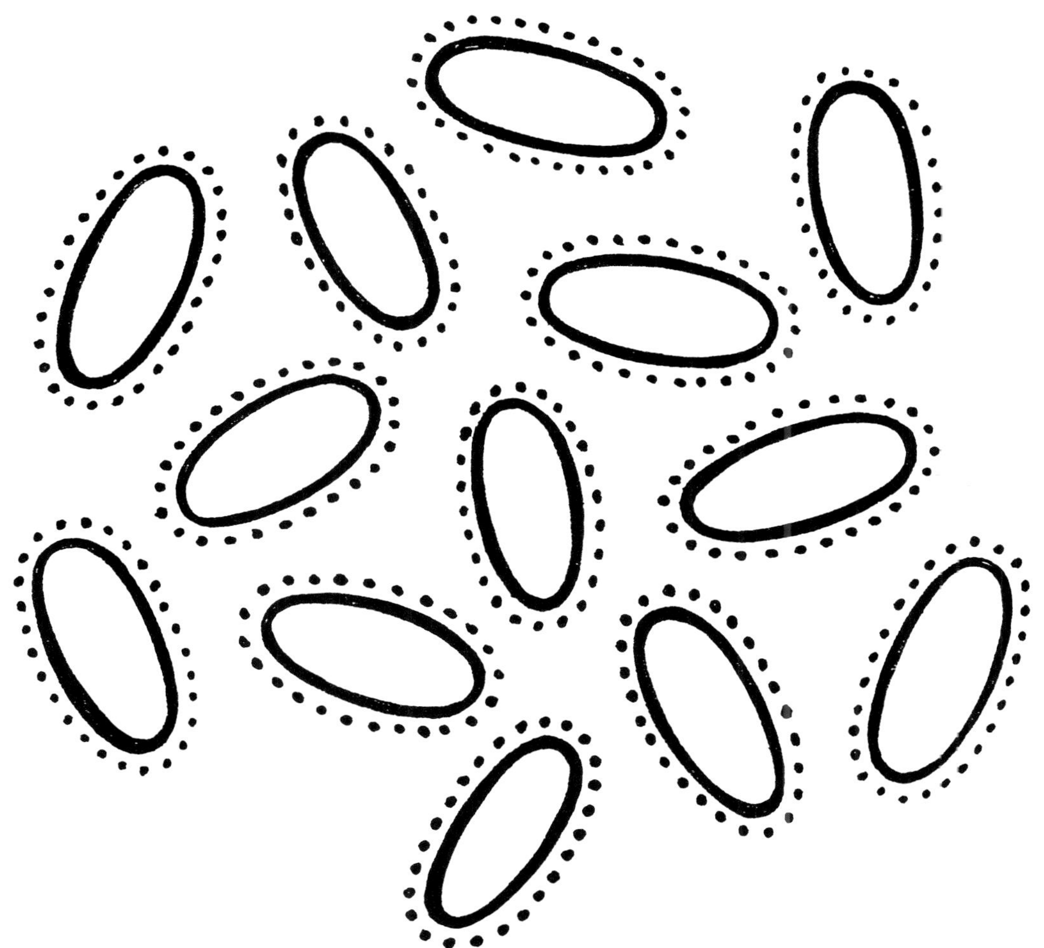

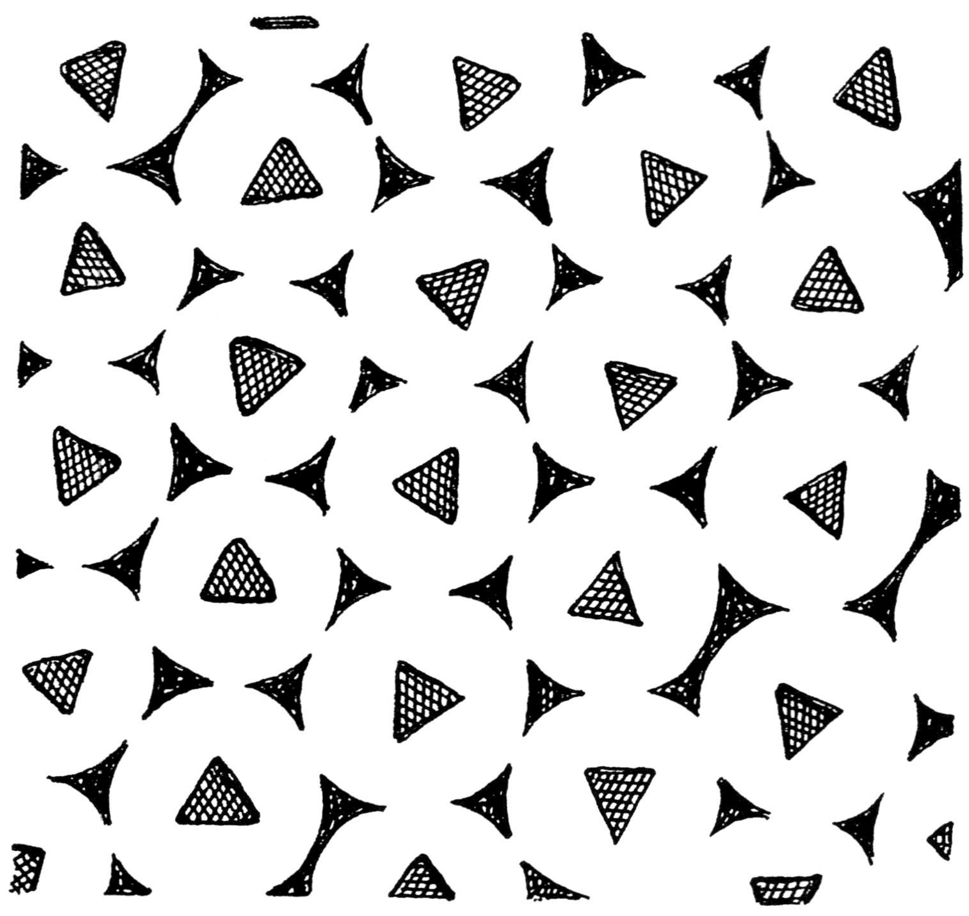

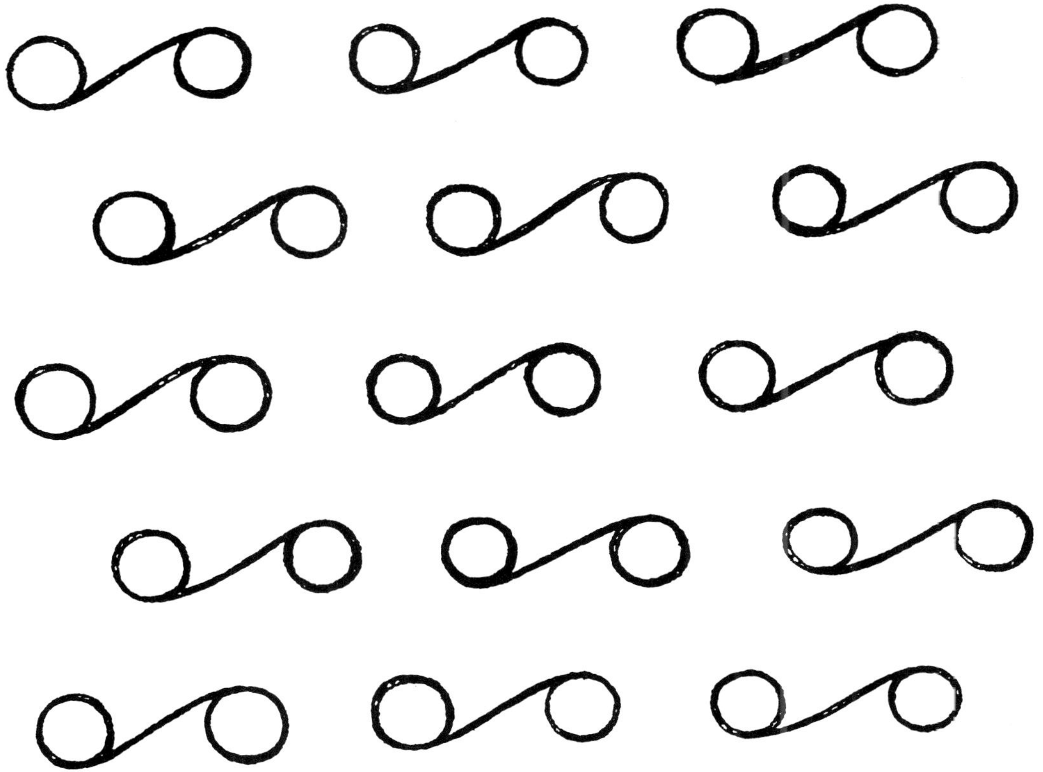

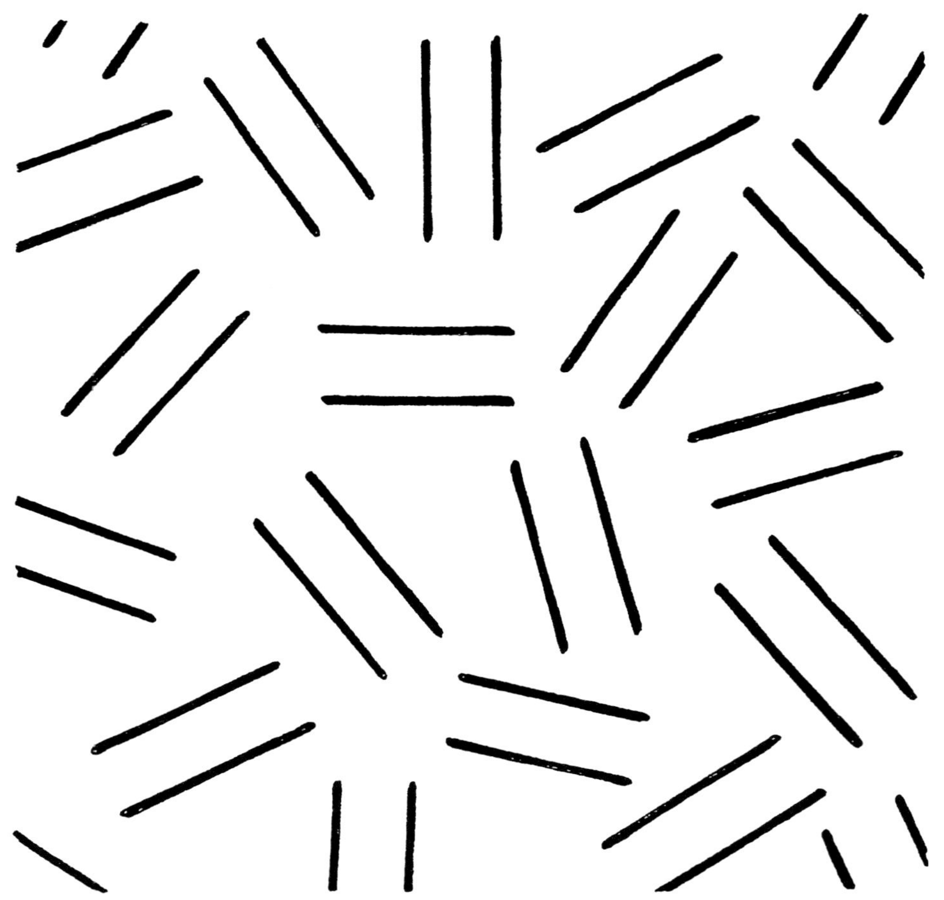

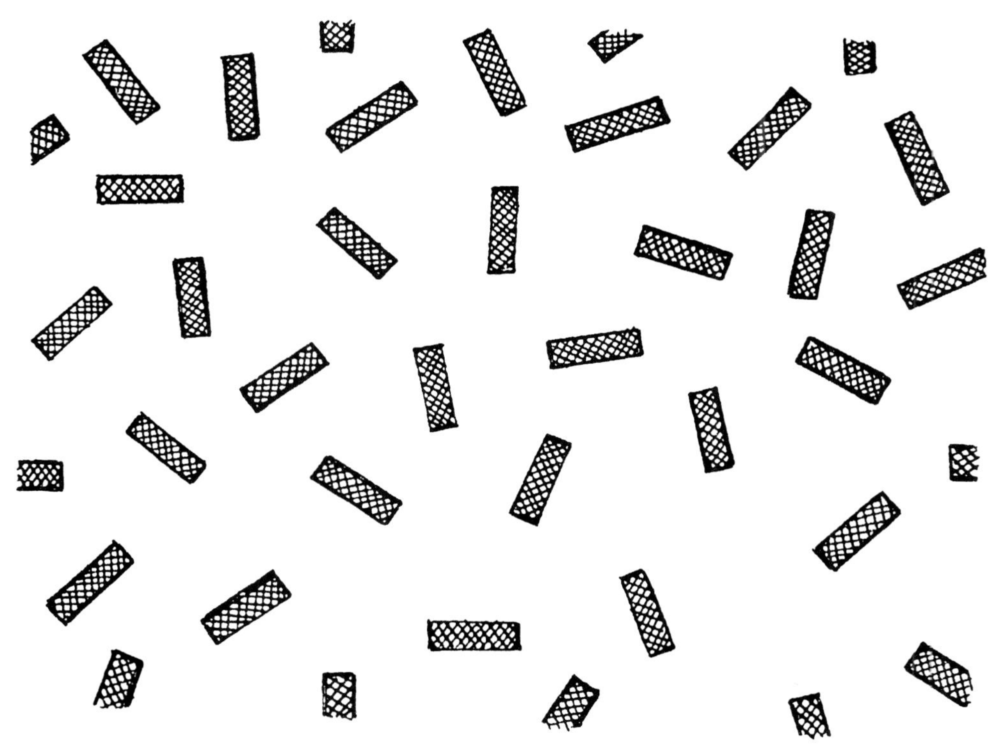

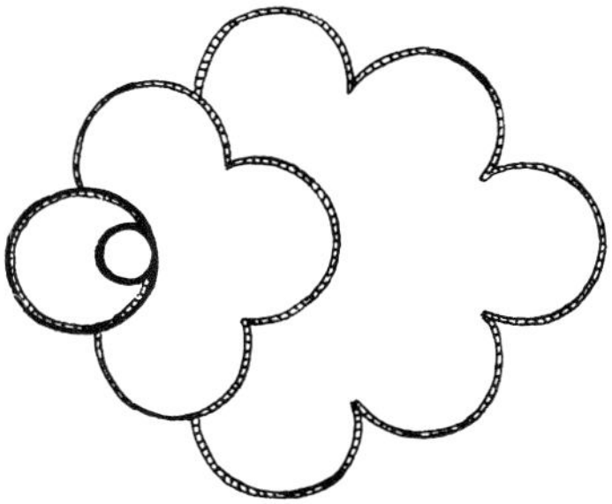

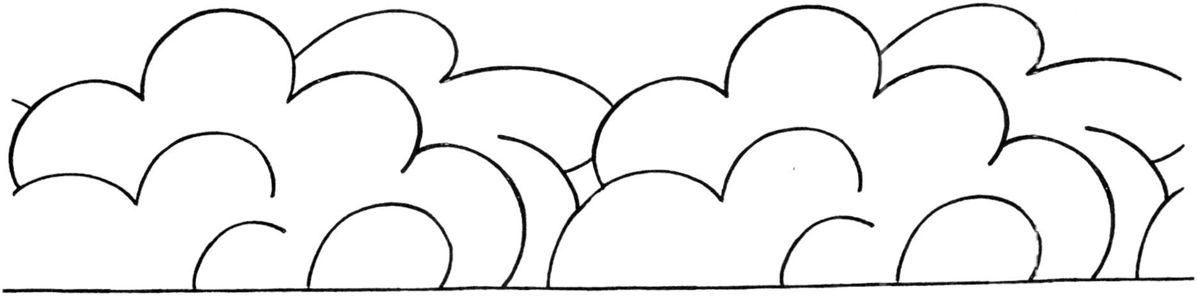

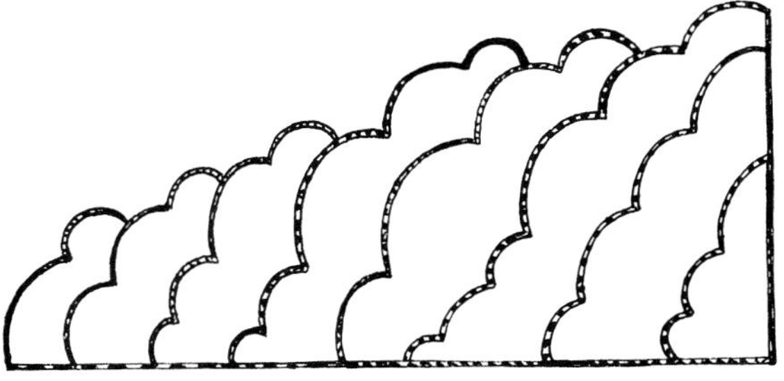

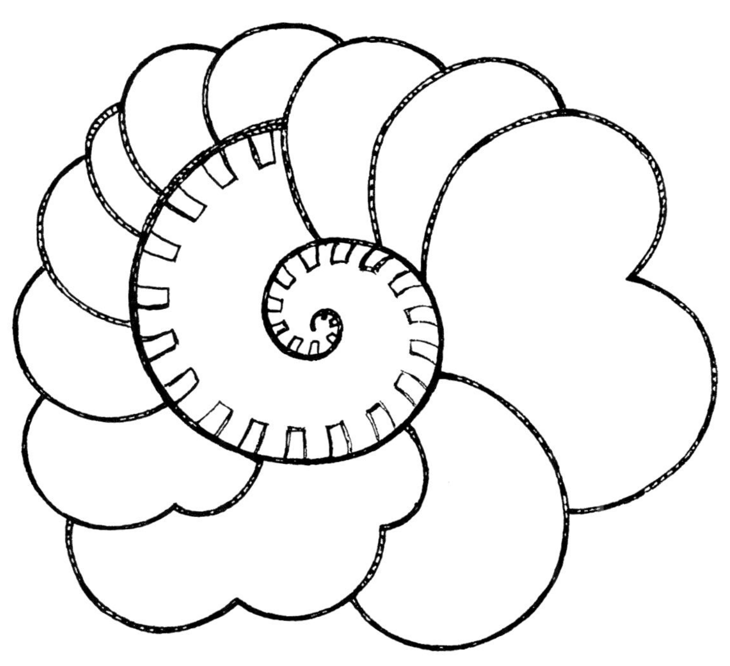

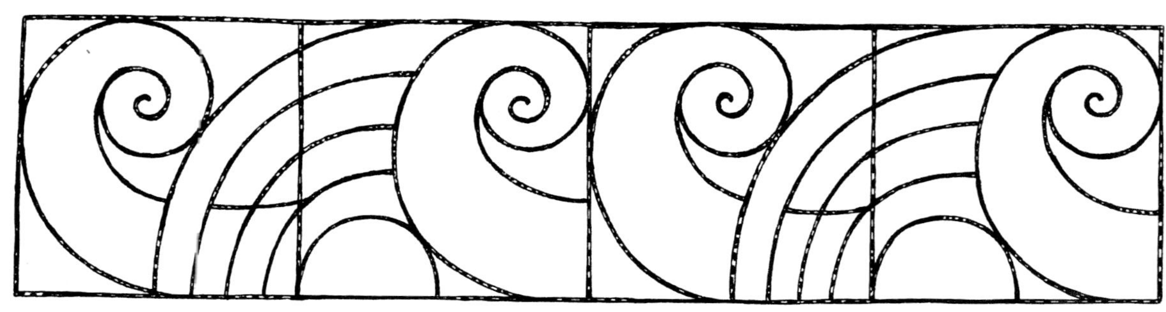

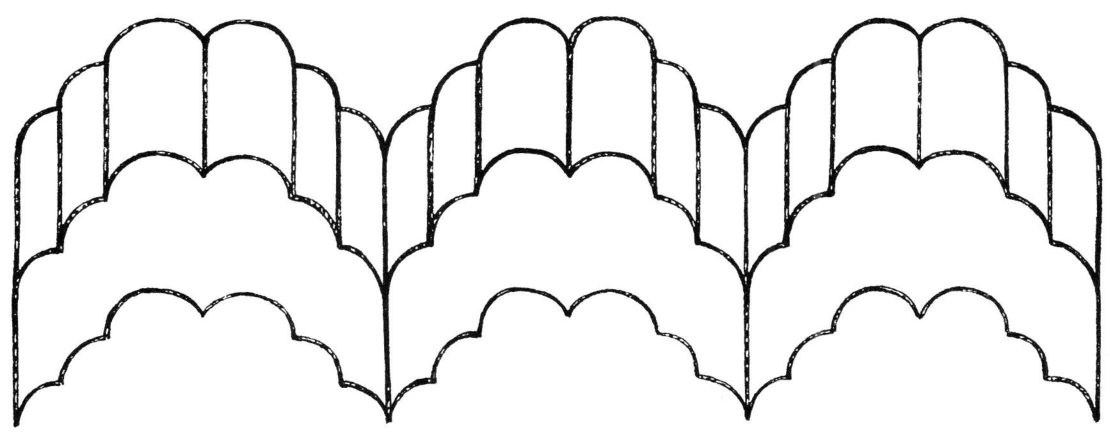

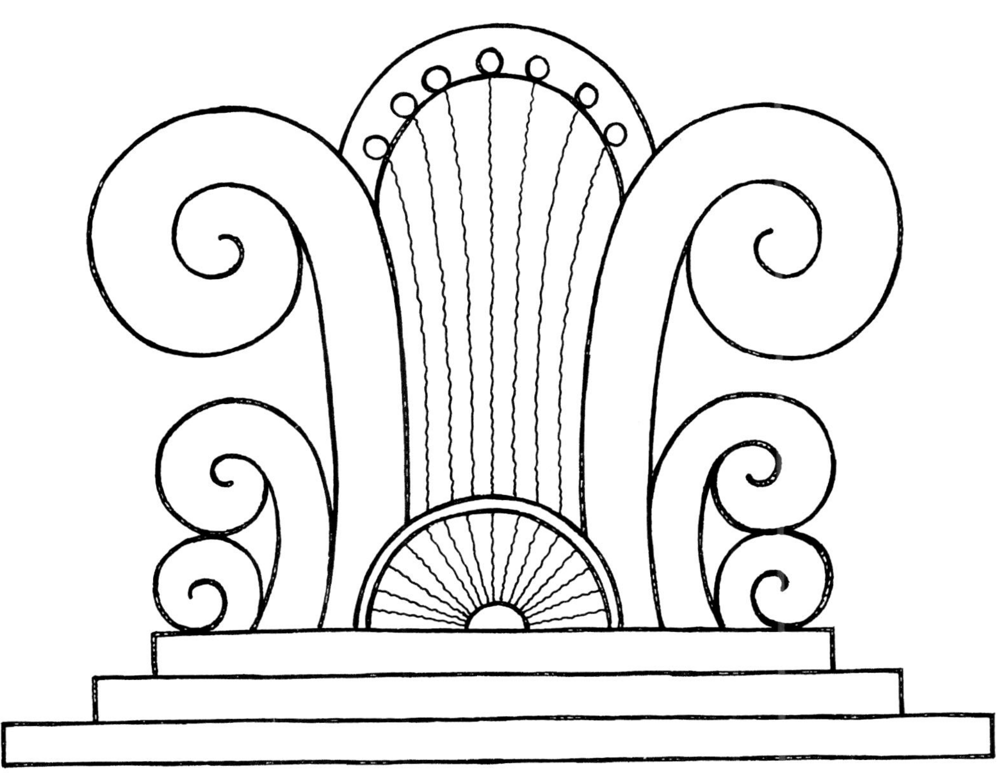

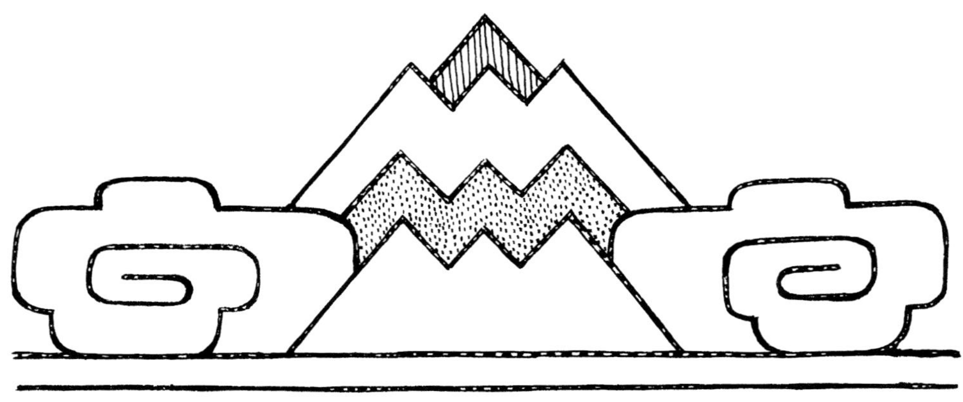

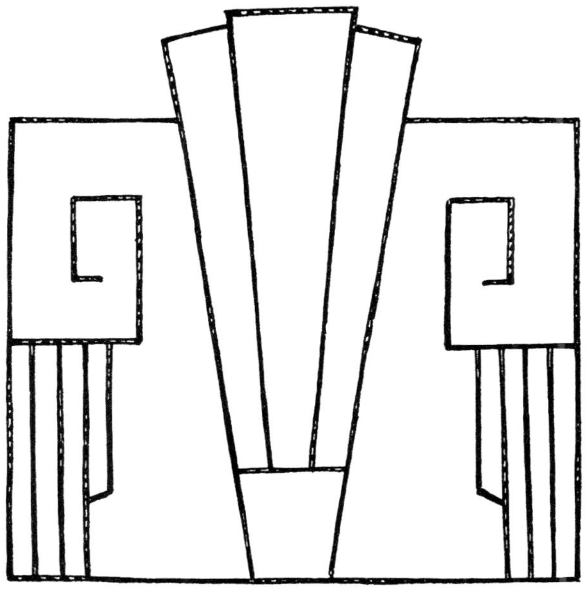

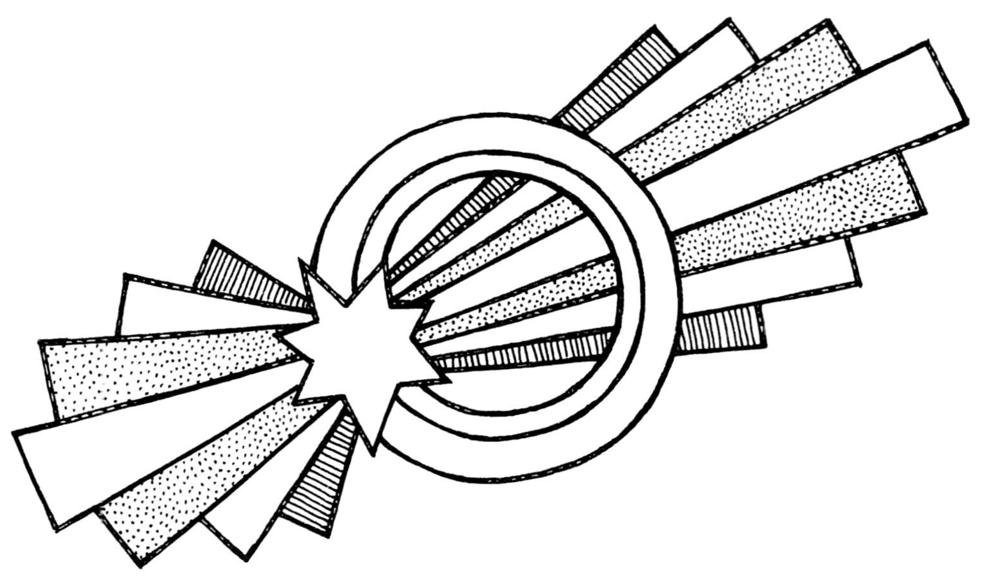

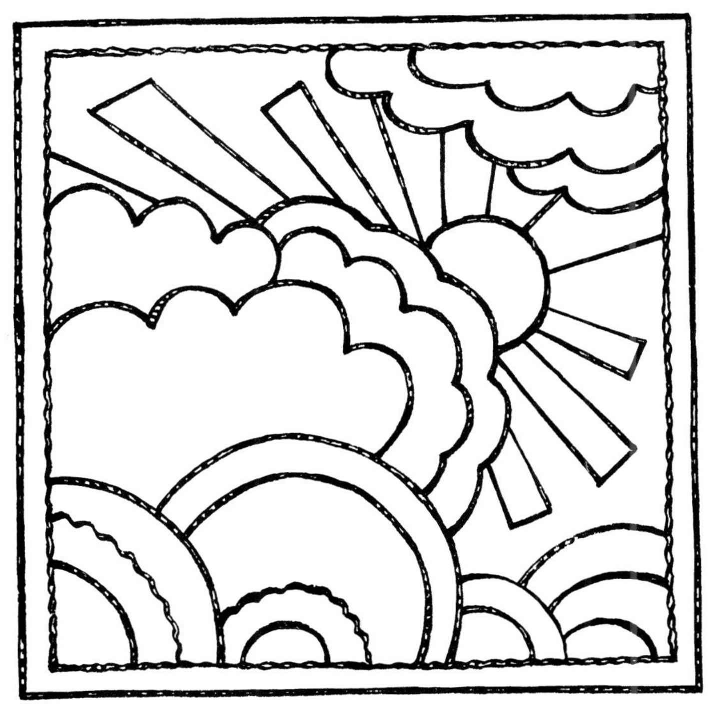

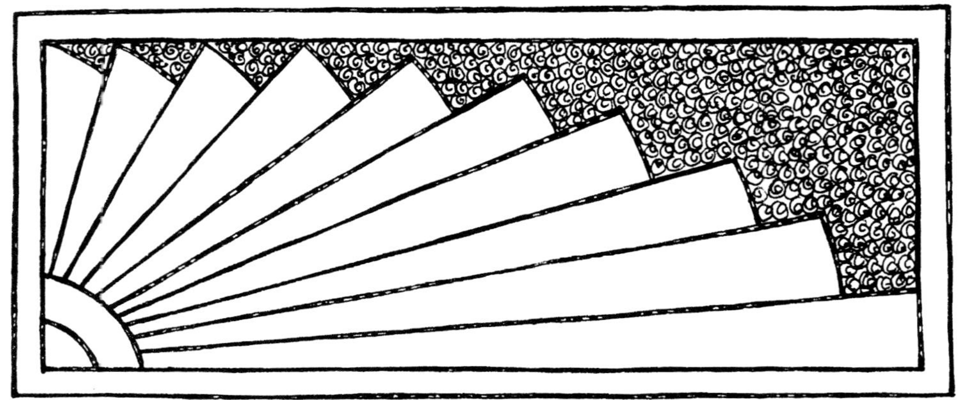

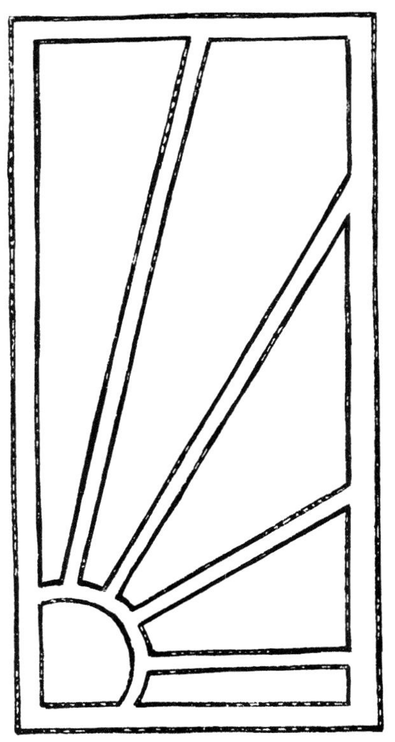

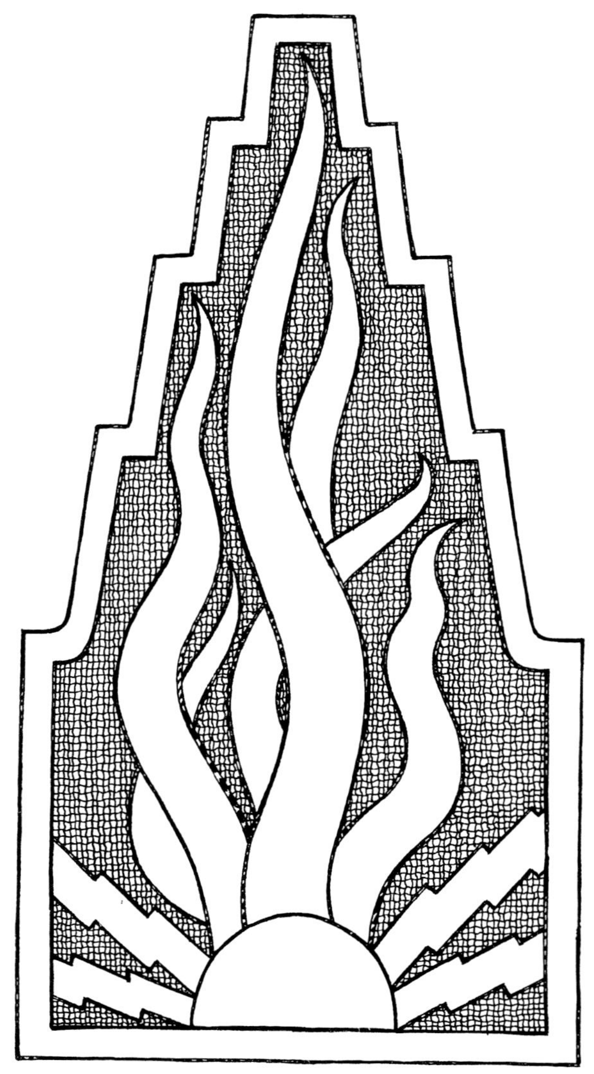

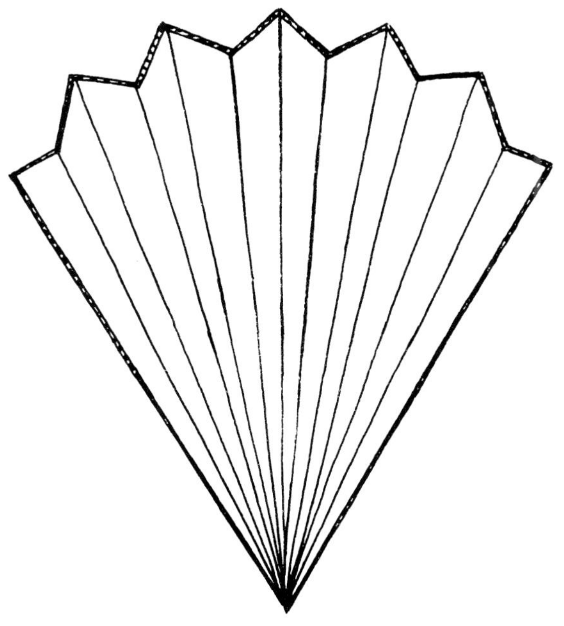

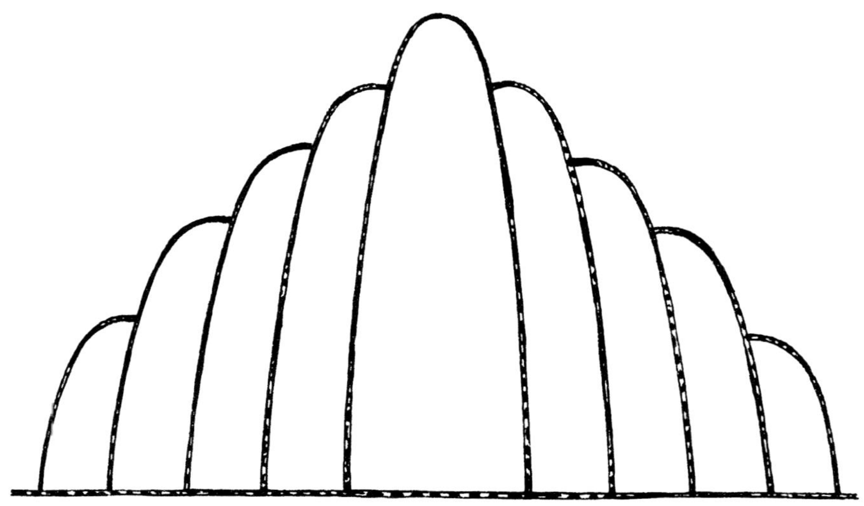

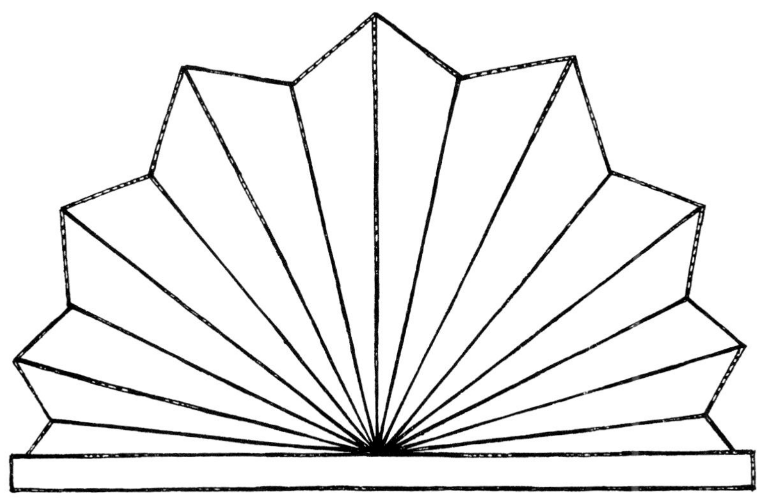

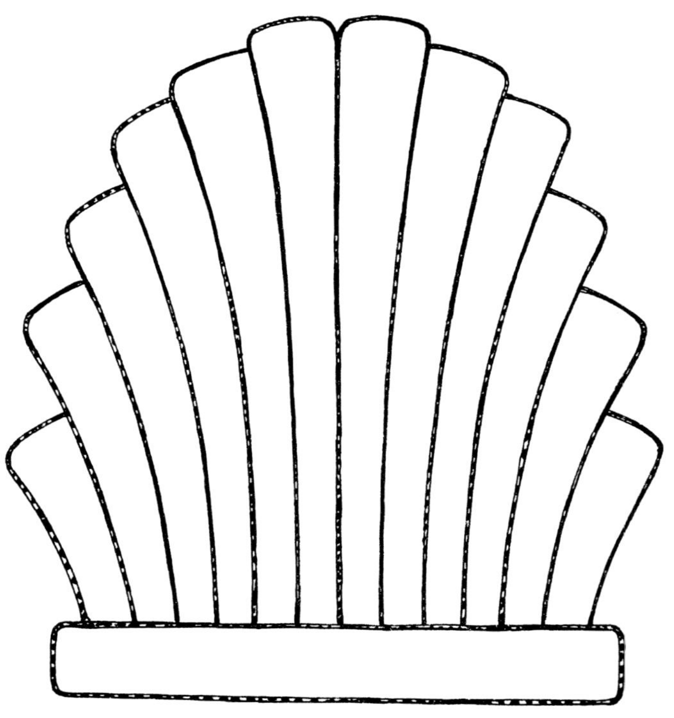

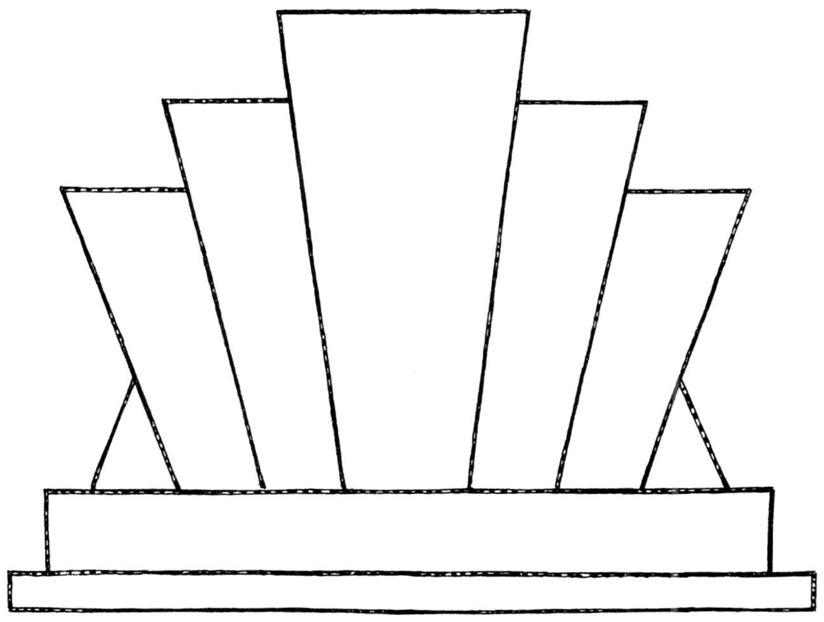

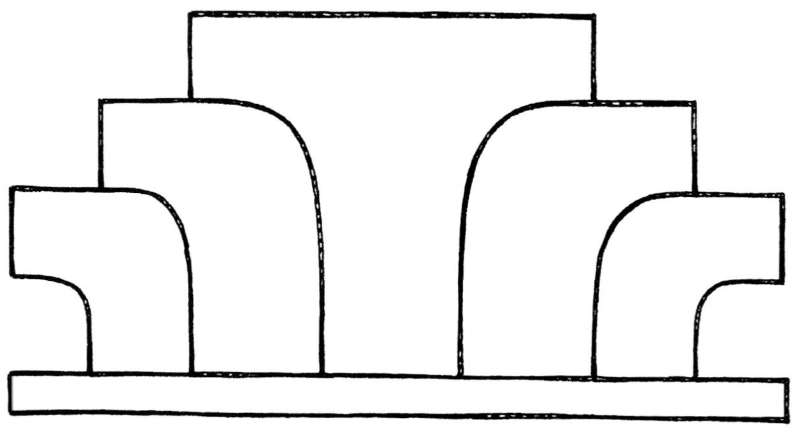

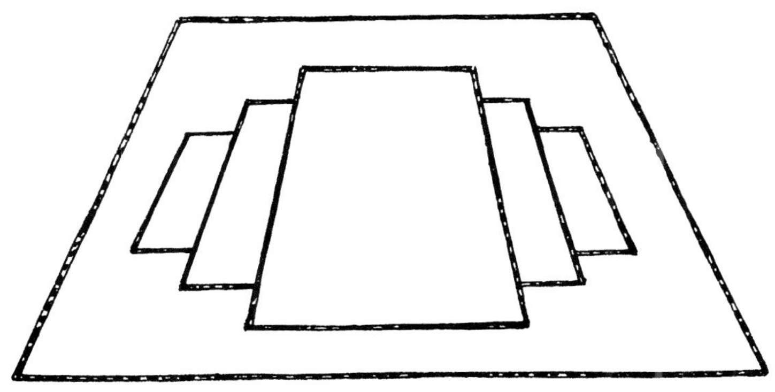

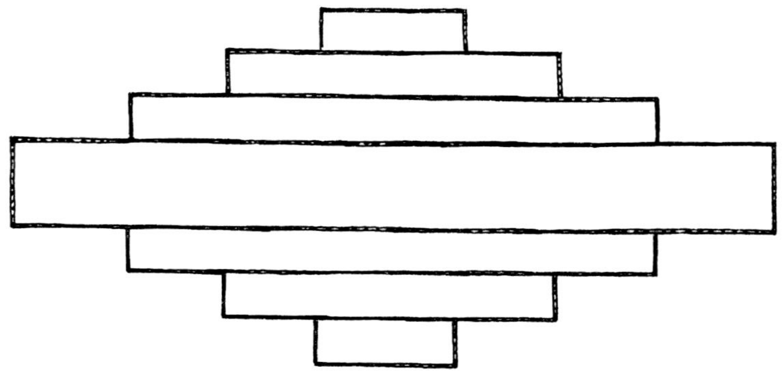

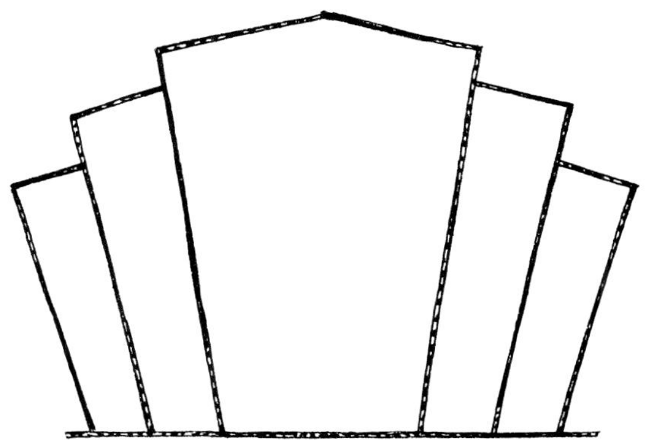

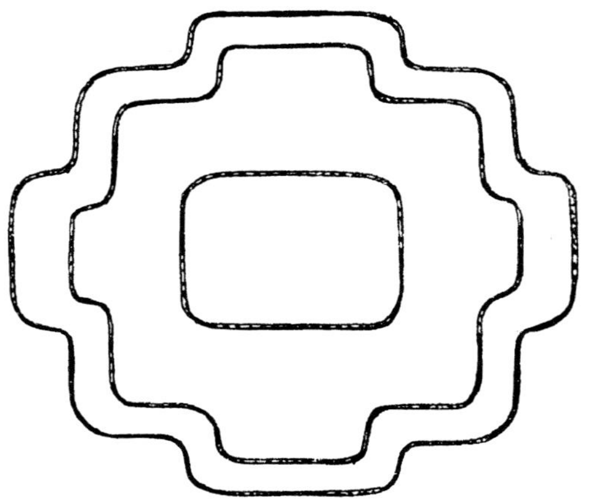

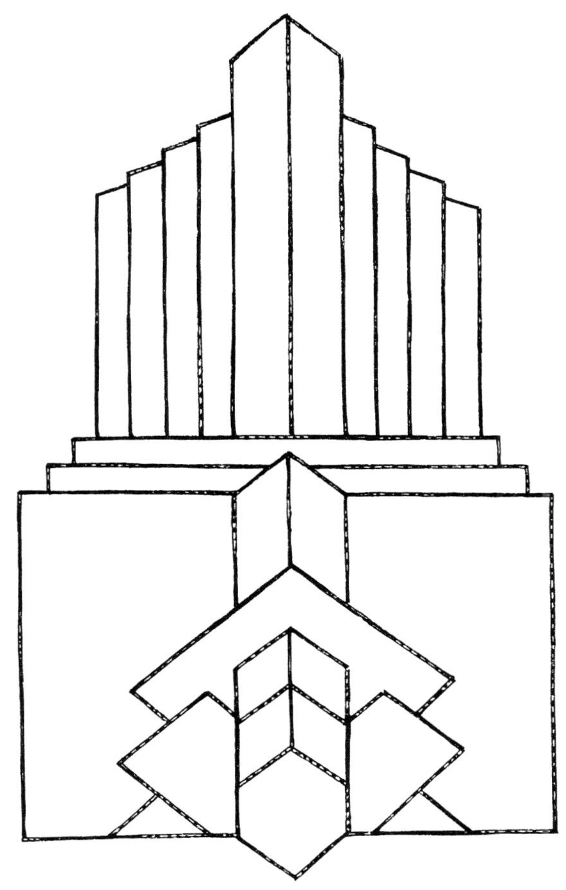

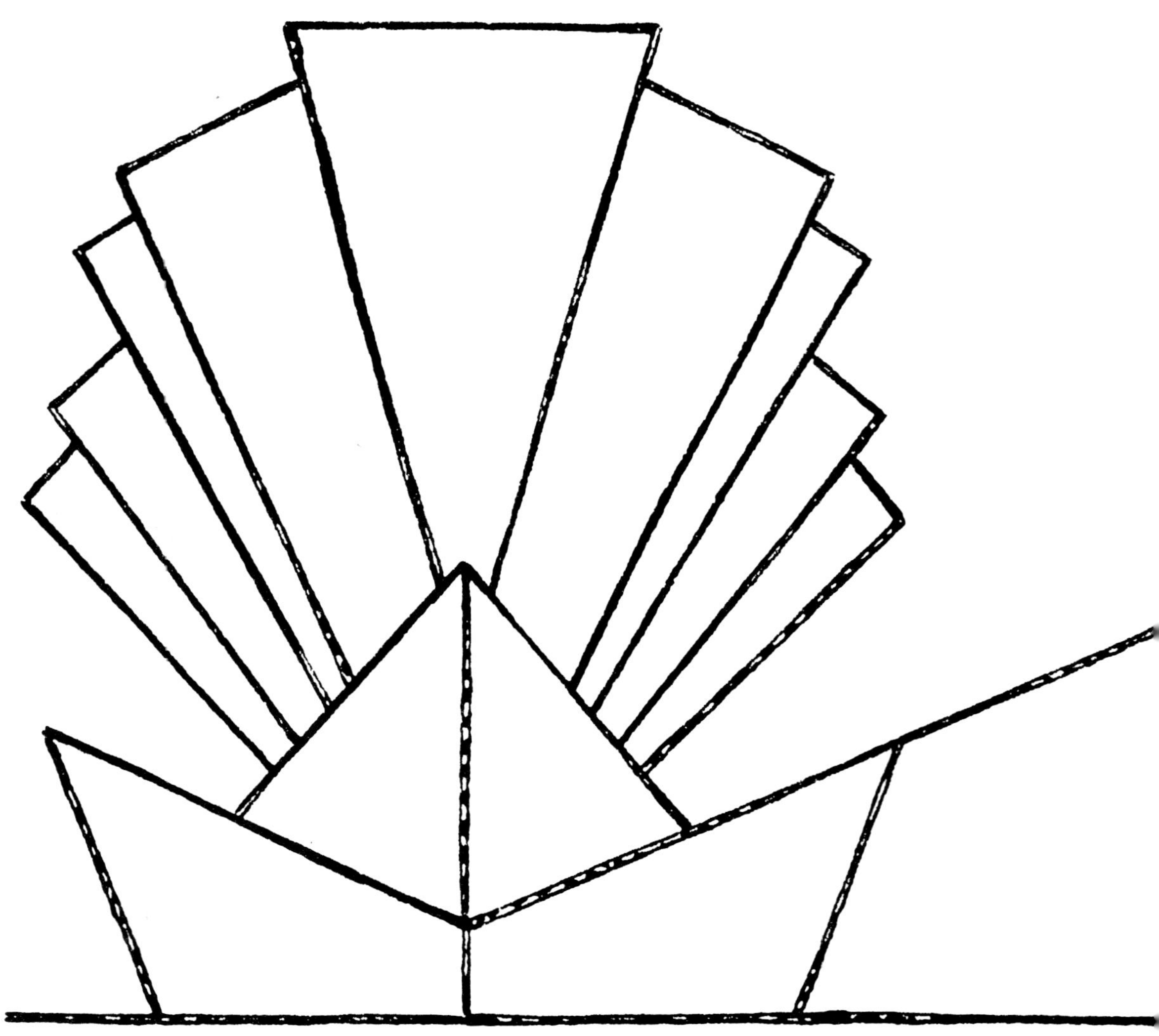

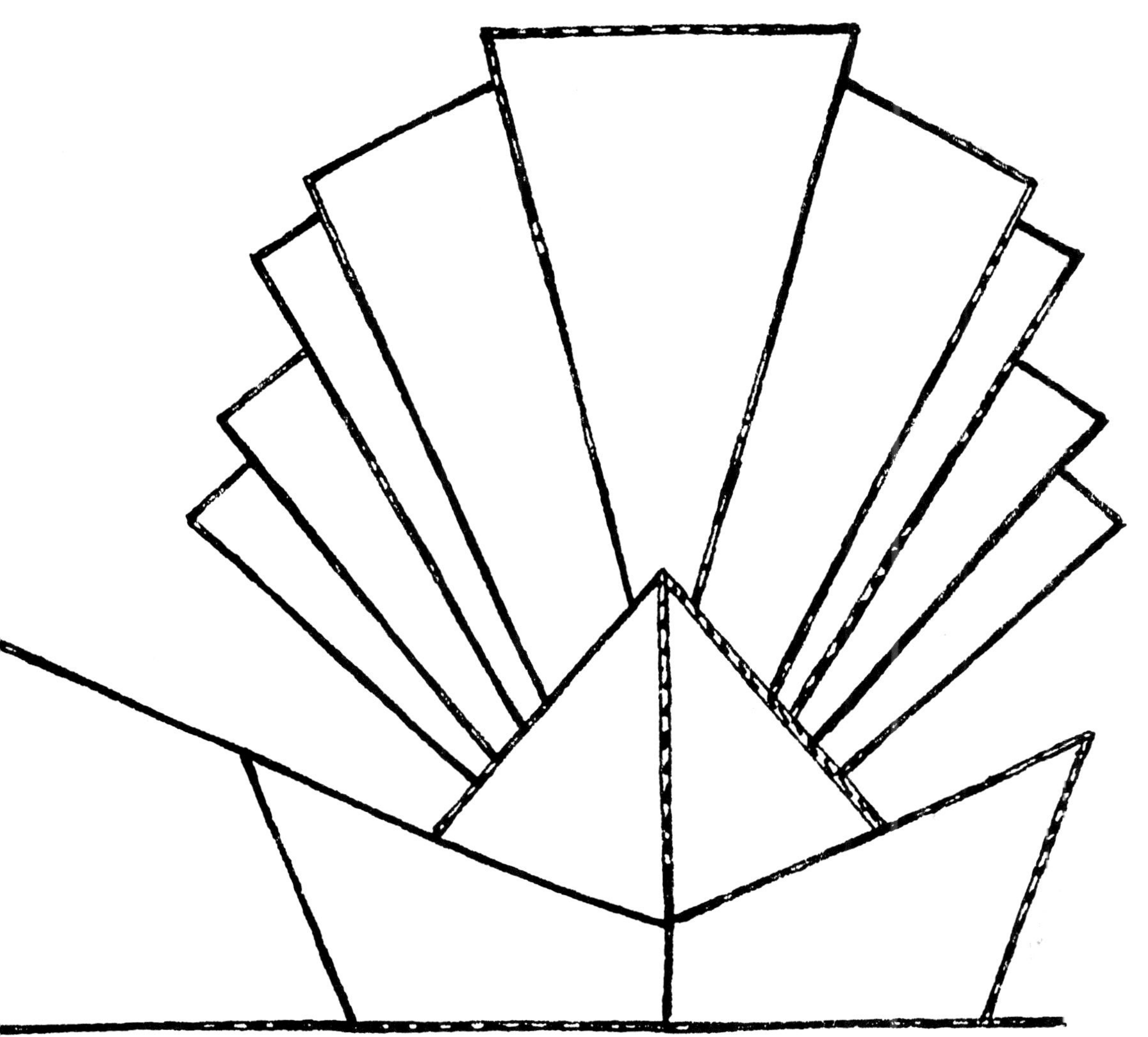

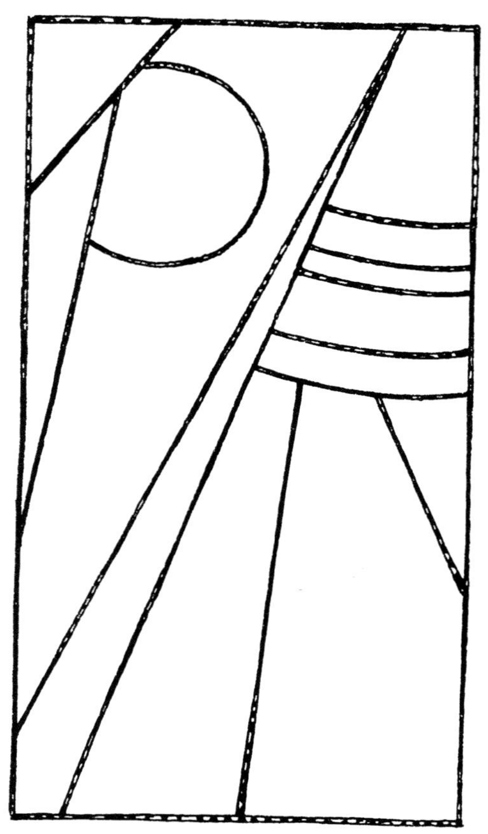

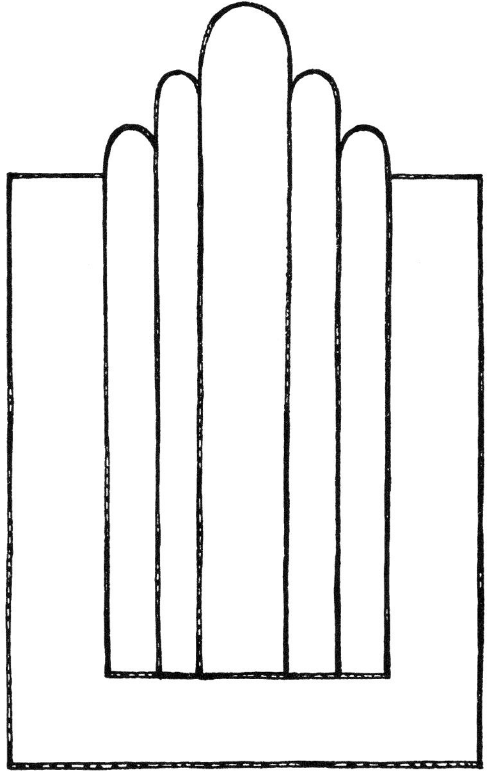

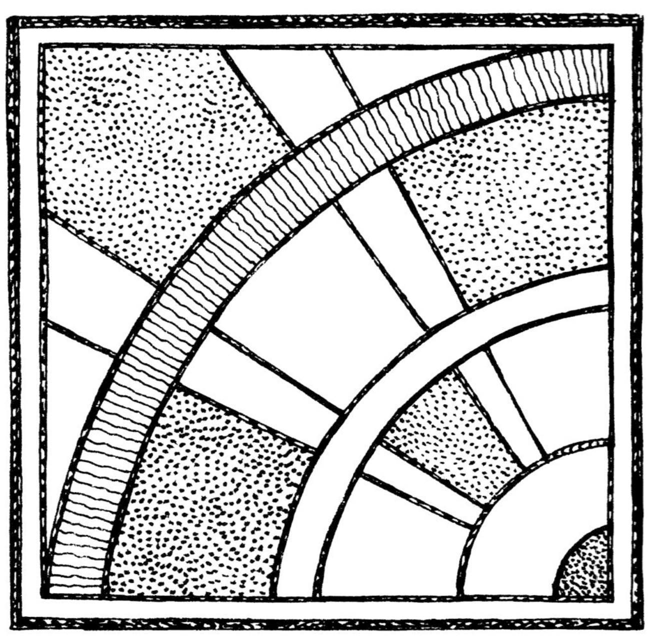

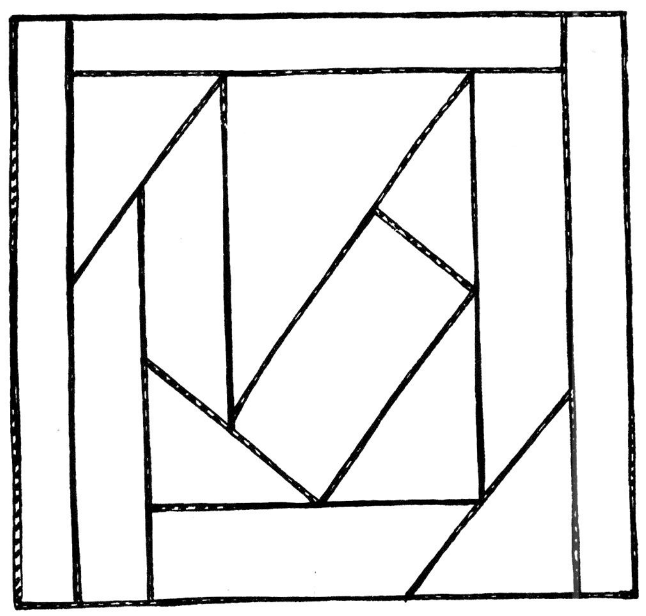

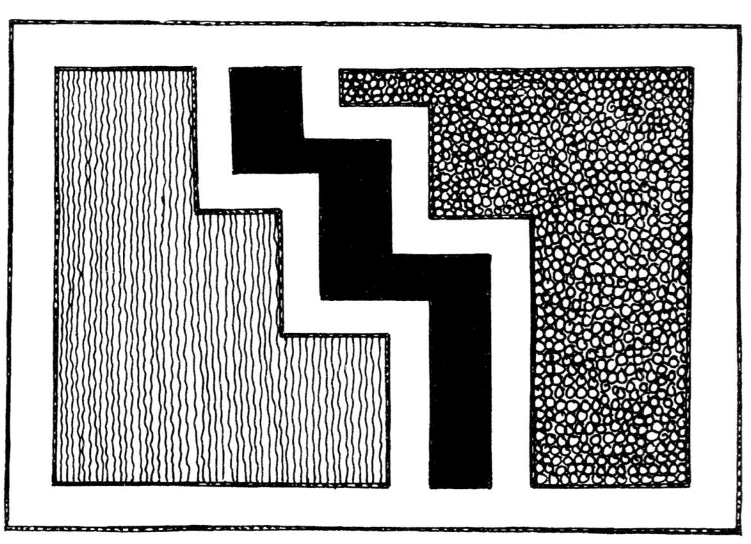

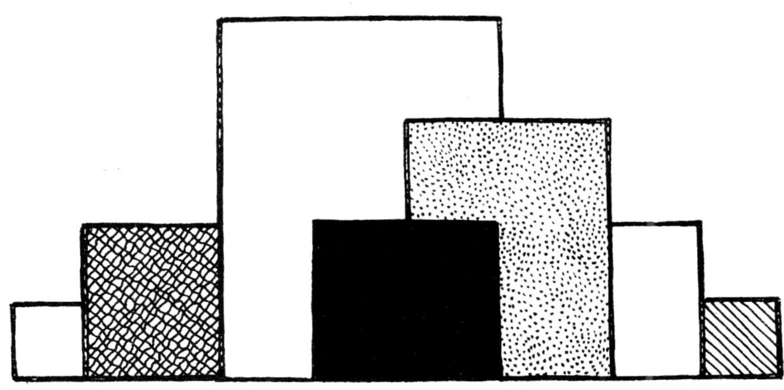

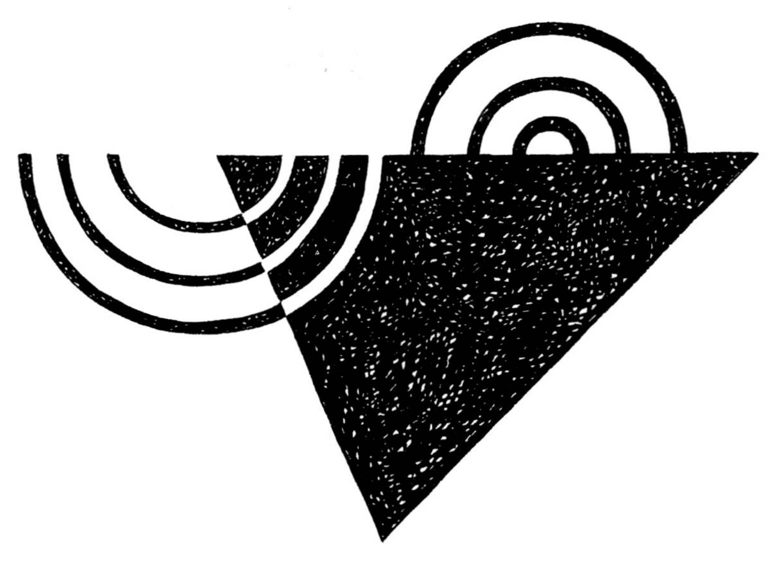